THE REMARKABLE CASE OF DOROTHY L. SAYERS

Photograph and signature of Dorothy L. Sayers from the Marion E. Wade Center, Wheaton College, Wheaton, Illinois, U.S.A.

The Remarkable Case of Dorothy L. Sayers

Catherine Kenney

THE KENT STATE UNIVERSITY PRESS
Kent, Ohio, and London, England

AA℥ o 18)

© 1990 by Catherine Kenney
All rights reserved
Library of Congress Catalog Card Number 89-39714
ISBN 0-87338-410-5
ISBN 0-87338-458-X (pbk.)
Manufactured in the United States of America

Permission has been granted by David Higham Associates, on behalf of the Estate of Anthony Fleming, to quote material by Dorothy L. Sayers from *The Divine Comedy, The Just Vengeance, The Zeal of Thy House, The Mind of the Maker,* and various unpublished manuscripts and letters.

Second printing and first paperback issue, 1991

Library of Congress Cataloging-in-Publication Data

Kenney, Catherine McGehee, 1948–
   The remarkable case of Dorothy L. Sayers / Catherine Kenney.
   p. cm.
   Includes bibliographical references.
   ISBN 0-87338-410-5 (cloth : alk.) ∞ — ISBN 0-87338-458-X (pbk. : alk.) ∞
   1. Sayers, Dorothy L. (Dorothy Leigh), 1893–1957—Criticism and interpretation.   2. Detective and mystery stories, English—History and criticism.   3. Christianity in literature.   4. Women in literature.   I. Title.
PR6037.A95Z74   1990
823'.912—dc20

                                   89-39714
                                     CIP

British Library Cataloging-in-Publication data are available.

To JPK

with love and gratitude
for risking the adventure

Contents

Contents

Preface

There are incidents in one's life which, through
some haphazard coincidence of time and mood,
acquire symbolic value.

—Gaudy Night

With the perfect clarity of hindsight, I can now see that such an incident occurred in my life, on that frozen February evening in the late seventies, when I first picked up *Gaudy Night*. I cannot say what moved me to try something by Dorothy L. Sayers at that point, but it was a perfect conjunction of time, mood, story, and reader. Here was a book that seemed to speak directly to me, a book that raised some of the most important questions of my life and stated them in terms I immediately recognized. *Gaudy Night* astounded me with its wit and infectious good humor, its mellow portrayal of the human comedy, and perhaps most of all, its richly imagined, lovingly evoked sense of life.

Innocent that I was then, I knew nothing of the controversy over the relationship between mysteries and mainstream novels, nor of Sayers's intention to bring the detective story back into the central tradition of English fiction. Yet, after only a few pages, I knew what any reader of *Gaudy Night* can know: here is a genuine novel, filled with people acting from human motives and wrestling with human perplexities, created by a masterful storyteller.

At that time, I had recently joined the faculty of a women's college, and I was amused to meet my colleagues—and myself—on every page. And as Sayers knew from bitter experience, anything remotely murderous appeals to those incarcerated in school. I remember flipping back to check the publication data inside the front cover, only to discover the astonishing fact that the novel was older than I was! Who was this Dorothy L. Sayers, who had made such a book?

I proceeded to try to find out, first by reading everything she ever wrote, then by looking at what had been written about her. Not since adolescence had I so greedily devoured an author, with no object other than pleasure in sight. Little serious response had been made to her work at that point, although the now-infamous biography by Janet Hitchman, *Such a Strange Lady*, was available. Reading it, and a number of later studies, I found that I did not quite recognize the woman I had met in the novels and essays. Clearly, *my* Dorothy L. Sayers was different from the author many others knew. This is, I suppose, the strongest reason for writing a book about anyone.

The Hitchman book served an important purpose for Sayers studies, however; by revealing some significant details of the author's life, the book motivated the Sayers-Fleming estate to authorize a major biography by James Brabazon, which came out in 1981. The biographical studies provided a provocative and poignant glimpse of the enigmatic woman behind the books. Knowing something of the personal cost at which these lively books had been created made their author at once more fascinating and more sympathetic. The more I learned about Dorothy L. Sayers, the more I realized that she was a challenge I could not ignore. But it was Sayers the writer whom I wanted to know, and with few exceptions, the people interested in her were not approaching her work seriously as literary art.[1]

Like most detectives at the beginning of an investigation, I did not know what I had stumbled upon when I first discovered Dorothy L. Sayers. Only later did I learn that there had been other witnesses at the scene. I was gratified by the discovery that my response to DLS was shared by some of the literary people I most admire, including Nina Auerbach and Carolyn G. Heilbrun, whose early essay, "Sayers, Lord Peter, and God," remains one of the best critical introductions to Sayers's work.

I also did not foresee the wide world which would be opened to me as a result of coming upon Dorothy L. Sayers. She has led me to consider—or to reconsider—the wonders of Wilkie Collins and Conan Doyle and Dante Alighieri; the history of broadcasting and the marketing of mustard; the nature of art and the meaning of work; and the role of Christianity and tradition in the modern world. Spurred by her richly eclectic mind, I have romped once again through the fields of medieval romance, followed controversies about chemistry and crime, explored the sites of fen floods, and charted the history of detection. How exhilarating it is to break out of the narrowly defined academic mold into which most of us are cast.

Sayers's range is also a bit daunting. No less a critic than C. S. Lewis has commented that "the variety of . . . [her] works makes it almost impossible for anyone to deal properly with it all."[2] I agree with this assessment, and in fact, do not deal at length with her Dante studies. I knew when I began this book that Barbara Reynolds was working on a study of Sayers and Dante, and judged that she was the best person to tell that particular story.[3]

It is a great irony that a writer who repeatedly asserted the limitations of the biographical approach to literature has been the subject mainly of biographical studies. Perhaps when a writer attempts to evade questions about his or her personal life, the very attempt calls more than usual attention to that life. In addition to the Hitchman and Brabazon books, there is the junior biography by Alzina Stone Dale, now long out of print, a book by Mary Brian Durkin, O.P., in the Twayne series, and a literary biography by Ralph Hone. The Hone book is also, in my opinion, the best survey of Sayers's work.[4]

What follows is not a biography or a survey, but an assessment of Sayers's major contributions to modern letters and culture. Considering her novels, essays, and plays, I will attempt to ascertain what constitutes her best work. What I judge to be her three main accomplishments serve as the organizing principle of this book: first, her transformation of the modern detective story into a serious novel of social criticism and moral depth; second, her penetrating critique of the situation of modern women; and finally, her compelling work as a lay theologian and interpreter of Christianity. Thus, the book proceeds, not only in roughly chronological order, but also from the work that most readers know best to what they know least.

This book assumes some familiarity with Sayers's fiction, but it is not intended for specialists. Indeed, I would like to think that it is appropriate for the same kind of reader DLS had in mind when she wrote. I hope that it will appeal to those who already admire the work of Dorothy L. Sayers, and that it may bring others to appreciate her. And let the reader be warned: I will not spare details of the mysteries' solutions in my discussion. Since I am offering in-depth analyses of various texts, it would be impossible to skirt around these facts, for often the nature of the mystery and its solution are crucial to understanding the novelist's intentions. If there are any readers of this preface so lucky as to have never read *The Nine Tailors* or *Gaudy Night,* they are herewith sent to do so before continuing with this book.

I bring to this study of Dorothy L. Sayers the biases and standards of a literary critic, specifically one interested in fiction as a genre. One of the most fascinating comments often made about Sayers is that she wrote "real" novels. I wish to consider the question of why her mysteries tend to strike astute readers this way, and in so doing, to suggest her place not only in the history of detection, but in the larger tradition of the English novel, which she admired. On first reading *Gaudy Night,* I was haunted by its resemblance to other novels, but only upon reflection realized its similarities to nineteenth-century English fiction, especially the novels of Jane Austen. The links between these authors have important implications not only for literary and social history, but also for our growing understanding of the subtle relationship between gender and genre.

The core of my critical terminology is derived from Sayers's own literary criticism, since this provides the best clues to her goals and values as an artist. I will attempt to approach her work in the spirit she brought to the reading of literature, a spirit alert, open, keen, and sympathetic. I can think of no writer who more enthusiastically celebrates the books she knows. Surely her own work merits such attention.

If Dorothy L. Sayers is still read with excitement and reread with delight today, almost three-quarters of a century after the publication of her first book, it is because of her strength as a writer, a maker with words. It has been said that there are two kinds of people who read mysteries: people who read only mystery fiction, and those who read only Dorothy L. Sayers. I want to understand why this is so. Why, after all these years, is she often named as a favorite author, not only by inveterate detective fans, but by some literary types who ordinarily express nothing but scorn for popular writers?

Finally, I will try to articulate what I find so appealing in the work of Dorothy L. Sayers. I hope that the following discussion retains some of the excitement and sense of wonder I felt when I first encountered this remarkable writer.[5]

Acknowledgments

In my experience, there are only two moments of unalloyed joy during the making of a book. One is that unexpected moment when the idea of the book comes, unbidden, into the writer's solitary consciousness. The other, much later and more sociable, is when one has the opportunity to thank those who helped bring the book out of the heavens and into something approximating reality.

From the inception of this project, I have been blessed with readers, editors, supporters, and questioners who have added much to my understanding of Dorothy L. Sayers. This book is better for each of them, but its errors and "lamentable lacunae" are, of course, mine alone.

The Remarkable Case of Dorothy L. Sayers was made possible in part by a grant from the American Association of University Women Educational Foundation. This grant enabled me to spend much of my sabbatical from Mundelein College in England. I am happy to have this opportunity to acknowledge the AAUW's support of this project, as well as their significant contribution to the higher education of women.

Anyone who is seriously interested in Sayers today must use the rich collection of her published and unpublished works available at the Marion E. Wade Center of Wheaton College. I am honored to have been a co-recipient of the Wade's Clyde S. Kilby Research Grant in 1984. During the years I have been immersed in Dorothy L. Sayers, the Wade staff has helped me in too many ways to mention. I want especially to thank its director, Lyle W. Dorsett, and associate director, Marjorie Lamp Mead, both of whom also took on the onerous task of reading parts of the manuscript, as well as staff members Evelyn Brace and Brenda Phillips.

Sayers scholars and fans, present and future, owe a special debt to Ralph L. Clarke, president of the Dorothy L. Sayers Society, whose unstinting energy and unfailing kindness have done much to encourage interest in her work. I cannot thank him enough for the help he has given me on this project, including a careful and lively response to the manuscript. Two other English members of the Society, Gerald Pressey and Philip L. Scowcroft, its research officer, also vetted the manuscript and cheerfully answered innumerable questions. My thanks to them, and to Christopher Dean, the Society's secretary, who kindly checked the archives for me.

Before his death in 1984, Anthony Fleming, Sayers's son and literary executor, answered many queries and responded with acuity to early drafts of this book. He also granted me permission to read restricted manuscripts, for which I am most grateful.

A number of people who knew DLS made themselves available for personal interviews, including James Brabazon, her authorized biographer; Sheila Hodges, formerly an editor with Victor Gollancz Ltd.; and Kathleen Richards, Sayers's secretary during the war years. Others who answered questions and made relevant materials available include Pauline Adams, librarian of Somerville College, Oxford; Livia Gollancz, chairman of Victor Gollancz Ltd.; and David Winter, head of Religious Programmes, Radio, for the British Broadcasting Corporation. In addition, I wish to thank the librarians at the Bodleian Library, Oxford; the British Library; and the BBC's Written Archives and Play Library, for granting me access to their collections.

Barbara D'Amato and Alzina Stone Dale, my colleagues in Mystery Writers of America, and Jessica Mann, member of London's hallowed Detection Club, generously spent time reading this manuscript and discussing it with me when they should have been writing their own books. Nancy L. Winder not only read the book with great care, but also enlisted other readers with expertise in matters theological, including Ronald F. Marshall and Jon R. Nelson. On the literary side, I am indebted to Mary De Nys, Agnes Donohue, and Carole Hayes, who provided helpful critiques of this study. Lois Leidahl Marsh made two essential contributions: a nonspecialist's skeptical reading of the manuscript, as well as the care and feeding of my Vizsla pup while I was off investigating Sayers locations in England.

I am grateful as well to the members of my seminars on Sayers and detective fiction at the Newberry Library in Chicago and in the Master of Liberal Studies Program at Mundelein, who challenged and stimulated me during the formative stages of this study.

For starting me on the road to this book, I thank Mary Griffin, who requested my first article on DLS and would not take no for an answer. This request came shortly after my discovery of *Gaudy Night,* and the opportunity to write such an essay helped crystallize my response to Sayers early on. I also wish to acknowledge the help of the late Peter Brogno, who, as my department chairman, made it possible for me to have a clean, well-lighted place in which to work for a few brief years. And to Jeanne West, formerly of the Kent State University Press, my sincerest thanks for expressing an early interest in this book and for hounding me to finish it.

To all of these and other friends: to everyone who aided and abetted in the execution of this project; to those who put up with me during the ordeal of incarnation and listened patiently while "I tired the sun with talking" of things Sayersian; and especially to my husband, who made this book his by doing all these things and more, I have only this left to say:

I am so grateful, that while I breathe air
My tongue shall speak the thanks which are your due.

(*The Divine Comedy* 1.86–87, trans. Dorothy L. Sayers)

The Documents in the Case

The novels of Dorothy L. Sayers are widely available in so many different editions that I have chosen to cite chapter numbers, rather than pages, in referring to them here. Although some of these books were originally issued in the United States under different titles, I use their original English titles. These are, in fact, the titles that the books carry on both sides of the Atlantic today, and only American readers who are using very old editions will notice any difference.

Many of Sayers's essays have been published and reprinted in a number of places. Some are the transcripts, often lightly revised, of lectures. I have attempted to sort this out in my comments and to indicate the differing dates of lecture and publication, where this is significant. I have also chosen to cite essays according to their first publication in a collection. Thus, "Are Women Human?" is cited from *Unpopular Opinions,* in spite of the fact that it was delivered as a lecture some years earlier and has been published since in other anthologies.

A wealth of unpublished and manuscript material is available to researchers. DLS was remarkably prolific as well as diverse, and those seriously interested in her work face reading thousands of letters (often many pages in length), scores of notebooks, and the drafts of stories, poems, plays, lectures, and essays, both published and unpublished. The vast majority of this material is held in the Marion E. Wade Center of Wheaton College, Wheaton, Illinois, but the Dorothy L. Sayers Society also has substantial archives. The present address for the Society is in care of its secretary, Christopher Dean, Rose Cottage, Malthouse Lane, Hurstpierpoint, West Sussex, England BN6 9JY.

Whenever referring to unpublished material, I have indicated the collection where I saw the document in question. If the original manuscript was numbered by the author, I have also included page numbers. Thus, a citation to "Wade ms. 37" means the thirty-seventh page of a manuscript in the Wade Center. Many of the manuscripts are, however, unpaginated and undated; some are untitled as well. The majority of the letters cited are also owned by the Wade, but others are in the collections of the Bodleian Library, Oxford; Smith College, Northampton, Massachusetts; the BBC's Written Archives, Reading; the British Library; and the Sayers Society. Although I worked at the other collections, Anthony Fleming allowed me to see photocopies of the letters owned by Smith College.

Always at hand was *A Bibliography of the Works of Dorothy L. Sayers,* published by Colleen B. Gilbert in 1978. No bibliography of such a prolific writer could ever be complete, of course, but the Gilbert book is a model of bibliographic scholarship and an essential resource for anyone trying to trace the development of Sayers's art or her publishing history. A good deal of unpublished material has come to light since the publication of this bibliography, however, and a number of the manuscripts to which I refer will not be found in it.

Readers may note that I have also relied heavily upon the factual information provided in James Brabazon's *Dorothy L. Sayers* (1981). Although our opinions and judgments about this subject sometimes differ, Brabazon deals honorably with primary materials and does an admirable job of sorting out Sayers's somewhat complicated life. The following chapter will present those details of her life and times which are essential to understanding the kind of writer she became.

I

A Detective in the House of Fiction

> All art and myth-making disclose the universal pattern of things
> and may therefore be taken as symbolic presentations of truths
> greater than themselves.
> —"Oedipus Simplex"

> What a piece of work is man, that he should enjoy this kind of
> thing! A very odd piece of work—indeed, a mystery!
> —*The Omnibus of Crime I*

1

The Making of a Mystery Writer

It is impossible to say precisely what drove Dorothy L. Sayers to choose the detective story as her genre in the early 1920s, a time she would later characterize as "that spiritually ragged period"[1] and which she drew with great precision in her novels. After graduation from Somerville College, Oxford, in 1915, she spent some difficult years casting about for her life's work. Like most educated women until very recent times, she tried to use her university education as a schoolmistress,[2] first in Hull, for just over a year beginning in January of 1916, and later in London, beginning in the autumn of 1920. She never really wanted to be a teacher, however, and between these two short-lived experiences, took time out for a two-year stint at Blackwell's in Oxford, beginning in 1917. At Blackwell's she was a sort of publisher's apprentice in which it was her job to learn "the whole business, from discount to the three-colour process."[3] This job, which at least superficially suited her literary aspirations better than did the teaching positions, ended when Blackwell's changed from an emphasis on *belles lettres* to textbook publishing. It is likely that Dorothy Sayers was also something of a challenge to deal with in that office, for in Basil Blackwell's judgment the brilliant, exuberant young woman seemed "a racehorse harnessed to a cart."[4]

Her next job was as an assistant (in a secretarial rather than a teaching capacity) to an Oxford friend, Eric Whelpton, who had a teaching position at a school near Paris after World War I.[5] To readers of Sayers's novels, perhaps the greatest significance of this experience at L'Ecole des Roches, in Verneuil sur Avre, was its likely influence on the development of the writer's distinctive—and rather un-English—Francophilia, the strong admiration of French culture and mores which informs much of her work.[6]

Sayers seems to have been temperamentally unsuited to the job of teaching, and to her credit realized this early on and decided to do something else. It must be remembered that, for a woman in the first quarter of this century, such a decision carried greater liabilities than it does today, when women's choices are wider. It has never been easy to support oneself by writing, and Sayers's decision to attempt to do so was courageous, although she would probably refuse such a label. In 1955, she described her job history in a letter to *The Church Times,* which had run a rather garbled account of her life, implying that what she had really wanted was a fellowship at Oxford. The petulant tone is characteristic of such missives:

> Allow me to inform you that I never at any time either sought or desired an Oxford fellowship. If anybody entertained such hopes on my behalf, I am not aware of it, and if I disappointed anybody by my distaste for the academic life, that person has my sympathy. . . .
> Neither was I "forced" into either the publishing or the advertising profession. . . . Nor do I quite understand why earning one's living should be represented as a hardship. (After all, even Oxford fellows have to do some work nowadays to justify their existence). "Intellectual frustration" be blowed! . . . it was all very good fun while it lasted. (Hone 180)

That last sentence is a key to understanding the life and work of Dorothy L. Sayers. A woman of deep and wide-ranging enthusiasms, she enjoyed many types of experience—all great fun while they lasted. At different periods of her richly varied life, and in different moods, she engaged in novel writing, advertising campaigns, Dante studies, religious drama, literary criticism, and social commentary because it pleased her to do so. One of the reasons her work is pleasurable is that it communicates this sense of fun and pleasure in the work done. Sayers addicts—of which there are a goodly number—are fired by her enthusiasm, which they match in the intense interest they bring to her work.

In spite of her disavowals and indeed the evidence of her life, it has become something of a cliché to characterize DLS as a failed scholar who missed her chance in academe and then "settled for" writing popular fiction. Even so astute and sympathetic a reader as Robin Winks, himself a historian at Yale as well as a great aficionado of detective fiction, has asserted that "Sayers wanted all her life to be a don" (*Modus Operandi* 35). Perhaps one of the reasons for this confusion was her statements in the mid-1930s, around the time of *Gaudy Night,* to the effect that she had always expected to grow up to be an Oxford-educated scholar.[7] As the only and very gifted child of an Oxford man, this was a reasonable expectation,

4

especially since Dorothy Leigh Sayers had been born in the old Choir House at Christ Church College, Oxford, where her father was then Headmaster, just as the movement to admit women's colleges to the University was gaining real momentum. It is perhaps not idle to speculate about what kind of difference it might have made in her life if the Reverend Henry Sayers had fathered a son as well as a daughter.

We should not equate Sayers's wanting to be a scholar with a desire for becoming a professor or don, however; her life and work suggest that she herself did not equate the two. It is true that she eagerly sought membership of the University of Oxford, and that she wished to be considered part of the wider community of scholars. This she certainly accomplished, and not just by virtue of her First Class Honours Degree in Modern Languages (French) from Somerville, which was finally recognized as a full-fledged part of the University in 1920 at a ceremony where DLS was among the first group of women ever to be awarded an Oxford degree. Perhaps in a bizarre way that day made up for centuries of waiting, for those women were awarded BA's and MA's at the same ceremony, five years after DLS had completed her work at Somerville. Yet the final proof of her scholarship came in her life and work. The evidence shows that she approached experience as a scholar: in the integrity she brought to writing fiction and criticism, in her capacity for change and growth, and in her energetic employment of well-honed skills in the study and translation of medieval French and Italian works, most importantly the first Penguin edition of Dante's *Commedia*. There is much of Dorothy L. Sayers in Harriet Vane's happy realization when she returns to Oxford in *Gaudy Night:* "They can't take this away, at any rate. Whatever I may have done since, this remains. Scholar; Master of Arts; Domina; Senior Member of this University . . . a place achieved, inalienable, worthy of reverence" (ch. 13).

Superior though her intelligence and classical though her education might have been, Dorothy Sayers wanted, even demanded a larger, more exciting stage than that offered by the Oxford she loved and would remember affectionately in *Gaudy Night*. As we shall see in the discussion of that novel, she was acutely aware of the perennial tension between Town and Gown, and though attracted to both, chose Town when it mattered most—just as Wimsey and Vane do. In the summer of 1919, after her job with Blackwell's had folded, she wrote to her parents that she intended to leave Oxford: "I want . . . a thorough change," she declared (Brabazon 75). By 1920, she had effectively turned away from the security of both college walls and the indulgent arms of family, away from university and vicarage forever, and into the clamorous uproar of London. This move seems the crucial one in her path to becoming a writer, and it influenced greatly the novels she wrote. Though she would return to the university through the years, lecturing on occasion at both Oxford and Cambridge, she came back as a scholar-citizen of the world, a status explored in some detail in *Gaudy Night,* which remains one of the best college novels ever written.

In May of 1922, owing perhaps as much to her experience at Blackwell's as to her Oxford degree, Sayers landed the job of copywriter at S. H. Benson's, then England's largest advertising agency, where she was to make her bread and butter for the next decade as she turned out increasingly complex novels at the rate of roughly one per year. It is easy for her admirers to belittle this position at Benson's. It was a kind of drudgery for the gifted young woman, and it did deplete much of her time and energy. Equally important, however, is the fact that it provided steady income and a relatively stable life for the aspiring novelist; as such, it effectively supported her writing habit until she was well enough known, in the early thirties, to command good advances on her books. The ebullient evocation of office life in *Murder Must Advertise* also suggests that at the advertising agency, she found some of the camaraderie she must have missed since her college days.[8] The job taught her much about the use and abuse of language in the modern world, which became the theme not only of *Murder Must Advertise,* but of many of her later essays and lectures. Certainly this experience in advertising, combined with her thorough knowledge of book publishing, made her an unusually astute writer when it came to the business of contracts, publication schedules, permissions, and book promotion. It was, at any rate, a propitious combination of experiences to prepare a writer who was to see the novelist's job as both art and craft.

According to her authorized biographer, James Brabazon, by August of 1929 DLS had secured a contract with an American publisher that guaranteed her a steady income from her writing (*Dorothy L. Sayers* 142). From 1930 on, she was effectively that rare bird, a self-supporting freelance writer, and after that time, focused increasingly on the kind of book she wanted to do. Indirectly, this argues for how little she was actually motivated by money-making in her writing.

Like many fiction writers, DLS had begun by composing verse in childhood, and she penned some rather derivative, highly stylized and conventional poetry while at Oxford and in the years immediately following. Some of this poetry was collected in *Op I* and *Catholic Tales and Christian Songs,* slim volumes brought out by Basil Blackwell in 1916 and 1918 respectively.[9] She continued to write poetry intermittently throughout her life, and Brabazon believes that she always considered herself a poet rather than a novelist (126). If so, it would appear that she suffered from an inability—common among writers—to judge her own work. Though her poetry was an attempt at writing "real" literature and was closer to the literary models she had studied in school than her detective fiction was, Sayers had little to contribute to the development of modern poetry, while her fiction includes some of the greatest mystery stories ever written.

Although it is not as effective as her prose, her poetry shares with her fiction a love of tradition, legend, and myth, and in subject matter and theme, often anticipates her later religious writing. The early work in poetry provided useful practice in the careful employment of language and attention to form that was later to distinguish her novels from the average detective story or indeed from most popular fiction. Her life-long work as a poet was also essential preparation for the monumental task she would take on in the 1940s, after ceasing to write mysteries, of translating the *Divine Comedy* into English poetry, although her infelicity with verse is sometimes noted as a weakness of that translation. Much as she may have wanted to be, Dorothy L. Sayers was not a great poet. But she was a great storyteller. Her narratives are filled with unforgettable characters living in a fully realized world that is presented in inimitable style. After fifty years, even her approach to Dante as a storyteller seems the freshest and best aspect of her admirable work on him.[10]

The future novelist—and the Dorothy L. Sayers that most of the world was to know—was prefigured, not in the early verse-making, but in the little girl who enjoyed making up wildly dramatic stories to act out in the isolation of her childhood homes, the rectories of Bluntisham and Christchurch in the remote fen country of East Anglia.[11] One thinks of a parallel in the young Jane Austen, in other vicarage, at another time, acting in little dramas of her own invention, although Sayers did not share with Austen the benefit of a large family audience for her earliest "work." This proclivity for story-telling is the hallmark of Sayers's art, informing everything from the detective novels through her approach to Dante.

In the early 1930s, when Sayers reflected on her childhood following her parents' deaths, she praised her mother's intelligence and commitment to her daughter's education, but also concluded that if her mother could have enjoyed the opportunities of a later generation of women, she probably would have been a writer herself. DLS decided this because her mother's letters displayed a "great gift of humorous narration."[12] Is there a better explanation for the success and enduring appeal of works by the daughter of Helen Mary Leigh Sayers than that she inherited, or perhaps absorbed, this gift for telling a story with wit and humor? It was a glad gift that the novelist fully appreciated. In her "Hymn in Contemplation of Sudden Death," a poem published in *Op I,* she cites as one of the things for which she is most grateful this God-given ability "to view the whole world mirth-fully." The known details of Dorothy Sayers's life suggest that this remarkable sense of humor helped her through many difficult times, just as it has kept several generations of readers coming back to her novels.

Since the autobiographical fragments, "My Edwardian Childhood" and "Cat O' Mary," are products of middle age, they are both, in a way, Sayers's fictional rendering of her own story, the narrative of her life reconstructed from the tissue of memory and experience. Thus, one could conclude that hindsight made it easy for her, as a successful novelist, to maintain in her memoirs that she had always known it was her destiny to be a writer. But the force with which she describes her childhood and adolescent fantasies of becoming a maker, a creator of new worlds, is convincing. While most of her experiences at school were disappointing or embarrassing, Dorothy Sayers learned early that she could control any situation in which language was central. As a novelist, she would make Lord Peter Wimsey's facility with language and civilized chat his most distinctive characteristic, the talent that helped him solve cases, win his lady, and even forestall the coming war. In "Cat O' Mary," DLS vividly describes a child's first realization of having this creative ability, and the feeling of empowerment that attends such a realization, especially if it comes, as such fantasies usually do, when the child is otherwise quite miserable and helpless. The language of the passage suggests the God-like image of the human creator which Sayers would develop later in *The Mind of the Maker:*

> One day I will show them [the other school children, from whom she was essentially alienated]. I will set my feet on their heads, put the world in my hand like clay and I will build, build, build—something enormous—something they never even dreamed of. It is in me. It is not in them and I know it.[13]

She "knew" this, of course, through the writer's empathic imagination, which permits glimpses into the hearts and minds of others. Many artists' autobiographies contain such passages, including vivid descriptions of the realization that they were somehow different from their peers, especially in their ability to view their experience as onlookers as well as participants.

The precocious young girl, who did not leave home for boarding school until she was sixteen and who spent childhood mornings happily reading with her mother, probably read widely in her father's library as well. It was her learned father who taught her Latin and introduced her, at the age of four-and-a-half, to the *Alice* books, which she obviously loved, given her novels' many allusions to them ("My Edwardian Childhood" 7, 9–10). Her fiction also reveals a familiarity with the major English novelists from Richardson to Dickens, as well as with the rich vein of detection running from Wilkie Collins and Conan Doyle into her own time.[14]

One characteristic of classical detective fiction is to refer to other works in the genre. Throughout her career, Sayers alludes to the Sherlock Holmes canon more than any other detective stories; this is true even after her own version of the detective novel had moved far from the formula. As late as *Gaudy Night* and *Busman's Honeymoon,* which many people refuse to consider proper mysteries,[15] she was still seeing Wimsey and the detective process partially in reference to Holmes (*Gaudy Night* ch. 14, and *Busman's Honeymoon* ch. 13). Considering the number of writers in the genre between Conan Doyle and herself, it is interesting that she always saw her work in relationship to his. Perhaps this was based in an unconscious realization of her place in the development of the genre: at least one historian of detective fiction has concluded that after Sir Arthur Conan Doyle, Dorothy L. Sayers is "the dominant figure in the genre," a judgment I see no reason to refute (Winks, *Detective Fiction* 11).

Equally striking in Sayers's mysteries are the allusions to mainstream novelists, including references to *Northanger Abbey* in *Clouds of Witness;* Dickens, in *Busman's Honeymoon;* and in the same book, Mr. Rochester of *Jane Eyre.* In addition, her novels are filled with quotations and appropriations from the Bible and from the great English poets, most notably Shakespeare, Tennyson, Milton, and Donne.[16] Indeed, many modern readers must have met the work of John Donne first, or perhaps only, in the novels of Dorothy L. Sayers—an extraordinary fate for a Metaphysical poet. It is clear from her practice, therefore, that Sayers saw her fiction in a rich, multidimensional context, and was willing to invest it with her considerable learning.

DLS was truly catholic in her tastes, and never hesitated mixing popular culture with the greats. In fact, her vigorous and eclectic mind tended to stampede the barriers erected by more pedestrian souls. During a holiday from Somerville in 1913, she wrote to a fellow student, Catherine "Tony" Godfrey, that she had been indulging in an orgy of novel reading.[17] Some years later, Eric Whelpton was surprised to find the would-be writer devouring penny dreadfuls during leisure hours at L'Ecole des Roches. In his own memoir, *The Making of a European,* Whelpton recalled:

One day, when I teased her for reading such rubbish, she told me that she was part of a team . . . who were deliberately preparing to create a vogue in detective novels; she suggested that I should join them. I replied rather sourly that I did not imagine for a moment that the public would fall for such rubbish and that I would have nothing to do with it. (Hone 35)

9

If this is an accurate memory, Sayers was clearly more in tune with what the world wanted than Whelpton was. Thus, in addition to her solid work in modern and classical languages and her reading in medieval romance and the greats of English literature, it is clear that sometime between her childhood fascination with *The Three Musketeers* and the publication of her first detective novel in 1923, she had become an avid reader of crime fiction, high and low. Such reading prepared her to take on the genre as a practitioner, critic, and innovator.

In many ways, the detective genre suited her perfectly. In the particularly literate version to which she was attracted, the detective story had the swagger, the ritualism, and the irrepressible sense of fun and high spirits she craved. Its formal structure appealed to her essential classicism. And, though later in life she would sometimes speak disparagingly of her novels as not being the kind of work for which her education had prepared her,[18] the fact remains that the detective story-cum-novel has always appealed to a rather intellectual group of writers and readers.

By Sayers's own reckoning, the detective story was invented by one of the great literary critics of his day, Edgar Allan Poe (*Tales of Detection* viii), and major developments in the genre have come largely from those with sound classical educations or strong literary histories. In fact, her explanation of E.C. Bentley's place in the history of detection could be a description of her own. His *Trent's Last Case* was a landmark in detective fiction, she argued, precisely because "it was the work of an educated man, with the whole tradition of European letters behind him, who was not ashamed to lay his gifts of culture at the feet of that Cinderella of literature, the mystery novel."[19] Even Raymond Chandler, whose work is often considered the model of the anti-intellectual hard-boiled detective story, was himself a liberally educated man who set about creating a literary style to embody the language of the streets; Chandler himself was no more Philip Marlowe than Mark Twain was Huckleberry Finn. Chandler speaks disdainfully of the English mystery, especially of DLS, in "The Simple Art of Murder," but a curious fact in the history of detective fiction is that both he and Poe, who are usually considred prototypically American writers in the genre, were schooled in England.

Though a liberal education may seem, at first glance, fairly remote from the marketplace for mystery and murder, Sayers characteristically defined the work of the mystery-monger in scholarly terms. In her introduction to *The Omnibus of Crime II,* she warned that the detective story cannot be "thrown off at a white heat. . . . The central idea may be the result of inspiration, but the details must be worked out in a mood of calm and almost scholarly leisure" (2). This description of the business of the mystery novelist goes a long way toward explaining the appeal of this manifestly popular form to scholars, who are notorious readers of mysteries and often write detective fiction under assumed names. Perhaps this surreptitiousness fits the form, with crime writers, like their subjects, invoking aliases to hide their trails. Prominent examples of mysterious dons include "Michael Innes," or J. I. M. Stewart, a scholar of English literature who taught at Oxford, and "Amanda Cross," the cover for Columbia University professor Carolyn G. Heilbrun, whose professional respectability reached its apex as the 1984 President of the Modern Language Association of America. In the same year, the MLA's annual convention included a standing-room-only seminar devoted to the topic "Academics Who Write Detective Fiction." (Even so, one panelist refused to disclose the pseudonym under which his thrillers had been published.) Professor Heilbrun has suggested that the form appeals to intellectuals because people generally like to read about characters at least as intelligent as they are ("Sayers, Lord Peter, and God" 457); with the exception of the great detectives, twentieth-century fiction has not been particularly rich in intelligent characters.

Part of the mystery story's appeal lies not so much in trying to outwit the detective, as in watching the workings of a superior mind while it posits, in scholarly fashion, numerous hypotheses—all gloriously wrong—until the last one, in which reality is recast by looking at the evidence in a new way. In the best detective stories, this final revelation suggests scientific discovery in the hands of a poet, a creative "synthesis of experience" (*The Mind of the Maker* 31; cf. *Whose Body?* ch. 8). What Sherlock Holmes calls "the game" of detection, the exciting intellectual hunt for the one correct, rational explanation of the mystery, is not, therefore, so much a contest between reader and detective to see who can explain the mystery first. It is more the intriguing experience of following the detective's moves, including all the false starts and dead ends, until the discovery of the one possible path out of the maze and into the right conclusion. When this happens, the tension and suspense carefully created by the story are exploded in a wonderful moment of blinding insight when the reader exclaims, "Yes, I see; I should have seen that all along!" This experience is curiously similar to reading a good poem, which forces us to see reality in a new, but immediately understandable way. As Jacques Barzun has argued, detective fiction gives intelligence a place it has in no other literary form, with its plot providing instance after instance of "the spectacle of the mind at work" (*The Delights of Detection* 17). Sometimes called "the sport of noble minds"[20] the classical detective story is a "severe and civilised form" which "demands much fundamental brain work of those who write in it," according to C. S. Lewis, himself no great fan of detection ("Panegyric" 95). I

11

would add that the better efforts in the genre demand similar "brainwork" from their readers as well.[21]

Sayers has a good bit of fun with the cerebral, even academic habits of the detective in her very first novel, *Whose Body?*, where she allows Wimsey the better part of a scene to reconsider all of the evidence in the mystery. He does so, he tells us, "by following the methods inculcated at the University of which I have the honour to be a member" (ch. 5). Like his creator, Wimsey is, of course, a product of Oxford. A good detective story *is* entertaining, but its peculiar pleasures are much like those provided by university debating societies, the rough and tumble of scholarly investigation, the invigorating rigors of the tutorial and the examination. In this connection, it is interesting that the plot of *Whose Body?* was suggested by an Oxford parlor game, in which guests were challenged to explain the odd circumstance of finding a dead body, nude except for a pair of pince-nez, in a bath (Brabazon 87). Perhaps such games and devices are so appealing because, contrary to the standard intellectual position of this century, their problems are capable of both precise statement and final solution.

In addition to sharing the scholarly or intellectual tendencies of much detective fiction, Sayers unabashedly filled her novels with the knowledge of a liberally educated mind. To the consternation of some readers and the delight of many others, she infused her books with classical allusions, puns in several languages, and literary quotations from far and wide.[22] Her books all display a "wicked facility in quotation" (*Gaudy Night* ch. 12), and since the allusions are often included without quotation marks and are frequently twisted into hilarious malapropisms and puns, it is possible for readers who are less conversant with English literature than Sayers to miss the point. This could well include most readers today, for DLS not only knew a vast range of Western literature, but also had so absorbed it into her way of looking at the world and expressing herself that it was actually part of her style and vocabulary, rather than a product of the nearly always fatal practice of tacking on a few lines from the masters to create an appearance of erudition.

Often, these allusions and verbal pyrotechnics serve to illustrate the character of her detective-hero, Lord Peter Wimsey, or members of his entourage, or, especially in the later novels, Harriet Vane. Sometimes, as in "The Article in Question"[23] or *Gaudy Night*, passages in French or Latin provide key details in solving the mystery or in understanding a subplot. In all her work, they are testimony of Sayers's wide and enthusiastic reading, her joy in language and wordplay, and her overflowing, irrepressible love of this world and all its artifacts. Like her characters, Dorothy Sayers had remarkable conversational stamina; C. S. Lewis remembered liking her "for the extraordinary zest and edge of her conversation—as I like a high wind."[24] To put this comment into perspective, we must recall the brilliant minds with whom Lewis was conversant. It is fair to say that the Sayers wind has blown over many a less responsive or hearty auditor, but those who love her do so largely for the intoxicating breeziness of her unmistakable voice.

Her manuscripts reveal that allusiveness was indeed a habit of mind; Sayers's allusions fit into the fabric of her fiction as easily as descriptions of people and dialogue.[25] Her habit of quoting, usually without acknowledgment of source and almost always without checking the quotation, was something she shared with a lifelong friend from Somerville days, Muriel St. Clair Byrne, and indeed with generations of literate people.[26] In fact, the tone of a typical Sayers scene is reminiscent of the kind of chatter one may hear whenever real book lovers get together. It is not surprising that literary people should exhibit such behavior, for what is more natural, more human, than to want to possess the things we love?

The second epigraph on the first page of part 1, "What a piece of work is man, that he should enjoy this kind of thing! A very odd piece of work— indeed, a mystery!" is a characteristic Sayers allusion, borrowing easily from *Hamlet,* specifically the speech on man's "noble reason," while discussing one of the more trivial results of the human capacity for reason, the mystery story. The original lines run: "What a piece of work is a man! How noble in reason! How infinite in faculty! . . . in apprehension how like a god!"—a good metaphor for the detective's godlike role of seeing all and distributing justice (*Hamlet* 2.2). As is typical of Sayers's allusions, one need not know the source to get the point, but knowing it adds to the enjoyment and understanding of the passage.

Though all her novels are peppered with allusions from classical and modern literature, in the early books Wimsey seems to be quoting and punning more for the reader's benefit than for the other characters in a scene. When he meets Harriet Vane, a woman of similar education, tastes, and habits, Wimsey's natural allusiveness is really unleashed. He has finally found the perfect conversational partner, reason enough for a Sayers character to fall in love. Harriet mocks Wimsey—speaking perhaps for the reader—when she declares in response to his impetuous proposal of marriage, "If anybody ever marries you, it will be for the pleasure of hearing you talk piffle" (*Strong Poison* ch. 11). The last two novels, which focus on Harriet and Peter, are studded with quotations and allusions. Sayers seems aware of this near saturation of allusions, for she has Harriet pointedly ask Wimsey, "Do you find it easy to get drunk on words?" He admits that, regarding language, he is rarely sober (*Gaudy Night* ch. 4). In *Busman's*

Honeymoon the reader and the newly married Wimseys veritably reel with intoxicating language; here, they even encounter a Shakespeare-quoting police superintendent, to add to the mood of linguistic lunacy.

Sayers's devoted readers, many of whom regularly re-read her books, must be married to her work, at least partially, for the pleasure of hearing her talk piffle. Such piffle is, for better or worse, the common currency of people who share a cultural history and who can take for granted a knowledge and love of the books which communicate its patterns. In the world of readers, texts are landmarks as recognizable as more tangible aspects of the landscape, and often more beloved. One of Sayers's greatest compliments to readers of the manifestly popular form of the detective novel was her assumption that they shared her cultural background and would understand her allusions, even or perhaps especially when they are made in jest.

It is not always easy to determine the butt of these literary jokes, however. For example, consider the implications in the Dowager Duchess of Denver's garbling of one of the best-known lines of Alexander Pope, who though quoted widely himself, was also capable of doing a bit of literary borrowing on his own. Lord Peter's birdlike mother, one of Sayers's most felicitous creations, chirps blithely into his ear this apparently nonsensical comment: "What oft was thought and frequently much better expressed, as Pope says—or was it somebody else? But the worse you express yourself these days the more profound people think you—though that's nothing new" (*Clouds of Witness* ch. 9). Beginning with a pun on the elegant and familiar neoclassical line, the speech ends as a smashing attack on modern vapidity and sloppiness, with each turn in the delightfully balmy labyrinth of language suggesting a slightly different meaning. Such allusions seem curiously contemporary because of their offhandedness and self-mockery, as though nothing, including proverbs and philosophy, quite merits being taken absolutely seriously.

The dense fabric of allusion in Sayers's novels is similar to that found in much twentieth-century literature, including the more literary versions of the detective story,[27] and is an aspect of what is now fashionably called "intertextuality." Perhaps in a time when things fall apart, when the function and future of literature is daily questioned and the alienation of human beings from one another is so severe, texts have to talk to each other to make connections. Perhaps, even worse, in these incoherent times only texts *can* speak to each other. Yet one need only look back to Shakespeare (and to Renaissance and neoclassical writers generally) to realize that such borrowing and refashioning of texts is a venerable habit. At any rate, the novels of Dorothy L. Sayers are emphatically not for the reader who wishes to believe that nothing of interest was written before 1900 and that history began in the modern period.

One might predict a diminishing demand for such books as the world becomes seemingly less bound to literary traditions, but the testimony of the marketplace is irrefutable; the fact is that, more than a half century after they were written, Sayers's novels still sell. One of the most literary of all her books, *Gaudy Night,* sold very well from the beginning, and continues to be wildly popular. It would appear that, even in these culturally arid days, there is still an appreciation of the special pleasures provided by one whom Paul Foster once described as "this luminously humane writer," who admittedly may be "too consciously literary, too maddeningly well-read; but her erudition serves the purpose of underlining the great part books play in extending the common territory of the human race, its knowledge of reality" (*Writers of To-day* 117). It is hard to imagine praise that could have pleased Dorothy L. Sayers, the humanistic scholar, more.

Sayers once said that it is by an author's assumptions, by what he or she takes for granted, that we can really know the writer.[28] In addition to assuming that her readers are familiar with the literature she cherishes, she also assumes that they share a certain sympathy—or at least a tolerance—for her world view, a view that endorses the traditional values of order and civility, as well as the concepts of personal responsibility and justifiable limits to human behavior. While the great detective, as an amateur, generally works outside the law, he does not work against it or seek to rend the basic social fabric. This essential conservatism informs most detective fiction, at least in England. Unless otherwise stated, my comments are relevant to the English mystery, rather than the modern detective story in the United States, which tends toward the anarchic.

The classical detective story is, in fact, a comedy, a form that is fundamentally accepting of the world it mirrors, even though that mirror reveals many things worthy of hearty laughter or derision. In the hands of Dorothy L. Sayers, the detective novel is very much in the tradition of high comedy, depending as it does upon verbal ingenuity and wit for its meaning and impact. For this reason, her deft manipulation of dialogue recalls the repartee in Congreve, Austen, and Wilde as much as it resembles the cleverness of Sherlock Holmes. Sayers's books reveal much about English society, including many of its weaknesses, but they are essentially comedies of manners, faithfully recording and basically accepting what they see, rather than biting social satire that seeks to change the world.

Julian Symons has described the traditionalism of the English detective story:

> In a social sense the detective story expresses in an extreme form the desire of the middle and upper classes in British society for a firm, almost hierarchical, social order, and for an efficient police force. Classical detective stories, with their strict rules, their invariable punishment of subtle and intelligent wrongdoers, and their bloodhound policemen supplemented by private detectives of almost superhuman intelligence and insight, are the fairy tales of Western industrial civilization. (*The Detective Story in Britain* 9)[29]

DLS concluded similarly that the character of Sherlock Holmes personified the civilized world's unending battle against chaos.[30] There are clear limits in her fictional world, as well as an assumption that violators of these limits will be punished. This is true, despite certain cases, like the sympathetic killer in *The Five Red Herrings,* in which both the detective and the reader wish for a way around traditional justice and the letter of the law. In *The Nine Tailors,* Wimsey questions the wisdom of his investigation as he begins to see all of its ramifications: "Why should we hang a perfectly decent chap for anticipating the law [quite a euphemism for vigilante justice] and doing our dirty work for us?" The more conventional policeman, Blundell, speaks for society when he replies easily, "Well, it *is* the law, my lord . . . and it's not my place to argue about it" ("The Slow Work"). In broad cultural terms, the English detective story is a striking popular artifact created by a society based upon laws, not persons.

Perhaps it is this complacence with social norms, with what DLS herself once called "the thraldom of British good form" (*Whose Body?* ch.11), that, oddly, makes her so appealing to Americans, who have never belonged to such an ordered society. I would also suggest that it is paradoxically this very quality that causes many contemporary English readers, as members of a society in transition, to dismiss Sayers's work as dated or embarrassingly snobbish.[31] Even the recent British television adaptations of the Harriet Vane novels would seem to be an instance of this attitude, by their relentless stress upon the works as period pieces. In his *Puritan Pleasures of the Detective Story,* Erik Routley is obviously answering some of Sayers's critics when he discusses Lord Peter Wimsey as an aristocratic renegade: "Once you have accepted his background and met his relations as rarely as is decent, you have heard the last of English high life. Not one of the stories is placed in a country house, and there are fewer aristocratic titles per story than there are in the Holmes or the Poirot adventures"(141). This last comparison is especially interesting and revealing.

Would the following musings of the newly married Harriet Vane Wimsey about her husband be necessarily embarrassing or offensive to most English readers today?

She understood now why it was that with all his . . . cosmopolitan self-adaptations . . . he yet carried about with him that permanent atmosphere of security. He belonged to an ordered society. . . . In London, anybody, at any moment, might do or become anything. But in a village—no matter what village—they were all immutably themselves: parson, organist, sweep, duke's son, doctor's daughter, moving like chessmen upon their alloted squares. She was curiously excited. She thought, "I have married England." (*Busman's Honeymoon* ch. 5)

Must this grateful acceptance of having an "alloted square" or place in life, which is at least historically accurate, offend members of a society that is still wrestling with its traditional social class system? Or, is it more to the point that such certainty just seems hopelessly old-fashioned to the inhabitants of an increasingly urban, fragmented, and therefore anonymous and amorphous world?

There is, even yet, a very real attraction to these values of stability and order, as the worldwide readership for classic detective stories attests. On almost any day, one may observe otherwise up-to-date people going to and from their work in large cities, clutching tightly onto a well-thumbed Sayers or Christie.[32] Indeed, what a paradoxical spectacle this common sight is: a late-twentieth-century American sitting on a commuter train, engrossed in a murder mystery written by a citizen of a country that was so relatively free of capital crime that the story of a murder seemed a delightful curiosity—while that very reader may be passing through territory in which he or she feels fortunate not to be assaulted with a deadly weapon.[33] If classical detective stories are escapist literature, from what is that particular reader escaping? Perhaps this familiar vignette suggests rather an escape *into* something, into that alluring region desired by the beleaguered college president, who was once overheard crying at the end of a particularly combative day: "What I need now is a nice English murder!"

There is about these books the illusion of an unspoiled Eden, an evocation of the pastoral Albion of history and legend. As W. H. Auden observes in his perceptive essay, "The Guilty Vicarage," the classical English detective story presents a closed and stable society that has just been disrupted by one small problem, the problem of a body in the library or a corpse on the drawing room floor. Once this little unpleasantness is corrected, the presumption is that the society will again be perfect. The illusion, then, is of a life in which problems are not only definable but solvable—a heady illusion indeed to citizens of the modern world. In *Whose Body?* Peter Wimsey finds his family seat at Denver a somewhat welcome change from the chaos of London, because "at Denver things moved in an orderly way; no one died sudden and violent deaths except aged setters—and partridges" (ch. 9). Contrary to the stereotype of the English country house murder of her day, Sayers does not confine herself to bucolic village and countryside, however; and at her best, she challenges as much as she confirms.

It is not particularly surprising that this quintessentially English writer should be so popular in the United States, which suffers from an intermittent and rather complicated case of Anglophilia. But it is curious that there is perceptible hostility toward Dorothy L. Sayers in contemporary England.[34] There are, of course, notable exceptions, including crime writers P. D. James and H. R. F. Keating, who have published their admiring views of her work, and the membership of the Sayers Society.[35] In general, however, it seems fair to say that, as a novelist, DLS is held in relatively low esteem in Britain today. Perhaps some of this antipathy is traceable to the influential criticism of Julian Symons (see *The Detective Story in Britain* and *Bloody Murder*). Yet it is an indication of Sayers's dominance of the form during earlier times that more recent writers, both American and British, should feel driven to react against her work. This is just another way of saying that she remains the touchstone against which all serious detective fiction is tested.[36]

2

Toward a Poetics of Detection

No practitioner of the art of detective fiction ever spent more time analyzing and criticizing the genre than did Dorothy L. Sayers. Her comments on the form in periodical essays, in introductions to landmark anthologies of the genre, and in reviews of mystery novels for *The Sunday Times* of London constitute some of the best historical and critical comments on the genre. This body of criticism would assure her a place in the history of detection even if she had never written a mystery novel herself. Yet, happily, she wrote twelve detective novels that have been continuously in print since the first, *Whose Body?*, was published in 1923.[1] Taken together with her criticism, these novels present a remarkable accomplishment in the genre and afford a rare opportunity to test theory in practice and to watch the development of an artist working in one of the most tightly structured and consciously defined of forms.

Sayers's excellent education, wide reading, and even her traditionalism prepared her for the dual job of criticizing detective fiction and charting a new path for it to take. Both assessment and innovation depend upon a firm grasp of what has gone before. When she considered the state of mystery fiction at the end of the twenties—midway in her career as a novelist and at the height of the so-called "Golden Age" of detection—she was troubled by the widening gulf she perceived between stories that appealed to educated readers and those enjoyed by the masses. What had changed since the days of Collins and Dickens, she concluded, was that the better sort of mystery, the kind that was well written and well planned, had ceased being read, or indeed being readable, by those "in the back-kitchens," and was instead "becoming a caviare banquet for the cultured" ("Present Status of the Mystery Story" 47). If the literature of detection was to last, she argued, it had to fuse the puzzle-story of intellect and reason with the novel of sensation; it had to appeal once again to "ordinary human feeling" as well as to the highly refined, detached intellect. Such statements show how little patience Sayers actually had with intellectual snobbery, although she is often charged with having had a very bad case of it.[2] She never accepted the modern banality which suggests that the masses can handle only inferior literature and language, and spent most of her life trying to reach the widest possible audience, whether as a novelist, scholar, or lay theologian.

In fact, one reason the detective story appealed to her must have been her thoroughgoing disdain for much "high" culture in her time, a time marked by a rupture between art and popular culture that may never be healed. Some of the funniest passages in her novels pummel the tedious pretensions of much "serious" modern literature, with D. H. Lawrence not surprisingly receiving especially bitter attacks. *Strong Poison,* for example, seems to imply that while the admirable Harriet Vane is a self-respecting mystery-monger with few illusions about herself as an "artist," her murdered lover, Philip Boyes, is not even worthy of sympathy because of his self-indulgent "artistic" temperament and pomposity. As Harriet's friends observe, such an artistic temperament—or common garden variety bad temper—is an indulgence usually granted to men, not women (*Strong Poison* chs. 4, 8). The point is made even more strongly in another novel written in the same year, *The Documents in the Case,* which resoundingly denies the argument of a special dispensation for artists in its punishment of Harwood Lathom and its ultimately sympathetic portrayal of his victim.

Gaudy Night's description of "The Book of the Moment" campaign offers a rollicking satire of contemporary literature. At a literary cocktail party, Harriet Vane is both amused and perplexed by the crowd's discussion of the winning book, which reportedly moved some critics to tears. It is not clear whether they were tears of boredom or "tears of merriment, called forth by the unintentional humour of the book." Authors passed over for this award continue to hope, a bit irrationally, for their work to be named the "Book of the Fortnight," but as the author of *The Squeezed Lemon* points out, this will happen only if their publishers buy enough advertising. When Harriet makes the naive mistake of asking what the award-winning *Mock Turtle* is about, she is greeted with vague replies and concludes that "it was one of those books that reflect the author's reactions to Things in General. Altogether, significant was . . . the word to describe it" (ch. 11). Although many complaints can be made against mystery stories, reacting to Things in General is not among them; mystery writers are granted no such indulgences. Obviously, DLS had little patience with either the pretensions or the fashionable cynicism of her age. Her savage parody of modernist art is not to everyone's taste, but it is remarkably similar to James Thurber's hilarious send-up of the 1930s New York literary scene in "Something to Say."[3]

Lord Peter would seem to speak for Sayers when he babbles to Inspector Parker that "it isn't really difficult to write books. Especially if you either write a rotten story in good English or a good story in rotten English, which is as far as most people seem to get nowadays" (*Unnatural Death* ch. 3). The commonsensical Englishwoman who created Peter Wimsey once had the courage to comment about "an endeavor to write a detective story in Freudian symbols" that such a fashionable approach "may be the height of brilliance, but it sounds to me perilously like bottomless depths of nonsense" (*The Sunday Times* 17 Dec. 1933). This is a most refreshing admission from a critic. What Sayers strove to do and in large part was successful in doing was to write an old-fashioned English novel, a "good read".that was also well-written. She was therefore working in the tradition of the eighteenth- and nineteenth-century English novelists, and readers find in her fiction the richly detailed, varied world associated with those writers.

One of her major critical statements about the mystery story, written in 1930, describes the unique combination of qualities she considered necessary for improving the genre, or for making any real contribution to literature:

> We find a deep and wide gulf extending to-day between the mystery-story of sensation and the mystery-story of pure intellect, and we need a great new popular genius to fuse once more these two widely-separated elements and give us a new *Moonstone* or a new *Sherlock Holmes*. . . . This combination of fine writing with common feeling is a rare gift, but it is the quality which gives to any work the unmistakable stamp of permanency. ("Present Status of the Mystery Story" 47, 48)

Bridging the often impassable gap between genuine art and popular culture, Sayers's fiction is the product of such combinations: by turns, her novels are witty, suspenseful, wise, and entertaining. And though her early books assiduously avoid one of the commonest of all human feelings, love, when she finally takes hold of the subject in *Busman's Honeymoon,* she seems unable to let go.[4]

It is impossible to read Sayers's critical statements on the mystery and believe her claims that she never really valued her work in this genre. She began writing novels in a deliberate attempt to bring the detective story back into the main tradition of English fiction, and before finishing some fifteen years and twelve novels later, had gone a long way toward accom-

21

plishing that goal. Although the question of Sayers's place in the history of detective fiction remains open, critics separated by as much time and taste as Howard Haycraft and Jessica Mann agree that she successfully grafted the mystery story back onto the great tree of English literature. In a recent study of crime fiction by women, novelist Mann concludes that, despite their flaws, "Dorothy Sayers's novels so far remain supreme in that nebulous area where a detective novel has pretensions to be read for more than its plot" (*Deadlier than the Male* 182).[5] This is to say that they come closer to being real novels than any other works in the genre. I would add that, by the end of the twenties, when Sayers began a series of experiments including *The Documents in the Case, The Nine Tailors,* and the novels featuring Harriet Vane, she was indeed beginning to write novels in the sense that the term is traditionally used, to distinguish narratives that emphasize character development and moral change while evoking a well-delineated world. These books deal with the essential mystery of human experience, and may be read again and again for their subtle characterizations and increasingly complex structures and thematic implications.

As a critic of detective fiction, Dorothy L. Sayers was astute and tough, but she was also characterized by the quality she appreciated in her Oxford tutor, Miss Mildred Pope: the generous eagerness to praise others' achievements, which DLS considered the hallmark of a great mind.[6] Perhaps this generosity of spirit resulted partially from Sayers's characteristic ability to define her task in rather simple terms. She once remarked, vis-à-vis her monumental study of Dante, that there are really only two questions at the foundation of all good criticism: What is the writer trying to tell us? and What does this statement mean to us today?[7] Such startling simplicity sets her criticism apart from most, and reveals an essential, refreshing humility in the face of art.

Although DLS began studying the detective genre by 1920, most of her published criticism of mystery and detection was done from the late twenties through the mid-thirties, that is, just when she was most productive as a writer of fiction. It should be interesting and instructive, therefore, to see how the values that emerge from her work as a reviewer/critic relate to her own development as a novelist. There is no fairer or more appropriate way to judge a writer than by invoking the terms and standards she uses to judge others, especially her contemporaries. Thus, the following discussion will rely heavily upon the practical criticism DLS published as a mystery reviewer for *The Sunday Times.*[8] Considered along with her essays on the form, these reviews constitute a kind of Poetics of Detection, for they examine what has been done in the field and, from those particulars, formulate some rules of the game.

All of Sayers's own novels fall into the category of detective fiction, since their narrative structure follows the work of a detective (sometimes more than one) in the logical solution of a mystery. Thus, they may be called mystery novels as well, although this is a larger, more ambiguous term that includes many stories without a detective. In fact, her novels became increasingly concerned with evoking a general atmosphere of mystery: as her treatment of the detective problem became more subtle and ambiguous, her novels became increasingly absorbed with the ineffable mystery of human life that no amount of ratiocination will explain. In 1936, she distinguished among the varieties of crime fiction, noting that modern writers should reserve the label of "detective story" for

> those stories of crime and detection in which the interest lies in the setting of a problem and its solution by logical means. Psychological studies of the criminal mind are more properly called "crime stories"; while criminological problems whose solutions are arbitrarily revealed by coincidence or accident, or by straightforward explanations by the author, are styled "mysteries" or "thrillers."
> (*Tales of Detection* vii)

It is interesting that the terms "mystery" and "thriller" are equated in the last sentence. In England today, the term "thriller" is the common designation for what is called a mystery in the United States, where the more informal label of "murder mystery" is also used, despite the fact that some books in this category do not involve a murder. All may be included under the general rubric of "crime fiction," but detective stories in the classic sense are not the dominant mode today.[9]

In another context, DLS contrasted the detective story and the thriller in terms of how each tells a story and what kind of response it evokes in the reader: "The difference between thriller and detective story is mainly one of emphasis . . . . in the thriller our cry is 'What comes next?'—in the detective story, 'What came first?' " (*Sunday Times* 28 Jan. 1934). This simple distinction explains how the thriller manipulates the emotions, while the detective story appeals chiefly to the intellect. Though Sayers could effectively create suspense (as *The Nine Tailors* and *Gaudy Night* demonstrate), her novels are essentially detective fiction, not thrillers. She was capable of writing both kinds of work, as the variety of her short stories shows,[10] but her preference was to embed a detective story with sound intellectual appeal into a novel that could also evoke a wide range of human feeling and reflect a richly detailed pattern of life. By the time she wrote *Gaudy Night* and *Busman's Honeymoon,* the element of detection was so subordinated to other novelistic considerations, including theme and character development, that some readers felt she had abandoned the genre. I would suggest that she had redefined it.

It is true that her early books, through *The Unpleasantness at the Bellona Club* (1928) and including *The Five Red Herrings* (1931), which was a throwback to the earlier type, focus on the solution of the detective problem more than do her later novels, where our attention is turned upon increasingly interesting characters and their human predicaments. The most extreme version of this is in *Gaudy Night,* where the real interest lies not in solving the case of the Shrewsbury poltergeist, but in the delicate unfolding of Harriet Vane's personal dilemma. This duality would be a serious flaw in the novel if Vane's predicament of choice—work or Wimsey, head or heart, marriage or autonomy—were not inextricably linked to the detective problem. But the novel is thematically whole, and for this reason represents Sayers's final transformation of the modern detective story into a genuine English novel of character.

Before effecting such a transformation, she had to know the genre and its tradition well. The detective story, which is often compared to the sonnet because of its strictly imposed form, seems always to refer, implicitly and explicitly, to its tradition. The great detectives talk about each other, quote other mysteries, borrow techniques, habits, and phrasings from each other, generally parodying the form while practising it. Sayers knew the outline of detective fiction by 1921, when she began working on the story that would become *Whose Body?* (Brabazon 1). Her first novel includes numerous references to Sherlock Holmes and presents the London of Wimsey's sleuthing in the conventional, even hackneyed terms of November fog encircling the elegant, inviting, but faintly unattainable bachelor flat of the great detective. This invocation of convention is conscious, indeed self-conscious. While Wimsey prattles on about how this "real" case differs from a detective story (just as many early novels went to great lengths to present themselves as "histories"), he is at the same time floridly dramatizing himself as the stereotypical detective. As the game begins, he exclaims, "Exit the amateur of first editions; new motive introduced by solo bassoon; enter Sherlock Holmes, disguised as a walking gentleman."[11]

When he is happily trailing the murderer and finding clues, Wimsey tends to whistle, reminiscent of E. C. Bentley's urbane Philip Trent, with whom he also shares the habit of literary allusion.[12] Since it appears that DLS began working on her abortive critical/biographical study of Wilkie Collins around this time, we may conclude that by the early 1920s, she knew enough about the classics in the tradition to begin developing her own brand of mystery.[13] The culmination of all her study came mainly in the developing art of her fiction and in the scholarly authority she brought to the critical essays and reviews she was to publish from the end of the decade through the thirties.

Manuscripts in the Wade Center at Wheaton reveal that DLS was also doing a good deal of lecturing on mystery and detection at least until the early 1940s.[14] This is not surprising, for she was always in demand as a speaker. With her sweeping intelligence, lambent language, and rapier wit, she could distill a great deal of history and interpretation into a few memorable paragraphs or pages. Like Lord Peter Wimsey, she had an engaging and "funny way of talking about books . . . as if the author had confided in him [or her] beforehand, and told him how the story was put together, and which bit was written first" (*Whose Body?* 145). Though I do not suggest having had any such intimate conversations with Sayers, I believe that I recognize her voice when I hear it.

That distinctive voice comes through in the published version of her 1935 Oxford lecture, "Aristotle on Detective Fiction." Just the anachronism of this title, mocking as it does the modern temptation to define everything as premodern, should alert us that Sayers is having a bit of fun, but some have taken the essay rather literally as an explication of the detective story according to Aristotle's *Poetics*. Though Sayers does not—could not—mean that Aristotle actually had the modern detective story in mind when he claimed he was writing about Greek tragedy, she is seriously borrowing some of his observations about art and showing their relevance to detection. Most important of these are his emphasis upon a coherent plot—a detective story, unlike much modern fiction, must have "a beginning, middle, and end"; his stress upon mimesis, or art as a reflection of reality; and his observation that it is better for a story to depend upon the probable-impossible than upon the improbable-possible (*Unpopular Opinions* 178–90). Of course, the fact that Sayers attempted to apply Aristotle's aesthetic principles to the detective story at all manifests not only her classical sensibility, but also the seriousness with which she considered the form. As always, she has great fun playing with an unlikely connection, and the topic is discussed in the witty, engaging tone of her novels. For example, she speaks of the difference between the detective story and "the kind of modern novel which, beginning at the end, rambles backwards and forwards without particular direction and ends on an indeterminate note, and for no ascertainable reason except the publisher's refusal to provide more printing and paper for seven-and-sixpence" (181). This is a fairly lively statement of classical principles.

Yet Sayers did not greatly admire the standard detective story of her day, either. In the essay "Gaudy Night" (1937), which may be regarded as her literary autobiography, she explains her intention of creating something

25

"less like a conventional detective story and more like a novel" (*Titles to Fame* 75). The development she foresaw for the genre, therefore, was in a sense a creative move backward in time, a return to how the mystery had been handled in the nineteenth century by novelists like Collins and Le Fanu (*Titles to Fame* 76). This conception of the mystery as a genuine novel with claims to consideration as literature was Sayers's fundamental critical precept, the fountainhead of all other statements, and the impetus behind her own increasingly complex fictions. It is also the fundamental assumption in my discussion of her work. Sayers's insistence upon claiming a place for the detective story in the house of fiction is not really surprising when we recall that Defoe was a crime writer, and Richardson's *Clarissa,* which many consider to be the first great English novel, is the story of a rape. Ian Watt even links the development of a "well-defined criminal class" with "the rise of the novel," in his book of that title (95). Crime literature has interpenetrated English fiction from the beginning.

Though working in what many consider a sub-literary genre, DLS clearly wanted to write books that would last, and concluded that this would be possible only if detective novels took on the delicate task of studying human nature in addition to playing out the chess game many of them had become. Even a detective story, she argued repeatedly, must be *about* something, if it is to be worth anything. While stating her position as a critic of detection, she indirectly described the ideal for which she strove in her own fiction:

> They [the higher type of mystery] impress, not merely by the ingenuity of their construction, but by the possession of a certain inner power and force, so that we remember their atmosphere and can re-read them with undiminished, or even increased, pleasure, even when the plot is familiar to us. Of them we can, and do, instinctively say: 'These are great mystery-stories—not merely competent, nor merely clever, but *great*—the classics of their kind.' ("Present Status of the Mystery Story" 51)

In trying to determine what gives a mystery "that authentic stamp of permanency which we call classical quality," she concludes that it lies in the notion of mystery itself:

> Does the book, or does it not, strike that interior note of essential mysteriousness which is part of the nature of things? Death behind a locked door is no more truly mysterious than death unqualified. If the glamour be not there to remind us of the ineluctable mystery of things, then the whole super-structure of clue and false clue is artificial and lifeless. (51–52)

26

The writer's ability to engage the reader and to convince him of a new world is directly related to a deft use of language. If the mystery-monger is not a good writer, none of this is possible, for "it is not possible that a mystery story should be 'great but badly written' " (52). All of this is to say that, while working in a narrowly defined form with all of its inherent limitations, the mystery writer must first and foremost be a real writer, attentive to "that unreasonable poetry of things which informs English narrative and dramatic literature from Chaucer and Shakespeare to the present day" (49). If the mystery novel is to become a permanent part of the house of fiction, it must be evocative of living character, as well as large and serious in conception,

> for it is a mistake (and a very common one) to suppose that a mystery story cannot have the element of greatness. It cannot, perhaps, claim to be one of the greatest literary types—though there is always the great cautionary example of *Hamlet*, set like a sign-post to show how far blood-and-thunder may go on the road to Parnassus—but within the necessary restrictions of its form, it is as capable of its own proper greatness as a sonnet within the restrictions of octave and sestet. (50–51)

Later, in the analysis of individual texts, I will attempt to assess how far along the road to Parnassus Dorothy L. Sayers's work goes, by determining how closely she follows her own critical principles.

In addition to the essays and reviews already cited, the bulk of Sayers's thought on the genre of detective fiction is incorporated into her introductions to the massive *Omnibus of Crime* anthologies and *Tales of Detection,* as well as her published and unpublished work on Wilkie Collins.[15] In the first *Omnibus* (1929), she takes a long view of the history of detection, trying to see it as both part of the general literature of Western culture, and as a form distinct in itself:

> The art of self-tormenting is an ancient one, with a long and honorable literary tradition. Man, not satisfied with the mental confusion and unhappiness to be derived from contemplating the cruelties of life and the riddle of the universe, delights to occupy his leisure moments with puzzles and bugaboos.
>
> These mysteries made only to be solved, these horrors which he [the mystery reader] knows to be mere figments of the creative brain, comfort him by subtly persuading that life is a mystery which death will solve, and whose horrors will pass away as a tale that is told. (9)

At this point, DLS still considered detective fiction "part of the literature of escape and not of expression," an entertaining game to be played out with "sportsmanship," or fair play, for both the reader and the criminal (44, 12). Even so, she strikes a familiar chord here, arguing that mystery characters need to be brought up to the standards of mainstream fiction, instead of existing "more or less on the *Punch* level of emotion" (40). Such a development would lead detection away from the story of adventure and in the direction of the comedy of manners tradition where it belongs. She adds that the highly polished contrivance of the detective story is the modern version of the medieval romances of Roland and Lancelot (43), an enlightening comment from the creator of Lord Peter Wimsey, that supreme exemplar of gentleman, scholar, and hero out of the old mold. To a world that is increasingly ambiguous and anonymous, the modern detective story offers a powerful promise of meaningful action in the character of the detective-hero, that strong, clear-sighted individualist who rights an often topsy-turvy world and protects those weaker than he.[16]

The first *Omnibus* introduction also includes an interesting aside, which asserts that the sophisticated use of point of view is the modern detective novelist's most important skill (34). This opinion is not surprising from the author of *The Documents in the Case* and an admirer of *The Moonstone*, but it is one of those curiously sweeping generalizations that fill Sayers's prose and provoke as many questions as they answer. She herself experimented a bit with point of view, not only in the epistolary *Documents*, but also in *Busman's Honeymoon*, where Police Superintendent Kirk has his own chapter, and in *The Five Red Herrings*, where each suspect's story is recounted in turn by an omniscient narrator. Once Harriet Vane gains center stage in her novels with Wimsey (*Have His Carcase* and *Gaudy Night*), the entire Sayers world, including Wimsey, is turned on its ear, for we begin seeing it through Vane's particular consciousness. Ironically, it is only after the creation of Vane that Sayers gets into Wimsey's mind at all. Notable examples of her penetrating Wimsey's consciousness include his letters to Harriet in *Gaudy Night* and in the later "Wimsey Papers," as well as in a powerful scene in *Busman's Honeymoon*, where the narrator purposely shifts between the newly married couple's different angles of vision to dramatize their complicated responses to the new relationship (ch. 14). Such conscious manipulation of point of view is, of course, one of the distinguishing characteristics of modern fiction, and is evidence of Sayers's growth as a novelist and the seriousness she brought to the writing of narrative.

By the time of the second *Omnibus* three years later, DLS could say that the detective story was improving in quality because it was becoming a self-conscious art form, with better language and style and "real atmosphere," all necessary qualities for serious fiction (1–2). One of the reasons for these changes, she concluded sensibly, was the relative largesse of publishers, who were by this time able to accept longer books (in the 100,000- to 120,000- word range), unlike the spare volumes published immediately after the First World War (6). This additional space allowed for the thorough development of character that often distinguishes the best novels from pedestrian fiction.

It is impossible to calculate the extent of Sayers's own influence, as both novelist and critic, on the development of crime fiction during this period, but it was considerable. In keeping with the trends noted in her criticism, her own novels tended to become longer and more complex over the years, with increasing attention to developing minor characters and to painting in the elements of a detailed and rich atmosphere.[17] When considering possible reasons for her virtual abandonment of the detective novel after the thirties, it should be kept in mind that the Second World War created the same paper shortages as the First. Perhaps these constraints, along with a sense that people who were facing real annihilation should not be so interested in reading murder mysteries for fun, influenced Sayers's retreat from the form she had chosen during the period of unquiet peace between the two great wars. She certainly said as much in a variety of contexts during the war years.[18]

The struggle between plot and character is persistent in detective fiction, with many purists asserting that any time spent on character development needlessly obscures the mystery plot. Sayers once offered an interesting description of the genesis of a mystery novel from intellectual idea to particulars; in it, she reveals much about the relationship between character and plot in her own brand of detective story: "The 'idea'. . . usually presents itself in a flash of insight. . . . For a few days the mystery-monger goes about wrapped in a happy glow of murderous enthusiasm." Then the writer must sit down to work, doing some "solid thinking" about plot, while also giving much attention to the psychology of her characters. Since the characters' future is "fixed" by virtue of their function in the plot, the writer must be careful to see that they fit the plot they are to enact (*Omnibus II* 4).[19] Given this line of development, both character and plot acquire significant weight in Sayers's concept of the mystery novel.

Such novels are clearly an offshoot of traditional fiction, which has always looked to action to reveal character. Yet an essential playfulness is reflected in the typically Sayersian description of the perfect mystery reader, who must cooperate with the author by providing "an alert and amiable mind" for the hunt: "the reader we . . . really like to lead for our little walk up the garden comes out like an intelligent terrier, ears cocked and tail wagging, ready to run after what is thrown to him and to root cheerfully among the shrubbery till he finds it" (*Omnibus II* 12). This paradoxical sense of indulging in serious game-playing, while enjoying the results of seemingly effortless artistry, contributes to the intoxicating effects of a good mystery.

Sometimes, the inescapably serious annals of true crime inspire mystery novelists, and as an indefatigable researcher, DLS was conversant with the major British murder cases. In an essay on "The Murder of Julia Wallace," she looks at the facts of a historical case as if it were fiction, seeking to understand the possible motivation of its "characters." The writer of fiction, she suggests, must always look at a situation in at least two ways, for "where human nature is concerned, there can never be any certainty; it all depends on the way you look at these things" (*The Anatomy of Murder* 160). Thus, all fiction deals with the essential mystery of human experience, and the manipulation of point of view is not merely an exercise for the mystery writer, but is intrinsically related to the nature of mystery itself and its potential for rendering reality. By this time, Sayers was not considering the characters in a detective story as mere chessmen to move about the board, but something more: as well-developed fictional characters, with the capacity to reveal something about human nature and to comment upon life.

By 1935, when the third *Omnibus* was published, she was considering the genre in a still more serious light, invoking Milton in her explanation of the relationship between mystery, detection, and horror. These types of fiction have much in common, she observes, because "Death and Sin are the undoubted parents of the entire brood."[20] The allusion to *Paradise Lost* is fitting, because the detective story focuses on the loss of innocence and attempts to restore it. DLS goes on to say that detective novelists believe that "your sin will find you out" (2), a fascinating line from the author of *Gaudy Night,* published in the same year, and one redolent of deep psychological meaning for the novelist herself. Though she chose the form earlier, how much of its appeal to her was linked to her own repressed secrets?[21] A substantial part of the mystery story's general appeal must lie in its dispassonate, ritualistic, and therefore acceptable investigation of such repressed information, as it explores one of the most universal of all taboos, the subject of death. The faintly erotic quality of much English detective fiction, especially that of Sayers's period, perhaps results from the tantalizing implication of tasting forbidden fruit that accompanies any discussion of death, especially if that death be violent or unnatural. I would not go so far as Geraldine Pederson-Krag, however, who has argued that the intense curiosity provoked by the detective story is rooted in its ritualistic reenactment of the Primal Scene.[22] In *Busman's Honeymoon,* Sayers plays with the explosive connection between love and death, and the lost Eden of the Wimseys' honeymoon cottage is evoked through allusions to the poetry of Shakespeare, Donne, and Milton (see especially chs. 16–18).

On the old question of whether a love interest is good or bad for a detective story, DLS was fairly conventional in the early period, assuming that "a detective married was a detective marred" ("How I Came to Invent the Character of Lord Peter"). Yet she eventually authored one of detection's great romances when she created Harriet Vane and made Wimsey fall in love with her. The reasons for this radical change will be discussed in the chapter on *Gaudy Night*.

Dorothy L. Sayers knew enough of both traditional fiction and the detective story to draw large conclusions about the relationship between them. In 1936, in the introduction to her last anthology, *Tales of Detection*, she offered a short survey of the masters of detective fiction in the nineteenth century, observing that

> these writers approach the subject in the spirit of the novelist. . . . They are interested in the social background, in manners and morals, in the depiction and interplay of character; their works have a three-dimensional extension in time and space; they all, in their various ways, offer some kind of 'criticism of life.'

In this category, she places Dickens, whom she praises for "delighting in humour and humanity," as well as the French writer Gaboriau, whose witty pictures of provincial life sometimes eclipse the detective element. She characterizes Sheridan Le Fanu, whose work Harriet Vane is studying during the campaign of the poison-pen, as a master at evoking "an atmosphere of spiritual evil" (ix), an apt description of the mystery that Vane is trying to solve at Shrewsbury College.

The list of worthies ends with Wilkie Collins, whom she praises for being capable even in so rigorously plotted a mystery as *The Moonstone* of creating "rounded studies of life and character" (*Tales of Detection* viii, ix). Unlike Conan Doyle, whom she credits with initiating readers into "the romantic adventure of the intellect" (xi), the writers she most admires were novelists first and foremost—not simply tellers of detective anecdotes. She concludes by saying that the future of the detective novel should be defined by "a delicate balance of the humane and the intellectual elements" (xiii), an amalgam of the two kinds of detective story typified by Collins and Le Fanu, on the one hand, and Poe and Doyle on the other.

Though Sayers's novels refer more often to the Sherlock Holmes canon than to any other detective stories, her criticism gives more attention to the work of Wilkie Collins, whom she considered the prototypical writer of the

31

English mystery. This dichotomy is not surprising, given the different audiences for whom she was writing as novelist and critic. Readers of Sayers's novels in the twenties and thirties—and indeed, those since—were more likely to be familiar with Conan Doyle than with Wilkie Collins: is there any fictional character as universally recognizable as Sherlock Holmes?

DLS spent years working on a projected biography of Collins, which was left unfinished but undoubtedly had considerable influence on her attitudes toward the mystery genre. E. R. Gregory edited and published the fragment in 1977, but there is another important and virtually unknown manuscript on the subject. Entitled "Wilkie Collins 1824–1889," it is a manuscript of some 20,000 words that is seemingly the text for a lecture, but of a length that would likely have precluded its being delivered at one time. Even though it is roughly half the length of the fragment edited by Gregory, this manuscript may in fact represent Sayers's most significant statement on Collins. In typical Sayers fashion it was written in a notebook that also includes early drafts of the story that was to be published in 1927 as *Unnatural Death*. Therefore, it would seem safe to say that by the mid-1920s Sayers had done an exhaustive study of Collins's work, since the lecture manuscript focuses on literary analysis, including an excellent critique of *The Woman in White*.[23]

In a variety of contexts, DLS praised Wilkie Collins for his admirable accuracy with scientific and legal matters, and his careful attention to fair play (*The Moonstone* vi, v), both important tenets of Golden Age detective fiction and of the Detection Club which Sayers helped to found in 1929. Beyond his meeting these special requirements of the detective story, however, Collins was, in her view, preeminently a successful novelist, a "master of constructional form," and a real innovator in the history of English fiction who introduced the mystery novel with a plot as closely woven as that of classical drama (*Wilkie Collins* 61, 83). Sayers judged that, along with Dickens and Reade, Collins had accomplished wedding the novel of plot to the novel of character, thus making a permanent place for the mystery story in the mainstream of English fiction (84). This was the tradition out of which she saw her own novels developing.

Wilkie Collins was, of course, a popular writer, and it is not surprising that Dorothy L. Sayers found his freedom from the more self-conscious pomposities of "Art" refreshing, or that the creator of Harriet Vane respected Collins's ability to see women as individuals.[24] She considered Collins worthy of serious consideration because he attempted a criticism of life in his books, and was not just a teller of the puzzle-anecdote story, as Poe, Doyle, and their successors had been. (While DLS never mentions her contemporary, Agatha Christie, in this connection, Christie's stories typify the anecdotal, bare-bones mystery.) Perhaps more than anything, Sayers admired in Collins the "power to invent a spacious world populated with interesting and entertaining people" (*The Moonstone* xi), as good a description as any of a traditional novelist. Sayers's own fictional world, which grew larger and more complex over time, is marked by just such spaciousness and largeness of conception, even as her voice is distinguished by the humor she admired in Wilkie Collins (*The Omnibus of Crime I*, 25). Although they often allude to the stories of Sir Arthur Conan Doyle, Sayers's novels are more in the richly detailed novelistic tradition of Collins and Dickens, or for that matter, of Richardson, Fielding, and Austen.

Sayers's *Sunday Times* reviews show at least a limited appreciation of books that do not match this large conception of the mystery. They make room, that is, for the "good read" as well as the classic, for the heart-pounding excitement of the thriller as well as the more subtle analysis of behavior and reality found in the greatest mystery stories. The catholicity of Sayers's taste may be indicated by listing those writers she praised, in some way or another, during two years of writing this column: Sir Arthur Conan Doyle, G. K. Chesterton, John Rhode, Erle Stanley Gardner, R. Austin Freeman, Francis Iles, H. C. Bailey, Ellery Queen (although she regarded the work of these collaborators as flawed), Agatha Christie, Mary Roberts Rinehart, John Dickson Carr, P. G. Wodehouse, Sheridan Le Fanu, and John Meade Falkner. It is certainly a generous mind and an expansive definition of mystery fiction that will admit such a motley crew. It is also ironic that Sayers herself could enjoy many more crime writers than do most of her admirers. The sheer volume of work represented by these reviews, dealing as they do with several authors or books each week, constitutes a considerable as well as a considered response to Golden Age detective fiction.

Since Sayers regarded the mystery as legitimate fiction worthy of serious scrutiny, her reviews also reveal a great deal about her attitudes toward literature, language, and culture generally. An edition of these reviews would be a welcome contribution to the literature of detection and to the general criticism of fiction. While considering individual texts, the reviews range eclectically through literature and legend; in one opening paragraph, for example, DLS refers with ease to both Jane Austen and Mark Twain, two writers who have rarely coexisted so peacefully in any medium (27 Aug. 1933). This ability to make connections between disparate types and periods is one of Sayers's defining characteristics, infusing her prose with great vitality and forcing readers always to reconsider common distinctions.

When she began reviewing for *The Sunday Times* in 1933, DLS had

33

completed eight novels and an impressive body of criticism. Her editing of the massive anthologies had necessitated a wide-ranging study of mystery and detection from its earliest roots and had provided her with a sound perspective from which to judge the writers of her day. To the task of reviewing she brought her characteristic energy, enthusiasm, and wit, along with a well-developed critical acumen. She was as comfortable referring to medieval romance and Greek drama as to the latest version of the Body in the Library. Yet one of the first things to strike a latter-day reader of these reviews is their good humor, their attempt at being fair about the novelist's goals and limitations, and their generosity in distributing praise— especially their encouragement of new writers. In fact, in looking over the reviews, which were published from 25 June 1933 until 18 August 1935, one is most forcefully struck by the largesse of this reviewer, who took on the weekly task of reading and responding to numerous books—some frightfully bad and many all but forgotten today—while she was writing the novels of her maturity.

One review develops a wonderfully English metaphor to explain her delight in the just-published work of a less experienced novelist:

This stylish-looking youngster is not yet a finished racer, but he takes my fancy immensely. He is thoroughbred, coming of the fine King's English strain, by Humour out of Deduction, and I shall look for some first-class performances in classic events from the same stables in the near future. (*The Sunday Times* 9 July 1933)

Unfortunately, Mr. Johnston Smith, whose *Murder in the Square* she was praising, is not remembered as a writer of "classic" mysteries. Indeed, Sayers's reviews are of interest today primarily because of the light they throw upon her own work or upon the history of crime fiction, so forgotten are most of the titles she considered. The surprising and well-turned phrase, "by Humour out of Deduction," encapsulates the particular appeal of her own witty mysteries, as well as the personality of Lord Peter Wimsey.

One might expect the author of *The Documents in the Case* or *The Nine Tailors* to be rather arch in her consideration of lesser or lesser-known writers, but this was not so. There are two things that bring out her rancor, however; pretentiousness and slaughter of the King's English. For example, she begins one review with the invective that "Mr. Ellery Queen is determined to be literary or die," and goes on to deride *The American Gun Mystery* for being filled with "intolerable affectations" (*Sunday Times* 2 July 1933). Perhaps this is just subtly inverted snobbery on her part, but at least it is motivated by a genuine concern for quality rather than petty rivalry.

These reviews coincide with the theoretical statements made in the essays cited earlier; they insist upon accuracy in scientific and legal details, upon adherence to the "fair play" rule of detection—which holds that the reader must have every clue the detective has—and upon the importance of the mystery novel's being considered genuine literature that is thus judged by the same standards. Like her comments on Wilkie Collins, Sayers's reviews also stress the importance of humor in fiction.[25]

The reviews attack, among other things, clichés of both language and plot; American slang, which seems to have been a particular irritant (DLS was capable of commenting that a book was a "plain thriller . . . and—though American—written in plain English"); and the preponderance of blood and gore in a certain type of mystery, the "Hard-Boiled" school to which many American crime writers of the thirties belonged (2 Sept. 1934). Above all, the reviews castigate dullness. One writer's cheeks must have burned upon reading in the morning newspaper that his "book's inexcusable fault is nearly 300 pages of excessively dull, bad writing—the one sin which can and should never find forgiveness" (2 Dec. 1934). Yet even Sayers, who describes herself as a "most austere mental disciplinarian," is willing to "read shockers 'for fun,' provided that the fun is there and that the shocks do not shatter the grammatical foundations of language" (27 Jan. 1935).

The better type of mystery story, DLS says, rewards readers with a "feast of reason," providing them with "an exquisite English style, many entertaining characters, and a wealth of witty comment on life and manners" (13 May 1934). I could suggest no better description of her own formula for fiction than this short passage, in which she is praising the achievement of Father Ronald Knox. While she was able to enjoy both the exquisite refinement of the pure-puzzle story and the spiritedness of the thriller, Sayers clearly preferred the more complex mystery story-cum-novel and assigned it a higher value (cf. 29 July 1934 and 11 Feb. 1934).

Essays are, of course, a literary form in themselves, and it is interesting to note the novelist's touch and the genuine literary quality in many of Sayers's reviews. Praising a novel based upon an actual case, she evokes a whole period in this short tableau:

The background [drawn in the novel] has the authentic feeling of the early years of the century, that tightly stuffed period of hips and busts and padded hairdressing and overblown hats, when trimmings ran riot, and the frou-frou of silk petticoats was at once the hall-mark of worldly standing and the siren-song of hidden allurements. But the book is not merely a costume-piece; still less a study of morbid psychology; it is a fine novel of human passion and suffering. . . . (7 Oct. 1934)

This vivid description of the mores and morals of a particular time could be the germ of a novel and suggests the author's attitude toward the previous generation. Its imagery also calls to mind the sexually charged atmosphere of repression and respectability that permeates *The Documents in the Case* and *Have His Carcase.*

Again and again in her reviews, DLS asks whether the book *as a novel,* has a serious aim; whether it presents believable characters in a realistic setting; whether it incorporates a criticism of life into its pages; that is, whether it has something of importance to say. Above all, since she believes that mysteries should be regarded as literature, she demands that they be well-written. Her highest praise is reserved for those novels with genuine stylistic distinction, for it is by the quality of their writing that all books are finally judged.[26] It is clear that Dorothy L. Sayers wanted the mystery story to rise above the level of "something to read on the train." In a review entitled "Style in Crime Stories—Why Good Writing Pays," she put forward her case for the literate mystery novel:

No book intended for intelligent readers gains anything by bad writing. . . . those thoughtful and hand-picked minds that enjoy an intellectual puzzle are merely affronted and repelled by . . . a mess of sloppy cliché and incoherent syntax. The most intricate plot ever woven will never carry bad writing; but good writing will often carry a thin plot and really inspired writing will carry almost anything. That is why, in reviewing crime stories for an intelligent paper, I lay what some people may consider an exaggerated emphasis on style. Bad English has not even the excuse of expediency. It is a criminal blunder, and its perpetrators should, and frequently do, commit financial suicide by hanging themselves in their own participles. (25 March 1934)

What a wonderful scene: death by dangling participle to all bad writers! DLS publicly executed such writers in reviews like "Sins of the Crime Writers—Murder of the King's English." She even created a special circle of critical hell for them in her scathing survey of "The Week's Worst English," a section that was appended to some of her final review columns. It was as much for their slaughter of the King's English as for their ridiculously unrealistic plots that Sayers condemned many detective novelists of her day.

What an experience it must have been to serve as the public target of her rapier wit. In the everlasting ignominy of cold, black type, she charges one

36

writer with inflicting on readers "the . . . torture of an exasperating style" (9 Dec. 1934), while another is singled out for having "brought platitudinous dullness to the pitch of a fine art. Light dies before his uncreating word" (18 Aug. 1935). At the end of one review, she cries, "Dear Heaven! What has the English language done to be served up in this dismal mess of rehashed phrases, like a resurrection pie?" (12 Aug. 1934). The most haunting accusation, however, remains: "The book is so ill-written in parts as to read like a bad translation . . ." (4 Feb. 1934). It is easy to imagine why DLS had so little patience with schoolchildren.

Like teachers, reviewers rarely know what effects, if any, their comments have. But John Creasy has courageously recorded his response to being reviewed by DLS:

> Dorothy L. Sayers had true greatness in the crime story world, and although I never met her, she influenced my writing and my life more than any other writer. In 1935 she said of my fifth book: "This is a thriller with all its gorgeous absurdities full blown . . . if the author cannot think of the right word, anything approximate in sound will do."
>
> About five years later when I could utter the name of DLS without wanting to reach for an axe, I read the book through. To my mortification she was right. From then onwards I began to revise new books until, today, they have at least ten readings, four by independent readers, before my publisher sees them. And it is a fact that as the revision work grew, so did the sales.
>
> I often wish I had met her to tell her so.[27]

Sayers habitually uses humor—including humorous exaggeration—to make a point, and her reviews have the engaging style and tone of her novels. These reviews sometimes employ verbal irony and understatement to feign that peculiarly English pose of casual calm and slight amusement in the face of death and destruction—the same manner that refers euphemistically to a murder as "the unpleasantness at the Club" or demurs, "we seem to have had a spot of murder here." This jolly tone goes back in English crime literature at least to Thomas De Quincy's "Murder as One of the Fine Arts" (1854). In such a playful mood, Sayers speaks in a New Year's column of wishing for "twelve months of clotted crime" (7 Jan. 1934). In another, she gleefully describes the case of "a real murderer [who once] deposited a corpse in a railway cloakroom and threw away the ticket" as "this incident of abiding charm" (27 May 1934). This is the same amused and amusing, slightly acerbic voice (a voice characterized by what she once called "sub-acid wit" in another writer) that narrates her novels. An urbane and irrepressible wit is one of the characteristics of this voice, along with a strong self-assurance, a remarkable fluency and energy, a definite taste for mixing high and low vocabulary and style in one piece, and a great capacity for verbal play, exaggeration, and sheer fun.

As a critic, Sayers could invoke humor to praise as well as mock. Writing about the distinctions of Ronald Knox, whom she calls unhesitatingly "one of the most brilliant of modern stylists," she admits that he makes all his characters as witty as himself—a comment equally apt about Sayers herself, I should think. She dismisses this as a slight imperfection, however, since to her mind, detective fiction has too little wit in it anyway. She also praises Father Knox for writing books in which "the follies of the modern world are shrewdly castigated . . . [books, that is, that are] full of hard Knox" (27 June 33). The placement of this pun at the end of such a passage suggests a writer who is not only very sure of herself, but who also keeps in mind that the one unforgivable sin for a writer is to be dull (2 Dec. 1934). Sayers the novelist, the popularizer, sought to entertain and engage as well as to inform, because she knew that if the reader were lost out of boredom, nothing else would be possible. Her understanding of the writer's task made her unusually flexible and alert to her readers' needs, but it also moved her to use techniques which others might reject as vulgar or banal.[28]

It should not be surprising to a reader familiar with Sayers's novels that, in her book reviews, she considers the mystery as an essentially comic form. Thus, not only does she praise witty mysteries, she also goes on to define the detective story itself as representing a comic view of the world:

> Murder and madness must always contain the elements of tragedy, but it is the achievement of the comic artist to weave these lurid threads so closely into the stout warp of daily life that the garrulities of small gossip, the fond fancies of young love, the bitter jealousies of thwarted desire, and the distorted fancies of the unbalanced mind, form a texture like shot silk, dark and bright by turns, but all one cloth. (3 June 1934; cf. "The Comedy of Horror")

How well this metaphor, with its characteristically mundane and yet vivid images, describes the intricate fabric of Sayers's own novels, calling to mind especially the rich portrayal of the human comedy in books like *The Documents in the Case, Gaudy Night,* and *Busman's Honeymoon.* Her fictional imagery is, appropriately enough, often dark and light by turns. For example, consider the harlequin episodes of *Murder Must Advertise,* which is set in "the gloom and gleam" of London (*Whose Body?* ch. 2), or the patterns of light and darkness that fill *Gaudy Night.* These details lend an aura of both beauty and mystery to the Oxford novel, where the quads are lit at night "with cold washes of black and silver" reflecting Harriet

Vane's confused attitude toward herself and the college. Just as Harriet finishes an enigmatic conversation with Miss de Vine, the narrator paints a beautiful, provocative picture of the two women moving under the ancient Shrewsbury beeches, which "cast over them a dappled and changing shadow-pattern that was more confusing than darkness," an apt setting for a mystery at once more subtle and more complicated than the average detective story (ch. 2, 20, 23). These mysteries are "dark and light by turns," not only because they mix humor with seriousness and laughter with death, but also because their main characters' perceptions of the world are in constant flux.

Though Sayers supported the "fair play rule" of Golden Age detective fiction, she was able to take such technical facility for granted by the early 1930s, and perhaps for this reason stressed it less in her reviews than one might expect. On July 28, 1935, she discussed "Crime Writers at the Turning Point," a piece that is a kind of summation of her position on the genre:

> It is now . . . generally accepted that the author should play fair, avoid coincidences, tuck in his loose ends, and get his poisons from the chemist instead of distilling them out of his own fantasy. . . . But now comes the moment when, having made our rules and got them by heart, we can begin to experiment and play about with them. And this will bring us face to face with a whole set of new problems, most of which will turn out to be questions of balance and treatment.

By the time this was written, Sayers herself had experimented with the detective story, especially in terms of its style, subject matter, and emotional range. The real challenge to modern mystery writers, she concluded, was to develop the genre into something more than a slick mechanism: "Plot is not everything; style is not everything; only by combining them can we get a detective story that is also good literature." This is the goal toward which she had been working as a detective novelist.

A characteristic rave review by Dorothy L. Sayers is the "Salute to Mr. Punshon" published on 20 August 1933. She is best at theorizing when she begins with a particular text or experience, and in the process of responding to Punshon's *Information Received,* she raises some of the most basic and perplexing questions about literature:

> What is distinction—that quality whose name is so often taken in vain . . . . which is so hard to define and so instantly recognisable when seen? . . . The few who achieve it step—plot or no plot—unquestioned into the first rank. . . . In the mere mechanics of puzzle-making, Mr. Punshon has his masters, but all his books have that elusive something which makes them count as literature. . . .

Good writing and good characterisation—the secret, I suppose, lies there and in Mr. Punshon's . . . sub-acid wit. . . . [This] is not realism in the dull and pedestrian sense of the word. . . . [His works] have that enhanced and glorified reality which is the highest art.

This "enhanced and glorified reality," which is reality evoked and transformed through well-chosen language, is named again and again in Sayers's reviews as a hallmark of good fiction. Her remarks on Punshon conclude with the highest praise: "This is a real book, not assembled by a journeyman, but written, as a book ought to be, by a man who is a writer first and foremost."

In her reviews, Sayers often uses the word "glamour" to suggest this elusive quality of good fiction, glamour in the sense of a transfiguring of reality through art (4 Nov. 1934 and 30 July 1933). Although this may seem a curious choice to readers today, since the word has been so abused, Sayers was undoubtedly thinking of its original signification when Sir Walter Scott introduced it into literary language to mean "magic," "enchantment," or "spell." This power of enchantment is one of the oldest acknowledged qualities of literary art, and was one of the reasons that Plato objected so strongly to fiction. Sayers herself was always attracted by language's ability to enchant, to transform experience, as her early story-telling suggests.

Is there a more appropriate word than glamour to describe the multifarious attractions of Peter Wimsey? Glamour surrounds him, with his superhuman prowess and his elegant flat, his ease in any situation, his effortless charm and erudition, his endless supply of money, power, energy, élan. And glamour he brings to whatever he touches: he appears in people's lives just at the right moment, as if by magic—to set innocents free and send the guilty to eternal punishment. A charmer in two senses of the word, his wit is glamorous not only by virtue of its exquisite refinement, but by its transformation of the dull world of the everyday into an almost incandescent experience. If his creator's voice is distinctive, so is his; Lord Peter is "absolutely unmistakable" (*Gaudy Night* ch. 14) and a reader should be able to identify most of his speeches after a half-line or so. Like his precursor, Sherlock Holmes, the very streets Wimsey travels, the places he frequents, as well as his clothing, mannerisms, and personal effects carry about them a special aura. Perhaps this is what Chesterton meant when he said that detective stories were the first literature to re-create, from the conscious symbolism of the city, "the poetry of modern life."[29]

Sayers clearly valued the affective function of literature, its power to amuse and charm as well as to inform and challenge. She was even capable of enjoying the "thrills" provided by works that had little else to recommend them. This was a woman who teethed on melodrama, who spent school holidays happily reading "rubbish." Later, as a critic and writer of note, she could end an otherwise lackluster review by admitting that the book was not a total loss, for "thrills are thrills, and this is an exciting chase from the first to the last" (18 Feb. 1934). In another, she unabashedly praises "a full-blooded thriller" for its climax, which she says "reaches an unparalleled pitch of horror and excitement" (1 Oct. 1933). These statements are very much in keeping with her ideas on "The Importance of Being Vulgar," a typically provocative title for one of her lectures, by which she meant the importance of a writer's being able to speak to the common emotions and desires of all human beings. In this context, the word "vulgar" also implies the writer's facility with the vulgate, or the idiom of common speech, for communication with the public. Thus, Sayers was neither creating nor demanding a "high-brow" version of the mystery.[30] She was simply asking for craftsmanlike attention to language, style, and structure, and recommending some risk-taking when it came to characterization and choice of theme—all for the purpose of transforming the modern detective story into a genuine literary form.

Though Sayers would testily tell interviewers during her last decade that she had written her novels just for fun, or just to make money, her criticism reveals, as do her novels themselves, the seriousness with which she approached the art of detection. In reply to some imagined or actual criticism, she wrote in one of her later review columns that people had been accusing her of taking detective stories too seriously, since she had been "expressing approval of the efforts made of late to give the detective story a more reasonable psychology . . . and to link it up with problems of less empheral interest than the barren ingenuities of murder mechanics" (23 Dec. 1934). While Dorothy L. Sayers had a great capacity for fun, her concept of it is revelatory of her seriousness: how many people in this world would say that writing books, of any kind, is fun? Yet, in spite of the fact that she wrote novels primarily to entertain, she was also concerned with creating something of lasting value. One might argue that her ability to entertain, in its deepest sense, is largely responsibile for her enduring appeal, for while the writing of books may not often be considered entertaining, most people read fiction primarily because it gives them pleasure. This is even more true of detective novels, which no one reads to impress others and which are often devoured surreptitiously. With rare exceptions, detective stories are not taught as literature in school, a practice that ensures a kind of immortality to other types of books that might never be read otherwise. Crime writers survive only because readers want them.

A couple of years before Sayers ceased writing detective fiction, she warned that "no author who takes the writing of English seriously will be content to spin ropes of sand for ever. One day he will want to put some passion into his work, and if he may not put it into his detective stories, he will go away and write some other kind of thing. Then we shall again have all the detective stories badly written . . ." (23 Dec. 1934). Was this comment a kind of distress signal from the novelist? In *Gaudy Night,* Harriet Vane is facing just this problem as a writer; perhaps her finding a way of putting some passion into her detective stories signalled the readiness of her creator to go on to other kinds of writing. *Gaudy Night* is, at least, the best example of the type of mystery novel toward which DLS had been pointing during this period of development and study. And in its sequel, *Busman's Honeymoon,* she considers the range of human passion, acknowledging in the book's subtitle that it is really "a love story with detective interruptions."

With bold simplicity, Sayers once reminded her readers that the critic's task is two-fold: "to discover . . . [the writer's] aim and then, and then only, to pronounce whether the aim has been well or ill achieved" (*The Sunday Times* 23 Dec. 1934). If the writer's aim is trivial, as is true of much popular fiction, then the best a critic can say is whether or not the writer has achieved this limited goal. From her reviews, critical essays, and lectures, we are able to deduce Sayers's goals as a novelist: First, she was interested in learning as much as possible about detection and putting that knowledge to use by employing, refining, and playing variations on the formula. Then she was consumed by the possibility of taking genre fiction and turning it into genuine art.

Dorothy L. Sayers saw the detective story as a potential and proper subgenre of serious fiction, and therefore believed it should have the distinction, imagination, humor, and thematic content that characterizes genuine novels. It should present memorable and believable characters acting in a recognizably human landscape. The goal that Sayers set for herself as a mystery writer was large and ambitious. Even though working in what many consider the glory days of detective fiction, she was not content with the status quo.[31] Like all authentic artists, she wanted to stretch her form and herself to the limit.

Having elucidated her critical principles, we can now turn to an analysis of Sayers's own fiction. The following three chapters will consider the pattern of her career and attempt to determine how successful she was in achieving her stated goals. Can we say that her novels—any of them—are great mysteries according to her own definitions? The best of their kind?

Do they reveal some of the ineluctable mystery of things, or disclose clues to the timeless pattern of the universe? That is, how well do they hold up as literature today, more than a half century after they were written? And, as works of art, to what things larger than themselves do they point?

3

The Development of a Novelist

When Sayers evaluated her fiction in the 1937 essay, "Gaudy Night," she decided that she had failed in the early books because she did not know enough about life to write a real novel: "Re-reading *Whose Body?* at this distance of time I observe, with regret, that it is conventional to the last degree, and no more like a novel than I to Hercules." Characteristically hard on herself in this assessment, she added that her failure was not surprising, "because one cannot write a novel unless one has something to say about life, and I had nothing to say about it, because I knew nothing" (*Titles to Fame* 75).

Thanks to various biographical studies, we now know something of how life came rushing in on Dorothy Sayers during the years following her first high-spirited romp with a detective novel. Experience—often raw and difficult—came in the form of disappointing love affairs, a son (born in 1924) by a man to whom she was not married, and later (in 1926), a marriage of compromise to a man with whom she seems to have had little in common. Through the years, she faced the grinding financial responsibility for herself, her son, and finally, her husband, who like her fictional hero, Peter Wimsey, was left nerve-scarred by World War I.[1] If Sayers felt cheated of life experience before her thirtieth birthday (her age at the publication of *Whose Body?*), she was rewarded with rich, often painful experience in the following decade.[2] This experience undeniably influenced her fiction's movement away from the artificial puzzle plot and into real human problems.

She also noted in the "Gaudy Night" essay that *The Documents in the Case* (1930) and *Murder Must Advertise* (1933) were conscious steps toward her goal of writing serious fiction. Both exhibit well-delineated, believable settings and offer critiques of modern culture, although it is interesting that, at least regarding *Documents,* some topical references were added to the text during final revisions, in a deliberate attempt to give the book contemporary flavor.[3] Yet Sayers does not acknowledge the social criticism embedded in an even earlier book, *Unnatural Death* (1927), which is memorable chiefly for its subplot involving Miss Climpson and the Cattery. This was also the first of her novels with a well-developed theme, namely the destructive power of possessive love, which serves as the faint prefiguring of an idea that informs two of her best works, *The Documents in the Case* and *Gaudy Night.*

In 1931, following publication of *The Five Red Herrings*—the timetable/alibi story that is the most conventional and least characteristic of all her later books—the author wrote to her publisher, Victor Gollancz, saying that she was finished trying to predict what the public wanted and planned to concentrate in future on never writing anything careless or meretricious (1 Jan. 31). Does this statement imply that, according to her own lights, she had been writing sloppily, hastily, or cheaply until this point, that she had been trying to satisfy the baser aspects of the marketplace?

It is hard not to see some intended self-criticism in her words, yet again she seems to state too strongly the case against her early fiction. The fact remains that from the first, with *Whose Body?* (1923) and *Clouds of Witness* (1926), Sayers incorporated social criticism into her fiction. Wimsey's nerve-shattering experience in the First World War is always in the background, as are the questions (raised in the character of Sir Julian Freke) of head versus heart and the role of science in modern life. The changing status of women, typified in Lady Mary Wimsey's confusion about her role, is another significant theme, which is first relevant in *Clouds of Witness* and becomes central to the mystery of *Unnatural Death. The Unpleasantness at the Bellona Club* (1928), which effectively ends the first period of Sayers's fictional development, is also the most successful of her early books, coupling as it does a slick detective plot with vivid details of postwar English life. Indeed, to the extent that a realistic depiction of everyday life constitutes social commentary in fiction, all of Sayers's books make pointed comments about her society. She once asserted that the detective story—as opposed to the detective or mystery novel—is essentially an anecdote,[4] and *The Unpleasantness at the Bellona Club* is a tightly constructed little drama based upon the old joke about an English men's club so stuffy that its dead members cannot be differentiated from the living—a potent comment upon the society so described. During a decade and a half of novel-writing, Dorothy L. Sayers increasingly expanded the detective anecdote into a full-fledged novel.

Few novelists of any stripe present a world as richly varied as hers; one must go back to Dickens to see as many levels and types reflected in the fictional mirror. In the novels of Dorothy L. Sayers, one may come to know England as it was between the two great wars. Here are the radical reformers, the Chelsea eccentrics, the Fleet Street clowns, the beleaguered office workers. In her wide world, there is a place for the London of shop-girls as well as the Bloomsbury literati, for the remote country village and the crowded Underground. Her characters are salesmen, clerks, farmers, shopkeepers, mechanics, and policemen, as well as the vicars, solicitors, county families, and ambiguous academics and celebrities usually associated with the English mystery. It is almost as though, in a nation poised on the point of rending social change, Sayers gathers all England together for one long, last family portrait. It may be that she looks upon this sight with the complacence of one who has enjoyed much of the best in her culture, but she also brings to the portrait a real sympathy for the human condition in all its manifestations. Perhaps it is this very richness of her novels that makes her short fiction seem dry and mechanical by comparison. Sayers herself considered her short stories poor, and they pale in comparison to even her most conventional novels.[5] She needed the big stage, the wide possibilities of the novel to express her view of human life.

The character of Lord Peter Wimsey, who dominates all the books until *The Documents in the Case,* speaks of England's glorious past while making tentative steps toward an uncertain future he knows is not his own. Wimsey is a brilliant, tireless aristocrat, born a bit out of his time, who seeks a suitable object for his abundant talents and energy—which is to say, he searches for a meaningful existence. In Wimsey, Sayers planted the seeds of what would become the central theme of her entire canon: the signal importance of creative, satisfying work in human life. She bestowed great wealth upon Wimsey to ensure his ability to deal with any eventuality, and wisely made him the second son of a duke. As the second-born, he can enjoy the family status without having to accept the responsibility, a fact that permits him the freedom to take up whatever interests him. Sayers has been accused of romanticizing the aristocracy and the wealthy, but she is no more romantic than Jane Austen on the question of money. Although neither writer considers money an unalloyed gift, both regard it, quite pragmatically, as requisite to survival. And both speak from some experience with genteel poverty.[6]

If in no other way, the well-delineated personal world of Peter Wimsey, with his rudimentary biography sketched into the first novel, sets him apart from most fictional detectives.[7] Even Watson thought of Holmes as being without family or origin ("The Greek Interpreter"), but Wimsey—who is destined to be the hero of genuine English novels—must have a family, a background, a personal history. His world and character are so real, in fact, that Wimsey matures along with the books in which he appears, a notable concession to realism, and an uncommon trait for a character in a fictional series.

In the earliest stories, Wimsey's sleuthing may appear to be just a curious antidote to ennui. Like Sherlock Holmes, the early Wimsey could assert that his "life is spent in one long effort to escape from the commonplaces of existence. These little [detective] problems help me to do so" (*Adventures of Sherlock Holmes* 57). Yet by the time of *Gaudy Night*, the basic human need for proper, productive work is a full-blown theme, the critical problem informing both the detective and the romantic plots. This is a particularly apposite theme for the detective story, which is a form that appeals generally to a rather leisured class and which flourished during what has been called "The Long Week End" between the First and Second World Wars.[8] In this sense, the form speaks to the very situation that creates its audience, perhaps as a means of diffusing guilt about having so much time on one's hands, while suggesting, in the detective's work, creative and socially beneficial ways of using such time.

A born storyteller, Sayers demonstrates even in her early fiction remarkable facility with characterization and dialogue. All of her books are also enlivened by her inimitable sense of humor, although *Unnatural Death* is relatively humorless except when Miss Climpson is on the scene. In these early books, we are introduced to the core of Sayers's fictional world (with the notable exception of Harriet Vane, who brings revolution to it later on): her detective-hero, the incomparable, immortal Lord Peter Death Bredon Wimsey; his irrepressible mother, the Dowager Duchess of Denver; his heavily competent brother, Gerald, Duke of Denver; Denver's largest millstone, his wife, Helen; his sister, Lady Mary, who grows into responsible adulthood in the novels; his impeccable "man," Bunter; his friend, colleague and future brother-in-law, Inspector Charles Parker of Scotland Yard; and his chief accomplice in crime-solving, Miss Alexandra Katherine Climpson. DLS once remarked that Agatha Christie's greatest strength was her ability "to compel belief in her characters," but this is doubly true of Sayers's own creatures. She regarded this ability as "the great gift that distinguishes the novelist from the manufacturer of plots" (*The Sunday Times* 6 Jan. 1935). In her 1935 review of *Three Act Tragedy*, DLS notes that such characters are created by Agatha Christie when she "is writing at the top of her form"; unfortunately, this quality faded through Christie's long and prolific career.

Sayers's first four novels employed various standard conventions of the detective genre in her day: the murder by unusual (some would say, impossible) means (*Unnatural Death*); the country-house mystery (*Clouds of Witness*); the murder without trace of the victim (*Whose Body?*); and the murder in which alibi and time of death (that sticky wicket to which crime writers seem fatally attracted) are central to the solution (*The Unpleasantness at the Bellona Club*).⁹

By the end of the twenties, however, when she was working on the massive anthologies of mystery and detection and becoming an important critic of the genre, DLS began some interesting and risky experiments in her own fiction. Though she was able to come to this only because of her experience with the earlier, more conventional books, from 1930–37 she wrote the novels of her maturity, ones that are distinctively hers. One might imagine, with some stylistic changes, another writer of this period producing *Clouds of Witness* or *Unnatural Death;* one cannot imagine *The Documents in the Case,* the books featuring Harriet Vane, or *The Nine Tailors* being written by anyone other than Dorothy L. Sayers.

The Documents in the Case seems the pivotal text in Sayers's development as a novelist. In it, she tries a new narrative method, the epistolary form used by Collins in *The Moonstone* and by other major English novelists from the earliest days of fiction-writing in the eighteenth century, and she abandons Wimsey and his cohorts, who though charming, must have been getting rather tiresome to their creator by this point. When she returns to Wimsey in *Strong Poison,* he will be transformed from his earlier self partially by becoming more like Jack Munting, the center of consciousness in *Documents.* This latter novel also makes a substantial leap into serious, sustained social criticism, with its letter form permitting a leisurely consideration of complicated questions about the relationship between the sexes, the politics of marriage, the limits of personal responsibility, and the role of art, science, and religion in the modern world. Howard Haycraft has called the book Sayers's "graceful tribute in its narrative method to Wilkie Collins's *The Moonstone*" (*Murder for Pleasure* 137). It certainly shows Collins's influence, not only in its form, but also in its razor-sharp delineation of contemporary manners, and its penetrating, unsettling study of the sexes.¹⁰

Although this is the only novel whose title page acknowledges that Sayers was assisted by another writer—the pseudonymous Robert Eustace—there is no reason to conclude, as some have done, that Eustace actually shared the writing of the text itself.¹¹ Eustace was the pen name of Dr. Eustace Barton, a physician who co-authored detective stories with other writers, including L. T. Meade. The extant manuscript of this novel is entirely in Sayers's hand, and an extended correspondence between the collaborators reveals that although Eustace gave Sayers the idea for what she dubbed her "mushroom story," she developed the narrative itself and depended on him primarily for forensic information. He queried basic scientists regarding the properties of muscarine and provided a scientifically trained ear for Sayers to test ideas on as she progressed with the text. He also suggested some details for the laboratory scenes (DLS to EB, 24 July 1928; 1 Aug. 1928). The one known literary contribution made by Eustace weakened the book's structure a bit, because he insisted upon adding the anticlimactic notice at the end, specifying the murderer's fate (DLS to EB, 4 Jan. 1930).

It should be noted that, despite her university education, Dorothy Sayers had no formal training in the natural sciences—a fact that makes the generally accurate employment of scientific details in her detective stories even more impressive. As a scholar, she appreciated the role of expert knowledge in specialized areas, and was always disposed to consult experts on questions of fact. This made her choice of experts all the more crucial, however, and left her open to easy refutation by other experts—a fact that figured prominently in her conclusion, shortly after the publication of *The Documents in the Case*, that she had made a serious mistake in its scientific evidence. It is one of the great ironies of her career that in this book, for which she carefully sought and followed the advice of experts, she also created the greatest controversy over scientific accuracy in all her fiction. In a proverbial case of life imitating art, time has proved the novel's explanation of the physical properties of muscarine correct, but the book seemed to perpetrate a real "howler" when it was published.[12]

Perhaps the most significant thing about this collaboration is that while Eustace suggested a fairly conventional murder mystery involving poisons and their properties, DLS turned the book into an extended discussion of the nature of reality, a prime example of how she was to take the conventions of the detective story and fashion them to new uses.[13] The forensic point on which the book turns is a clever idea, but a reader who already knows the solution to the book's detective problem can return to it again and again, to savor its remarkable characterizations, its cogent comments on modern life, and its insights into human relationships and motivations.

In her next book, *Strong Poison,* Sayers introduces into an otherwise conventional mystery plot the troublesome character of Harriet Vane, and dares to do the unthinkable to her detective by making him fall in love. Like most writers of the classical detective story, she had until this point believed that a love story would spoil the detection, even though she had always admired two classics in the genre which place a romance at the center of the mystery: Wilkie Collins's *The Woman in White* and E. C. Bentley's *Trent's*

Last Case. Thus, after years of asserting that the English mystery should return to the tradition established by Collins, Sayers herself finally made that move in the novels she wrote in the early 1930s. With *Strong Poison* and the three subsequent books developing the Vane-Wimsey romance, she took up Collins's subject of the tenuous position of women in society, especially as it is affected by marriage. The politics of marriage is, of course, one of the central concerns of traditional English fiction, and a major preoccupation of the nineteenth-century novel. As we shall see, the introduction of the marriage question into the modern detective story was the final step in allying Sayers's novels with the main tradition in English fiction.

The Five Red Herrings (1931) is the only oddity of her middle period, and she was correct in judging it a throwback to the puzzle-problem type of story ("Gaudy Night"). As timetable stories go, it is brilliant, but many of Sayers's most devoted readers, myself included, find its painstaking and even tedious reenactment of time sequences more a display of the writer's capacity for detail than an engaging story. It should also be admitted that, as one might expect, some readers who do not like Sayers's work on the whole do enjoy the technical brilliance of this particular tale. It is, as DLS herself knew, more of a "Freeman Wills Crofts story" than a Dorothy L. Sayers (DLS to VG, 20 Sept. 1930). Yet even this novel provides something special in the lovingly evoked Scottish atmosphere; the little artist's colony where the action takes place is the real town of Kirkcudbright, where Sayers and her husband, Oswald Arthur "Mac" Fleming, spent summer holidays, and where they must have experienced some happiness. But for this exquisitely detailed atmosphere, which provided useful practice for the rich scene-painting of *The Nine Tailors,* the book leaves little memory of itself.[14] Coming as it does directly after *Strong Poison,* the highly intellectualized detective problem of *The Five Red Herrings* may be regarded as Sayers's attempt to evade the messy human problems raised by interjecting Harriet Vane, a real human being, into the Wimsey books.

By the early 1930s, Sayers was self-conscious enough as an artist to realize the route her fiction was to take. She admitted to Victor Gollancz that she had written *The Five Red Herrings* partially in response to some unfavorable reviews of *Strong Poison,* and partially because she feared stagnation as a novelist and wanted to try writing a pure-puzzle story (22 Jan. 1931). But she also seemed to sense that the puzzle was just a detour on the way to her ultimate goal; in the same letter, she describes the novel on which she is working, *Have His Carcase* (1932), as a return to the human interest story. In this book, novelist Harriet Vane refuses to deal with a love interest in her latest detective story, while in her personal life, she erratically evades the amorous moves of Wimsey and the glimmerings of passion they raise in her. The narrator informs us that Vane's current novel is not going well, trouble she seems to have until a crucial moment in *Gaudy Night,* when Wimsey convinces her to put some real life and feeling into the story, even if it "hurts like hell" (*Have His Carcase* ch. 15; *Gaudy Night* ch. 15). Clearly, these details about Vane's painful growth as a novelist are one of Sayers's ways of working out this problem in her own fiction. When Wimsey and Vane discuss the difficulties and perils of injecting life into the glittering mechanism of a detective story, they are, in a sense, two sides of their creator's mind debating on a topic of crucial importance to her.

Sayers once began a review with the sweeping statement that "the greatest peril that besets the detective story is that of over-mechanisation" (*The Sunday Times* 23 July 1933). In the character of Harriet Vane, we see her struggling against this peril, a struggle made all the more difficult because of the ease with which she could follow the detective formula and the corresponding uncertainty of charting other paths. Like Vane's books, *Have His Carcase* is flawed, but it does show Sayers reaching for another, more realistic kind of detective novel. In its opening scene, Harriet is forced to look at the actual world, at life, as if it were a detective story. When this artful manufacturer of murder plots finds a real dead body, she thinks her way through the action as if she were a character in one of her own novels, the ultimate test of their realism. *Have His Carcase* is, therefore, Sayers's way of examining the conventions and limitations of detective fiction in the form she understood best, a story.

The unwieldy structure of this book reveals that she had not yet solved the problem of combining realistic narrative with the detective story, however. *Have His Carcase* does indeed need "much more of the chisel on its padded frame" (Hannay 41), but the problem is not a simple one of length. *Gaudy Night* is longer, and yet structurally sound. The defect in *Have His Carcase* is that the Vane-Wimsey plot is at best tenuously related to the murder plot, and neither is intrinsically related to either the setting or the elaborate detailing of ciphers. The book seems to dart off into several different directions at once, as though its author is not yet sure of her way, and at times, it even lapses into the clichés of second-rate romantic fiction (ch. 13).

In *Murder Must Advertise* (1933) Sayers was able to avoid much of the newly created problem of dealing with Wimsey as a human being because Harriet Vane does not appear in the novel's action, and the plot dictates Wimsey's being disguised throughout the story. Even so, he has a "real" job in this book, seemingly the only time in his privileged life that he earned a salary, which he does as his creator has done, by working in an advertising agency. According to her own judgment, DLS made another step in this

51

novel toward fusing social comment with detection ("Gaudy Night"). Here, at least, the theme of the novel—the debasement of modern life and culture by various opiates and seductions—is directly connected with the setting in an advertising agency and the mystery plot. As such, *Murder Must Advertise* is a necessary preamble to the classical unities of theme, place, and action achieved finally in *The Nine Tailors* (1934) and *Gaudy Night* (1935). And its realistic depiction of the urban office, which is an uncommon setting in fiction despite its commonness in the daily life of millions, is timeless.[15]

With this general outline of Sayers's earlier fiction in view, it should be enlightening to examine in detail the best of her mature novels—*The Nine Tailors* and *Gaudy Night*—to see how well she accomplished the goals implied in her criticism and to what extent she refined the detective tradition. These two books typify the different sides of Sayers's art and the different types of mystery at which she excelled, so that knowing them may highlight both the range and distinctiveness of her art. We shall consider them in light of the earlier books which led to them, and in terms of their distilling the essential preoccupations and strengths of their creator.

4

The Nine Tailors and the Riddle of the Universe

Many readers who can remember nothing else Dorothy L. Sayers created recall, with warm admiration, the "story about the bells." *The Nine Tailors* is a complex work of art and, as such, is about a good many things that cannot be put into one sentence, but on a very basic level, the novel is in fact a story "about bells." It is, more precisely, about church bells and change-ringing, that distinctively English avocation and eccentricity, which is "like most English peculiarities, unintelligible to the rest of the world" ("The Bells Are Rung Up"). Although such peculiarities may be unintelligible to the rest of us, DLS happily took on the task of communicating Englishness, and *The Nine Tailors* is a fascinating study of her culture.[1] The novel's plot and theme are inextricably linked with the tolling of bells throughout remembered history in the tiny East Anglian parish of Fenchurch St. Paul, a fictional re-creation of the Fenland villages she remembered from her childhood in that remote part of England.

Avoiding overtly autobiographical references in her writing until this period, DLS began a change of course with the use of an actual and familiar setting in *The Five Red Herrings* (1931). Around the same time, she undertook the abortive autobiography, "My Edwardian Childhood," which was apparently begun during a spell of "middle-agedness" in 1932. This fragment was shortly thereafter turned into the lightly fictionalized "Cat O' Mary," also never finished, although it was announced for publication in 1935. "Cat O' Mary" itself led eventually to *Gaudy Night,* which is set in the Oxford of Sayers's birth and college days.[2] While she was working on *The Nine Tailors* for two long years, she had to turn out *Murder Must Advertise* (1933), just "to keep the wolf from the door."[3] That novel, interestingly enough, is set in the landscape of her adult life, the London of advertising and Fleet Street, of high crimes and misdemeanors. She had previously set novels in London, but never before was the background so well-wrought or so obviously the product of experience rather than imagination or literary convention. *Murder Must Advertise* demands its particular setting, and only one familiar with the workings of an advertising agency and with urban office life could have written it so convincingly. This novel is as faithful to contemporary life as *The Nine Tailors* is permeated with history and the timeless quality of rural experience. It is testimony to Sayers's great versatility and fluency that such a self-proclaimed pot-boiler is as good as it is, especially considering how different its strengths are from those of *The Nine Tailors*, the other novel on which she was working at the same time.

Why this increased willingness to use elements of her own life in fiction? DLS often asserted that a truly creative writer begins with invention, rather than with experience (*The Mind of the Maker* ch. 9), but perhaps by this time, she felt that she had invented enough to return to parts of her biography with impunity. Certainly there were things in her private life, including the birth of her son, that she never wanted revealed—reason enough to avoid any semblance of autobiographical fiction and to argue against the propriety of readers' interest in a writer's personal life. Yet one of many profound ironies in the case of Dorothy L. Sayers is her attempting major biographical studies of both Wilkie Collins and Dante as a means of understanding their art, while maintaining that an author could be, and should be, known only through his work.[4]

In spite of all her claims to the contrary, like any writer, Dorothy Sayers lived a personal life that affected her work. Perhaps by the early 1930s she had lived long enough to realize that she could not continue to run away from herself, a flight she has Peter Wimsey admit to in *Gaudy Night* (ch. 15). At any rate, her confrontation of the past was to generate the richest products of her imagination, *The Nine Tailors* and *Gaudy Night*. While working on *The Nine Tailors*, she turned forty (in 1933), a milestone usually accompanied by stock-taking and reassessment. Then there was the fact of her son, born in 1924, who was growing up, even in her absence.[5] Perhaps most significantly, both of her parents had died within a year of each other, between September of 1928 and August of 1929. Their deaths must have forced Sayers, an only child, to look her own mortality full in the face.

Her novels after this time treat death in a markedly different way from the jolly corpse-chasing of *Whose Body?* I do not wish to overstate this change: Wimsey matures in each of the books, and in so doing, becomes slowly more aware of the real horror of death and the actual implications of proving someone guilty of murder. But there is a noticeable shift in the

54

novels written after 1929. Wimsey does not even appear in *The Documents in the Case* (1930), where the merciless death scene fills the heart of the book and evokes pity for the victim as it flashes back to his lonely death agonies. This makes it impossible for the reader to regard the crime with the cool detachment proper to a purely intellectual game of Whodunit?

In *Strong Poison,* also written in 1930, Wimsey is genuinely frightened by the spectre of mortality. This is largely because his infatuation with Harriet Vane, who is facing a death sentence for murder, forces him to admit his own limitations:

> As the taxi lurched along the rainy Embankment, he felt for the first time the dull and angry helplessness which is the first warning stroke of the triumph of mutability. Like the poisoned Athulf in the *Fool's Tragedy,* he could have cried, "Oh, I am changing, changing, fearfully changing." Whether his present enterprise failed or succeeded, things would never be the same again. It was not that his heart would be broken by a disastrous love—he had outlived the luxurious agonies of youthful blood, and in this very freedom from illusion he recognised the loss of something. From now on, every hour of light-heartedness would be, not a prerogative, but an achievement—one more axe or case-bottle or fowling-piece, rescued, Crusoe-fashion, from a sinking ship. (Ch. 8)

What Wimsey feels palpably in this moment is the ceaseless flow of time and his own submersion in it, a recognition that is necessary on his way to becoming a real human being and not just another "priggish superman" of a great detective, as Auden called him ("The Guilty Vicarage").

In the earlier *Unpleasantness at the Bellona Club* (1928), Captain Fentiman is on the brink of hysteria when he cries that everyone at his club is dead in a way, but since the focus is not upon him and his misery, the tone of death as a bad joke is sustained. At the beginning of *Have His Carcase* (1932), however, Harriet studies minutely the blood-soaked corpse; later, she cannot take her eyes off the pitiful, lost old women at the ironically named Hotel Resplendent (ch. 3). Harriet's preoccupation with these images of mortality becomes ours, because we see the action through her eyes: the narrative holds up a mirror in which she sees herself, and we, too, are forced to glimpse our own reflection.

By the time of *The Nine Tailors* (1934), Sayers takes on the subject of death directly, spinning a long meditation on time and change, with the ancient church bells, which ring for both weddings and funerals, standing above human existence as implacable reminders of both individual mortality and racial history. The novel's time sequence follows the march of the seasons through an entire year, adding to our sense of time's inevitable passage and of humanity's frenetic, doomed race against it. Surely part of the impetus for this great book, which lovingly reconstructs the terrain of Sayers's childhood, was the loss of the father who had introduced her to the beloved *Alice in Wonderland* and the mother who had spent mornings reading with her so many years before.

The Nine Tailors examines the subtle relationship between life and art in a dialogue between Wimsey and the aspiring writer, young Hilary Thorpe, who, like Harriet Vane, is left to face adult life without parents (*Strong Poison* ch. 1). Hilary begins by saying that writing, or the process of objectifying experience, is a way of dealing with life's harder bits:

> "It really makes things easier to do a little wondering, I mean, if you're interested in a thing it makes it seem less real. That's not the right word, though."
> "Less personal?"
> "Yes. . . . You begin to imagine how it all happened, and gradually it gets to feel more like something you've made up."
> . . . "If that's the way your mind works, you'll be a writer one day. . . . Because you have the creative imagination, which works outwards, till finally you will be able to stand outside your own experience and see it as something you have made, existing independently of yourself." ("Lord Peter Is Taken from Lead")

Sayers will develop this concept of the artist later in *The Mind of the Maker.*

The Nine Tailors opens with Wimsey crashing his car off the narrow, snow-packed road and into the drain near Fenchurch St. Paul. An unconventional murder mystery, the narrative does not even acknowledge the fact of a mysterious death until the second part, but images of death permeate the opening scene and prefigure the novel's theme. Beyond the ditch where Wimsey's car is interred in a blanket of snow, "the black spikes of a thorn hedge stood bleak and unwelcoming," starkly proclaiming the death of nature. All about him, "the fen lay shrouded. . . . the snow that had fallen all day gave back a glimmering greyness to a sky like lead." With Bunter beside him, Wimsey forges on through "an eternity of winter," seeking any sign of life "in this frozen desolation" ("The Bells Are Rung Up"). It is a great relief when he finds the lovable rector, Mr. Venables, who takes him "home." When Wimsey enters the parlor of the rectory, it is almost as though his creator, too, is reentering her past, reclaiming some warm memory across the cold years in between:

> Mrs. Venables, a plump and placid figure in the lamplight from the open door, received the invasion with competent tranquillity. . . .

"Agnes, my dear, have you explained to Emily that Lord Peter will be staying the night?"

"That will be all right," said Mrs. Venables, soothingly. "I do hope, Theodore, that you have not caught cold."

"No, no, my dear. I have been well wrapped up. . . . Ha! What do I see? Muffins?"

"I was just wishing for muffins," said Wimsey. . . .

Wimsey gratefully took in the cosy sitting-room, with its little tables crowded with ornaments, its fire roaring behind a chaste canopy of velvet overmantel, and the silver-tea-vessel winking upon the polished tray. "I feel like Ulysses, come to port after much storm and peril."

How often must the young Dorothy Sayers have watched her own mother greet, with "competent tranquillity," such hapless visitors to the rectories of Bluntisham and Christchurch. And how often must she have longed, in the years since leaving home, for such a warm homecoming—complete with the comical, winking teapot—after her own years of "storm and peril." This is not to say that the Reverend Theodore Venables and his wife *are* Sayers's parents, or that she is Wimsey. Rather, it is to suggest the way in which particular autobiographical and psychological details may be transmuted into art.[6] Part of what is being dramatized in this scene is Wimsey's remarkable good nature and civility, but he is quite changed from the cosmopolitan epicure readers met in the earlier books. It is almost as though the experience of *The Nine Tailors* cleanses and purges him in preparation for his becoming the fully realized, fully human man of *Gaudy Night* and *Busman's Honeymoon*.

Reading is a substantial part of life for any writer, and Sayers herself said that another book, John Meade Falkner's *The Nebuly Coat* (1903), inspired *The Nine Tailors* (DLS, letter to Mr. Lakin, 27 Jan. 1935). There are obvious similarities between the two novels. Both are set in villages where a great old church is the center of the atmosphere and much of the action. In *The Nebuly Coat*, the cries of the church's arches fill the air as does the sound of bells in Sayers's book. Perhaps the architect's restoration of the old church in *The Nebuly Coat* was also in the back of her mind when she wrote *The Zeal of Thy House* in 1937. Falkner's novel includes a would-be writer, Anastasia, but unlike Hilary Thorpe, who is an adolescent Harriet Vane, Anastasia is mocked rather than taken seriously (and therefore may have been a model for Agatha Milsom in *The Documents in the Case*). In Falkner's book, the gothic feeling emanating from both church and inn, which is named rather unsubtly The Hand of God, creates an atmosphere of impending doom that is similar to the tone of preternatural evil evoked in *The Nine Tailors.* Finally, both books exhibit the comedy of social classes so typical of the English novel.

In one of her *Sunday Times* reviews, DLS recalled the impression Falkner's novel had made on her, declaring that those "who love it cherish it in their hearts with a shy and secret passion." (Yet she was obviously unafraid of publishing her literary passions in the newspaper.) This review does not acknowledge a direct influence by Falkner on *The Nine Tailors,* but it suggests their relationship by noting that "the chief character in [Falkner's] story is the great church tower that dominates the whole of the atmosphere and action." Sayers's discussion of Falkner's turn-of-the-century book appears in a review of E. C. R. Lorac's *The Organ Speaks,* and what she says about that novel is relevant to an appreciation of *The Nine Tailors:* "The 'personality' of the music pavilion does . . . permeate the book, and this gives a continuity and aesthetic value to the work. . . . Mr. Lorac knows his musical 'stuff' inside and out, and uses that technical knowledge very skilfully to produce effects of mystery and beauty."[7] By substituting the word "church" for music pavilion and change-ringing or campanology for "musical stuff," one can make the same claim for *The Nine Tailors.* She goes on to state a general maxim for the mystery story in her time, arguing that "an infusion of beauty is what the detective story needs to-day if it is not to die of desiccation but to remain a living branch of the great tree of English fiction" (3 Feb. 1935). Sayers had always written a clean, crisp, and witty English prose, but her style becomes richer, more complex, more "literary" after the Bellona Club mystery, and *The Nine Tailors* is a particularly beautiful book.

Not everyone would agree on this point. Perhaps the most biting indictment of the novel was published by Edmund Wilson in a follow-up to his now infamous article, "Who Cares Who Killed Roger Ackroyd?," an essay in which he lashed detective fiction in general. Wilson knew very well who cares about mysteries, and that was what irritated him most: they have too many devoted readers, readers he chastises in a rather provincial fashion by warning of the sorry effects of "Wasting Time." The tone he adopts would be suitable, perhaps, for a new edition of the New England Primer or an eighteenth-century English tract against the evils of novel-reading. After the publication of Wilson's initial attack on detective stories, many readers wrote to him, suggesting that he hated detective fiction only because he was not reading the right books. The overwhelming majority recommended that he try a novel by Dorothy L. Sayers, particularly *The Nine Tailors.* After he had done so—more or less—he reported that he was not convinced, calling it "one of the dullest books I have ever encountered in any field." This is a rather odd way to talk about a novel; what *is* its "field," anyway? He added that he had skipped over all the passages dealing with campanology and much of the villagers' dialogue. Setting aside for the moment the inanity of such a response, which would damn any freshman English student to oblivion, one must ask what is left of the book, once its plot mechanism (the ringing of changes), its characterization, and its idiom are deleted. Yet Wilson goes on relentlessly, asserting that Sayers does not write well, but only seems good because she affects a literate style in a genre that is usually considered sub-literary.[8]

To such charges there is no final answer. One person's subtlety is another's abstruseness; vulgarity to one is refreshing candor to another. But I would argue that for the reader who does not skip through this book and who will take the time to savor its special flavor, it repays with the pleasures peculiar to a soundly constructed, largely imagined work of art. It is, furthermore, the culminating work in one type of mystery story at which Sayers excelled: the hyper-intellectual puzzle, which structures the tale and discloses much specialized knowledge on a particular subject. In this case, of course, the specialized knowledge is campanology.

The novel is also filled with a panoply of richly imagined, carefully evoked characters in a vividly realized human situation. It is expansive, even panoramic in its depiction of the fens and their inhabitants, filled with minor characters worthy of Dickens while evoking an atmosphere and setting reminiscent, in its richness of detail and palpability, of Hardy's "Wessex" or Le Fanu's pictures of old village life in Ireland. In addition, *The Nine Tailors* presents a coherent, serious theme that emanates from its particular setting and emerges from its plot. In other words, it is a novel by Sayers's own definitions.

In a DLS review of a Mary Roberts Rinehart mystery, published while she was working on *The Nine Tailors,* she contrasts the cramped, minimalist detective story typical of her day with the broader canvas used by the nineteenth-century practitioners she admired. Her contemporaries tend to suffer from "a lack of spaciousness," she observes, whereas

when we open 'The Woman in White' or 'Wylder's Hand,' we step into a world of people having their roots in time and space and a life which extends beyond the limits of the immediate problem. Larger issues are at stake than the precise method by which the arsenic is administered, and the strings are pulled by a more awful puppet-master than a Chief Inspector of Scotland Yard. (1 Oct. 1933)

Sayers's own novels grew increasingly complex and large in this sense, and by the time of *The Nine Tailors,* she was capable of creating a very spacious story indeed. It is hard to think of another mystery story—with the notable exceptions of *The Moonstone* and *Bleak House*—as richly detailed or massively constructed as *The Nine Tailors*.

While working on this novel in 1932, Sayers wrote to Victor Gollancz that she considered it "a labour of love" (Brabazon 149). Love she does lavish on it, from its careful portraiture of many engaging characters, to its symphonic depiction of the East Anglian landscape, to its lushly beautiful prose. And surely love was part of what drew her back to the home she had left so resolutely in youth, before the years of striking disappointment and accomplishment. The sincerity of her earlier commitment never to write a careless or meretricious book is manifest in the care with which she went about constructing this impressive tale.

The existing notebooks from *The Nine Tailors* record the extensive spadework the author did before beginning to write. The first notebook contains sixty-three pages of change-ringing material, including forty pages devoted to changes themselves (which are worked out in numerical charts) and the remainder with notes on bells and changes. One of the first leaves in the notebook is graced by an amateurish drawing of a bell, which has been struck through, presumably by the author herself. This drawing suggests curiously that to its author, also, this was a book about bells. Another folder holds maps of the actual fen dam and sluice system, as well as sketches of the mythical church. As DLS often did in plotting a novel, there are also lists of characters, outlining the relevant parts of their lives vis-à-vis the plot, especially its crimes. She seems to have worked out all or most of the change-ringing material first, as well as the chapter headings, which are drawn from campanological terms. Again, as is typical of the Sayers notebooks and manuscripts in the Wade Center, there is little revision of the text once the story begins. For this reason, it is likely that these manuscripts are not first or working drafts, and some would even appear to be fair copies prepared for a typist. Yet they are the only known manuscripts of the novels, and may in fact demonstrate the remarkable verbal facility of their author.[9] Certainly her many letters, which tend to be long, chatty, and well-wrought, are evidence that she was very fluent.

Since she grew up as a rector's daughter in the fens, it is perhaps surprising that DLS had never heard changes rung before writing this book, and indeed had to do what can only be called research on the science of campanology before making it an integral part of her novel's plot and theme (DLS to Maxwell Fraser, 13 Dec. 1936). For her efforts, she was rewarded by bell-ringers' acknowledgments that the book contained only a few minor errors in its change-ringing material, and with an order from her physician to take three weeks of complete rest after finishing the manuscript. She had thoroughly exhausted her immense supply of energy on this book.[10] Regarding technical accuracy, Harriet Vane admits that she has never published a book with fewer than "six major howlers" (*Gaudy Night* ch. 3). Her creator would surely be gratified to realize that today, the *Oxford Companion to Music* refers interested readers to *The Nine Tailors* for a lucid account of the highly specialized subject of change-ringing (Durkin 71).

This authenticity is what critics have meant when they have praised the novel as one of the finest examples of a mystery story incorporating specialized knowledge. Such specialized knowledge is a bonus provided by a certain kind of detective fiction, and is enjoyed, even craved, by the intelligent terrier of a reader for whom Sayers wished to write. As a scholar, she enjoyed "getting up" or researching new areas. As a popular novelist, she also knew that a form which combines new or esoteric knowledge with genuine suspense and imagination will always have an audience, because "to listen-in on other people's 'shop' is the most entertaining thing in the world" (*The Sunday Times* 4 Feb. 1934). This is just another way of putting the cliché about fiction's appealing to the insatiable human appetite for gossip, or what Austen calls "news" (*Pride and Prejudice* ch. 1).

Aside from campanology, readers of Sayers's novels can learn something about advertising and newspapers (*Murder Must Advertise*), college governance and the academic life (*Gaudy Night*), English law and the House of Lords (*Clouds of Witness*), modern science (*The Documents in the Case*), and ciphers and tides (*Have His Carcase*). In addition, her novels make numerous references to the work habits of both visual artists and writers; one mystery, *The Five Red Herrings,* depends upon a knowledge of a painter's palette for solution. Wimsey, of course, knows something about everything, so that just being in his company provides readers with endless tidbits of history, science, literature, music, and philosophy, in addition to details of the well-worn detective preoccupations of fingerprints, time of death, poisons, and alibis. Some of this is slap-dash, especially in the early books, and it is tempting to conclude that Wimsey knows too much, that no one could be so knowledgeable. Of course, one person is as knowledgeable as he—his creator. In this connection, it is interesting that Wimsey's mental gymnastics are always more convincing than his physical ones. Think of the improbable escapades of *Murder Must Advertise,* for example. Dorothy L. Sayers was an intellectual, not an athlete, and Wimsey is her child.[11]

Edmund Wilson would have been justified in skipping all of the material on bell-ringing in *The Nine Tailors* if it had been, as he suggests, extraneous to the story and only a tedious example of its author's pretentiousness. But *The Nine Tailors* is a coherent work of art because its obvious subject-matter, change-ringing and fen churches, is intrinsically related to its plot, its narrative structure, and its theme, much as whaling is integral to

Melville's *Moby Dick*. In one of her book reviews, Sayers observed that this kind of unity is essential for a mystery story that is also a work of art. She argued, in a review of *The Looking-Glass Murders,* that any good novel's idea must be

> integral to the structure of the book. . . . However entertaining the background of a story may be, yet, if the same story might equally well have been worked out against another background, then the setting is exterior to the structure, and the book, as a work of art, is incomplete. But here the setting is significant, because the theme of the action is also the theme of the book, and this is artistically right. (*The Sunday Times* 10 Feb. 1935)

Yet consider how many mysteries have almost interchangeable settings: the generic village, the standard country house, the lightly sketched great city. Some readers like—or find comfort in—this formulaic approach, but art does not seek to comfort us or to confirm our expectations. Nor is it exhausted by one reading. The generic nature of many mysteries is part of what makes them eminently forgettable, a quality that W. H. Auden believed was one of the symptoms of addiction to the detective story—an addiction he admitted having. A hallmark of such fiction, he said, is that "I forget the story as soon as I have finished it, and have no wish to read it again" ("The Guilty Vicarage"). Given his disparaging comments about Lord Peter Wimsey in the same essay, it is apparent that Auden did not admire Sayers; but her novels, especially the later ones, disprove his general thesis about the detective story, for they are among the select group of mysteries that linger in memory and often enjoy multiple readings.[12]

One of the reasons for this is that Sayers's novels offer more than a puzzle, more than a clever anecdote. From the beginning, she spent a good bit of time developing character and painting in the background of her stories. Over the years, she became more adept at evoking atmosphere, and one can say that three of her latter novels *must* take place in the settings used: *Murder Must Advertise, The Nine Tailors,* and *Gaudy Night.* To a lesser extent, the men's club named for Bellona, the goddess of war, is a fitting backdrop for a story that takes place on Armistice Day, especially since the effects of the First World War on English society are felt throughout the book. The vulgar and depressing "watering-place atmosphere" of *Have His Carcase* is similarly appropriate to its tale of seduction and betrayal; and presumably, the drama of a "suburban vamp" (*The Documents in the Case*) must take place in dreaded suburbia, or at least what Sayers understood of suburbia in 1930.[13] In these books, she was clearly working toward the kind of well-wrought artistic unity she would be able to effect in *The*

Nine Tailors. One could say of her Fenland mystery what Sayers herself once said of *The Album* by Mary Roberts Rinehart: "The book is so largely conceived that its outlines retain their massive purity in spite of their load of detail" (*The Sunday Times* 1 Oct. 1933).

All of the chapters in *The Nine Tailors* are headed with change-ringing terms, from the opening "The Bells Are Called Up" to the final "The Bells Are Called Down." In between are the bells running through their courses, as the detective runs through the puzzle, changing direction here and there, falling behind and dodging ahead, until reaching the final solution (or resolution, in the case of the bells). Throughout, bell-ringing is a metaphor for the detective process, which in turn becomes a metaphor for life. The solution to the whereabouts of the Wilbraham emeralds, one of several interrelated mysteries in this complexly woven narrative, is revealed by decoding a peal. Wimsey makes this discovery, not through using his reason, however, but by virtue of the creative mistake of Venables, who glances at the cipher without his eyeglasses and concludes that it is a peal. It is both cipher and peal, of course, and provides one of the book's many examples of the detective story's greatest lesson about the "reading" or interpretation of experience: namely, that it is almost impossible to know exactly what it is that one sees or to determine its significance. Poe, Conan Doyle, and Christie each demonstrate this quality of detective fiction in different ways.[14] In a detective story, everything must be considered important until proven otherwise, in direct contravention of the ordinary approach to experience. In *The Nine Tailors,* the discovery of the emeralds leads to other discoveries, until the central mystery of Deacon's death is finally solved. Through Venables's felicitous "mistake," the novel seems to imply not only the limitations of human reason, but also the need for more than clear vision and intense study to solve the real mysteries of this world—an ironic conclusion for a mystery novel.

As Wimsey wrestles with the mystery at Fenchurch St. Paul, he admits that, instead of the puzzle's being illuminated by investigation, it is only growing "curiouser and curiouser." How fitting that he appropriates the language of another logician cum fabulist, Lewis Carroll, whose ghost haunts these pages as it haunted their author's mind. The narrator uses the word again, commenting that "curiously enough, it was the Rector who solved the cipher," while Venables himself demurs that his discovery "was pure accident . . . and due entirely to my failing vision. That is a curious thing." The rector adds a statement which adumbrates the novel's final revelation, saying that this fortuitous accident "has given me the idea for a sermon about evil being over-ruled for good. But I never should have thought of the possibility that one might make a cipher out of change-ringing" ("Lord Peter Follows His Course Bell"). Until this point, no one trying to solve the mystery had thought of it either, nor of the astounding possibility that change-ringing would turn out to be not only the solution of the crime, but its perpetrator as well.

What Wimsey learns in this book is the impossibility of playing the game of detection, or of working out the permutations of a change with neat mathematical precision, without also invoking ambiguous human consequences. This is a lesson he was promised as early as *Whose Body?*, when his friend Inspector Parker warned him that, as an essentially serious human being, he would one day have to accept responsibility for his actions and stop playing at life (ch. 7). Wimsey's participation in ringing that New Year's peal, which Mr. Venables regards ironically as "really providential" because the great detective's being stranded in Fenchurch St. Paul was an accident ("The Bells Are Rung Up"), is more providential than either of them could know. No one could have guessed at the tale's opening that divine justice was operating through Wimsey, although the book continually reminds us that God works in mysterious ways—even to the point of permitting the indirect execution of a wicked man. For Wimsey this experience is a crucial step in his development as a human being: he cannot run away from the fact that, by being a bell-ringer and running through the prescribed courses, he was also taking a man's life and leading to the discovery of dark secrets held by some sympathetic characters. What started as an idle occupation becomes an act of overwhelming moral significance.

The great puzzle-solver learns that every solution leads to another type of mystery and carries with it the awful burden of knowledge. Like the Alice books to which it repeatedly refers, *The Nine Tailors* takes logic and turns it on its ear, implying that old habits of thinking are inadequate. At one point, a frustrated Wimsey says of the deceptive fens, "It's like Looking-Glass Country. Takes all the running we can do to stay in the same place." In response, the police superintendent scans a landscape that seems "flat as a chess-board, and squared like a chess-board with intersecting dyke and hedge" ("Plain Hunting"). This recognition of the limits of the "game" of detection, and of the inadequacy of human strategies to cope with this world and to solve the "problem" of life, is necessary before Wimsey takes on the consummate challenges of *Gaudy Night,* where his defenses are dropped and the chess-board itself is obliterated (ch. 20).

The Nine Tailors' ostensible subject, therefore, is fundamentally related to its plot, and is the mechanism for revealing its theme. The bells not only provide a metaphor for detection, but are, in a still-controversial stroke of imagination, also one of the most ingenious examples of that classic convention of detective fiction, death by unexpected means. The thief Geoffrey

Deacon was rung to death, we learn in the last chapter, the victim of nine hours' exposure, in the bell chamber of Fenchurch St. Paul, to the joyful noise of holy bells. The narrator is careful not to explain the exact etiology of the man's death, but even so, forensic scientists have had a bit of fun ridiculing the cause of death.[15] No one has been willing to test Sayers's idea, however, and for most readers the description of Wimsey's reaction to a few minutes in the bell chamber is proof enough of its murderous intensity (see "The Waters Are Called Home"). As Sayers herself once commented about a forensic point in an Anthony Rolls novel: "I have no idea whether the medical details . . . are correct, but I am quite ready to accept anything that is told me by so convincing an author" (*The Sunday Times* 11 Feb. 1934).

"Nine Tailors Make a Man," the bells' inscription tells us, and in the course of the novel, we learn that the nine tailors can even bring a wicked man to justice, acting as the hand of God. Thus, this book is both the most extreme example of Sayers's idea that answering the question "How?" in a murder mystery will lead to solving the more trite question, "Who?" and a subtle dramatization of her essential Christian belief that, in this world, good and evil are inextricably mixed, and, further, that good can even come from evil.

Her notable earlier attempts at focusing on the "How?" question include the equally controversial murder method used in *Unnatural Death,* namely the injection of a large bubble of air into an artery, which can cause death but is highly unlikely. "How?" is also the main mystery in *Strong Poison* and *Documents,* but *The Nine Tailors* ranks supreme in this mode. Although searching for clever new methods of killing people is partially the result of the mystery writer's need to keep the reader confused, DLS also saw it as linked ultimately to the novel's realism. As she once pointed out, in real life the problem for the police is usually not identifying the criminal, but understanding the crime well enough to convict him (*The Sunday Times* 22 July 1934).

Readers familiar with *The Nine Tailors* should not have been surprised when, a few years after its publication, DLS began writing religious drama and became an energetic, rational voice for Christianity in the modern world. In both subject matter and theme, this novel is a religious and distinctively Christian book, dealing as it does with questions of guilt, responsibility, suffering, and redemption. If, as its narrative suggests, human beings cannot solve the riddle of the universe by dint of intellect and imagination, it is not surprising that they should look to a higher power for some of the answers, as the following exchange between Mr. Venables and Lord Peter makes clear:

"So I think I'd better go," said Wimsey. "I rather wish I hadn't come buttin' into this. Some things may be better left alone. . . . I know all about not doing evil that good may come. It's doin' good that evil may come that is so embarrassin'."

"My dear boy," said the Rector, "it does not do for us to take too much thought for the morrow. It is better to follow the truth and leave the result in the hand of God. He can foresee where we cannot, because He knows all the facts."

"And never has to argue ahead of His data, as Sherlock Holmes would say?" ("The Quick Work")

As is true in *The Documents in the Case,* here a proper understanding of science and religion permits them to coalesce and even to vindicate each other.

It would appear to be no coincidence that the detective story, which both celebrates and tests the power of the intellect and of scientific inquiry, emerged at just the point in Western history when science had finally captured the popular mind but was increasingly challenged by the intelligentsia. Even Sayers's earliest fiction reveals a fear of trusting science and the intellect too much, as her hideous portrait of Sir Julian Freke shows (see *Whose Body?*). In a sense, Freke, the freakish half-human, is the dark side of Wimsey—and perhaps of his overwhelmingly cerebral creator—or at least is what Wimsey could become if his heart were never engaged and tempered by experience. The development of Wimsey's character, and of Sayers's art, is partially a development away from the brittle cleverness of the detective story and into the ambiguous path of an education of the heart. Given what is known about her life, it is also possible that through these novels she was examining her own tendency toward trusting the intellect too much, of denying the claims of the heart.[16] It is almost as though her novels ask what is the most one can expect from the intellect, and having determined that, move on to discover another order of experience.

In *The Nine Tailors,* the setting of the old church calls to mind not only humanity's relationship to history (or time), but its relationship to God (or eternity), with the church's tower imaging a link between the two. Through numerous scenes of ascent into the tower, the novel suggests that human beings must crawl out of themselves and reach beyond the earth for an understanding of the essential inscrutability of the universe, that lingering sense of mystery that is left when all soluble problems have been settled. Bits of the earthly mystery are cleared up by these ascents, notably in Hilary Thorpe's finding the cipher in the bell tower early in the story, and Wimsey's final climb at the novel's resounding climax, when his own pain reveals to him how Deacon died. The scene is one of Sayers's most powerful:

As his head rose through the floor, the brazen fury of the bells fell about his ears like the blows from a thousand beating hammers. The whole tower was drenched and drunken with noise. It rocked and reeled with the reeling of the bells, and staggered like a drunken man. Stunned and shaken, Wimsey set his foot on the last ladder.

Half-way up he stopped, clinging desperately with his hands. He was pierced through and buffeted by the clamour. Through the brazen crash and clatter there went one high note, shrill and sustained, that was like a sword in the brain. . . . It was not noise—it was brute pain. . . . He felt himself screaming, but could not hear his own cry. . . . this unendurable shrill clangour was a raving madness, an assault of devils. . . . The belfry heaved and wheeled about him as the bells dipped and swung. . . . Mouth up, mouth down, they brawled with their tongues of bronze, and through it all that shrill, high, sweet, relentless note went stabbing and shivering. ("The Waters Are Called Home")

This is the imagery of waking nightmare, the intolerable horror of facing some final, irrevocable truth. Employing a whole range of poetic devices, including personification of the bells, alliteration ("drenched and drunken," "rocked and reeled," "brawled . . . bronze"), internal rhyme ("bells fell," "heaved and wheeled,"), and onomatopoeia ("It rocked and reeled with the reeling of the bells"; "Mouth up, mouth down, they brawled with their tongues of bronze"), the language makes the reader hear, feel, and see what Wimsey experiences. Is it any wonder that Charles Williams called this ending "quite unsurpassable"?[17]

When Wimsey finally reaches the roof, he is surrounded by "an enormous stillness," as though he has travelled through one last dark and cacophonous night of the soul and found peace. The scene causes the words "Childe Roland to the dark tower came" to echo in the reader's mind—with Wimsey, like the knights of old, representing the forces of civilization against barbarism, of light against darkness. This time when Wimsey leaves the tower he knows the solution to the novel's main mystery, for he has almost died in the way Deacon died. This experience represents a radical transformation of sleuth-hound into mortal man, through an indentification of criminal and detective, hunter and hunted, crime and solution. This paradox makes the great detective's insight here as humbling as it is heroic. As Lionel Basney has written, "Wimsey's profound discomfort . . . completes, without releasing us from, the moral tension of the murder itself" (Hannay 35). Such purposeful ambiguity places this tale within the realm of art, and encourages richly varied interpretations.

Through the series of ascents, the tower also comes to represent the effect of perspective, or angle of vision, on experience. When Hilary climbs to its top, she sees in one still moment the intersection of past, present and future:

> Far away beneath her lay the churchyard, and, while she looked, a little figure, quaintly foreshortened, crawled beetle-like from the porch. . . . [It was] Mrs. Venables going home to lunch. . . . A brown spot in the churchyard caught her eye and her heart seemed to turn over in her body. Here . . . her mother lay buried. ("Mr. Gotobed . . .")

From the almost godlike perspective of the ancient tower, the young girl is able to comprehend not only the essential triviality of human lives but also their excruciating brevity, a lesson as ambiguously frightening and reassuring as life itself.

In a laudatory review of G. K. Chesterton's *The Scandal of Father Brown*, DLS argues that Chesterton's gift to detective fiction was his bringing God back into the story. The review asks, "Is the detective to figure only as the arm of the law or as the hand of God?" In *The Nine Tailors*, Wimsey and all of the bell-ringers function literally as the "hand of God"; by bringing their hands to pull the ropes, they unwittingly kill the evil Deacon in the course of a religious observance. Thus, they bring divine justice to a man who has wronged society. This is accomplished through a maze of coincidences that would seem melodramatic except for their everyday nature: a car accident, a case of the flu, a chance meeting, a lost key. In the context of the story, which continually reminds us of humanity's relationship to God and the eternal, this maze of coincidence is elevated to the domain of providence. Again writing on Chesterton, Sayers explains indirectly her emphasis on the eternal in *The Nine Tailors:*

> If we wipe out God from the [detective] problem we are in very real danger of wiping out man as well. Unless we are prepared to bring our murderers to the bar of Eternity, we may construct admirable jig-saw puzzles, but shall certainly never write a "Hamlet" . . . [Chesterton] showed us how to enlarge the boundaries of the detective story by making it deal with real death and real wickedness and real, that is to say, divine judgement. (*The Sunday Times* 7 April 1935)

The sweeping vistas of *The Nine Tailors*—up to heaven, out to the last reaches of the horizon on the endless fen flatlands—dramatize Sayers's enlargement of the detective story in patently physical terms.

In a most intriguing discussion of this novel, John Cawelti has suggested that Sayers even had the temerity to make God "the least likely person" in the sense that God permitted the series of actions and coincidences that brought Deacon to his death in the bell chamber (*Mystery, Adventure, and Romance* 124). If we can accept this rather waggish interpretation of a divine "Whodunit?" at Fenchurch St. Paul, we need only add that, by using the bells as the method of death—bells hanging there, like the purloined letter, in the open for anyone to see at any time—Sayers has used all of the detective essentials created by Poe: the clue that is concealed by virtue of remaining in plain view; death by unexpected means; and the murderer as least likely person (*Tales of Detection* viii). In keeping with the conventions of her own day, Sayers has also adhered brilliantly to the practice of fair play. No one can say that the means of death is not prominently displayed, along with much discussion of the bells' potential for harm. Nor can the author be charged with withholding important information about bell-ringing from the reader. Sayers has, therefore, employed the chief conventions of classical detective fiction even in this novel, which moves far beyond the ordinary boundaries of the tale of detection and into a meditation on the unanswerable riddle of the universe.

Yet in spite of all its emphasis on the supernatural, there is an essential realism about this novel that is lacking in Sayers's earlier books. Much of this new realism is created by changes in her hero. Here, Wimsey is himself threatened with death when he enters the bell chamber; throughout the story, he is dwarfed by his surroundings and subjected to the torments of the seasons; and his inner torment about the moral implications of detection, which has developed throughout his career, grows measurably in this story; it will reach a pitch of frenzy in the final scene of *Busman's Honeymoon*.

Perhaps one of the most striking differences in this book is Wimsey's separation from his usual world. He wrecks his magnificent car (a modern knight's steed) at the story's beginning, and must proceed on foot through a blinding snowstorm; he is far from the luxuries and enticements of London and the Piccadilly flat; he is separated from his family and friends during most of the action; and even Bunter, who is in attendance, seems relatively remote most of the time. Wimsey, the overweening sophisticate, is rendered childlike in his dealings with Mr. and Mrs. Venables: he thankfully shares their oxtail stew and courteously helps Mrs. Venables with chores in the parish. She pities him when he cannot solve the mystery, and her husband attends to his uncertainties as a kindly guardian would. The Wimsey that readers first met in 1923 was a self-conscious caricature of the Great Detective and English gentleman, resembling more the archetypal man-about-town than a real human being. How different—and how much more sympathetic—is this ignominious picture of him:

> Lord Peter Wimsey sat in the schoolroom at the Rectory, brooding over a set of underclothing. . . . the vest and pants [of the dead man] were spread upon the table. . . . They had been washed, but there were still faint discolorations upon

them, like the shadow of corruption, and here and there the fabric had rotted away, as the garments of mortality will, when the grave has had its way with them. Wafted in through the open window came the funeral scent of jonquils.

The last line, carrying the "funeral scent of jonquils," is reminiscent of the opening lines of Eliot's *The Waste Land*. Even after much study of these miserable reminders of mortality, Wimsey is no closer to a solution. In his rank frustration, he looks more the part of a schoolboy having trouble with arithmetic than the great thinking machine he seemed in earlier novels: "Lord Peter thrust his fingers into his hair till the sleek yellow locks stood upright. 'Bless his heart!' thought Mrs. Venables, looking in upon him through the window. She had conceived a warm maternal affection for her guest" ("Tailor Paul Is Called Before . . ."). Contrast this image with what is perhaps the apex of Wimsey's "priggish superman" career in *The Five Red Herrings:*

> "This," said Lord Peter Wimsey, "is the proudest moment of my life. At last I really feel like the Sherlock Holmes. A Chief Constable, a Police ector, a Police Sergeant and two constables have appealed to me to decide between their theories, and with my chest puffed like a pouter-pigeon, I can lean back in my chair and say, 'Gentlemen, you are all wrong.' " (Ch.26)

Bracing stuff if you expect fictional heroes to enact common fantasies of superhuman prowess, but a bit *outré* for a believable character in a realistic novel.

Sayers had often stated her preference for the realistic novel of character, and it is a significant moment in her development as a novelist, and in the life of her hero, when he admits to Superintendent Blundell, after "a restless day and night" spent trying to solve the Fenchurch mystery:

> "I think I have been the most unmitigated and unconscionable ass that ever brayed in a sleuth-hound's skin. Now, however, I have solved the entire problem, with one trivial exception. . . ."
> . . . "What's the bit you haven't solved, by the way?"
> "Well, the murder," said his lordship, with an embarrassed cough. "I can't quite make out who did that, or how. But that, as I say, is a trifle." ("The Quick Work")

This is a remarkable statement from the great detective who has spent his career solving murder mysteries, but the mystery at Fenchurch St. Paul is deeper than the question of one man's death. This novel evokes some of the essential mysteriousness of things to which the greatest mystery stories point, accomplished here through its evocation of the gothic atmosphere of church and churchyard, its insistent imagery of the bells as almost preternatural creatures with minds of their own, and its delicate probing of the mystery of human action and responsibility. It seeks finally to comprehend the incomprehensible riddle of the universe, while dramatizing the impossibility of finding any clear solution to the problem of life. When Wimsey learns that the detective problem is "trivial," at least in the larger scheme of things, he has learned an important lesson in perspective.[18]

Though Wimsey dominates the book, the novel's large cast of characters contribute significantly to its power. Sayers always handled minor characters well, but she lavished more attention on them as she matured. Bunter, Wimsey's too-perfect valet, has some wonderful scenes in this novel, especially the mock-tragic episode of the bottle that was accidentally washed clean of its fingerprints ("Emily Turns Bunter from Behind"). This is among Sayers's most comical episodes, one in which the comedy of classes reveals the insufferable snobbery of what used to be called "the lower orders."

The novel's most memorable character is Mr. Venables, who effectively takes Bunter's place as Wimsey's partner in crime-solving. Venables, a richly comic figure, is one of Sayers's finest characterizations, and the attention she lavishes on his portraiture demonstrates how far she has come toward writing a traditional English novel. Venables is described initially as scholarly and gentle, that is, as a very "type" of the old-fashioned parson, but it is his marvelous, almost Dickensian eccentricities that bring him to life: his unreasonable passion for campanology and church history, the compulsive tooting of his horn at the shrubbery, the mild banter that conceals great wisdom. Sayers's insight into and compassion for Venables are apparent:

The service was devoid of incident, except that Mr. Venables again mislaid the banns, which had to be fetched from the vestry . . . in his sermon, he made a solemn little mention of the unfortunate stranger whose funeral was to take place on the morrow, whereat Mr. Russell nodded, with an air of importance and approbation. The Rector's progress to the pulpit was marked by a loud and gritty crunching, which caused Mrs. Venables to mutter in an exasperated tone, "That's the coke again—Gotobed *will* be so careless with it." ("Lord Peter Is Called into Hunt")

Venables is a real human being, drawn with a mixture of amusement and exasperation, mockery and tenderness, and his portrait evokes strong sympathy and identification in the reader, who recognizes the human face.

In the brief, sparsely outlined detective story of Conan Doyle and most of his emulators in the twenties, including Agatha Christie, there is no place for such character painting or close scrutiny of manners—unless they are directly relevant to the mystery—but these details add immeasurably to a full-blown novel in the English tradition. Indeed, in a sense, they *are* the novel.

Venables brings to mind Fielding's Parson Adams, who accompanied Joseph Andrews on his manic adventures and who was based upon the greatest comic idealist of them all, Don Quixote. These men, who are seemingly so out of touch with mundane reality, manifest through their good humor, loving hearts, and profound simplicity an essential truth about life. In a way, the venerable Venables is Wimsey's teacher, reminding him of the persistent mystery of experience, reassuring him about his role as detective, helping him, indirectly, solve the mystery. Though he may be a prototypical absent-minded scholar—losing the keys to the tower, setting his clock always ahead because it is inaccurate, forgetting his place in conversation—Venables reveals great wisdom when he cautions Wimsey that the problem with solutions is that sometimes they only intensify the mystery. In this imperfect world, he warns, it is possible that "the interpretation is even more perplexing than the cipher" ("Lord Peter Follows Course Bell"). Yet he also encourages the detective in his frustrating work, drawing a metaphor from the bells: "Even if you have to lie still a whole pull now and again, you'll soon find yourself back in the hunt," he suggests kindly. When Wimsey acknowledges that it irritates him to "lie behind" for the whole way and get no nearer to a solution, Venables takes the opportunity to make a little joke that strikes at the heart of the detective's struggle: " 'There's always something that lies behind a mystery,' said the Rector, mildly enjoying his little witticism. 'A solution of some kind" ("Lord Peter Is Called Wrong"). Obvious, perhaps, but a reminder that Wimsey and every curious soul needs: do not ask questions if you cannot stand the answers. Just as the dammed-up water must break free in the terrible flood at the novel's end, so must the results of Wimsey's detecting, or indeed of any human action, be made manifest. As this novel dramatizes again and again, human beings cannot foresee many of the consequences of their actions, but consequences there will inevitably be ("The Slow Work").

The novel's rich tapestry also includes wonderful cameo appearances by a whole panoply of characters who fill out our sense of English village life in the early part of this century. As is true of all profoundly realistic novels, this attention to the particular manners of a particular place also implies something universal in human experience. A half-century after they were created, we recognize as real the intriguing wildness of Potty Peake, the village idiot reminiscent of Faulkner's Vardaman, who tempts us to trust too much what he says by playing on our strong temptation to seek wisdom in such unlikely places; the contentious bell-ringers, who fight the immemorial battles of people living in close proximity to each other while vying for some paltry distinction within their small world; and Mr. Ashton, a "farmer of the old school . . . [who] spoke in a series of gruff barks and held himself so rigidly that if he had swallowed a poker it could only have produced unseemly curves and flexions in his figure," an economical way of suggesting a personality and a whole way of life. His wife is undaunted by such rigidity, however, declaring in one unforgettable line that she makes her own cowslip wine because "this nasty stuff you get at the shops . . . [is] good for nothing but to blow out the stomach and give you gas," ("Lord Peter Dodges"). Though some readers today are offended by Sayers's attention to the distinctions of social class, including dialect, her fine ear permitted her to write English as it was actually spoken. If this ability tends to highlight the differences among people in her society, it does so in the service of realism. And one could argue that this willingness to hear others in their own voices is an indication of an essential respect for their individuality and their right to be who they are.

On the difficult subject of social distinctions, few are as eloquent as the most refined Mrs. Gates, who spends an entire scene bleating about the vulgarity of other villagers to Superintendent Blundell. She is a virulent cross between Austen's Miss Bates, that "great talker upon little matters" (*Emma*), and the pretentious Mrs. Elton. The encounter between Mrs. Gates and Police Superintendent Blundell demonstrates Sayers's talent for delineating manners, especially as they relate to social class and reveal character: "When a highly refined lady, with a grey glace gown and a grey glace eye, addresses a full-blown Superintendent in plain clothes as 'officer,' the effect is not soothing, and is not meant to be so." Even though he is offended, Blundell does not blunder as Mrs. Gates reacts to the placement of her wreath at the funeral. His exchange with this "lady" is worthy of Austen or Dickens:

"Miss Thorpe is one of the Family," said Mrs. Gates, "and the Family are always considerate of other people's feelings. True gentlefolk always are. Upstairs are not."

"That's very true, indeed, ma'am," said the Superintendent, with so much earnestness that a critical listener might almost have supposed the remark to have a personal application. ("Lord Peter Dodges . . . .")

In the novel's sardonic narrator, Sayers has provided just such a "critical listener," of course, and the combination of irony and understatement in this scene is devastating.

All of this attention to manners is not only a hallmark of English fiction, but is also an essential part of the detective process. As Sherlock Holmes knows, what a man wears or how he speaks discloses essential clues to understanding him and any mystery surrounding him. For this reason, the more stratified a society is, the more likely it is to foster the classical detective story of observation, ratiocination, and solution. Today, with all sorts of distinctions blurred almost into oblivion, such deduction from appearances is more difficult and less certain.[19] Although manners and their meaning cannot be taken for granted anymore, crime remains with us; hence, the general post-war shift away from detective fiction to crime literature, which tends to be preoccupied with the criminal mind, or with details of the crime, not with its explanation or punishment.[20]

The exquisitely detailed East Anglian landscape is itself almost a character in *The Nine Tailors*. The book provides readers, especially Americans, with a short history of the fens and their churches, as well as an understanding of the central role of the parish church in English village life. This role is radically different from the church's function in American culture, based as it is on diversity and an official separation of church and state that precludes one church's representing the totality of communal life or history.

One can learn a great deal about English history, architecture, and culture from *The Nine Tailors*. This material is not gratuitous, because, as with the change-ringing passages, it is relevant to the novel's theme and the moral development of its hero. Wimsey is carried away by his first sight of the inside of Fenchurch St. Paul, carried up and out of himself and his own time, a necessary movement in the development of his character on the road to *Gaudy Night:*

At first glance he felt himself sobered and awe-stricken by the noble proportions of the church, in whose vast spaces the congregation . . . seemed almost lost. The wide nave and shadowy aisles, the lofty span of the chancel arch—crossed, though not obscured, by the delicate fan-tracery and crenellated moulding of the screen—the intimate and cloistered loveliness of the chancel, with its pointed arcading, graceful ribbed vault and five narrow east lancets, led his attention on and focused it first upon the remote glow of the sanctuary. Then his gaze, returning to the nave, followed the strong yet slender shafting that sprang fountain-like from floor to foliated column-head, spraying into the light, wide arches that carried the clerestory. And there, mounting to the steep pitch of the roof, his eyes were held entranced with wonder and delight. Incredibly aloof, flinging back the light in a dusky shimmer of bright hair and gilded outspread wings, soared the ranked angels, cherubim and seraphim, choir over choir, from corbel and hammer-beam floating face to face uplifted.

"My God!" muttered Wimsey, not without reverence. ("The Bells in Their Courses")

This is obviously Sayers's native territory; there is not an awkward or impatient move as the camera eye luxuriates in every detail. Even Wimsey, the irreligious child of eighteenth-century rationalism, is moved by such an edifice. The experience forces him to recall the Biblical text, "He rode upon the cherubims and did fly; He came flying upon the wings of the wind." Some two hundred pages and many months later, these very words help him solve the mystery, suggesting one of the values of allusion and memory, that is, as a key to understanding ourselves and our experience.[21] This is just one of many looking-up scenes in *The Nine Tailors,* each drawing the human detective ever closer to eternal reality.

It is interesting to drive through the fens today and note the literal, physical dominance of the terrain by its stunning churches. A visitor to the tiny village of Bluntisham, where the Sayers family moved from Oxford when their daughter was only four, may be astounded by the magnificent reach of the spire of its parish church. The height of the spire is somewhat exaggerated because the church itself stands on a slight rise and looms up out of the otherwise relentlessly flat land. Walking through the churchyard, one may also be rewarded with the pleasant shock of recognition in finding members of the local Thoday family buried there.[22] Their mossy tombstones bear lasting testimony to the veracity of the novelist's claim that she used names remembered from childhood in her story of the fens.

An interesting historical perspective on Fenland churches is offered by Frank Morley in his *Literary Britain:*

A characteristic of the Fenland that had emerged in early times was that when floods stood in the land, any eminence was a haven for whatever strange company the emergency might bring together. Where a church was built if only on a slight rise, upon occasion it could be equal sanctuary, for the moment at least, for any refugee, inlaw or outlaw. Church towers came to have a double function as landmarks by day and by night, when so required, as lighthouses. . . . The development of very early hermits' chapels into the later lantern churches, each by both bell and beacon offering a haven, was a theme with which Dorothy Sayers had special sympathy. (43)

As *The Nine Tailors'* dramatic ending shows, the church—both as building and social institution—is the heart of this society. During the flood at the novel's end, Sayers effectively has her little world reenact the Biblical

Flood, thereby suggesting the timeless dimension of reality. But the flood is also the means of gathering all her characters back into the church, on stage for the final act. The novel ends as it begins, in a communal celebration of place, history, and tradition.

To understand how far this novel is removed from the classical tale of ratiocination on which it is based, it is interesting to consider how Sir Arthur Conan Doyal might have written it. He would, perhaps, have young Hilary Thorpe come to London, seeking Holmes's advice about the "Curious Case of the Corpse with No Hands." She would request the assistance of the great detective in determining how a stranger's body came to desecrate her mother's grave. Holmes and Watson would speed off to the country on the train, and would probably spend about twenty-four hours poking around the only-too-innocent looking village before Holmes would announce, in a few paragraphs at the end, who the man was and how he died. Watson would be astounded, Hilary would be delighted, and Holmes would have displayed just enough knowledge of bells, English churches, and the effects of sound on the central nervous system to explain away the mystery. How Holmes comes to know these things is often the greatest mystery in the story, however, and he explains the salient points *after* he has discovered something of importance, not as he is detecting. In this regard, Conan Doyle's narrative method is quite different from the fair-play rule of Sayers's day. Such a story would include—*pace* Edmund Wilson—none of the infernal stuff on campanology, nor the exquisitely detailed village life, nor the large cast of believable minor characters, nor the jewelled prose. And the mystery of Deacon's death would remain singular, pristine, and explainable, with none of this murky metaphysical business about the ambiguity of guilt, responsibility, and expiation.

If Holmes chastised Watson for degrading "what should have been a course of lectures into a series of tales" by daring to put a bit of "colour and life" into the record of Holmes's cases ("The Adventure of the Copper Beeches"), the wizard of Baker Street would, for once, be speechless at what Sayers has done with the mystery story. For many purists, she has gone too far in expanding the detective anecdote into a fully imagined novel. But one leaves *The Nine Tailors* with a deepened sense of life, especially its complexity and ambiguity, which is the kind of revelation that emerges from genuine works of art. This is a novel that even Dorothy L. Sayers herself could not have accomplished without all the writing and living she had done since beginning to write detective stories.[23]

The Nine Tailors shows that one mystery leads to another, that there are "wheels within wheels," as Mrs. Venables says, and that in this dark world, human beings have only momentary flashes illuminating real truths and final causes. To dramatize life's ambiguity, Sayers portrays Wimsey as increasingly unsure of himself and his function in a multi-faceted mystery. It is no longer a simple question of what he will find behind the locked door, in the old tower, at the base of the obvious and relatively trivial mystery. As Venable hints, the puzzle-solver may find more than he was seeking at the end of his quest, something about life that cannot be explained away, something he may prefer not to know. From *Oedipus* forward, the greatest mysteries suggest a ritualistic reenactment of the Fall: fuelled by the insatiable desire to know, their principals cannot bear the knowledge once gained.[24] Curiouser and curiouser, indeed.

As we have seen, in "The Guilty Vicarage" Auden avowed that he never remembered detective stories, but *The Nine Tailors* resonates in memory as the great bells at Fenchurch St. Paul resonate through the wild, windswept wastes surrounding them:

> the bells gave tongue: . . . rioting and exulting high up in the dark tower. . . . Out over the flat, white wastes of fen, over the spear-straight, steel-dark dykes and the wind-bent, groaning poplar trees, bursting from the snow-choked louvres of the belfry, whirled away southward and westward in gusty blasts of clamour to the sleeping counties went the music of the bells—little Gaude, silver Sabaoth, strong John and Jericho, glad Jubilee, sweet Dimity and old Batty Thomas, with great Tailor Paul bawling and striding like a giant in the midst of them. Up and down went the shadows of the ringers upon the walls, up and down went the scarlet sallies flickering roofwards and floorwards, and up and down, hunting in their courses, went the bells of Fenchurch St. Paul. ("The Bells in Their Courses")

This passage, which adroitly mimics the rhythm of the bells and causes us to feel their power through an insistent use of parallelism, repetition, and alliteration, calls our attention both up and out, away from ourselves and the particulars of time and place.

The classic mystery story, Sayers said, points to something larger than itself. To what does this novel point, but to the ineluctable mystery of things, to the bar of eternity and the insoluble, irresistible riddle of the universe? Subtitled "Changes Rung on an Old Theme," *The Nine Tailors*'s theme is indeed the oldest: man against nature, human mortality against the backdrop of eternity. Sayers generalizes by having the little village stand for a microcosm not only of English society, but of the human race, as it reenacts the Flood. To Dorothy L. Sayers, the church is the ark, the place that cannot be taken, and those who make the journey to it—good, bad, or indifferent—will not die. This may seem a strange message to communicate through a mystery novel, but it is the very statement that its author was to make more directly in the coming decade, as England was besieged by forces as terrible and as real.

Flannery O'Connor, who is in most ways lightyears away from Dorothy L. Sayers, has nonetheless made some comments on the relationship between mystery and fiction that serve to illuminate the latter's work. O'Connor boldly asserts that "it is the business of fiction to embody mystery through manners," and while she is not speaking of the mystery genre per se, her comment is pertinent to the kind of mystery novel at which Sayers excelled. The O'Connor essay also points to the essential link between the mystery story and the comedy of manners strain in the English novel, and suggests a reason for considering the mystery as a legitimate novel form. In another context, O'Connor adds that it is the novelist's "dramatic need . . . to know manners under stress" (*Mystery and Manners* 124, 208), a possible explanation for why the Golden Age of detective fiction came at just the historical moment, after the First World War, when England was facing momentous social change. The phrase "manners under stress" is powerfully suggestive of any society in crisis or transition.

Writing explicitly about detective fiction, Robert Barnard suggests a connection between historical currents and this form of popular literature. Admitting that "one should not take the comparison between the classic crime story and the comedy of manners too far," he goes on to assert that

the parallels are striking. In 1660 in Britain the metropolitan upper class had just been through two gruelling decades. . . . Through Restoration comedy they built a new wall around themselves, to keep out the realities of a changed world. . . .

In 1920 the English middle classes had seen empires crumble, new Bolshevik republics established, Labour parties flourishing, a whole battalion of middle-class standards collapse. They suspected, like the Restoration nobility, that their world was gone forever, and they took refuge in a form of literature that was hedged with rules and conventions. . . . (Keating, *Who Dunit?* 31)

Perhaps the most famous reflection on the loss of the old world was Robert Graves's bitter autobiography, *Good-Bye to All That*, but the cataclysmic effects of the 1914–18 war were felt throughout the world. That war's aftermath stimulated much important fiction by the generation of American writers whom Gertrude Stein first described as "lost."[25] It is interesting to scan Barnard's list of what happened to postwar English society, and realize that all of these changes and stresses are somehow reflected in Sayers's novels.[26]

DLS was not really nostalgic, as some writers of English-style mysteries are, but was clearly writing at the turning point in a way of life. Her novels offer a kind of affectionate backward glance at England's past, while maintaining a steady eye on the manners that reveal its tenuous hold on the present and suggest its future. Like the very best detective stories, *The Nine Tailors* is, in addition to everything else that may be said of it, a fine piece of social history.

Flannery O'Connor perceived a link between social upheaval—which she herself observed in modern Southern culture—and the stuff of all fiction: "Manners are of such great consequence to the novelist that any kind will do. Bad manners are better than no manners at all, and because we are losing our customary manners, we are probably overly conscious of them; this seems to be a condition that produces writers" (*Mystery and Manners* 29). Such a condition produced Dorothy L. Sayers, as it had helped to produce the novel form itself in the tumultuous eighteenth century. Though Sayers's comedy is much warmer, more accepting than O'Connor's, both were moved to write by such displays of manners and mannerisms. As novelists, they knew that manners reveal the person and typify the culture in which the person acts. Thus, all of the attention to dialect, to class, to pretension and social dis-ease, is the novelist's means of penetrating the mystery of human nature that is both revealed and concealed in manners. While O'Connor was a more patently Christian novelist than Sayers was, her description of the fictional world of the Christian writer is particularly fitting for *The Nine Tailors:*

> The chief difference between the novelist who is an orthodox Christian and the novelist who is merely a naturalist is that the Christian novelist lives in a larger universe. He believes that the natural world contains the supernatural. And this doesn't mean that his obligation to portray the natural is less; it means it is greater. (*Mystery and Manners* 175)

The spacious world of *The Nine Tailors* is firmly grounded in a reality as recognizable as the English countryside where it is set, but this palpably natural world is also permeated by the supernatural reality in which Sayers believed. As O'Connor observed, "fiction is so very much an incarnational act" (*Mystery and Manners* 68); in faithfully recreating a time-bound, particular, human world, Dorothy L. Sayers implies a whole universe of timeless reality.

The Nine Tailors is a monumental achievement: a thoroughly satisfying mystery with an ingenious plot; a wonderful evocation of East Anglia and its people; a short course in campanology and church architecture; a rumination on sin, suffering, guilt, and redemption; a rollicking comedy of particular manners and universal truths. In it, Sayers accomplished her goal of writing a mystery novel as largely imagined as those by Collins and Dickens. She could not have written this novel without the increased tolerance for subtlety and ambiguity achieved in *The Documents in the Case,* or the new willingness to face death attained in *Strong Poison* and *Have His Carcase,* or the practice in creating an organic relationship of plot, setting, and theme attempted in *Murder Must Advertise.* From the height of *The Nine Tailors,* she was ready to reach for her crowning achievement, *Gaudy Night.*

5

Gaudy Night
and the Mystery of the Human Heart

If *The Nine Tailors*, with its focus upon the exquisitely elaborate hunt for a rational solution to mystery, is Sayers's supreme achievement in the detective story tradition, her penultimate novel, *Gaudy Night*, is the culmination of the other major strain that has been flowing in her work since the beginning: the rich novel of character that is the cornerstone of traditional English fiction. In *Gaudy Night*, she finally accomplishes her goal of marrying the detective plot to the English novel and achieves the most complete expression of thematic concerns that had been implied in her work from the beginning. *Gaudy Night* is a mystery story, but in it, the focus is upon the human perplexities revealed through the mystery, rather than upon the detective problem per se. Thus, the novel raises more questions than it answers, and troubles the reader into thinking about real human problems and real human life.

In many ways, *Gaudy Night* could not be more different from *The Nine Tailors*, and their existence—written as they were within a space of three highly productive years—is eloquent testimony to the breadth and versatility of Sayers's talent as a novelist.

As in the early books, Lord Peter Wimsey is the central character of *The Nine Tailors*, isolated in the tiny village, a modern knight on his lonely quest for truth. Though the story is filled with interesting minor characters, they are brought on stage primarily for working out the mystery, and the great detective is left to himself and his ratiocination much of the time. Conversely, Harriet Vane is the central character of *Gaudy Night*, and she is surrounded by a college full of people, people from whom she cannot escape. Her world is essentially the tightly bound world of human relationships and quarrels; her task, the heroine's traditional lot of working within such social groups and boundaries. In both spatial and psychological terms, therefore, *The Nine Tailors* and *Gaudy Night* suggest, respectively, masculine and feminine experience, or at least what has been regarded traditionally as such.

To simplify and bring their differences into bold relief, we can say that *The Nine Tailors* focuses upon the eternal, while *Gaudy Night* is caught up in the temporal; the first is expansive and metaphysical, while the second is intensive and psychological. The earlier novel's imagery suggests, through many movements of ascent, that human beings must look up to heaven and out to the farthest reaches of the Earth for answers to their problems. The structure of *Gaudy Night* forces its characters inward, into territory that proves even more challenging and frightening—inside the university, inside the college walls, inside the quad, inside the room, finally inside the lonely spaces of their minds.

In her introduction to the first *Omnibus of Crime,* DLS noted a similar turn toward psychological realism in crime fiction: "the study of psychology has produced . . . a new kind of terror—the nightmare country between sanity and madness; the pressure of mind upon living mind, and the lonely horror of the dark places of the soul" (45). It is into this nightmare country that Harriet Vane ventures in *Gaudy Night,* where she falls prey to the "pressure of mind upon living mind," to the point that she questions the sanity of everyone in the story, including herself. With a pervading sense of evil more potent than that found in most murder mysteries, "these chapters convey more real eeriness and discomfort than you could get from gallons of blood" (*The Sunday Times* 16 July 1933) and point the way toward the psychological thrillers of Ruth Rendell and P. D. James.[1]

This movement away from the artificial puzzle-plot and into the mysterious regions of the human heart had been Sayers's general direction since *The Documents in the Case,* and she recognized that for many detective fans, it was tantamount to an abandonment of the genre. In a 1935 review she wrote:

Some readers prefer their detective stories to be of . . . [the] conventional kind; they like to enjoy the surface excitement without the inward disturbance that comes of being forced to take things seriously. But I believe the future to be with those writers who can contrive to strike the note of sincerity and to persuade us that violence really hurts. (*The Sunday Times* 26 May 1935)

In *Gaudy Night,* the novel on which she was working when she made these observations, we see real seriousness and real pain caused by even the threat of violence, while the inward disturbance of everyone in the story—

particularly of Harriet herself—far exceeds the surface display of violence. In fact, this novel is so remote from the detective formula that there is not even a murder in it, though there is an insistent threat of death. Thus, its detective plot is a more extreme version of the mystery of *The Nine Tailors,* where the body is not discovered until the second part of the book and is not actually a victim of murder at all. The consequent delay in setting up the Fenland mystery helps build the rich East Anglian atmosphere and establish the old church and its brooding bells as main "characters" before distracting us with the small matter of Geoffrey Deacon's death. This is to say, such a chronology creates a proper perspective from which to view the matters of life and death considered in the story.

In her first four novels, Sayers followed the pattern of most Golden Age detective stories, commencing the action with the discovery of a body or the discussion of a murder. Once again, *The Documents in the Case* is the pivotal text in her breaking from convention. That epistolary novel permits extended discussions of morality, marriage, art, science, philosophy, psychology, and religion largely because it retells the story of Harrison's death by building up to it, in a flashback, midway in the book. If the narrative had begun more conventionally, with the discovery of a body, as it does in *The Unpleasantness at the Bellona Club,* for example, the assumption is that even loquacious Jack Munting would have been forced to interrupt his philosophical ruminations and focus upon the detective problem; it is a bit riveting to come upon a corpse, after all. As soon as a writer starts focusing on something other than the investigation of a crime, the detective story's boundaries are widened—some would say blurred—and some readers have dismissed *Gaudy Night* as an unsatisfying mystery, for it includes no body, no murder, and the novel pays so much attention to other subjects and lines of action that the detective process is often obscured, even to the detective herself.[2]

Harriet becomes so immersed in her personal dilemma, in fact, that she cannot interpret the evidence before her. That is, she reacts as a real person would, not a detective in a story. As she looks at Miss Hillyard's shoe, she thinks, "It was evidence—of something. But of what? The whole business of the Poltergeist seemed to have retreated over the horizon, leaving behind it the tormented shell of a woman staring blindly into vacancy under the cruel harshness of the electric light" (ch. 20). Such a statement encapsulates the transformation of the detective story into a modern psychological novel. What could be more modern than this image of a "tormented shell of a woman," at once illuminated and stunned by the harsh glare of an electric light, staring blankly into nothingness? Because Sayers herself was capable of seeing more than vacancy in human experience, the novel is not frozen in

Miss Hillyard's blank gaze, however. This apparent distraction from the detective process proves to be the very evidence Harriet seeks, for she sees something of herself reflected in Miss Hillyard's tormented face. This recognition is a key to unlocking the mystery of Harriet's heart, which is the real subject of *Gaudy Night*.

While it is an exotic and singular variant of the detective tradition, *Gaudy Night* has that all-pervading sense of mystery and impending doom that characterizes the greatest mystery stories, like *The Woman in White*, which has a similar atmosphere. In both novels, most of the action involves women cut off from the world and attempting to cope with a sinister environment that is all the more threatening for being superficially normal. Neither the characters nor the reader can name the terror, but that only intensifies the suspense.

The mystery that lurks within the walls of Shrewsbury College, which is clearly modelled on Somerville, is not the easily stated question of guilt or innocence in a murder investigation, but rather a cluster of unanswerable human perplexities. The essentially insoluble dilemmas facing most of the characters in this complexly woven narrative can be stated in boldly thematic terms as the competing claims of freedom and responsibility, intellect and emotion, love and work, self and other. Sayers believed that "it is always a healthy sign when we encounter a central intellectual idea in a detective story" (*The Sunday Times* 8 Oct. 1933), and in *Gaudy Night* she employs all of these ideas to dramatize the moral development of Harriet Vane.

The novel is the history of Vane's developing consciousness, which is the angle of vision through which we see everything, including Wimsey. His portrayal since *Have His Carcase* (1932) had been increasingly subtle, primarily because Sayers had begun to scrutinize him through Vane's eyes.[3] This shift makes the later novels at once more intimate and more realistic, for Vane's proximity to Wimsey and her confused interest in him moves readers closer to this once-distant and larger-than-life hero. Wimsey's unsuccessful attempts to woo Vane also humble the former superman, who has been used to getting whatever he wants.

One scene in *Strong Poison*, the first of the Harriet Vane books, reveals Sayers's intention to transform this perfect image of an English gentleman and consummate thinking machine into a real human being Harriet can accept:

The stately volumes on his shelves, rank after rank of Saint, historian, poet, philosopher, mocked his impotence. All that wisdom and all that beauty, and they could not show him how to save the woman he imperiously wanted from a sordid death by hanging. And he had thought himself rather clever at that kind of thing. The enormous and complicated imbecility of things was all round him like a trap. He ground his teeth and raged helplessly, striding about the suave, wealthy, futile room. The great Venetian mirror over the fireplace showed him his own head and shoulders. He saw a fair, foolish face . . . a monocle clinging incongruously under a ludicrously twitching brow; a chin shaved to perfection, hairless, epicene. . . . He snatched up a heavy bronze from the mantelpiece—a beautiful thing, even as he snatched it, his fingers caressed the patina—and the impulse seized him to smash the mirror and smash the face. (Ch. 15)

There is something of Prufrock in the studied elegance of Wimsey's uniform, with its "rather high collar, faultlessly starched, a tie elegantly knotted," an interesting correspondence given Eliot's propensity to see himself in the guise of the stereotypical English gentleman (cf. T. S. Eliot, "The Love Song of J. Alfred Prufrock," lines 42–43). But now Wimsey sees the image as repressive and wishes to be free of it. Sayers saves the best touch for last, denying her hero even the satisfying self-indulgence of such histrionics:

The inherited inhibitions of twenty civilised centuries tied one hand and foot in bonds of ridicule. What if he did smash the mirror? Nothing would happen. . . . And next day a new mirror would be ordered, because people would come in and ask questions, and civilly regret the accidental damage to the old one. And Harriet Vane would still be hanged, just the same.

From this point, the novels proceed to dismantle the image in that mirror; like Alice, Wimsey goes through the looking glass and into a new order of reality. In the process, he becomes a fully realized human being, capable of suffering pain and exhaustion, filled with little vanities and imperfections, wholly mortal—a necessary transformation of the super-sleuth into a proper hero for a realistic novel.

It is interesting to note that in the books of this period from which Vane is absent, Wimsey not only reaches the height of his deductive powers (literally, in the tower at Fenchurch St. Paul), but also retreats into the role of superman (in *The Five Red Herrings* and *Murder Must Advertise*). Though office life at Pym's Publicity is richly detailed and eminently believable, with its intense pettiness and claustrophobic atmosphere, some of Sayers's most embarrassingly melodramatic writing is found in *Murder Must Advertise,* including the passages describing Wimsey's impossible physical stunts (ch. 4). It is not surprising that she slipped back a bit on characterization and became less subtle in this book, which was written to pay bills while she was finishing the monumental *Nine Tailors*.

In the essay "Gaudy Night," DLS explains that she wrote *Strong Poison* "with the infanticidal intention of doing away with Peter, that is, of marrying him off and getting rid of him" (*Titles to Fame* 78). She says that she chose marriage rather than death as an end for her great detective's career, because she did not want to risk being faced with Conan Doyle's embarrassing predicament of killing a popular sleuth only to have to resurrect him later to appease outraged readers. This proved to be a practical concern; long after she ceased writing mysteries, readers continued to pester her for more Wimsey novels.

It is difficult to know how closely Sayers's proffered explanation actually describes her conscious motivation for introducing a love story into the Wimsey saga. Novelists, especially detective novelists, specialize in "the art of framing lies" (DLS, "Aristotle on Detective Fiction"), and Sayers can compete with the best of them when it comes to leading the reader up the garden path. It could be that she only discovered this pattern in her work in retrospect, but no matter: whether it was done consciously or not, the pattern that "Gaudy Night" describes is in Sayers's fiction, and she put it there. What is most fascinating is that, even as she describes wanting to "do away with" Peter Wimsey, she admits a realization that he will not die.

By using a marriage plot to end Wimsey's sleuthing days, DLS effectively chose a vehicle which would assure her of achieving her often-repeated goal in writing detective fiction, that is, of returning it to the house of English fiction. As Ian Watt established in *The Rise of the Novel,* the English novel, from *Pamela* until the advent of modernism, has been preoccupied with the marriage question. In the very act of attempting to do away with her detective, therefore, Sayers moved the modern mystery closer to its historic home and began the series of novels that would culminate in her finest achievement, *Gaudy Night.*

Like many mainstream novelists before her, DLS discovered that settling the marriage question is never easy for two realistic and self-respecting characters, and that it cannot be effected cheaply by a writer of integrity. While working on *Strong Poison,* she found herself in a strange predicament. She had planned a melodramatic ending for the novel: the marriage of her detective and Harriet Vane, who has been wrongfully accused of murder. Wimsey falls head over heels in love with Vane when he first sees her in the dock at the Old Bailey. This is, to say the least, an inauspicious beginning for a serious love story. Sayers quickly realized that she could not bring off the marriage in this book, even though such an ending would have been no more melodramatic than the plots of the Victorian sensation writers she enjoyed. Rather than offering Wimsey an easy way out of the detection business, however, Harriet Vane presented new, more human challenges to him and to his creator. Indeed, Vane complicated things to the point that several more novels were needed to develop the relationship before the two could marry and yet retain their self-respect. The novelist discovered that she "could not marry Peter off to the young woman he had (in conventional Perseus manner) rescued from death and infamy" because [she] "could find no form of words in which [Harriet] could accept him without loss of self-respect; in every way, their situation was false and degrading" (*Titles to Fame* 79). Since Harriet was a real human being from the beginning, she could not be forced into marrying a caricature.

Rather than patching up their relationship and sending them off together in a contrived resolution, DLS did the artistically right but difficult thing. She resolved to do "radical surgery on Peter," to turn him into a whole human being from the bits and pieces of biographical and psychological data she had placed into even her earliest books. This decision shows that as an author, she had as much self-respect as she bequeathed to her characters. Her description of the tough-minded process of transforming Lord Peter is also rather comical, especially considering the number of people who have accused her of being in love with her fictional hero: "I laid him out firmly on the operating-table and chipped away at his internal mechanism through three longish books" (presumably *Have His Carcase, Murder Must Advertise,* and *The Nine Tailors,* unless she was counting *Gaudy Night* itself), in order to make him into a man an intelligent woman could accept (*Titles to Fame* 80). In *Gaudy Night,* Sayers is obviously recalling this process in Harriet's torment over "Wilfrid and Co.," her new novel, which has "gone sticky" as a result of her trying for greater realism. To understand the gradual transformation of Wimsey, and of Sayers's characters generally, into fully realized human beings, is to understand the development of her art and to see *Gaudy Night* as its apex.

James Brabazon believes that, after settling on the marriage plot as a way to get rid of her detective, Sayers realized she still needed the money that could be had from more Peter Wimseys, and that this was the real reason she did not marry him off at the end of *Strong Poison* (ch. 13). While the subsequent Wimsey books were financially successful, it is hard to accept that money was the main motivation for writing them. *The Nine Tailors* could certainly have been turned out less elaborately and in less time, and it is at least arguable that a simpler story would have sold better. DLS herself did not expect a large readership for *Gaudy Night,* as she assumed that academic life and academic women were not of much interest to many people (*Titles to Fame* 83). This is comparable to Jane Austen's assumption, while she was working on *Emma,* that its heroine was someone "whom no one but myself will much like." Although Emma Woodhouse is unlikable in multitudinous ways, her story has captivated readers ever since

Austen created her. Usually an astute judge of markets, Sayers was really wrong about *Gaudy Night,* which had the largest sales of any of her novels, and now enjoys a readership spanning several generations. Furthermore, in the same year as the first Harriet Vane novel, she had published *The Documents in the Case,* her only non-Wimsey novel, proving that she could compose a successful mystery without her series detective. Thus, it seems that the hard-nosed intellectual integrity which is the theme of *Gaudy Night* was important enough to its author to make her admit that her original plan for getting rid of Wimsey would not work. Just as Harriet could find no form of words in which to accept Wimsey's first impetuous proposal of marriage, so her creator was unable to find words to effect their union without doing serious damage to her fiction and her own self-respect. In a characteristic pun, DLS once explained this kind of artistic integrity by declaring that "it profits a book nothing to gain the whole circulating library, and lose its own soul," hardly the comment of a hack (*The Mind of the Maker* 133).

All of the Wimsey-Vane books demonstrate Sayers's increasing unwillingness to indulge in formulaic narratives, melodramatic resolutions, and stereotypes. She always courted challenge, and in this new romantic interest, had created one monumental challenge for herself. Only the very best mystery novelists, such as Collins, Dickens, and Bentley, had ever succeeded in combining a love story with a mystery. Both Dupin and Holmes were aggressively men without women, and through the twentieth century, most detectives have indulged in romance very much off stage, if at all. As a historian of the genre, DLS knew this; but with typical vigor, she attacked the problem of bringing a believable love story into the life of one of the greatest fictional detectives of all time. This experiment constituted a conscious revision of the detective story of her day, which she believed "had perfected a polished and heartless mechanism upon which all genuine feeling was a mere intrusion. Either the reality of the passions made the detective business look cheap, or the austerity of the detective interest made the passions look tawdry." When Sayers wrote these words in 1933, she concluded that uniting the two types of story was the greatest challenge facing detective novelists of her time, adding that "no one has as yet perfectly resolved the problem" (*The Sunday Times* 5 Nov.). Yet a few years earlier, in *The Documents in the Case,* she herself had made great strides in this direction, via the love letters of Jack Munting and Elizabeth Drake.

Five years later, in *Gaudy Night,* with its subtle integration of mystery plot and love story, DLS achieved a thoroughly satisfying resolution of this problem. This novel and its sequel, *Busman's Honeymoon,* develop a profound love story between two believable and sympathetic characters whose union represents a proper balance between the intellect and the emotions, the personal and the ethical, just as the villain of *Gaudy Night*'s mystery plot represents a terrible imbalance in these values. *Busman's Honeymoon* was Sayers's last completed detective novel, and it might never have been written if Muriel St. Clair Byrne had not encouraged her to write the play about Wimsey upon which it is based.[4] A final attempt at another Wimsey novel, "Thrones, Dominations," was left unfinished. Perhaps after accomplishing what she herself considered the greatest challenge facing modern detective fiction, Sayers was effectively finished with the genre.

Because of her basic honesty and integrity, Harriet Vane is unable to fall into Wimsey's protective arms at the end of *Strong Poison*. Knowing this, he demonstrates his own integrity, leaving without comment before she is released from custody. When they next meet, in *Have His Carcase,* a novel whose atmosphere is permeated by sexual frustration and suspicion, they dance and swim together, yet never does he make one move to seduce her. In both this novel and *Gaudy Night,* the would-be lovers are alone together for extended periods of time, but when they are not sparring verbally, they are engaged, at least superficially, in the intellectual game of clue-following, cipher-solving, and alibi-checking. For Wimsey, the experienced, passionate lover trained by Continental mistresses, this is a fairly rigid schedule of patience and denial. *Gaudy Night* places the couple tantalizingly into scenes from melodrama and romance, where our expectations are that either he will take advantage of the romantic possibilities in the situation (in the punt, in the field demonstrating evasive techniques, on the roof of the Radcliffe Camera, where it is he who backs away from an emotional exchange), or that she will be finally worn down by his insistent presence and succumb. None of this happens, which reveals not only Sayers's ability to manipulate the reader by invoking stock formulae, but also her increasing rejection of formula and consequent movement toward realistic fiction. That she was conscious of this shift is revealed in the narrator's description of Harriet's thoughts in *Gaudy Night,* as she reflects on her interaction with Wimsey:

mentally turning the incidents of the last hour into a scene in a book (as is the novelist's unpleasant habit) and thinking how, with a little vulgarity on both sides, it could be worked up into a nice piece of exhibitionism for the male and provocation for the female concerned. With a little manipulation it might come in for the chapter where the wart Everard was due to seduce the glamorous but neglected wife, Sheila. He could lock her to him, knee to knee and breast to breast in an unbreakable grip and smile challengingly into her flushed face; and Sheila could go all limp—at which point Everard could either rain fierce kisses on her mouth, or say, "My God! don't tempt me!" which would come to exactly the same thing in the end. "It would suit them very well," thought Harriet, "the cheap skates." (Ch. 19)

This scene shows that, as a writer of realistic fiction, DLS has come a good distance from that embarrassing moment in *Have His Carcase,* when Wimsey "flung himself on his knees in a frenzy of remorse and agitation" and cried, "Harriet! darling! angel! beast! vixen!" (ch. 13). So many exclamation points! Have we somehow wandered into *Wuthering Heights?* It is hard to imagine this speech emanating from any real human being, but it is impossible to believe it of Wimsey. When DLS envisions such a scene in *Gaudy Night,* she regards it as an object of satire, and her fiction is more believable as a result. In Harriet's reflection on the latter scene, the novelist clearly enjoys mocking the clichés and conventions of pulp fiction, while implying that if there is to be a resolution between these lovers, it will be hard-won (cf. ch. 14 of *Busman's Honeymoon,* where Wimsey himself uses such language mockingly).

Thematically, Wimsey's unwillingness to abuse power also reveals his capacity for nonpossessive, selfless love, which is sorely tried in both *Gaudy Night* and *Busman's Honeymoon.* This quality makes Wimsey a particularly good example of what Sayers once called "the gentlemanly tradition of the English detective story" (*The Sunday Times* 3 Sept. 1933), a form that celebrates the right of every person, no matter how weak, to a fair chance. Wimsey also recalls such earlier gentlemanly lovers in English fiction as Fitzwilliam Darcy, who similarly refuses to use emotional blackmail on Elizabeth Bennet (*Pride and Prejudice* ch. 52). The newly married Harriet Wimsey invokes such language in *Busman's Honeymoon,* when she refuses to take advantage of her own power over Peter: "If we disagree, we'll fight it out like gentlemen. We won't stand for matrimonial blackmail" (ch. 17).

Playing fair extends to how writers should treat their characters. In *The Mind of the Maker,* Sayers engages in a little dialogue with a fictional reader, who asks why an author cannot force a character to do or to be whatever the author desires. Her sub-acid wit is in full display in the response: "You shall not impose either your will or mine upon my creature. He is what he is, I will work no irrelevant miracles upon him, either for propaganda, or to curry favour, or to establish the consistency of my own principles. He exists in his own right and not to please you. Hands off" (13). Although this was written some years after the last Wimsey novel was completed, it seems that Sayers was blessed with this kind of objectivity in her own novel-writing. She would not force Harriet to marry Peter, nor did she even "make" Peter himself. As she once explained, she did not remember ever inventing Peter Wimsey, but recalled only the kind of spontaneous visitation that marks the creation of character in a truly imaginative mind:

> I do not . . . remember inventing Lord Peter at all. My impression is that I was thinking about writing a detective story and that he walked in complete with spats and applied in an airy don't-care-if-I-don't-get-it way for the job of hero. . . . Later on I gathered more details about his personal tastes and habits . . . I . . . discovered that he was two years older than myself. This difference in age persists, and we are looking forward to growing old together. ("How I Came to Invent the Character of Lord Peter")

Sadly for the legions of Wimsey-lovers around the world, he was not permitted to grow old with his creator, but was near fictional death when she offered this witty description of his birth. Yet Wimsey is so real—real in a way that only great fictional characters can be real—that this description of his serendipitous creation rings true.

In one of *Gaudy Night*'s longest and most memorable scenes, the real Wimsey, the human being inside the brittle, glittering facade, is finally revealed to Harriet, and thereby to the reader. While Harriet is immediately swept up into the detective process in this novel, Wimsey does not appear in the action until just over half way through the plot, a well-orchestrated delay that makes his appearance just that much more dramatic. As Dawson Gaillard has observed, Wimsey enters the action of *Gaudy Night* as a magical man (*Dorothy L. Sayers* 74). He appears at Oxford one beautiful, clear morning following a terrible storm that images Vane's restless state of mind and presages an end of the sexual tension and psychological torment that have permeated her view of Shrewsbury and her years of resisting Wimsey. Though on the surface Wimsey may still seem only "a specimen of the pedigree animal" (ch. 18), Harriet's stay at Oxford permits her, even forces her, to see him as he really is. When they go out on the river one afternoon, in the close quarters of their punt, she studies him more closely, more minutely than ever before. The effect is explosive:

> she studied his half-averted face. Considered generally, as a facade, it was by this time tolerably familiar to her, but now she saw details, magnified as it were by some glass in her own mind. The flat setting and fine scroll-work of the ear, and the height of the skull above it. The glitter of close-cropped hair where the neck-muscles lifted to meet the head. A minute sickle-shaped scar on the left temple. The faint laughter-lines at the corner of the eye and the droop of the lid at its outer end. The gleam of gold down on the cheekbone. The wide spring of the nostril. An almost imperceptible beading of sweat on the upper lip and a tiny muscle that

91

twitched the sensitive corner of the mouth. The slight sun-reddening of the fair skin and its sudden whiteness below the base of the throat. The little hollow above the points of the collar-bone. (Ch. 15)

This detailed portrait is not the same person we saw in the early books, but could be the same man seen at closer range or through different eyes. A sensual but unromantic portrait of the lover, the very specificity of its details has caused some readers to conclude that Wimsey must have been drawn from life. It is just as possible that his portrait demonstrates Sayers's fertile imagination and gift for detail; there is no reason to conclude that an imagined person cannot be described in at least as much detail as an observed one.

What *is* remarkable about this description is that it is the portrait of a man, drawn in great physical detail, by a woman. Men have traditionally paid more attention to women's physical appearance than vice versa, and such attention has usually been more, shall we say, encompassing than the chaste head and neck description offered here, which ends with a touch of flirtation about the collar bone. Interestingly, Wimsey, the hyper-intellectual detective, is studied by his equally intellectual lover from the neck up. This is not to say that the scene is not passionate; it is. But as its author said in another context, "where the intellect is dominant it becomes the channel of all the other feelings. The 'passionate intellect' is *really* passionate. It is the only point at which ecstasy can enter" (Brabazon 263). Until Harriet Vane was introduced to Wimsey's world, there was scant attention to passion at all, although there were occasional references to his international love-making; and unlike Sherlock Holmes, he was always potently sexual. Even in *Whose Body?*, where Wimsey is his most bloodless, Sayers lets her *rara avis* show his true colors: "Lord Peter roamed in, moist and verbena-scented, in a bath-robe cheerfully patterned with unnaturally variegated peacocks" (ch. 5). Harriet finally allows him to "spread the tail of vanity" in *Gaudy Night* (ch. 14) when they embark upon their little journey on the Cher, and the mating dance begins.

The very first description of Wimsey in print is no more sentimentalized than *Gaudy Night*'s portrait, but it is more stereotyped. We must glance back to that early image of Lord Peter if we are to appreciate how far he has come. On the first page of *Whose Body?* we are told that "his long, amiable face looked as if it had generated spontaneously from his top hat, as white maggots breed from Gorgonzola." (For those who assume that Sayers was in love with her fictional creation, is this a woman's description of her beloved?) Later in the same chapter, the novelist adds the accoutrements of a monocle and a "beautiful Malacca walking-stick with a heavy silver knob" to complete the trappings of his type. Wimsey parades around London, we are told, "looking . . . like an advertisement for gents' trouserings" (ch. 4). The stereotypical nature of the early Wimsey perhaps explains the long American love affair with his character: with the notable exceptions of his talkativeness and his appreciation of *haute cuisine,* Lord Peter Wimsey conforms to type so well as to be almost a caricature of the English gentleman, while eschewing the least attractive characteristics often ascribed to that type, i.e., his real disdain for snobbery; his deep capacity for sentiment. In Wimsey, ambivalent colonials can have their aristocrat and like him, too.[5]

After *The Unpleasantness at the Bellona Club,* Wimsey evolves slowly into a real human being. Luckily, Sayers had planted enough details about his life, habits, and personality throughout the early books for him to flower easily into a realistic character in the later novels. And, unlike Conan Doyle, she was remarkably consistent in these biographical details from book to book. In *Busman's Honeymoon,* Harriet finally removes Wimsey's monocle in a gesture of intimacy that represents the complete transformation of caricature into human being (ch. 3). It also becomes clear in this last book that Wimsey's manner has been as much a defense as a weapon: the endless chatter, the stinging wit, the manic activity all wind down into a quiet revelation of self at the book's heart (ch. 16). It is hard not to perceive something of his creator in this revelation, for the strident and difficult manner that Dorothy Sayers seems to have developed over the years—her own habit of "being everlastingly tightened up to face things" (*Busman's Honeymoon* ch. 14)—was very likely her way of attempting to protect herself from being known, and by implication, from being hurt.[6] At any rate, she writes of both the terror and the wonder of intimacy as one who has known both.

A measure of how much Sayers's fiction always focused on character is revealed in the fact that, while she was working on the first Wimsey novel, she referred to it simply as "Lord Peter" (Brabazon 2). His character is the center of her fictional world until *The Documents in the Case,* and even after that point, he dominates *The Five Red Herrings* and *The Nine Tailors.* To a large extent, a Dorothy L. Sayers mystery is just what its dust jacket proclaims it to be, "A Lord Peter Wimsey." She came to penetrate his world more completely and with more understanding as she matured, after developing her powers of characterization in the panoply of minor characters surrounding him. Even Raymond Chandler, who had little regard for her novels, considered these wonderful minor characters evidence that she could write about real people, although he dismissed Wimsey as a hero of "exquisite and impossible gentility" ("The Simple Art of Murder").

While Harriet Vane, Sayers's most believable character, lives in a world easily recognizable to most of us—a world of limited resources, painful mistakes, and mundane responsibilities—Wimsey is larger than life. This is part of his charm, and was surely one of the reasons Sayers created him. At the beginning of her career as a novelist, she was playing a clever joke on her readers, as much as anything. The ageless imp of the perverse, the early Lord Peter was Sayers's own whimsy, her fun, her protection against earth-borne cares. Much of this was conscious and deliberate: she once explained that she had given Lord Peter a large income because

> it cost me nothing and at that time I was particularly hard up and it gave me pleasure to spend his fortune for him. When I was dissatisfied with my single unfurnished room I took a luxurious flat for him in Piccadilly. When my cheap rug got a hole in it, I ordered him an Aubusson carpet. When I had no money to pay my bus fare, I presented him with a Daimler double-six, upholstered in a style of sober magnificence, and when I felt dull I let him drive it. ("How I Came to Invent . . .")

Because the fantasy is so patent, so obviously fantastic, this would seem an unusually harmless way to handle the depression and anxiety that often attend the transition period between finishing a university education and finding a niche in the "real" world.

Such a fantasy also has wide appeal. Like Dorothy Sayers, most of us can only look in upon the world of Peter Wimsey. When Parker first enters Wimsey's flat, we are told it seems to him "not only rare and unattainable, but friendly and familiar" (*Whose Body?* ch. 2). It is familiar because it conforms to type. Wimsey lives in the manner one would expect of a man who is "caricatured . . . as a typical aristocrat" by the Labour-papers (ch. 3). And 110A Piccadilly is a suitable domicile for a descendant of Holmes and Dupin, though it is more luxurious than their habitats. Its very luxury makes it both more unattainable (to most of us) and more familiar (because it matches our own fantasies). Wimsey's flat is assertively masculine, urban, and urbane, filled with the odor of pipe smoke and old port. Richard Tillinghast makes an interesting comment about this quality, concluding that the Wimsey stories present the mysteries of masculine behavior as perceived through fascinated female eyes ("Dorothy L. Sayers" 30). When the venue changes from the Piccadilly flat to the modest Elizabethan country house in *Busman's Honeymoon,* the last Wimsey novel, which is appropriately subtitled "A Love Story with Detective Interruptions," Wimsey has been transformed. The cosmopolite detective has become a realistic hero by being returned to his pastoral English roots and allied with the general bias in English fiction for the country over town. This bias is manifest in Wimsey's stated preference for Talboys over "the Hotel Gigantic," somewhere on the continent, and in the scene in which he and Harriet bedeck themselves with vine-leaves and see themselves in pastoral images (ch. 16).

Who was Peter Wimsey? Generations of readers have tried to answer this question, a testament to his enduring fascination and credibility. There seems to have been a rather stronger than usual tendency to conclude that he was based upon a particular man in Dorothy Sayers's life. It is tempting to guess or to hope that his creator enjoyed the companionship of a Peter Wimsey in real life, but her biography suggests no such thing. Indeed, her own love affairs and marriage seem to have been so flawed that there has been an opposite tendency to dismiss Wimsey as the pitiful wish-fulfillment of a woman who was perpetually disappointed in love. Though there was little of Sayers's husband, "Mac" Fleming, in the scholarly, aristocratic detective she created years before meeting him, it is hard not to read some compassion for Fleming into the final scene of *Busman's Honeymoon*, where Harriet is faced with the nervous wreckage of a husband still haunted by the First World War. A perplexing, curious, and seemingly unanswerable question is how Sayers came to write so convincingly of mature love at a time in her own life when, as far as we know, her marriage had deteriorated beyond repair.[7] Seen against this murky domestic backdrop, her attempt to explore the limits and power of love in both *Gaudy Night* and *Busman's Honeymoon* becomes at once more poignant and more noble. Dorothy Sayers knew only too well "how difficult it . . . [is] not to be embittered by personal experience" (*Gaudy Night* ch. 3), but her novels stand as proof that such embitterment is not inevitable.

Eric Whelpton, an Oxford friend for whom she undoubtedly had some kind of affection, assumed that she was in love with him, a love he did not return. This assumption has caused some readers to see Whelpton's high forehead reflected in Peter Wimsey's profile. On the other hand, Sayers's undergraduate crush on Dr. Hugh Allen, the director of Oxford's Bach Choir in her time, may be the source of Wimsey's passion for Baroque music. The novels themselves refer to Wimsey as a latter-day Sherlock Holmes, who had a similarly beaked countenance and deductive turn of mind. They also compare him to Bertie Wooster, whose gibberish resembles a parody of Wimsey's patter at its most ridiculous, while Sayers's comments on *Trent's Last Case* suggest that Philip Trent was another conscious literary model for her detective.[8] Lord Peter Wimsey is also a glorious remnant of an earlier time, recalling both Roland and Lancelot, and reminding us that his creator was a medievalist. And when Harriet pointedly calls him "Mr. Rochester" in their honeymoon book, we can perceive the link between nineteenth-century fiction and the Vane-Wimsey romance.[9]

Though books were a central part of Dorothy Sayers's life, Wimsey was surely not drawn entirely from convention and imagination; great fictional characters rarely are. There is, in the cadence of his rather absurd name, the suggestion of his being inspired by one Maurice Roy Ridley, who became Chaplain of Balliol, Wimsey's old college. Sayers herself once identified Ridley as "the *perfect* Peter Wimsey. Height, voice, charm, smile, manner, outline of features, *everything*." James Brabazon accepts the pretense of this letter, written to Muriel Byrne in 1935, that it is describing a man DLS has just seen for the first time during a trip to Oxford (*Dorothy L. Sayers* 155). However, there is a much earlier letter, written in 1913 to another Somerville chum, Catherine Godfrey, that describes Ridley with the same effusion. A youthful Dorothy Sayers exclaims in this earlier letter that she has fallen hopelessly in love with Ridley, who has just gone down from Balliol, after hearing him read a poem as though he felt it. Since she does not actually know the man at this point, she is obviously having great fun with the idea of being in love. Presumably part of Mr. Ridley's peculiar attraction lies in his name, which reminds her, she says, of a dime novel's hero (DLS, letter to Catherine Godfrey, 29 July 1913). Is there not, in this youthful experience, some hint of Peter Death Bredon Wimsey, the Balliol man who would astound Harriet Vane years later with his ability to compose a metaphysical conceit? (*Gaudy Night* ch. 18).

The temptation to conclude so is encouraged by Sayers's describing, in the same letter, the formal question put to the University of Oxford upon graduating its students. This ritual, which impressed her sufficiently for her to describe it in some detail, becomes years later the form of Peter Wimsey's successful proposal of marriage to Harriet Vane: "Placetne?" the doctors of the university are asked; does it please them to graduate the students before them? "Placet," they reply.[10] Thus, this one letter implies the full circle of Sayers's career as a novelist, and demonstrates why her letters are an invaluable resource for understanding her work.

Yet, the question remains: "Who was the real Peter Wimsey?" The answer, thanks to Sayers's narrative talent and whimsical intelligence, is that Wimsey is all of the above, and more. The "real" Peter Wimsey may be found yet at 110A Piccadilly, where his primrose-and-black drawing room overlooks the Green Park. Like Mac Fleming, Wimsey loves Daimlers, while he shares with Fleming's wife a passion for detection and odd bits of scholarship. Devoted to murder and his mater, Wimsey talks piffle and whistles Bach. One can know Peter Wimsey in a second by the animation of his birdlike profile, the spring in his step on the way to the Yard, his sensitive, graceful hands, his irresistibly disarming back-chat. As DLS once wrote of Christie's Poirot, Wimsey is " 'real,' in the sense that we never stop to enquire whether his words and actions are suited to his character; they *are* his character, and we accept them as we accept the words and actions of any living person" (*The Sunday Times* 6 Jan. 1936). According to his old college friend, Peake of Brasenose, who sees him during that memorable afternoon on the river in *Gaudy Night,* Wimsey is, after all the years, "absolutely unmistakable" (ch. 14).

Lord Peter Wimsey's greatness as a fictional creation is witnessed by his fans' ability to speak of him as if he were an actual, historical person, with a life that extends beyond the pages of his stories or the limitations of his time and place. This is considerable praise for any novelist's invention, and aside from any other of her strengths, assures Sayers a kind of literary immortality. Although he appears in only eleven novels, the last of which was published over a half-century ago, Wimsey lives as vibrantly today as ever in the minds of Sayers's readers. Like the acolytes of Sherlock Holmes, Wimsey-worshippers enjoy writing biographies of him, following in his footsteps, or just talking about his preferences in wine, women, and song. These devoted Wimseyans, who are otherwise seemingly rational folk, will even debate about what Lord Peter *would do* in a given situation; there is no stopping him. In the words of his creator, "The Incomparable Peter is more fatally than ever Peter the Ineluctable. Formerly a periodic visitation, he has become a permanent resident in the house of my mind. His affairs are more real to me than my own . . ." (*Titles to Fame* 93). Perhaps it is this sincere, almost childlike belief in her own creation that makes Sayers's hero, finally, so believable to the rest of the world.[11]

This is the complicated man whom Harriet Vane studies in the punt on that early summer Sunday at Oxford. After years of fleeing, she is forced close enough to see Wimsey, and finally sees into her own heart as a result. During her close scrutiny, "He looked up, and she was instantly scarlet. . . . So, thought Harriet, it has happened. But it happened long ago. The only new thing that has happened is that now I have got to admit it to myself." When Wimsey falls asleep later, she is surprised by her inability to laugh at him, "for another person's sleep is the acid test of our own sentiments. . . . From a height of conscious superiority we look down on the sleeper, thus exposing himself in all his frailty . . ." (ch. 15). But Harriet finds that, just as she was unable to take advantage of her superior position in communicating family business in a letter to him some days before, she cannot do so now. This is a crucial realization in her moral development. Until this point, she has felt markedly inferior to Wimsey, a feeling that has driven her to indulge in gratuitous cruelties, just to see him wince (ch. 15). What she wants, she now realizes, is not the upper hand, but an equal relationship, a fact suggesting her suitability for a mate who also foregoes power plays. By the end of her soul-searching journey in this book, Vane is able finally to see herself as Wimsey's equal, a realization that will make their union possible.

Wimsey's sleep—the longest period of quiet and repose in these bustling books—permits Harriet to examine him, and her feelings for him, minutely. While rummaging through his pockets looking for matches, she finds a copy of *Religio Medici,* and stumbles upon these unsettling, pertinent words from it:

> "When I am from him, I am dead till I be with him. United souls are not satisfied with embraces, but desire to be truly each other; which being impossible, these desires are infinite, and must proceed without a possibility of satisfaction." That was a most uncomfortable passage, whichever way you looked at it. She turned back to the first page and began to read steadily, with critical attention to grammar and style, so as to occupy the upper current of her mind without prying too closely into what might be going on beneath the surface. (Ch. 15)

This passage reveals much about Vane, and perhaps her creator as well. Of special interest is its anxious retreat into the mechanics of a text as a way of avoiding any messy personal applications of its message. Because the real plot of *Gaudy Night* is the story of Harriet's discovery of her own heart, the novel does not focus on a detective problem that is soluble, but as Browne's text suggests, on a human predicament that must be faced even with full knowledge that it is "without a possibility of satisfaction." This is the difficult thing, the insoluble human enigma, with which Harriet has refused to deal in her own detective novels, and from which she flees in both fact and fiction until the end of *Gaudy Night.*

Harriet Vane's fear of passion and its expression is integral to the mystery plot of *Gaudy Night,* for it is this fear that makes her misunderstand the clues she is able to assemble with professional acumen. When Wimsey reviews the pieces of information she has been collecting, he remarks that, since she is usually better at synthesis, he must conclude that her mind is being blocked by some "personal preoccupation." Admittedly, he is hardly disinterested in the matter, but his point is well-taken. He asserts to Harriet that, "having more or less made up your mind to a spot of celibacy you are eagerly peopling the cloister with bogies," which is to say that she is projecting her own sexual anxiety onto others and thereby distorting reality (ch. 15). Again and again, detective fiction dramatizes such effects of bias on human perception, revealing our inability to see anything we do not expect and the concomitant predisposition to see things that are not there. What separates the detective from the average person is what DLS calls "the detective's gift of distinguishing the important from the unimportant," that is, of detecting the real significance of what is seen (*The Sunday Times* 3 Sept. 1933).

In a sense, this is an important lesson of mainstream fiction as well; novel after novel reveals the limitations of individual perception and the history of lost illusions. The detective story's extraordinary emphasis upon the meaning of manners and mannerisms, upon detail-watching and scene-decoding, thus results in a kind of super-realism which may be regarded as an extended parody of one of the English novel's distinguishing characteristics. This is presumably what Sayers meant when she observed that the English mystery story is "steeped in that unreasonable poetry of things that informs English narrative literature from Chaucer and Shakespeare to the present day" ("The Present Status of the Mystery Story" 49).

In this connection, it is interesting that the ascendance of detective fiction in the nineteenth century paralleled the height of realism in conventional fiction and in one way may be considered its apogee. Conan Doyle was the contemporary of Henry James. Not only was the development of consciousness James's overriding preoccupation, but his narrative method also somewhat resembles the detective story. Or, if you prefer, the detective story is Jamesian. Consider this statement from *The Art of Fiction,* in which James outlines the novelist's task in language that could also be a description of the methods of Sherlock Holmes: "The power to guess the unseen from the seen, to trace the implications of things, to judge the whole piece by the pattern, the condition of feeling life in general so completely that you are well on your way to knowing any particular corner of it—this cluster of gifts may be almost said to constitute experience." James's famous order to the artist and the center of consciousness would be equally appropriate for the detective: "Try to be one of the people on whom nothing is lost." In a detective story, the discovery of reality usually consists of the detective's learning the truth of some situation outside himself, the truth about someone else's actions. In *Gaudy Night,* as in most serious fiction, this discovery takes place within the center of consciousness, that is, within Harriet Vane herself. Although this shift into psychological realism makes *Gaudy Night* a genuine novel, it does not make it less of a mystery, for there is no greater mystery than that of the human heart.

In the slowly unfolding mystery of *Gaudy Night,* Harriet notices a great deal around the college, but does not fully understand what she sees. In fact, she misdiagnoses the problem of the Shrewsbury poison-pen as exactly the opposite of what it turns out to be. As Sayers explained, "It was necessary for my theme that the malice should be the product, not of intellect starved by emotion, but of emotion uncontrolled by intellect" (*Titles to Fame* 83). One thinks again of Jane Austen, whose *Sense and Sensibility* has an analogous theme. For a twentieth-century writer, this emphasis is particularly effective, because it overturns a standard expectation of the modern age, which holds that there is more to fear from the purely intellectual life than from its polar opposite in the overly emotional one. It is also fitting because it highlights Vane's personal dilemma: whether to choose work or love, her head or her heart. But the novel is not as simplistic as Sayers's statement suggests, for the range of characters in the college demonstrates many variations on the head-versus-heart dilemma in which Vane finds herself. The mystery plot and the romantic plot of this intricately structured narrative play contrapuntally against each other, resembling the strains in Peter's beloved Bach fugues, separate but interdependent variations on the same theme. Appropriately enough, the novel's climax comes just after a concert, in which such strains come together at last (ch. 23).

Thus the novel manifests an elegant and essential artistic unity, and is neither a simple mystery story with a serious intention attached, nor a detective plot embroidered gratuitously upon a "straight" novel. It is a book that defies classification, which may explain some readers' discomfort with it. Yet it is surely the most persuasive evidence of its author's true powers of invention. *Gaudy Night* is, finally and quintessentially, a Sayers book, the one work that best reveals who she was. She herself sensed the importance of this novel. In the essay of the same title, which traces the development of her fiction, she describes her most important discovery while working on *Gaudy Night:* "By choosing a plot that should exhibit intellectual integrity as the one great permanent value in an emotionally unstable world, I should be saying the thing that, in a confused way, I had been wanting to say all my life" (*Titles to Fame* 81). This is the chief mystery that any writer seeks to comprehend in the act of writing.

The "villain" of *Gaudy Night's* mystery plot is not, as Harriet suspects, one of the unworldly dons, who are immersed to varying degrees in arcane projects. The face of evil here is mundane, domestic, and banal—as it usually appears in real life. It is embodied in the person of an overly emotional scout named Annie Wilson, who puts her heart—or its perversion—over everything, including honesty. One curious fact about this story is that, after starting to work on it, DLS learned that the case she had imagined had actually happened, so she had to change some details (*Titles to Fame* 83). The novel is just that realistic, just that true to life.

At the climax of the detective plot, when Wimsey forces the Senior Common Room and Harriet to see the truth about the Shrewsbury mystery as well as some hard truths about themselves, Annie is revealed as the culprit. She has been plaguing the college with vicious pranks because a new member, the rather unsubtly and ironically named Miss de Vine, once exposed Annie's husband for academic dishonesty and caused, in Annie's view, his eventual suicide. For this reason, Annie wants to destroy not only Miss de Vine, but her type. Annie Wilson sees educated women, en masse, as the real enemy, and in a way they are. They represent an attitude toward life that is radically different from hers, and Annie is incapable of seeing more than one side to any question.

As the novel has it, most of the dons are willing to let the truth come out, no matter how painful or disconcerting it may be, whereas Annie's perverted loyalty to family, to the claims of the heart, forces her to cover up any transgression. On this point—and it is a major point of the book—Sayers may be accused of idealizing the academy: truth *is* a stated value in academic life, but those espousing that life often fail miserably in the service of truth. When Harriet imagines what life inside the university would be like, she thinks of it as a haven from the human suffering she has known:

The fact that one had loved and sinned and suffered and escaped death was of far less ultimate moment than a single footnote in a dim academic journal establishing the priority of a manuscript or restoring a lost iota subscript. It was the hand-to-hand struggle with the insistent personalities of other people, all pushing for a place in the limelight, that made the accidents of one's own personal adventure bulk so large in the scheme of things. (Ch. 1)

Such a thought could come only to one who has not engaged in the hand-to-hand combat that often animates universities; the fact that the stakes may be as infinitesimal as a footnote in some dim academic journal does not diminish the ordeal. In fairness, it should be added that the quoted passage represents what Harriet thinks at the very beginning of the story, before she has been subjected to weeks of pressure from the insistent personalities within the college. While at Shrewsbury, she learns much about the competitiveness, pettiness, and prejudice that infects any human institution, academic or not.

In a moment of remarkable and selfless honesty, Wimsey forewarns Harriet of the frightening solution to the case, saying that "there . . . [is] no devil like devoted love" (ch. 20). This is hardly a sentimental speech from a would-be husband, but it is his very willingness to reveal to the woman he loves "the final baseness of which love was capable be-

101

fore . . . [asking] her to risk the adventure [of marriage] with him" that proves Wimsey capable of "that habit of intellectual integrity" which the novel presents as the one unshakable value in an unstable world. By forcing Wimsey to risk everything, Sayers has fully humanized him. In *Gaudy Night*, his future is at stake and his whole being is challenged and tested. Even solving the mystery threatens him with the loss of the one goal he now pursues: union with Harriet (ch. 20). Cursed (and blessed) with both a heart and a brain, Wimsey is left to face life as a complicated, vulnerable human being, no longer the exquisite caricature.

The novel implies finally that both polar reactions to life are inadequate, first by having the kindly scholar, Miss Lydgate, point out to the steely Miss de Vine that some tempering of the intellect by the heart, and of the fact by the human circumstance, is desirable. Pitying Annie, Miss Lydgate argues the intellectual's time-honored, quixotic belief that any problem can be mitigated by understanding it: "If only we had known, we could surely have done something to make her see the thing in a more rational light. Did it never occur to you, Miss de Vine, to inquire what happened to this unhappy man?" (ch. 12). Miss de Vine admits sadly that it did not, an admission that completes the circle: If Annie Wilson could have been more rational, if Miss de Vine could have been more compassionate, the implication is that there would have been none of the unpleasantness bordering on insanity that besets Shrewsbury College. Miss Lydgate is the Mr. Venables of this story: compassionate and wise, unafraid but humble, scatter-brained yet capable of teaching great truths, she represents the human dimensions of a moral life. By virtue of her closeness to this compassionate scholar, Harriet is able to perceive the possibility of charting a course between the extremes of Miss de Vine and Annie Wilson. Learning this middle way will not only enable her to come to terms with Wimsey, the passionate intellectual, but will also permit the integration of both sides of her personality so that she may live a fully human life.

The unfinished sonnet that plagues Harriet during the Shrewsbury investigation distills her dilemma. Upon her return to Oxford for the Gaudy, she is struck by the apparent peace of the place. Later, she begins a poem in which Oxford is imaged as "that still centre where the spinning world/ Sleeps on its axis," a refuge from the screaming vulgarity of the modern world. She is tempted to abandon London, that "swift, rattling, chattering, excitable and devilishly upsetting world of strain and uproar" (ch. 11) for the seemingly safe walls of Oxford. Yet she is unable to finish the sonnet in which she expresses this desire, and through her involvement in the investigation of the Shrewsbury poison-pen, comes to regard the college not so much as a quiet haven, but as a sinister encampment of madwomen. In a subtle interplay of mystery and romance, Vane's confusion on this point also intensifies the suspense created by the mystery plot, because her mistakes and misapprehensions mislead the reader as well. Her surname proves doubly appropriate; in addition to suggesting her blinding vanity and her ineffectual efforts to unravel the Shrewsbury mystery—efforts that are "in vain"—the name also recalls the function of a weather vane: to shift and point direction with every change in the wind. Such responsiveness to the atmosphere in which she finds herself has both a positive and negative side, for Harriet Vane becomes so changeable that she begins to lose touch with reality and doubts her own sanity (ch. 18). Her first moment of real clarity comes on the day after the storm, when an "all clear" is sounded and all of Oxford takes to the river (ch. 14).

Harriet's divided mind obscures her vision and prevents her from solving the mystery or making a decision about her future, until Wimsey completes her poem by invoking a device that links opposing forces. Unlike her original octave, his sestet does not celebrate stillness or even request it. Rather, it asks for a precarious existence, "poised on the perilous point," the tenuous compromise between competing forces that is the only suitable strategy for living in an ambiguous world. This is a vision Wimsey was prepared for in *The Nine Tailors*. When Harriet sees his resolution to her poem, and to her personal dilemma, she finally sees Wimsey and herself: "in the five years or so that she had known him, Harriet had seen him strip off his protections, layer by layer, till there was uncommonly little left but the naked truth." The naked truth revealed in Peter's sestet forces her not only to see, but to feel—a turning point in her sentimental education. After reading the completed poem, the sardonic narrator tells us, Harriet "went to bed thinking more about another person than about herself. This goes to prove that even minor poetry may have its practical uses" (ch. 18).

The practical use of Peter's "conceited, metaphysical conclusion" to Harriet's poem, which resembles John Donne by way of T. S. Eliot,[12] is in pointing the way for the last step in Harriet's moral development. This sonnet frees her from the blinding, bruised ego and permits her to care for another human being. As its metaphysical conceit images, the integration of head and heart, of intellect and emotion, is the essence of the wholly human, fully lived life. Perhaps, Harriet now thinks, she can have both sides of human experience and does not have to choose between them. Thus Wimsey himself is rewarded with life; by risking everything and revealing his own vulnerability, he opens the way for the passionate and intellectual fulfillment Harriet represents to him.

Following their afternoon on the river, Harriet remembers the prayer of "a well-meaning but incoherent curate," whose wonderfully mixed metaphor is particularly apt to her new knowledge of herself: "Lord, teach us to take our hearts and look them in the face, however difficult that may be" (ch. 15). When Harriet is forced finally to look into her own heart, she undergoes the kind of material change that so often distinguishes the hero or heroine of the great English novels. Her story is the history of a growth in perception, and Elizabeth Bennet's self-characterization could be hers. At the turning point in *Pride and Prejudice,* Elizabeth admits to herself:

> Of neither Darcy nor Wickham could she think, without feeling that she had been blind, partial, prejudiced, absurd. 'How despicably have I acted!' she cried.—'I, who have prided myself on my discernment! . . . Had I been in love, I could not have been more wretchedly blind. . . . I have courted prepossession and igno-rance, and driven reason away. . . . Till this moment, I never knew myself.' (Ch. 36)

Elizabeth does not fully know herself even at this point, of course. A young woman on the threshold of adulthood, she will have to grapple forever with a constantly evolving sense of self—with what Henry James calls "the terri-ble fluidity of self-revelation" (Preface to *The Ambassadors*)—that marks psychological realism in the novel as it marks real life. But the novel is the story of her initiation into this mode of experience.

In contrast to earlier literary forms, the novel has always had many fe-male readers and writers. Thus, it is not surprising that in traditional English fiction, the journey toward self-knowledge is often cast in terms of the marriage question. Marriage was the one striking choice open to bour-geois women in the eighteenth and nineteenth centuries, the choice that determined the entire shape of their lives. It is hardly surprising to find that the novel, which was on the ascendancy during this period, was preoccu-pied with one of the important social issues of its time.[13]

Harriet Vane is a distinctively modern woman in that she is capable of making a life without marriage or family at all, but she still faces the deci-sion to marry or not as a central issue in her life. When she glances down the corridor at students' rooms in Shrewsbury, she automatically divides them into the rooms of the future married and unmarried, just as she scans former students to determine how much marriage or spinsterhood has af-fected them (ch. 1). As the complicated history of her decision reveals, Vane's financial independence only makes the question of marriage more difficult. For this reason, her story is remarkably appropriate to our time, and is perhaps more like Austen's *Emma,* that detective story-cum-romance, whose strong-willed heroine is a woman of independent means.[14] Since marriage is not a financial necessity for either Emma Woodhouse or

Harriet Vane, they may truly choose to marry or not, as it pleases them. A real choice, with real consequences, fuels the drama of their situation and creates a problem of proportions large enough to generate wonderfully elaborate and richly complex narratives.

In the Victorian period against which Sayers reacted so strongly, Harriet's sexual history would probably have assigned her to Tess D'Urberville's fate, while her class and her lively, questioning mind would most likely have ordained that she share the lot of Bronte's governess, Jane Eyre. The great reconciliation scene atop the Radcliffe Camera in *Gaudy Night* calls to mind not only the tortuous path to love in *Jane Eyre,* but also the scenes portraying the reconciliation of lovers in *Pride and Prejudice, Emma,* and *Persuasion.* In each of these novels, the heroine and hero come together after much misunderstanding and misery because they have learned enough about themselves to face each other as equals.[15] That DLS was conscious of the link between the Vane-Wimsey romance and nineteenth-century fiction is revealed in Harriet's calling her new husband "Mr. Rochester" (*Busman's Honeymoon,* "Prothalamion"), an apt allusion because of Wimsey's age, experience, and passionate nature. Yet the Vane-Wimsey novels demand no melodramatic reversals of fortune to bring the lovers together, nor do they suffer from the excess of emotion that characterizes the Brontes. Rather, they follow two increasingly believable characters as they attempt to achieve that most delicate balance in personal relations through an argument of souls. This attempt to balance competing forces and to reason through an emotional labyrinth most resembles the classical sensibility of Jane Austen, another Englishwoman who was blessed with the capacity to see the whole world mirthfully.

Though some have found "Wimsey in love . . . a sorry figure" (Craig and Cadogan 190), I do not agree. By pushing him and his lover to this point, his creator has not only fully humanized him, but has also accomplished her goal of writing a traditional English novel. She has probed, with some sensitivity and subtlety, the endlessly fascinating mystery of the human heart. What began as a clever idea to effect a facile ending for the Wimsey saga became the means for accomplishing the kind of serious exploration of character and culture that DLS considered essential to the novelist's art.

In social terms, the marriage of Harriet Vane and the aristocratic Wimsey represents not only a needed revitalization of the old order,[16] but also the drama of acceptable social mobility in an increasingly bourgeois world. As is true of many great novels dealing with the marriage question, the relative inequality of these lovers must be realistically resolved before their union is possible. They begin with two types of inequality: there is the obvious class difference, as well as the more difficult problem of Vane's initial powerlessness and her debt to Wimsey for her life and freedom. As Sayers says in the essay, "Gaudy Night," the greatest problem in bringing these lovers together was to find a believable way of resolving their inequality: "at all costs, some device must be found for putting Harriet back on a footing of equality with her lover." This was found in the Oxford setting, which offered the only place where Harriet "could stand free and equal with Peter," that is, "on the intellectual platform" where "she had never been false to her own standards" (*Titles to Fame* 81). It seems likely that this is the way DLS regarded herself at this point in her life.

Thus, the Oxford setting is imperative not only for the mystery plot, which focuses upon the destruction caused by a lack of intellectual integrity, but also for the love story. At Oxford, Wimsey and Vane meet not so much as great detective and grateful client, nor even as Duke's son and doctor's daughter, but as colleagues, a fact dramatized by their literally fitting into the same Master's gown (ch. 14). And it is this possibility that distinguishes Sayers's heroine from her ancestors in the nineteenth-century novel: in addition to the lively mind of an Elizabeth Bennet and the tough moral fiber of a Jane Eyre, Harriet Vane has the immeasurable advantage of a liberal education. Darcy, Knightley, and Rochester all chose highly intelligent and fiercely independent women for mates, but in their day, no woman had a university education. Harriet's distinct advantage in this regard makes her facing the marriage question just that much more prickly, for her education has made her capable of both economic and psychological independence: "How could one feel fettered, being the freeman of so great a city, or humiliated, where all enjoyed equal citizenship?" (ch. 2). Vane's choosing to marry, since it is in every way a true choice, becomes both more difficult and more meaningful as a result.

Gaudy Night explores questions that were of pressing interest to Dorothy L. Sayers in 1935, but there is no aspect of her fiction that has travelled better into our own time. If anything, the novel is more timely today than when it was written, for the educated, professional woman is now more the norm than the striking exception. By addressing one of the important concerns of this century—the tentative emergence of women into all areas of society—in the timeless terms of realistic human psychology, Sayers created a classic novel. The book has survived many of its contemporaries in both the mystery genre and more ostensibly serious fiction because it is not a piece of social propaganda, but a work of art. Its author understood it as her duty "not to instruct, but to show forth; not to point a moral but to tell a story" (*The Man Born to Be King* 4). After all these years, *Gaudy Night* remains a gripping story.

The novel also evokes a palpable, unforgettable setting. Much has been said about the picture of Oxford and university life presented in its pages. Some readers have found Sayers hopelessly naive about academe and irritatingly nostalgic about Oxford. In their historical survey of women in crime fiction, Patricia Craig and Mary Cadogan have said that the impetus for *Gaudy Night* was partially nostalgia, adding that they consider nostalgia a "disabling pressure which signifies retreat" (191). As a critical principle, this assumption would seem to deny many of the great achievements of Western culture. What would one do with Proust in that case? Or, more to the point, with *Brideshead Revisited,* a man's remembrance of Oxford? Not sharing this assumption, I should think that a bit of nostalgia is even allowable in *Gaudy Night,* since Oxford was Sayers's birthplace and the scene of some of her happiest days. After her family's move into the fens, the town and university must have represented all the social life they had left behind, so that Oxford's attractions probably grew in the remembrance.

To regard this novel as a simple piece of nostalgia also ignores its generally amused and amusing look at college life. For example, consider this first glimpse of the faculty en masse:

> The procession came into sight beneath the archway; a small crocodile-walk of elderly people, dressed with the incongruous brilliance of a more sumptuous era, and moving with the slovenly dignity characteristic of university functions in England. . . . the female dons adopted a reverential attitude suggestive of a prayer meeting. (Ch. 1)

A picture as unsentimental as it is accurate.

Beyond any personal biases DLS may have had about the place, the choice of an Oxford setting was appropriate and perhaps inevitable. First, the college provides the kind of closed society that is typical of the classic detective story; something has happened, and the culprit must be an insider. The village of Fenchurch St. Paul functions similarly in *The Nine Tailors,* for example. The academic setting was also essential for working out an idea DLS had been struggling with for some time, "the idea of a 'straight' [non-detective] novel, about an Oxford woman graduate who found, in middle life, and after a reasonably satisfactory experience of marriage and motherhood, that her real vocation and full emotional fulfillment were to be found in the creative life of the intellect." This seems to be a description of the abortive "Cat O'Mary," on which she had been working in the early thirties. Then, in 1934, she was invited back to Somerville to "propose the toast of the University at . . . [her] College Gaudy dinner."

107

This event forced her to start thinking about what Oxford had done for her. Upon reflection, she decided that its legacy was "that habit of intellectual integrity which is at once the foundation and the result of scholarship." This habit of intellectual integrity, which was to become the theme of *Gaudy Night*, had stayed with Dorothy Sayers through the tough years and had encouraged her to extend the boundaries of detective fiction. Thus, she realized, an Oxford novel would solve her problem of marrying off Wimsey and would also allow her the opportunity to say something she had always wanted to say (*Titles to Fame* 81).

Though Sayers knew and loved Oxford well, it is important to realize that she was, in a sense, an outsider to the University. In her talk at the Somerville Gaudy, she underscored this feeling, remarking that she had never before walked the streets of Oxford in academic dress.[17] No wonder she has so much fun dressing Harriet and Peter in the same gown! Even as a student there twenty years earlier (in the days before any of the women's colleges were actually part of the University), DLS must have been aware of her essential separateness from the University, although she seems remarkably free of the bitterness that such exclusion prompted in Virginia Woolf. Yet *Gaudy Night* does address the delicate position of women at Oxford. In response to the thoroughly irresponsible behavior of Miss Cattermole, a student who does not really want to be there, Harriet Vane speaks eloquently of the duty of women students to behave well *because* they are not yet fully accepted by the men (ch. 8). This attitude was probably more relevant to Sayers's pre-war Oxford days than to 1935, when the novel was written, but it suggests a very practical reason for some idealization of the place.

It is true that DLS does not write of college faculty life with the same authority she brings to her description of the advertising business in *Murder Must Advertise* or with the authenticity of her East Anglian scenes in *The Nine Tailors*. But this is artistically right, since *Gaudy Night* tells the story from Harriet Vane's angle of vision and Harriet is herself a visitor to academe. She returns, with some misgivings, to Oxford at the novel's beginning, and by its end, has found that she cannot stay there, despite all its charms. In keeping with Vane's biases, Sayers presents an ideal and somewhat innocent view of the collegium in her portrayal of the Senior Common Room's unwillingness to put personal loyalties and comfort before the quest for truth. This was the nub of the complaint lodged in an article by Q. D. Leavis, which is the most savage attack on this novel and one of the most biting indictments of Sayers in print. Once Leavis gets going, it becomes apparent that—like many critics—she is attacking much more than the book under review: "The real draw of *Gaudy Night* was its offering the general public a peepshow of the senior university world. . . . If such a world ever existed, it does no longer. . . . It is time that a realistic account of the older universities was put into circulation" ("The Case of Miss Dorothy Sayers" 337). And of course the review proceeds to put such a picture into circulation. While I agree that *Gaudy Night* overstates the case for intellectual integrity among academics—who are unfortunately as ready as anyone else to indulge in personal vendettas or question-begging and often only add to the abuse by hiding behind such cleverly phrased concepts as "intellectual integrity"—the novel does not present a totally idealized portrait of these people. There is a whole range of human behavior demonstrated among them, from Miss Hillyard's reactionary hatred of men, to Miss Shaw's neurotic need to be needed by her students, to Miss Edwards's reassuringly blunt common sense. Even Miss Lydgate, who is the most sympathetic character in the college, is modified by her frailities and mistakes. She certainly would not be an easy person to live with, at least while she is working on a book, which seems to be a chronic disease in her case. Presumably, Miss Lydgate "has got a book"—a bad case of English prosody—as perennially as the undergraduates "have got an essay" (ch. 6). Nor is Miss Lydgate's opposite, Miss de Vine, turned into an ogre, but rather is seen as a severely limited person who is valuable within the narrow scope of her abilities. And the wonderful touch of the comical hairpins, which are always coming out of Miss de Vine's messy hair, suggests that her coolly cerebral "front" is only part of the story. As a scholar, Dorothy Sayers understood the limitations of specialists operating outside their sphere of competence, limitations she dramatizes through the variety of human behavior exhibited in this novel. The point is stated most clearly in Harriet's final realization that, after "the distorting-glass of suspicion was removed, they [the dons] were kindly, intelligent human beings—not seeing, perhaps, very much farther beyond their own interests than the ordinary man beyond his job or the ordinary woman beyond her own household—but as understandable and pleasant as daily bread" (ch. 23). As a culminating insight, this seems remarkably balanced, avoiding the pitfalls of being either fawning or caustic.

Thus Miss de Vine is not a villain, but a recognizably human character who, like the meddling Peter Wimsey of *The Nine Tailors,* unwittingly sets into motion a series of actions and reactions with terrible consequences. Her humanity does not make those consequences less frightening, however; in fact, the very mundane quality of her actions makes the story just that much more compelling and disquieting. If, after reading *Gaudy Night,* we return to the game-playing of *Whose Body?,* we can perceive the extreme disparity between the credibility of Sayers's early characters and her later ones. In the first novel, Sir Julian Freke is one-dimensional; indeed, that is his flaw. He is Sayers's most despicable villain, and his fatal error is that he totally intellectualizes life. He regards other human beings as specimens for the dissecting table. He is an analyzer to the extreme of becoming a destroyer; Wimsey, his opposite and better self, is the creative actor playing Sherlock Holmes to Freke's Moriarty. The third novel, *Unnatural Death*, presents Freke's counterpart, Mary Whittaker. She is another monomaniac who is willing to do anything to get what she wants, but her defect manifests itself in the guise of possessive love. These two villains are, in bold relief, the progenitors of Miss de Vine and Annie Wilson, but the increased subtlety with which Sayers draws such characters in *Gaudy Night* is persuasive evidence of her development as a novelist.

Vera Brittain remembered Dorothy Sayers from Somerville days as an "examine-every-atom-of-you-type" (*The Testament of Youth* 106), a telling clue to the young woman's destiny as a writer. In her passionate attention to the details of human behavior and the actual world in which they are manifest, the youthful DLS was accumulating the memory store of a novelist. Although she had a considerable talent for portraiture from the beginning, even in her childhood play-acting, she became more adept at characterization through the years, partially because she began to write longer books, which could afford her the space to explore character in some depth, and partially because of her experimentation with the epistolary form.

Beginning with her most fully developed and believable minor character, Miss Climpson, Sayers explored the possibility for character development and revelation through letters, a technique most elaborately implemented in *The Documents in the Case* and in the priceless comedy evoked in the introductory letters to *Busman's Honeymoon*. If one should wish a primer of Dorothy L. Sayers—her attitudes, values, and preferences; her wit, whimsy, and wisdom—it may be found in these delicious letters preceding the tale of Wimsey's haunted honeymoon. Such letters are as entertaining as those she wrote in her own voice in real life, and as true to character. Her increasing ability to get inside Wimsey's mind is manifest in his letters in *Gaudy Night* and in the "Wimsey Papers," in addition to the well-drawn interludes describing his state of mind in chapter 14 of *Busman's Honeymoon*. Had they continued, the "Wimsey Papers" would have constituted a fine epistolary novel in themselves and could have taken Sayers's fiction beyond The Long Weekend and into a world shaken once again by war. It is a tantalizing prospect: What *would* Wimsey have made of the death camps? Of the Bomb? And what new characters may have visited his creator's imagination?

Though her novels are saturated with references to her times and are, in a way, documents of them, the mysteries of Dorothy L. Sayers weave a rich tapestry of human relationships and personalities, which are essentially unchanging. The portraits of students in *Gaudy Night* are dead right for all time, revealing as they do both their creator's view of her world and something immutable in human experience. Is there any aggregate of students anywhere that is not blessed with "a Fresher with an urge for modernity and very little natural taste"? Is it possible to visit any college campus without experiencing the shock that Harriet Vane feels upon entering such a person's room? Though some of its particulars scream "1930s" to us now, the room remains regrettably familiar:

> The narrow bed . . . was covered with drapery of a crude green color and ill-considered Futuristic pattern; a bad picture in the neo-archaic manner hung above it; a chromium-plated lamp of angular and inconvenient design swore acidly at the table and wardrobe provided by the college, which were of a style usually associated with the Tottenham Court Road; while the disharmony was crowned and accentuated by the presence, on the chest of drawers, of a curious statuette or three-dimensional diagram carried out in aluminium, which resembled a gigantic and contorted corkscrew, and was labelled upon its base: ASPIRATION. (Ch. 1)

I am particularly fond of that lamp, swearing "acidly" at the writing table beneath it. Working up to a final sneer at the absurdly pretentious title of "Aspiration," the comic timing in this passage is masterful, moving the reader to laugh at both eternally feckless youth and the special barbarities of the modern age.

In the luxuriant elaboration of this novel, DLS is able to include a whole panoply of characters who are as fully realized as those filling the pages of patently "serious" English novelists. In addition to the wonderful snapshots of the dons, the novel has ample opportunity to scan the student body. There is, for example, one Miss Millbanks, who managed to carry "her intellectual attainments easily. She held a minor scholarship, . . . declaring publicly that she was only a scholar because she would not be seen dead in the ridiculous short gown of a commoner." Harriet meets another student whose shabbiness bespeaks an attitude that such mundane matters as clothing are "beneath her notice." The eating habits of others are not beneath her notice, however; she declares disdainfully, with the facility and certainty peculiar to the undergraduate temperament wherever it exists, that only "groupists drink cocoa." Then there is Miss Layton, who "did, indeed, contrive to look fragile and pathetic, and anything but learned. Nevertheless . . . Harriet discovered that she was an exceptionally well-fancied favorite for the English School. . . . If the dry bones of Philology could be made to live by Miss Layton, then she was a very dark horse indeed." Such portrait-painting is a vehicle for the detective process, because Harriet must study each person in college as a potential madwoman, and she concludes that "so unexpected a personality [as Miss Layton] might be capable of anything" (ch. 7). Each of these characters is brought to life through one or two telling details, and each is immediately recognizable as a real human being, the work of a genuine novelist.

This timeless portrayal of character exhibits "the ruthless realism which goes directly to essentials" (*The Mind of the Maker* 214). Quite a few of the characterizations in this book are, in fact, discomfortingly recognizable. There are Cattermoles and Bartons and de Vines aplenty in college communities. Yet there is no Freke in *Gaudy Night;* its characters are ambiguous human beings with unfathomable depths that even they only partially understand, flawed but not wholly evil. DLS had worked toward such realistic characterization in *The Documents in the Case* and *The Nine Tailors,* the two earlier books which most vigorously explored the mixture of good and evil in human life, and the ones that prepared her for evoking a truly artistic ambiguity in this, the finest of her fictions, a triumph of psychological realism.

Gaudy Night is also markedly realistic in its physical descriptions of Oxford, with its buildings lovingly sketched in, crowded spires of golden stone stretching against the sky; the Radcliffe Camera sleeping "like a cat in the sunshine" (ch. 11); the spring wind whipping against gowns of scholars and dons; the odor of old books lingering in Duke Humphrey's library. This is not mere scene painting or local color, but an evocation of the scholar's life. Since this novel is an examination, both gay and grave, of the scholarly approach to experience, such imagery is organically related to its theme. Sayers gets a good deal of poetry out of Oxford's old stones:

Mornings in Bodley, drowsing among the worn browns and tarnished gilding of Duke Humphrey, snuffing the faint, musty odour of slowly perishing leather, hearing only the discreet tippety-tap of Agag-feet along the padded floor; long afternoons, taking an outrigger up the Cher, feeling the rough kiss of the sculls on unaccustomed palms, listening to the rhythmical and satisfying ker-klunk of the rowlocks; . . . then, at night, the lit lamp and the drawn curtain, with the flutter of the turned page and soft scrape of pen on paper the only sounds to break the utter silence between quarter and quarter chime. (Ch. 11)

The beautiful cadence of this passage sings of the discrete pleasures of the life of the mind. Has it ever been made more attractive? Perhaps Dorothy Sayers rediscovered, upon her return to Oxford for that Gaudy night in 1934, something of herself in its "melodious silence"; perhaps, like Harriet Vane, she felt

> something . . . [come] back to her that had lain dumb and dead ever since the old, innocent undergraduate days. The singing voice, stifled long ago by the pressure of the struggle for existence, and throttled into dumbness by that queer, unhappy contact with physical passion, began to stammer a few uncertain notes. Great golden phrases . . . swam up out of her dreaming mind. (Ch. 11)

In such a mood, the beginning of a sonnet comes to Harriet, the beginning of a text that will eventually reveal her destiny.

Though the extraordinarily prolific Sayers never suffered from real "dumbness," her earlier books are more restrained, less musical than either *The Nine Tailors* or *Gaudy Night*. In fact, the luxuriant beauty of *Gaudy Night*'s prose has sent several generations of readers to visit Oxford, just to see what all the fuss was about. Jessica Mann even suggests that this novel has been responsible for many young women choosing to try for Oxford or Cambridge (*Deadlier than the Male* 179), a curious legacy indeed for a detective story. The novel toys a bit with Oxford's geography, but these changes are acknowledged at the beginning of the book, and a reader of *Gaudy Night* will recognize much in the Oxford of today. How ironic it is that many people see this ancient town and temple of learning through the eyes of a popular novelist. To appropriate the language of Sayers's praise for another Oxford novel, *Gaudy Night* has "the true Alma Maternal atmosphere, and . . . [is] so rightly contrived [that the] . . . Oxford story . . . could not very well have happened anywhere but in Oxford" (*The Sunday Times*, 10 March 1935).

Gaudy Night is not only an Oxford novel, but a "school mystery," a subgenre which had special appeal to the former teacher who wrote it:

> For some reason, nearly all school murder stories are good ones—probably because it is so easy to believe that murder could be committed in such a place. I do not mean this statement to be funny or sarcastic: nobody who has not taught in a school can possibly realise the state of nervous irritation that can grow up among the members of the staff at the end of a trying term, or the utter spiritual misery that a bad head can inflict upon his or her subordinates. (*The Sunday Times*, 9 Sept. 1934)

This observation is tellingly drawn from experience, and shows that DLS understood the particular pitfalls of the academic existence as well as its curious charms. When Harriet and Peter run into an old friend of his, a man who has remained at the University as a lecturer, they find in his depressing lack of development another argument against the academic life: "It's the one great drawback to living in this place. It keeps you young. Too young," Peter observes with acuity (ch. 14).

Sayers once asked rhetorically in a review why all school mysteries seem "so convincingly 'real' "—and then suggested that it is possibly "the poignant suffering undergone by assistant masters that wrings out of them . . . devastatingly accurate pictures of common-room friction" (*The Sunday Times,* 10 March 1935). This is a provocative image, especially when one thinks of the explosive scene in the Senior Common Room, where Wimsey "invades" the female territory and pushes the lot to the emotional wall as he reveals the solution to the Shrewsbury mystery. A prototype of all end-of-term crises and harangues, this scene functions as both a stunning climax to the novel's detective plot, and the final test of Wimsey and Vane in preparation for resolution of the romantic plot. Perhaps if Sayers *had* been a don, the novel would have focused upon the destructive tension generated within any educational institution, for a teacher's experience of a school is profoundly different from a student's. But that would be a different book. *Gaudy Night* emerges from a keen perception of both Town and Gown, and the inevitable clash between the two.

As the climactic scene in the Senior Common Room shows, there is a psychological realism about this book that is the result not only of faithful attention to human behavior, but of a brave consideration of the vagaries of the human heart. Harriet points to the underlying mystery of the novel, the inscrutability of human nature, as she muses to herself on the difference between a well-contrived detective story and real life:

> Human beings were not like that; human problems were not like that; what you really got was two hundred or so people running like rabbits in and out of a college, doing their work, living their lives, and actuated all the time by motives unfathomable even to themselves, and then, in the midst of it all—not a plain, understandable murder, but an unmeaning and inexplicable lunacy. How could one, in any case, understand other people's motives and feelings, when one's own remained mysterious? (Ch. 11)

During the course of the novel, Harriet must learn to see into her own heart before she is able to understand the Shrewsbury mystery. She learns this by articulating the central question of her life, which is also the basic question raised by the novel's mystery plot: "Could there ever be any alliance between the intellect and the flesh? . . . Easy for a man, and possible even for a woman, if one avoided foolish accidents, . . . Yet six centuries of possessive blood [Wimsey's inheritance] would not be dictated to by a bare forty-five years of over-sensitized intellect . . ." (ch. 21). In this short passage, Harriet articulates the main barriers she must surmount before she can accept Wimsey's offer of marriage: she must realize that there can be, for both men and women, an alliance of intellect and flesh, that these competing needs are not necessarily mutually exclusive; that she can, on some plane, meet her lover as an equal; and that though evil cannot be destroyed, it can be transformed into good. By the end of *Gaudy Night,* she is able to say that she is glad that the past five years happened, even though they included bitter unhappiness and her trial for a murder she did not commit, because they have led to something worthwhile, her new self-knowledge and her imminent union with Wimsey.

The difficult journey of self-discovery that Vane makes in this novel, and for which Wimsey has been prepared by his own trial of waiting for her, is not the story of a problem solved, but of an enigma articulated and faced. In Sayers's own judgment, the mystery or question around which this novel revolves "is not really a problem at all: it is a human perplexity" (*The Mind of the Maker* 190). The novel's emphasis upon this other, more significant plot is indicative of how far she had moved from the formula of conventional detective fiction by this point. As she explains in *The Mind of the Maker,* there is a

firmly implanted notion that all human situations are "problems" like detective problems, capable of a single, necessary, and categorical solution, which must be wholly right, while all others are wholly wrong. But this cannot be, since human situations are subject to the law of human nature, whose evil is at all times rooted in its good, and whose good can only redeem, but not abolish, its evil. The good that emerges from a conflict of values cannot arise from the total condemnation or destruction of one set of values, but only from the building of a new value, sustained, like an arch, by the tension of the original two. (191)

At the end of *Gaudy Night,* when the two lovers emerge from under the tangible arch made by one of Oxford's bridges and face each other at last, the novel's imagery suggests the meaning of their union, the creation of "a new value, sustained, like an arch, by the tension of the original two," or the resolution of conflict between self and other, head and heart, love and work, male and female. DLS later wrote that she admired Dante particularly as a practitioner of "great architectural art" (*Purgatory* 53). What one artist admires in another is always revelatory, and Sayers's own best novels,

The Nine Tailors and *Gaudy Night,* display this architectonic sense of form.

Gaudy Night denies the simplistic way of looking at the world by destroying the notion of life as an artificial detective puzzle. This is reflected not only in the richly ambiguous nature of its characters and theme, but also in the change that Wimsey convinces Harriet to make in her own fiction. He tells her that she has not yet written the book of which she is capable, and urges her to "abandon the jig-saw kind of story and write a book about human beings for a change." This she should do, he believes, even if it "hurts like hell," because it is the only way she can grow (ch. 15). It is possible that Dorothy Sayers had been pushed by someone in just this way, but this dialogue between Wimsey and Vane also represents the creator's internal struggle as an artist. In the essay "Gaudy Night," she identifies Harriet and Peter as two sides of the human personality and "two moods of the artistic spirit" (92); their story is thus the ageless story of the soul at war with itself.

In a powerfully suggestive image, the evil at Shrewsbury College—the spectre of real suffering and real madness—destroys the game by the literal crushing of Harriet's chess set. The set is of elaborately carved ivory, each delicate piece consisting of "a complicated nest of little revolving balls" (ch. 13), which are like Mrs. Venables's "wheels within wheels," imaging the unending revelation of mystery within mystery in human life. Harriet is bewitched by the set, "for which she . . . conceived an unreasonable affection," but she is unable to understand its strange appeal. Before buying it as a gift for her, Wimsey examines the set minutely, as Sayers had scrutinized the intricate mechanism of the detective story. Scholars both, neither could be satisfied with the second-rate or fake. (In chapter 19, Harriet herself connects the chessmen with the tortuous transformation of her detective stories into realistic fiction). Once the set is destroyed, however, she realizes that she valued it chiefly as a gift from Wimsey. It was the first thing she ever willingly took from him, and her newly learned ability to accept love makes her vulnerable to new pain and loss. Quite unexpectedly, the "game" has taken on a human dimension and is now valued in human terms.

The episode of the chessmen is a metaphor for Sayers's transformation of the brittle mechanism of the detective story into a novel of human relationships and desires, a change that forces her characters to face life without a game plan. She once observed that "There is one vast human experience that confronts us so formidably that we cannot pretend to overlook it. There is no solution to death" (*The Mind of the Maker* 195), a fact that, ironically, she learned from the inability of pure detective fiction to deal with human life. As *Gaudy Night* makes clear, there is no final solution to life, either. This purposeful ambiguity informs Sayers's novels increasingly after *The Documents in the Case* and reaches its height in *Gaudy Night:*

> Here, by an exercise on both sides of a strict intellectual integrity, . . . [Harriet and Peter's] situation is so modified that they are enabled to enter into a new relationship, presenting fresh situations with the prospect of further errors and misunderstandings. This "solution" is neither final nor complete. (*The Mind of the Maker* 190)

That is, her characters are now functioning as real human beings who must face life as a series of blunders, misunderstandings, temporary resolutions, and new difficulties.

James Brabazon suggests that DLS was able to do a book like *Gaudy Night* at this time because she had settled as many of the problems in her personal life as she could. In the interval between *The Nine Tailors* and *Gaudy Night* she had decided, it seems, to stay with her husband, even though they were apparently unhappy, and had gone as far as she ever would in acknowledging her son, who had been since infancy in the care of her cousin. At this point, Sayers "adopted" Anthony, which simply meant that, to the world, he was known as her son and carried the Fleming name. Of course, she could not have legally adopted her natural son, and the child never joined her household (Brabazon 148–51). It is poignant to think of how different the marriage of Wimsey and Vane was from the actual life led by their creator.

Strangely enough, it does not appear that Dorothy L. Sayers ever made a conscious decision to abandon the mystery genre. After *Busman's Honeymoon,* she would complete no other novel, although the unfinished manuscript of "Thrones, Dominations" shows that she continued to be interested in the Wimsey-Vane relationship and wanted to follow it into established married life. In that fragment, Uncle Paul Delagardie and Harriet are still interesting, but Peter Wimsey is a tired, faded image of his earlier self. Sayers's abandonment of the manuscript suggests that she realized the narrative was not working. "Talboys," a slight story finished but unpublished in her lifetime, reveals that the Wimseys had the kind of happy, challenging married life predicted for them in the last two published novels. (This story was published in the 1972 collection, *Lord Peter.*) Perhaps it was too much even for Dorothy L. Sayers to bring off an interesting novel about an essentially happy and fulfilling marriage, although *Busman's Honeymoon* makes a good start at such a series.

It was the late 1940s before DLS announced that "there would be no more Peter Wimseys," a decade after she finished her last novel. Her religious plays, the war, and her all-consuming passion for Dante separated the Sayers of 1948 from the creator of Lord Peter. Yet as late as that year, the BBC broadcast a new radio mystery entitled *Where Do We Go from Here?*, which DLS wrote for a series produced by the Detection Club. This play's existence reveals that she had not turned her back on the mystery genre entirely, and it is a curious work to place beside the scholarly research and theological writing usually associated with the last period of her life. And curiosity of curiosities, this inveterate storyteller began a novel as late as the early fifties, when she worked on a manuscript about Dante and his daughter, Bice.[18]

Regrettably, once she had become immersed in her Dante studies, Dorothy L. Sayers had not world enough and time to continue writing novels. This opinion may be regarded as "unsound, unscholarly," but I trust no one would think it "insincere" (*Gaudy Night* ch. 14). At her best, Sayers has no peer as a detective story writer who is also a genuine novelist. Her great characters are as vibrant today as the moment she conceived them; her stories and settings linger in memory and have become part of the English mythos and landscape for readers spanning several generations and numerous nations. *The Nine Tailors, Gaudy Night,* and just below them, *The Documents in the Case* and *Busman's Honeymoon,* are truly great mystery stories, the classics of their kind.

These exemplary mystery novels show that intelligence and fair play can be brought to bear on every aspect of life—including popular fiction—a hard but worthwhile quest. *Gaudy Night* carries the theme of intellectual integrity, and is itelf a prime example of such integrity. When DLS came to write *The Mind of the Maker* in 1941, she drew on her experience as a novelist and playwright to make some illuminating observations on the creative process: "The business of the creator is not to escape from his material medium or to bully it, but to serve it; but to serve it he must love it" (66). *Gaudy Night* is the creation of one who knew, loved, and served the mystery genre. Whatever else may be said of Sayers's motivation in writing detective fiction or her regard for it as a genre, the substantial evidence of her novels demonstrates the love she brought to their writing and the integrity with which she served her chosen medium.

Near the end of *Gaudy Night,* Harriet Vane stands on the roof of the Radcliffe Camera and surveys the crowded glory of Oxford, which must be one of the most over-developed plots of real estate in the entire world. Yet she focuses at last on one solitary human being, a "slight figure that crossed the cobbled Square, walking lightly under the shadow of St. Mary's into the High." In this contemplation of Peter Wimsey she discovers "all the kingdoms of the world and the glory of them" (ch. 23). This perception represents Sayers's final alliance with the traditional English novel of character and individual experience. *The Nine Tailors* sought reality in the cosmos, in the endlessly expanding universe, in the tower itself; but *Gaudy Night* peers into the inner chaos of the human heart and is firmly planted on this mutable earth, where the novel is most at home. The quiet, golden afternoon of Harriet's revelation seems to be the last day of the Long Weekend between the two great wars. Wimsey will be called away by the Foreign Office on the Monday morning, and there is a valedictory scent in the air, a supressed urgency about the coming conflict. *Gaudy Night* thus effectively closes not only the Wimsey saga, but a golden period in detective fiction.

II

Sayers on Women

An Inquiry into the Fatal Subject

> "What," men have asked distractedly from the beginning of time, "what on earth do women want?" I do not know that women, *as* women, want anything in particular, but as human beings they want, my good men, exactly what you want yourselves: interesting occupation, reasonable freedom for their pleasures, and a sufficient emotional outlet.
>
> —"Are Women Human?"

6

Assaying the Subject

The epigraph to this section is the culminating passage in one of the most succinct, witty, and cogent arguments ever constructed on the subject of women: a 1938 lecture with the typically provocative Sayers title of "Are Women Human?"[1] Some three years after delineating the dilemma of the modern educated woman in the fictional mode of *Gaudy Night,* DLS was invited by a women's group to speak on the feminist movement. The subject made her bristle. Saying she thought that the time for an "old-fashioned" or "aggressive feminism" was over, she went on to question the whole notion of women as a distinct subject of inquiry.[2] Later published as one of her self-proclaimed *Unpopular Opinions,* the talk is as freshly invigorating today as it was in the late 1930s, when its author turned her wit upon her audience's expectations:

> I am occasionally desired by congenital imbeciles and the editors of magazines to say something about the writing of detective fiction "from the woman's point of view." To such demands, one can only say, "Go away and don't be silly. You might as well ask what is the female angle on an equilateral triangle."[3]

While it remains unclear whether it is worse to be the congenital imbecile or simply the half-witted editor, Sayers's audience was undoubtedly awakened by such sardonic humor. The message to all looking for a woman's view of the world was clear: "No Thoroughfare."

As one might expect from a writer of classic detective stories—a form that celebrates the rights and responsibilities of the individual—DLS champions the cause of women as individual human beings, not as members of a class called "females." Speaking from a novelist's perspective, she observes that "the question of 'sex-equality' . . . is, like all questions affecting human relationships, delicate and complicated" (17). Undeterred by such complexity, she proceeds to argue that

what is unreasonable and irritating is to assume that *all* one's tastes and preferences have to be conditioned by the class to which one belongs. That has been the very common error into which men have frequently fallen about women—and it is the error into which feminist women are, perhaps, a little inclined to fall into about themselves. (107)

Taken together with its companion piece, an essay entitled "The Human-Not-Quite-Human," Sayers's "Are Women Human?" constitutes her most direct statement on the subject of women.[4] Though most of what she argues in these essays is implied in her fiction, especially *Gaudy Night,* the straightforward nature of nonfiction combines with her vigorous style of argumentation to leave little open to interpretation. Given these two essays, in addition to her scattered comments on women elsewhere,[5] it appears that she was not particularly interested in the question of equal rights, which has been the central feminist issue in contemporary America. Presumably she expected that an emphasis on the humanity of both sexes would take care of all forms of inequity.

Yet she emphatically encouraged women—and men—to choose any job that matched their abilities and interests, and her own highly productive and diverse working life is proof of her commitment to this idea. Of the notion that women should do something just because it has been traditionally considered a male job or prerogative, however, she was contemptuous. If her barbs at the Miss Cattermoles of this world are not clear enough in her fiction, she is unambiguous in "Are Women Human?": "It is ridiculous to take on a man's job just in order to be able to say that 'a woman has done it. . . .' The only decent reason for tackling any job is that it is *your* job, and *you* want to do it" (*Unpopular Opinions* 109; cf. *Gaudy Night* ch. 3). The record of Sayers's negotiations with publishers and broadcasters reveals that she expected to be treated as the professional she was.[6] But none of this was tied to her female identity, and I cannot imagine her thinking of her work as symbolic or as a political statement.

The acerbic "Human-Not-Quite-Human," which focuses not upon the humanity of women, but upon society's relentless denial of that humanity, takes up the cliché of the female's being the "opposite sex." The essay dissects this common metaphor, asking why the female should be considered "the opposite sex," for "what is the 'neighboring sex?' " (116). The whole discussion becomes a way of satirizing the idea of women as a race apart

124

from the general run of humanity. As the essay explores gender stereotypes, we can follow the keen novelistic eye penetrating an imagined character's sensibility and touching upon the fundamental destructive power of
stereotyping, namely what it does to a person's self-image: "Probably no
man has ever troubled to imagine how strange his life would appear to
himself if it were unrelentingly assessed in terms of his maleness; if everything he wore, said, or did had to be justified by reference to female approval." Once on this tack, Sayers exercises her formidable argumentative
skills as she inverts—and thereby makes ridiculous—the clichés of gender.
Whatever would become of a man, she asks, if all his life were as determined by gender as women's lives have been?

> If the centre of his dress-consciousness were the cod-piece, his education directed
> to making him a spirited lover and meek paterfamilias; his interests held to be
> natural only in so far as they were sexual. If from school and lecture-room, Press
> and pulpit, he heard the persistent out-pouring of a shrill and scolding voice,
> bidding him remember his biological function. (117–18)

Trying to survive in this upside-down world, "The New Man" would also
find all the books rewritten. In a sociology text, for example, "he would
find, after the main portion dealing with human needs and rights, a sup-
plementary chapter devoted to 'The Position of the Male in the Perfect
State' . . . People would write books called, 'History of the Male,' or
'Males of the Bible,' or 'The Psychology of the Male' " (118). Such titles
seem odd because they turn men into the "opposite sex" and imply a mystery of manhood, like the "Enigma of Woman" which men have generated
for centuries. This enigma represents not only the "otherness" of the female, but the inability of the male to comprehend her. As DLS observes in
her notes on Dante:

> When women write or talk (and they have always talked pretty freely) one gets
> the impression that Man as such is an open book to them. . . . The great love-
> lyrics, the great love-tragedies, the romantic agony, the religion of beauty, the
> cult of the *ewig Weibliches,* the entire mystique of sex, is, in historic fact, of
> masculine invention. The exaltation of virginity, the worship of the dark Eros,
> the apotheosis of motherhood, are alike the work of man: the Fatal Woman is his
> discovery (and so, indeed, is the Fatal Man: Faust and Don Juan, Lovelace and
> Manfred are not of woman born). (*Purgatory* 33)

Were these traditions reversed, however, and men were categorized as
women have been, simply by reference to their sexual attributes and roles,
it would be surprising if any individual male could retain some sense of

125

himself *as a human being.* If he could, he would be faced with an even greater problem, for his culture would then mock him as a freak of manliness. Patronizing (or should we say "matronizing"?) interviewers, come to investigate the new creature, would proclaim: "There is nothing in the least feminine about the home surroundings of Mr. Focus, the famous children's photographer. His 'den' is panelled in teak and decorated with rude sculptures from Easter Island; over his austere iron bedstead hangs a fine reproduction of the 'Rape of the Sabines' " (118). The image is both humorous and profound. If a man were subjected to such treatment, it would not be surprising if he then "presented the world with a major social problem" (119); indeed, it would be remarkable if he could survive with "any rag of sanity and self-respect" intact. Through satiric inversion, exaggeration, and superb comic timing, Sayers thus refuses the brutalizing imprisonment of category for any human being, female or male. In "Are Women Human?" she declares, "*All* categories, if they are insisted upon beyond the immediate purpose which they serve, breed class antagonism and disruption in the state, and that is why they are dangerous" (114–15). Such comments are either ignored by, or unknown to, those who characterize DLS as a conventional social snob.

Acknowledging women's fully human status would mean that they were treated, "not, as an inferior class and not, I beg and pray all feminists, as a superior class—not, in fact, as a class at all, except in a useful context" (114). This emphasis on the worth of the individual human being makes Sayers's comments liberating for both sexes. Arguably, men have suffered as much from gender stereotyping as women have.

Little as she would have chosen such a role for herself, cultural and personal history conspired to make Dorothy L. Sayers both a powerful critic and an exemplar of the modern woman. Though she always stressed the humanity of women—and their consequent kinship with, rather than differences from, men—DLS has, in spite of herself, come to represent the accomplished, independent woman to several generations. She would be somewhat uncomfortable in this role—as her testy response to the women's society makes clear—but it is not really surprising that Dorothy L. Sayers, the liberally educated scholar, the eminent social critic, the superior detective novelist, has become something of a touchstone for female accomplishment in our time. Indeed, her refusal to see herself as symbol, coupled with her steadfast commitment to personal responsibility and her chosen work, have only made her a more powerful model for others.

Though it may be ironic, the fact of Sayers's significance to contemporary women is not really antithetical to her views on what one of her characters once called "the fatal subject" of modern times, the so-called "women's question."[7] Indeed, I would argue that it is Sayers's reluctance to regard women as a special class that raises the value of her statements on a subject that has proved fatal for many. Though she aggressively rejects special pleading and unique categories for women, what DLS says about female experience is fundamentally liberating and truly revolutionary: women are human beings, she asserts again and again, as valuable and as interesting individually as any other human beings—no more, no less. This insistence upon the humanity of one half of the human race forces the amorphous "women's question" into sharp focus: "Every woman is a human being— one cannot repeat that too often—and a human being *must* have occupation, if he or she is not to become a nuisance to the world" (110). It is fitting that she should emphasize the importance of work in female experience, because for Dorothy L. Sayers, human beings are what they make and do.

In the bold thesis quoted at the beginning of this section, Sayers is answering not only Freud, who wondered aloud about what women could possibly want, but also a *Zeitgeist* of her day, which was summarized most boldly in the *Kinder, Kirche, Küche* school of thought perpetuated by the Third Reich.[8] Reiterating the hackneyed questions often raised about women, she offers new answers: What is a woman's place? What is her role? What on earth can she possibly want? According to Dorothy L. Sayers, as a human being, a woman's place is wherever her work, heart, and whimsy take her. Or, to use the terms enunciated in "Are Women Human?" a woman's life is properly composed of *love* ("sufficient emotional outlet"), *work* ("interesting occupation"), and *play* ("reasonable freedom for their pleasures"), just as any fully realized human being's existence is. What is most striking is Sayers's insistence on this humanizing trinity of experience for women, in which she was not only ahead of her own time, but also beyond much discussion of women's issues even today. Her three categories of human experience will provide the key terms for the following chapters in this section, which examine Sayers's fictional portrayal of women and demonstrate the interplay between her novels and essays of social criticism.

DLS mentions "interesting occupation" first because she considers having suitable work the primary human need—the stuff of which all authentic lives are made. This idea of work as the defining human activity informs her entire canon, surfacing even in the early novels. We will begin there, with a look at the curious character of the spinster-sleuth, a type that provides useful occupation for some of those "superfluous women" who have been accumulating in industrial nations during the last two centuries.[9]

7

Unnatural Death
and the Testimony of
Superfluous Women

Clouds of Witness, Sayers's 1926 novel of marital discord and betrayal, sketches Lady Mary Wimsey as a woman without occupation or
clear purpose—something of a nuisance to her world and thus a contribu-
tor to its violence and confusion.[1] But *Unnatural Death* (1927), her third
novel, brings the women's question to the fore. Its villain, Mary Whittaker,
betrays her calling as a nurse. By way of counterpoint, the mystery is solved
largely through the admirable work of another woman, Miss Climpson,
who makes her first appearance in this book.[2] The relationship between
this novel's villain and hero is prototypical for DLS: in the world of her
creation, good people do good work, while subverting one's work or occupation is an unfailing index of moral corruption.[3] The implication seems to
be that if a person is capable of descending to slipshod work, it should not
be surprising if she indulges in a bit of murder here and there. Since its
detective, murderer, and victims are all spinsters, and the subject of spinsterhood is addressed directly in many of the scenes focusing upon Miss Climpson, *Unnatural Death* exhibits a rudimentary integration of story, theme,
and character that shows DLS moving toward the massive artistic integrity
she would accomplish in *The Nine Tailors* and *Gaudy Night.*
    In the strong and strongly developed character of Alexandra Katherine
Climpson, DLS brings her characteristic humor and good sense to scrutinizing the lot of unmarried women in an urban, industrialized world. Miss
Climpson is introduced in the third chapter of *Unnatural Death,* a chapter
that bluntly announces its intention with the title, "A Use for Spinsters,"
and quotes Gilbert Frankau on the "awe-inspiring circumstances" of living
in a country in which "there are two million more females than males."[4]
Though this may have been an awe-inspiring circumstance for those men,

the Englishwomen of Sayers's generation also suffered from the shortage of marriageable men. The carnage of the First World War had claimed the lives of three quarters of a million of England's young men, and those who survived were often scarred seriously, as were Peter Wimsey, George Fentiman (in *The Unpleasantness at the Bellona Club*), and Sayers's own husband. This circumstance is another interesting parallel between DLS and Jane Austen; both lived in a world ravaged by war, and both reflected in their fiction one long-term consequence of war, namely an increasing number of spinsters.[5]

Sayers wrote *Unnatural Death* in the year of her marriage, and it is tempting to speculate about the connection between her personal life and the questions raised in this book. Brabazon covers this tumultuous portion of her life in detail, and cites persuasive evidence of her overwhelming desire to marry, which seems to have reached crisis proportions around this time (chs. 8–10). Even without reference to expressly biographical materials, however, a sensitive reader of Sayers's third novel may wonder to what extent her decision to marry Mac Fleming was motivated by the novelist's keen awareness of the scarcity of possible mates, especially for a woman of her age, experience, and intelligence. It is possible that she wrote this book, in part, to clear her mind about questions and fears she was facing in her own life around this time.

For whatever reason, this novel suffers from an uncharacteristic awkwardness, as if its author were not sure of herself and her destination. Its opening is tentative and needlessly prolonged, while its mystery is linked rather arbitrarily to the book's social criticism, which is its greatest strength. In *Unnatural Death,* DLS is clearly attempting something beyond her technical grasp at this point, but such attempts will lead to the superlative novels of the thirties.

The book also seems uncomfortable with female sexuality. On one level, *Unnatural Death* may be read as an exploration of the modern (1920s) woman's options, some of which the author apparently finds unsettling. The book's final image of that freak of nature, the eclipse, prompts the usually resilient, sunny Wimsey to ask, "What is the matter with the day? . . . Is the world coming to an end?" (ch. 23). The entire novel seems generated by a time that is out of joint: in this shaky world, a nurse murders her own patient, and an unnatural death leads to the discovery of the "unnatural" or unconventional life of the killer. *Unnatural Death* examines the fate of women who cannot, or will not, fulfill society's definition of the female role. It is a book about "odd" women, odd in the sense of their being unmarried and, therefore, not part of an even-numbered couple, but odd also in the sense of their living outside of society's heterosexual patterns.

Like most human beings, Dorothy L. Sayers displayed somewhat contradictory attitudes toward social convention. As her unfinished autobiographical novel, "Cat O'Mary," suggests, she herself was torn between desiring conventional acceptance as a woman and rejecting her culture's definition of the female—maternal, powerless, and dependent, a creature of feeling and instinct, not of reason or imagination (Wade ms. 43). Such contradictory impulses are not unusual; the desire to have it both ways would appear to be an endemic human trait. It is just that artists, if they are successful at reaching an audience, call attention to themselves, thereby highlighting habits and proclivities that go unnoticed in less prominent creatures—and Sayers has managed better than most to garner attention.

The focus in *Unnatural Death* is upon the unmarried woman, especially the indefatigable Miss Climpson, the novel's only significant female character who does not come to grief. It is no coincidence that she is also the woman who has found her proper job. Although she is not the first, Miss Climpson is one of the brighter and more believable examples of the female sleuth—a character type almost as old as the detective story itself. In the late nineteenth and early twentieth centuries, fictional female detectives were often spinsters or widows who took up detection as "an escape from the dreadful alternative of genteel poverty" (Craig and Cadogan 15), the most likely alternative for members of that growing pool of superfluous women who did not marry. Their unattached status presented them with both the freedom to pursue such work, and the necessity for doing so—a perfect marriage. As Miss Climpson says in one of the "Wimsey Papers," for those who do not marry or inherit wealth, finding gainful employment is no luxury, because "you can't have money unless you *make* it" (*The Spectator* 1 Dec. 1939, 770). She knows from experience the truth of another famous spinster's observation that "Single Women have a dreadful propensity for being poor" (*Jane Austen's Letters* 483).

The female detective character goes back at least as far as 1861, when W. S. Hayward's *Revelations of a Lady Detective* told the story of a woman working at Scotland Yard. This character predated the reality, but according to Craig and Cadogan's historical survey of women in crime fiction, twenty-five women were appointed to the London Metropolitan Police in November of 1918 (92). It is likely that this was one of many opportunities for women resulting from the shortage of men caused by the First World War. These contemporary police appointments make Miss Climpson's activities as a private investigator during the 1920s more believable, especially since she is not a freelancer, like so many of her sister-sleuths, but a proper employee of Lord Peter Wimsey. Because of her professional relationship with Wimsey, Miss Climpson becomes an agent for the social hierarchy of money, power, and influence that was (and often, still is) a man's domain. This is a notable concession to realism, distinguishing Sayers's treatment of the women's question from the standard fantasy of popular culture, which often shows women enacting roles they could never take in life. In this sense, Miss Climpson is more believable than Wimsey himself. While he faces the perennial difficulties of the amateur sleuth (including the all-important question of how and why he comes to be involved in the investigation of a crime), she has a thoroughly professional reason for her actions, a privilege indeed for a woman of her day. No self-appointed snoop, Miss Climpson's proper job is detection.

One of the first women to write detective fiction, the American Anna Katharine Green, created a subspecies of the type in 1896, when she introduced what has been called the "elderly busy-body detective."[6] The female detective—usually unattached, often spinsterly—has remained a staple of detective fiction ever since. The most famous example of this type is undoubtedly Agatha Christie's Miss Jane Marple, who did not begin her inquiries until a couple of years after Miss Climpson's appearance on the scene. Thus, women have figured prominently in detective fiction, as both writers and detectives, almost from the beginning. Given this fact, in addition to the large female readership for mysteries, it is not surprising to find the form addressing questions of particular interest to women.[7]

Perhaps women mystery writers have created female detectives partially as a way of relieving or checking the aggressively male, men's club type of atmosphere which fills so much detective fiction, from Poe and Conan Doyle on. Such an atmosphere pervades Sayers's own early fiction, with the exception of *Unnatural Death*. The even more elusive, and more fascinating, question of why women have participated so fully in the practice of the English and English-style mystery will probably never be answered. Perhaps one not-so-pretty reason is that, since the mystery genre is rarely considered high art, it has been more acceptable for women to work in it.

Exemplifying the differences between Sayers and Christie—two writers who are often compared infelicitously—Miss Climpson is a more rounded and sympathetic character than Miss Marple, and more importantly, the stories in which she appears emphasize the realistic depiction of character and social milieu over the slick detective story mechanism that was Christie's forte. This is to say that Sayers was working in a genuinely novelistic tradition, rather than the bald detective story mode at which Christie excelled.[8] The richly comic and thoroughly human charcter of Miss Climpson, developed as she is with great subtlety and sympathy, is one indication of her creator's movement toward writing a traditional English novel, a genre distinguished by memorable "minor" characters that are often its most striking feature.

Miss Climpson's character is so strong and interesting, in fact, that in *Unnatural Death,* she steals the show. The book's most vivid scenes focus on her, as she interrogates villagers, examines her own highly bred Christian conscience, and comments upon the varieties of female experience reflected in its pages. Until Harriet Vane appears, Miss Climpson is the only character in the Wimsey books who approaches the hero's intelligence and sensibility. As the scrupulously fair Inspector Parker notes on first meeting her, Miss Climpson displays "great acumen in seizing . . . the salient points" of an investigation. She is quick-witted and distinguished by intelligent gray eyes as well as by "a clear head and retentive memory" (*Unnatural Death* ch. 3). Eliciting high praise from the ultimate judge, Miss Climpson is regarded as both tactful and shrewd by the great Lord Peter, who can trust her to function as his alter ego wherever a male may not tread safely. She easily follows his instructions and can, on command, appear to be a person with an income of £800 a year (quite a bit more money than she had ever seen in one place), including a thorough understanding of what kind of undergarments would be suitable to her newly assumed station in life. Recalling Sherlock Holmes's affinity for disguise, she expands upon this question of linen in one of her inimitable letters to Lord Peter: "it is necessary that every detail of my equipment should be suitable to my (supposed!) position in life. I have been careful to *wash* the garments through, so that they do not look *too new,* as this might have a *suspicious* appearance!" (chs. 3, 4). As a Sayersian creature, Miss Climpson's work is her play, and we enjoy watching her detecting because it gives her so much pleasure. In a more enlightened and kinder age, Miss Climpson could have been "a very good lawyer," assuming that her father would not have continued to oppose the education of women (ch 3).

The spinster-sleuth is a striking example of detective fiction's tendency to reflect the particulars of its time,[9] in this case, the changing status of women and their quest for fulfilling work. Specifically, the type suggests a way of capitalizing upon the growing economic burden of that large group of women who had become "superfluous" or redundant—to use the more contemporary but equally cruel adjective—since the mid-nineteenth century, the time of the detective story's birth. Until the last century, the term "spinster" was blandly descriptive, with none of the pejorative connotations it carries today. Presumably, it took on negative connotations when the number of unmarried women became, in Nina Auerbach's words, "a social headache almost as great as that of the ubiquitous 'deserving poor.' "[10] Sayers's novels show that she was not only keenly aware of this social headache, which had been intensified by the Great War, but was also ready to suggest some anodynes for the condition.

The casting of a spinster in the role of detective may, in our time, appear conventional, even trite. Is the spinster-sleuth just another variation on the old joke about the old maid seeking excitement in the threat of violence? Perhaps the murder mystery itself, with its titillating and faintly erotic insinuations of forbidden action and information, is just a stylized sublimation of the sex drive. Detection at least constitutes an acceptable instrument for probing into other peoples' lives and psyches—dangerous territory indeed for a form often described as "cozy." It is interesting that today, when being an unmarried woman does not necessarily imply spinsterhood or virginity, female detectives created by writers like Amanda Cross, P. D. James, and Antonia Fraser may be unmarried, but one would not likely refer to them as spinsters, and they are certainly not spinsterish.[11]

Yet the character of Sayers's spinster may appear more stereotyped than it is. When discussing her suitability for detection, Wimsey stresses Miss Climpson's reasoning powers, not the patronizing notion of "woman's intuition," a notion that gets a satiric send-up in the hilarious seance she conducts in *Strong Poison* (chs. 17, 18). Like Holmes and Wimsey before her, Miss Climpson "reads" experience. For example, she once maintained—correctly—that she knew the accused in a murder trial was innocent, not because of any evidence presented in the case, but because she sensibly considered the person's "demeanor [which was calm and open] . . . part of the evidence" (*Strong Poison* ch. 4). Such deduction may appear to be mere intuition or guesswork, especially to those not literate in the language of appearances, but it is actually the result of learning to interpret experience in its smallest, most subtle details.

Miss Climpson does not employ intuition at all, unless we use the word to mean the learned ability to read appearances and pick up vibrations from the very air of social situations—a perennial survival skill for the powerless, whether male or female. As Wimsey knows, it is more likely that a woman will have acquired this skill, simply because, as a woman, she has learned to notice myriad things in order to negotiate the minefield of personal relationships that so often explodes into novels, as well as murder *anglaise*. Sherlock Holmes enjoins us to appreciate the "great issues that may hang from a bootlace," a task of no great difficulty for the intelligent female of the species, whose domestic role has routinely limited her to the scrutiny of such minute detail and whose survival has often depended upon it. But, as the spinster-sleuth dramatizes, detection also paradoxically allows flight from the prison of the personal; building upon everyday domestic skills, it allows the shrewd woman to move into the public sphere. Miss Climpson typifies "the woman detective [who] stands out as the most striking, and the most agreeable embodiment of two qualities often disallowed for women in the past: the power of action and practical intelligence" (Craig and Cadogan 246).

Some of the great nineteenth-century novelists understood the relationship between conventional female experience and unravelling the mystery of human relationships, beginning as early as Jane Austen, whose *Emma* has been called the "most fiendishly difficult of detective stories,"[12] and carrying down through the century to the novels of Henry James. His *Portrait of a Lady* is the slowly unfolding story of Isabel Archer's attempt to understand the mystery of her own life, specifically her marriage to Osmond, and the novel's scrutiny of quivering nuance documents her reading and misreading of experience. James himself is proof that such a comprehension of experience is not inherently female, but learned. To call such novels "detective stories" stretches the term too far and blurs necessary distinctions, but the point is that there is a historical, organic relationship between the traditional novel in English and its stepchild, mystery and detection.

More directly relevant is the work of Sayers's ideal mystery writer, Wilkie Collins. Collins's thoroughly unconventional but strangely alluring Marian Halcombe, from *The Woman in White,* must have influenced DLS, not only in the creation of Miss Climpson, but also in the development of Harriet Vane, the most important female character to emerge from her imagination. The fact that Harriet was originally named Marian Delaney, according to the draft of *Strong Poison* at the Wade, suggests that she was modelled, in part, on Collins's Marian. (Given the name change, another possible source is Richardson's clever Harriet Byron, in *Sir Charles Grandison.*) Even if Marian Halcombe is not the first female detective in fiction, as Nina Auerbach has suggested (*Woman and Demon* 138), she is certainly one of the most striking examples of the type in a traditional novel, the kind of book that Dorothy L. Sayers wanted to write, and the kind of book she finally achieved with Harriet Vane at its center. Surely Marian Halcombe, with her superior intelligence, courage, and resourcefulness, must also be one of the greatest spinster-sleuths of all time.

Of special interest here is the timing of Sayers's research on Collins and the writing of *Unnatural Death.* As discussed earlier, we know that she was working on her abortive critical/biographical study of the Victorian sensation writer as early as the mid-twenties. In addition, the Wade notebook in which an early draft of *Unnatural Death* (then entitled "The Singular Case of the Three Spinsters") appears also includes the text of Sayers's lecture/essay entitled "Wilkie Collins." This lecture manuscript discusses *The Woman in White* in great detail and lauds Collins for his sympathetic understanding of a woman's need to be respected as a person in her own right, without reference to her relationship, if any, with a man. The fact that these two manuscripts are in the same notebook does not prove that DLS was writing both the story that was to become *Unnatural Death* and what appears to be her most complete analysis of Collins at the same time, but it is highly likely. Such a connection would suggest an interesting source not only for her characterization of the spinster-sleuth, but also for her first novel focusing on the predicament of women, a subject of great interest to Collins himself.

In the spinster-sleuth, Sayers takes a stereotypically female activity, gossip, and rarifies the potentially destructive habit into an art and science. Only the most hypocritical novelist—or novel reader—will dare disdain gossip; where would fiction be without it? Accustomed to the role of confidante, which the spinster so often fulfills in fiction and presumably in life,[13] Miss Climpson makes a graceful, unobtrusive investigator who is able to "ask questions which a young man could not put without a blush." When this innocuous-looking "elderly spinster"[14] appears at the scene of a crime, Wimsey avers, "Of course she asks questions—everyone expects it. Nobody is surprised. Nobody is alarmed. And so-called superfluity is agreeable and usefully disposed of" (*Unnatural Death* ch. 3). Miss Climpson has thus found a "good job" in the real sense of the term: she has found *her* job. As "Are Women Human?" declares, "Once lay down the rule that the job comes first and you throw that job open to every individual, man or woman, fat or thin, tall or short, ugly or beautiful, who is able to do that job better than the rest of the world" (*Unpopular Opinions* 110). Such a gender-blind rule would be truly revolutionary.

Through Miss Climpson and the Cattery—the detective agency masquerading as a typing bureau where Wimsey employs countless superfluous women—Sayers comments with wit and insight upon a serious social problem facing her society. With typical confidence and panache, she suggests a commonsensical solution to the predicament of women for whom a wasteful and inefficient world seems to have no use. This is the first glimmering of the Dorothy Sayers who would emerge a decade later in the essays of incisive social criticism, and the link between this early novel and the latter essays reveals the essential integrity of her career. *Unnatural Death* also foreshadows the kind of social commentary that would inform her best novels dealing with contemporary issues and the women's question, *The Documents in the Case* and *Gaudy Night*.

Miss Climpson demonstrates one respectable and creative possibility for the "superfluous female"; she can devote herself to doing a socially beneficial job of work for which she is uniquely suited. Her creator was clearly conscious of her symbolic import:

> "Miss Climpson," said Lord Peter, "is a manifestation of the wasteful way in which this country is run. . . . Thousands of old maids, simply bursting with useful energy, forced by our stupid social system into hydros and hotels and communities and hostels and posts as companions, where their magnificent gossip-powers are allowed to dissipate themselves or even become harmful to the community, while the ratepayer's money is spent on getting work for which these women are providentially fitted, inefficiently carried out by ill-equipped policemen. . . ." (*Unnatural Death* ch. 3)

As this passage shows, it is inaccurate to consider DLS simply as a conventional conservative. Through Wimsey's statements, she suggests with humor—a most effective way of saying something which might otherwise by considered unacceptable—that these women are not really superfluous at all. Rather, it is some of the habits of their society, which discards so much human talent, that are wasteful and outmoded (cf. *Begin Here*). In the typical bombast of his early period, Wimsey even declares that one day England will have to erect a statue to him, inscribed "To the Man who Made Thousands of Superfluous Women Happy without Injury to their Modesty or Exertion to Himself" (ch. 3). Sayers enjoys playing up the Cattery as a parodic twist on the old notion of kept women: like Parker, the reader is manipulated at first to think that Miss Climpson is Wimsey's mistress. This is not difficult, because of the common belief that men can have only sexual motivation for relationships with women (ch. 3).

None of this is meant to suggest that Sayers's spinster-sleuth is merely a symbol or mouthpiece for the author's concerns about the situation of women in her time. Miss Climpson is revealed to us chiefly through her letters, with their wildly enthusiastic expression and profligate emphases. These letters present her as a fully realized character, a character whose mind the author understands as she has understood no other up to this point. Miss Climpson demonstrates Sayers's ability to imply the general in the specific detail, to embody the broad cultural truth in the individual human situation, which is one of her greatest strengths as a fiction writer. For all the social commentary embedded in these books, the novelist remains bound to the truth of individual experience. The essayist may ask, and propose an answer to, the general question of "Are women human?" but the novelist must be concerned with complex and ambiguous individual persons. Miss Climpson powerfully suggests the humanity of her sex precisely because she is so distinct an individual.

Since DLS had been studying Wilkie Collins around this time, it is possible that she was also experimenting with the epistolary form, which Collins had used in *The Woman in White* and *The Moonstone*. (In 1930, she would, of course, write her own stunning epistolary novel, *The Documents in the Case*.) More than a literary convention or a technical experiment, however, Miss Climpson was the flower of Sayers's actual experience. In spite of her talents and university education, DLS had faced unemployment and lack of suitable work. She had feared a future without marriage—Miss Climpson is what she could have become. As James Brabazon says, albeit with too little recognition of Peter Wimsey's representing an essential part of Sayers's personality: "Wimsey was fabricated for a purpose—Miss Climpson came from the heart" (128).

At any rate, Miss Climpson is one of those wonderful old-fashioned fictional characters that can be said to "emerge triumphantly in the round."[15] At a turning point in *Unnatural Death,* we are made privy to her struggles with her conscience, a fact that elevates the work from straightforward detective story to the realm of fable. When she faces the moral dilemma of detection and knowingly accepts both knowledge and responsibility, she effectively accepts the burden of being human in an imperfect world. And with Huck Finn–like irony, she decides to risk going to hell, anyway: "Well," said Miss Climpson, "if this is a sin I am going to do it, and may I be forgiven" (ch. 22; cf. *The Adventures of Huckleberry Finn* ch. 31). As a thoroughly human creature, Miss Climpson is blessed with responsibility along with her newfound freedom. In fact, she must be one of the first female characters in fiction to face a moral choice that has nothing to do with love, marriage, or personal relationships.[16]

Whatever happens to her soul, the detective in her is richly repaid. Reading the scattered words and phrases written down by an anguished young woman preparing for confession, she is able to deduce a great deal:

> From these few fossil bones, Miss Climpson had little difficulty in reconstructing one of those hateful and passionate "scenes" of slighted jealousy with which a woman-ridden life had made her only too familiar. . . . Humiliating, degrading, exhausting, beastly scenes. Girls' school, boarding-house, Bloomsbury-flat scenes. . . . Silly *schwarmerei* swamping all decent self-respect. Barren quarrels ending in shame and hatred. (Ch. 22)

Perhaps Dorothy Sayers had herself experienced or witnessed such scenes. She seems painfully aware of, and frightened by, the destructive tension created by inharmonious sexual relationships—especially when, in the absence of useful work, these relationships become the focus of life. In the later Vane-Wimsey romance, the issue of self versus other is debated at even greater length, and Sayers's letters show that possessive love particularly appalled her.[17] This seems to be more of a target than the lesbianism in *Unnatural Death*.

Because Miss Climpson has found her proper job, her spinster status actually becomes an advantage, since it frees her from the tedium and routine of family duties.[18] By referring to her as a spinster, Sayers suggests that Katherine Climpson is beyond the usual age for marriage, or at least the husband-hunting years, a fact which protects her from any suspicion of romantic or sexual motivation for her investigative activities. In this way, she is similar to most of the great male detectives, who tend to be either asexual, in the Holmesian mold, or at least do not mix romance with detection; examples include Dupin, Holmes, the early Wimsey, and Nero Wolfe. Yet Miss Climpson is "a spinster made not born—a perfectly womanly woman" (*Unnatural Death* ch. 16), her creator appears anxious to tell us, perhaps to differentiate her clearly from the novel's lesbians. Unlike them, Miss Climpson shows no disdain for men; her relationship with Lord Peter, for example, is consistently portrayed as one of great warmth and mutual respect. The assumption is that Miss Climpson would have chosen marriage as certainly as she would have chosen the law, but history made both choices impossible for her. Her sleuthing is the best job she can make of her life given the circumstances. To readers in the latter part of the twentieth century, this may not be a sympathetic position for DLS to take on the subject of marriage, but it is the position she seems to have taken in her own life: in some ways a surprisingly conventional person, she apparently concluded that a marriage of compromise was preferable to no marriage at all.

It is important to note that, although the villain of *Unnatural Death* is a lesbian and her possessive attachment to a young, self-effacing girl is one of her most awful traits, the novel presents other views of women without men. One, of course, is the happy occupation of Miss Climpson. Another is provided by glimpses of an older female partnership that is contrasted with the current generation. The surviving partner is the murder victim, but there is enough talk about what she and her partner were like as young women to make it clear that they were very different from Mary Whittaker. Here is a description of the young Clara Whittaker, Mary's aunt, by that most trustworthy of narrators, a loyal servant:

A rare young lady she was in them days. Deary me. Straight as a switch, with a fine, high colour in her cheeks, and shiny black hair—just like a beautiful two-year-old filly she was. And very sperrited. Wonnerful sperrited. There was a many gentleman as would have been glad to hitch up with her, but she was never broke to harness. . . . Well, there is some creatures like that. I 'ad a terrier-bitch that way. Great ratter she was. But a business woman—nothin' else. . . . The Lord makes a few on 'em that way to suit 'Is own purposes, I suppose. (Ch. 12)

As Miss Climpson shows, there is absolutely nothing wrong with being "a business woman—nothin' else," so long as one conducts that business honorably, as Clara Whittaker did. What fundamentally distinguishes both Miss Climpson and the old Miss Whittaker from the villainous Mary Whittaker, and indeed from many people, is that they love their work. The joy they experience in doing their chosen work, and in doing it well, is the best evidence that they are good people.

Sayers's insistence upon women finding satisfying or interesting occupation is most liberating, and most unusual. How rare it is for anyone, of either sex, to demand this level of interest from work. As DLS notes sardonically in *Are Women Human?*, few object to women working, as long as the jobs they do are sufficiently boring or unpalatable that no human being would want them. This is an astute point: there was little objection to lower-class women working in the fields or sweatshops; it was only when middle-class women, especially those attached to men through marriage, began working that society became inflamed on the subject. In fact, when a woman works for any reason other than minimal economic survival, she is often still regarded with puzzlement and hostility.

In contrast to Miss Climpson's ebullient detection, Mary Whittaker grimly manipulates other people and uses them as a means to her corrupt ends. Her material greed, which leads to the first murder, extends into a kind of consuming emotional greed, the rapacious possessiveness that masquerades as love. Mary Whittaker thus represents what is for Dorothy L. Sayers one of the most flawed of human actions, that of turning another person—or the personal side of life—into one's only and all-consuming "job." As Miss Climpson puts it to the besotted Vera Findlater, this is not love but idolatry, and it is "*out of proportion* to see everything through the eyes of another fellow-creature" (ch. 16). This is the same flaw that motivates the actions of the poison-pen in *Gaudy Night*. Seen in this light, it is Mary Whittaker who is acting out the stereotypical woman's role of emotional manipulator and who is bound up in the personal, while the detective investigating her crimes, the superficially conventional spinster, has transcended the female stereotype.

One of the most striking characteristics of the female stereotype is passivity, but we are told that Miss Climpson is by nature "an active woman" who

139

becomes anxious and depressed when she is "condemned to inactivity" (ch. 22). How oddly human of her! Without suitable employment, people do tend to become troublesome to themselves and others, as Sayers had warned: "A human being *must* have occupation, if he or she is not to become a nuisance to the world" (*Unpopular Opinions* 110). Such nuisances may take the form of petty irritations and gossip; they may escalate into emotional vampirism; their apex is the destruction of peace and order in the act of murder. The need for interesting occupation is a curious and yet oddly apposite theme for a detective story, a form which tends to flourish among leisured classes. The genre itself may, in fact, be regarded as one of the games invented by civilized people to occupy time in an interesting fashion, to provide innocuous employment for those who might otherwise become nuisances. And I should expect even the genre's detractors to prefer for people to read murder mysteries rather than act out their murderous impulses. The spinster-sleuth is, therefore, much like the displaced aristocrat, Peter Wimsey, who takes up detection as a way of doing a useful a job of work and warranting a place in this world. Their fundamental similarities point to the androgynous ideal implied in Sayers's fiction, most notably in the Vane-Wimsey novels.

When I consider all that *Unnatural Death* does and attempts to do, I am reminded of Howard Haycraft's comment that even her mistakes do credit to Dorothy L. Sayers (*Murder for Pleasure* 142). This novel is marred by one-dimensional clichés like Mary Whittaker; its murder-method is overly ingenious, and most experts would say, implausible;[19] and even Wimsey seems wooden here. But from this rather unsatisfying book emerges one of Sayers's most memorable characters, Miss Climpson, as well as some provocative and profound comments on modern culture. In *Unnatural Death,* we see a conscientious, serious artist haltingly approaching an understanding of her own greatest subject—the role of work in human life—as she was beginning to shatter the brittle artifice of the conventional detective story.

We shall not meet Miss Climpson again until *Strong Poison.* In the meantime, her creator will begin to explore the possibility of a woman's successfully combining marriage with interesting occupation in one coherent life.

8

Neither Gods nor Beasts

Men, Women, and *The Documents in the Case*

Immediately following *Unnatural Death,* a story which is, in Miss Climpson's deprecating phrase, "woman ridden," Sayers wrote *The Unpleasantness at the Bellona Club* (published in 1928), her foray into the overpoweringly masculine world of a London men's club. It could be that such an ambience appealed to her after the total submersion in female politics that characterized *Unnatural Death.* The Bellona Club mystery again considers inharmonious sexual relationships, but this time they are between men and women: one the troubled marriage of a prime suspect in the case, the other a fractured affair involving the murderer. A common denominator in these two unhappy relationships is the male's resentment of the growing emancipation of women during the postwar period (chs. 7, 16). As noted in the discussion of *Gaudy Night,* Sayers's detective novels resemble much traditional English fiction in their preoccupation with sexual politics and the institution of marriage. She is most interested in whether that institution can be reformed sufficiently to make it both equitable and appealing to modern women. This is a central question raised in several of her novels during the 1930s, beginning with that daring experiment entitled *The Documents in the Case.*

The Documents in the Case was daring because it took artistic—and, it would be fair to assume, financial—risks. With a popular series detective and a successful record of writing fairly conventional detective stories behind her, DLS decided to try a book without her great sleuth and with much greater thematic complexity than before. Thus, she risked not only disaffecting her readership, but also the possibility of failing to achieve more ambitious goals. Under the influence of Wilkie Collins's considerable stylistic charms, she adopted the epistolary form for this, her fifth novel, which is also the pivotal book in her development as a novelist. Although she had experimented with letters in *Unnatural Death,* this old standby for writers of fiction was essentially a new narrative form for DLS in 1930. James Brabazon regards the epistolary form as a natural choice for her, given her legendary letter-writing ability, as well as her love for another novel in letters, Richardson's *Sir Charles Grandison* (129). That she even attempted all these things is admirable, but more impressive is the book that resulted, which is far and away the best novel she had done to this point.

From the letters DLS wrote to her collaborator, Eustace Barton, we know that the idea, that is, the detective premise, for this novel was suggested by Barton.[1] What is interesting is how Sayers took this rather conventional, if clever, detective idea, and turned it into the basis of a serious novel of rich social criticism and psychological complexity. I do not know at what point she decided to use the epistolary form for this story, but the decision was felicitous. As Barton had foreseen, the theme of the book is the nature of reality, its detective problem hinging upon the difference between real and synthetic poison.[2] The letter form, which dramatizes the way that individual perceptions shape reality, is a perfect vehicle for the novel's theme; in a sense, it *embodies* the theme. The form also allows for extended discussions of such subjects as sexual politics, middle-class respectability, the relationship between art and life, and the possibility for belief in an increasingly secular world—quite a bit for a detective story to take up—but all rendered believable by the epistolary form, which allows the letter-writer to function effectively as both narrator and essayist. Letters permit the leisure, reflection, and subtlety that are necessary to the unfolding of this multidimensional novel of ideas, as well as the intimacy appropriate to the presentation of the kind of domestic tragedy the story relates.

To dramatize perception's profound influence on our understanding of reality, the story begins with the letters of a rather more than usually warped sensibility, one Agatha Milsom. Miss Milsom may be regarded as what Miss Climpson could have become if she had not been blessed with good sense and the salubrious outlet of the Cattery. The striking differences between these two spinsters reveals Sayers's ability to create distinct, living characters without resorting to type. Agatha Milsom has a job as housekeeper to the Harrisons but never seems to do anything useful, as she plays a kind of suburban Slip-Slop to Margaret Harrison's latter-day Lady Booby (cf. *Joseph Andrews*). Rather than doing an honest day's work, Miss Milsom babbles on about how cruel life is, her nastiness stemming from what Paul Harrison recognizes as a "disagreeable [case of] sex-antagonism" (document no. 49). Agatha Milsom's predicament reminds us that DLS was stressing the necessity of finding satisfying work, not the importance of paid employment. A bitterly discontented spinster, Miss Milsom's sex drive and need for satisfying occupation are sublimated in inexplicable cravings, wild fantasies, and bizarre avocations, all of which add to the destructive tension in the Harrison household that culminates in adultery and murder. Pathetically ridiculous but ultimately dangerous, Agatha Milsom typifies the frustrated female who has found neither love, nor pleasure, nor suitable work. (Miss Hillyard of *Gaudy Night* and Aggie Twitterton of *Busman's Honeymoon* are similar characters.) All of her energies are thus turned inward and upon the personal, including slanderous gossip about those around her.

Attempting to put the documents in the case of his father's death into meaningful order, Paul Harrison quotes the shrewd Rev. Perry on Miss Milsom's lot. Upon realizing that she has been finally "put away," Perry remarks with both acuity and sympathy that "in the days of faith—or superstition, if you like—a convent or a beguinage would have provided the proper asylum for such a case, with some honest work to do and a harmless emotional outlet—but nowadays they make you pay for everything, not only your pleasures" (document no. 49). This is a curiously compelling argument for a more faithful and traditional society.

Left to her own devices, Miss Milsom becomes absorbed in a spate of hobbies that represent a stinging portrayal of the amateurism that has afflicted women in the last two centuries, as urbanization, increasing leisure, and changing social expectations have conspired to make them unfit for anything more substantial. A knitter who cannot even produce a pair of socks the same length, Agatha Milsom nevertheless fancies herself "artistic" and expects the recipients of such gifts to be thrilled. Her disgusted employer, who has a right to ask that she bring some order to his household, complains of her littering "the place with wool and bits of paper which she calls 'art materials' " (document no. 24), a habit that not surprisingly offends the neat, workmanlike draftsman.

Miss Milsom even imagines herself a potential writer, wondering in her miserable confusion if "it would have been better for my health if I had had something to occupy my mind" (document no. 3). Latching onto the bankrupt romantic notion of authorship as a way of expressing unusually deep feeling, her doctor encourages her in the idea of art as "therapy." He adds that her "power of *feeling* things so intensely ought to make . . . [her] a really good writer," if only she can master "the technique of putting it down on paper" (document no. 4). This attitude toward writing is, of course, a distinguishing characteristic of the amateur, and it particularly appalled

DLS, neglecting as it does the role of both intelligence and discipline in art. This misconception is treated at some length in *The Mind of the Maker,* especially the chapter entitled "Scalene Trinities," where Sayers observes that "the distinguishing mark of the sonless is to be frustrate and inexpressive. They are those unhappiest of living men, the uncreative artists." This would seem to describe many of the destructive and self-destructive characters in her fiction, including the murderers who pervert work: "the uncreative artist is the destroyer of all things, the active negation . . . assuming leadership of the universe in the mad rush back to Chaos" (163).

Dorothy L. Sayers did not associate emotionalism with being either female or creative, and Agatha Milsom is the object of much derision. Of particular repugnance is her grotesque parody of the cliché that women are innately more sensitive and compassionate than men. Miss Milsom demonstrates what she has of these fine qualities in a letter to her sister, which is filled with extraordinary sensitivity and tact: "You are to be congratulated, Olive, on not being sensitive. Temperament is a great gift, but a very unhappy one, as I know so well from my own experience" (document no. 2). Such sensitivity would also seem to be an unhappy gift when those self-proclaimed sensitive souls pass it along to others. Like Mary Musgrove, whose sore throats were always worse than anyone else's, Agatha Milsom tyrannizes others with her weakness.[3]

The novel implies that a large part of Agatha Milsom's problem is that she is not mated, but it does not wholeheartedly endorse marriage either. That marriage is no escape for many is imaged in the predicament of the similarly miserable and inept Margaret Harrison, whose mind is filled with crack-pot ideas, including a surfeit of ridiculous attitudes toward love, gleaned from popular novels and the daily papers. She resembles Austen's Catherine Morland in this, with the substantial difference that the heroine of *Northanger Abbey* is genuinely trying to learn about reality and to enter adulthood, while Margaret Harrison seems forever addicted to a prolonged and ugly adolescence.[4] She suffers from the adolescent's self-absorption, fickleness, and intense emotionalism, yet she is also a dupe of the great middle-class god, respectability, which effectively ruins most of the lives in the story. She wants a lover, but is unwilling to give up her comfortable niche as a middle-class housewife; she craves freedom, but abdicates any responsibility for her actions: she is Ibsen's Nora, without the courage or decisiveness to slam the door on the cozy little sitting room. In fact, *The Documents in the Case* reminds us of Sayers's provocative observation about the little-acknowledged relationship between respectability and crime: "of all motives . . . respectability—the least emphasized in fiction—is one of the most powerful in fact, and is the root cause of a long

144

series of irregularities, ranging from murder itself to the queerest and most eccentric misdemeanors" (*The Sunday Times* 5 Aug. 1934).

Taking all of the different viewpoints of the letter-writers in *Documents* into consideration, the novel paints a strongly unsympathetic picture of Margaret Harrison (see especially document nos. 5, 37–44), although it is modified somewhat by her proclaimed desire to get a job and do something with her life. She has made it clear that she does not consider making a home a worthwhile endeavor, even though she seems to expect to be supported by her husband. When he chastises her because she does not care for her home, she plays with his language, saying "What kind of a place is my home, that I should care about it?" (document no. 41). Yet she accepts no responsibility for having a home so uninteresting or terrible. As one would expect, her hidebound husband refuses to accept her plan to return to office work, and she is left where she started, a young woman with nothing to justify her life, even to herself. One of the things *The Documents in the Case* dramatizes is how little of real interest or challenge is left to the mistress and staff of an average modern home. This is a point DLS explains in historical terms in "Are Women Human?," where she concludes with some asperity that "It is perfectly idiotic to take away women's traditional occupations," that is, the wide range of cottage industries, domestic duties, and childbearing responsibilities allotted to the female in preindustrial societies, "and then complain because she looks for new ones" (*Unpopular Opinions* 110). If the desire for respectability was part of the root cause of Harrison's murder, so was boredom.

Although sexuality permeates *Unnatural Death* and the story implies that Miss Climpson is lucky to have found a suitable way of substituting interesting work for sexual gratification, *The Documents in the Case* is much more direct on the subject. Agatha Milsom remembers having suffered as a young girl because of her mother's "old-fashioned ideas of what was 'nice' " (document no. 18), and even Margaret Harrison is pitiable in her thwarted desires. Mrs. Harrison imagines, briefly and rather unconvincingly, that having a child might have made her life happier (document no. 42), if only because she could have then assumed the role of mother, in lieu of being a wife. This is certainly the path many "oddly married"[5] women have taken, but whether happiness is ever the result of such accommodation is questionable. The tension in the Harrison household is masterfully rendered, with the marital misery of these two very ordinary people showing that, while life without a partner may be difficult, marriage is often no solution to the problem. As Miss Milsom's therapist declares, "half my patients come to me because they are not married—and the other half because they are!" (document no. 1).

145

According to Jack Munting, who functions as a sort of Jamesian center of consciousness in the novel, the Harrisons' thorny relationship may be interpreted thus:

> In theory, he was extremely broad-minded, generous and admiringly devoted to his wife; in practice, he was narrow, jealous and nagging. To hear him speak of her, one would have thought him the ideal of chivalrous consideration; to hear him speak to her, one would have thought him a suspicious brute. Her enormous vitality, her inconsequence, her melodrama (that is the real point, I think), got on his nerves, and produced an uncontrollable reaction of irritability. He would have liked her to shine for him and for him only; yet a kind of interior shyness prompted him to repress her demonstrations and choke off her confidences. "That will do, my dear"; "Pull yourself together, my girl," checked a caress or an enthusiasm. . . . Into the muffling of his outer manner, her radiance sank and was quenched. (Document no. 37)

This is a sadly familiar picture, drawn with the great capacity for ambiguity and complexity that distinguishes genuine art. Such statements from Munting show how little credence DLS gave to the notion that there is a special "woman's understanding" of the world, or even of female experience. Munting's analysis of the Harrison marriage is remarkable in its subtlety and sympathy—he is an avatar of the writer, reflecting Sayers's own ability to evaluate the situation between men and women with fairness. Since Munting is a novelist himself, we think perhaps of his similarity to Wilkie Collins, who displayed an uncommonly sympathetic imagination in his portrayal of women. We should recall, also, how often Sayers's fiction shows that marriage can be hard on men (see, for example, Farren of *Five Red Herrings,* Tallboy of *Murder Must Advertise,* and Sellon in *Busman's Honeymoon*). Such details create a balanced picture of male-female relationships and keep the narratives from become diatribes.

In a letter to his fiancée, even Munting falls back on the cliché that no woman can understand a man's point of view, just as no man can understand a woman's. This is a curious statement when one stops to consider that a woman created Munting, wrote these love letters for him, and gave him believable thoughts and expression.[6] She also created the woman he loves, a woman who is able to see things from his point of view well enough to deal with his somewhat difficult nature. DLS was amused by men who asked her how she managed to write realistic scenes involving their sex; she answered as one might expect, that perhaps her male characters were believable because she just let them act and talk as human beings do.[7] While she chided men for considering women "mysterious," thereby denying their essential, discoverable humanity, she thankfully did not indulge in the opposite mistake and regard men as hopelessly enigmatic. By creating believable and sympathetic male characters like Jack Munting and the later Peter Wimsey, DLS demonstrates that a woman can indeed understand a man.

One of the implied questions in *The Documents in the Case* is to what extent personal responsibility and morality can be mitigated by circumstances such as Margaret Harrison's miserable boredom and frustration, or Harwood Lathom's superiority as an artist over his victim. Margaret especially presents highly charged arguments in support of moral relativism, thereby adding the most unattractive touches to her generally repellent character. A veritable Goebbels of the bedroom, she writes to her lover: "What right have the useless people to get in the way of love and youth? . . . Get rid of the ugly and sick and weak and worn-out things, and let youth and love and happiness have their chance" (document no. 43). By the book's end, DLS has given a resounding no to such rationalization. This answer is in keeping not only with conventional morality, but with the English detective story tradition, which assumes that no person has the right to take advantage of another—no matter how unattractive or "useless" that person may be—and that individual desires must be kept in check by the law. When Munting realizes that Lathom murdered Harrison, all considerations of friendship and artistic values are overridden: he can do nothing but take the side of the law, and even more importantly, of the victim, against his old friend (document no. 52). The classic detective story has little patience with the seductive modern notion that people who turn to crime are "trapped" by their environment and therefore blameless. The human habitat may be sterile, debased, or abrasive—and in the American and some contemporary English detective stories it tends to be all three—but the detective genre acknowledges implicitly that individuals must live within the limits sanctioned by their society. There are exceptions to this, even as early as the Sherlock Holmes canon, but the English detective story goes against the law only after debate, not as a matter of course.[8]

On the issue of sexual morality, the book also rejects the relativism of Margaret's sentimental and self-justifying philosophy that "there is no sin," as though her adultery "had a consecration of its own."[9] Thus, in spite of her keen understanding of Margaret's predicament, Sayers judges women in the same way she does men—the surest evidence that she regards both sexes as fully human. Taking the side of traditional morality, as it does ultimately, this book goes against the kind of modern thinking that blames the world for the outcast's actions, or at the very least romanticizes rebellion. When Margaret argues against Nature itself, maintaining irrationally that it would be impossible for a pregnancy to result from her adulterous liaison, the book implies a link between conventional morality and what DLS

147

once called "the universal moral law" (*The Mind of the Maker* 9), something she herself had learned from bitter experience.

The Documents in the Case also shows that a rigorous adherence to justice is liberating. In allotting blame, the novel treats Margaret Harrison as a responsible human being, not as a victim of man's unfairness to woman. Mrs. Harrison may not be *legally* guilty of a crime, but her manipulation of Lathom makes her equally responsible, in moral terms, for the murder he commits. In a malapropism that also constitutes a particularly apt pun, Margaret's steamy, self-serving letters to her lover are, according to the sublime Mrs. Cutts, "excitements to murder" (document no. 49). There is no better way to show that women are indeed human than to treat them as such. In "Are Women Human?" Sayers says, "When it comes to a *choice*, then every man or woman has to choose as an individual human being, and, like a human being, take the consequences" (*Unpopular Opinions* 110–11). Although she may understand the reasons for Margaret Harrison's behavior, Sayers neither excuses nor rationalizes it; never does she display an automatic, unthinking alliance with women *because* they are women. Given her novels and essays, it should be safe to assume that Dorothy L. Sayers would not think much of the current fashion in the mass media for sentimentalizing and justifying women's retaliatory violence against men.[10] Her evenhanded treatment of the sexes is a refreshing outgrowth of an abiding belief in the primacy of the individual and in fair play. Thus, although *Documents* is a novel of astute social criticism, it is not a piece of propaganda, but a richly realistic work of art woven from particularly tough moral fiber.

Sayers had depicted unhappy marriages and troubled romantic relationships in each of her early books, beginning with *Whose Body?*, where the murderer is motivated by sexual jealousy. It is also obvious from the beginning of the Wimsey saga that the marriage of the current Duke and Duchess of Denver is particularly unattractive to DLS. The Denvers' marriage lacks all the things she valued most in male-female relationships, namely intellectual affinity, trust, honesty, passion, humor, friendship.[11] *The Unpleasantness at the Bellona Club* presents the acute marital suffering of the George Fentimans, as well as the miserable entaglement of Ann Dorland and Dr. Penberthy. In fact, the only happy and successful marriage to come out of the early Wimsey stories is that of Peter's sister, Lady Mary Wimsey—to a policeman. So much for refuge in convention. Some readers accuse Sayers of romanticizing the aristocracy and the status quo, but it is unclear how such readers would interpret this pattern of marriages, for never does she sympathize with what would be considered the "right" match in conventional terms. After much ado, even her hero makes what is considered by real snobs like Helen, Duchess of Denver, an embarrassingly poor marriage (see the "Prothalamion" to *Busman's Honeymoon*). In fact, breaking the conventional pattern seems to be her characters' only chance at marital happiness.[12]

The new angle in *The Documents in the Case* is not, therefore, its attention to unhappy sexual relationships, but its parallel exploration of a happy and satisfying alliance between Jack Munting and the woman who becomes his wife during the story, Elizabeth Drake. With a name powerfully suggestive of England's glorious age, it is possible that Elizabeth was named deliberately for the great English queen who, according to DLS, was lucky enough to have been born into the right "job" and courageous enough to sacrifice personal happiness to doing that job well.[13] As a modern woman, however, Elizabeth Drake does not have to make this ultimate sacrifice; she seems destined to have both a successful writing career and a satisfying marriage, and is thus charting new waters for female experience.

Although DLS abandoned Wimsey and his entourage for this story, considering *Documents* in the context of her entire career suggests that it was through the creation of Munting and Drake that the novelist discovered the direction the later Wimsey books were to take. This novel is more serious and complex than any fiction she had written to this point. In addition, the Muntings' relationship—discussed, planned, and analyzed at a length possible only for people who appreciate the power of the word and who are intellectual and introspective enough to tolerate such self-analysis—prefigures the relationship that Wimsey will eventually forge with Harriet Vane. Once Sayers discovered that she could not bring off a conventional melodramatic ending to *Strong Poison,* she was left with having to develop the Vane-Wimsey match along rather more serious and less expectable lines. *The Documents in the Case* may be regarded as her rehearsal for this task.[14]

We hear a faint echo of Peter Wimsey (and by extension, of Bertie Wooster) in Munting's nervous, "Hullo-ullo-ullo!" (document no. 37), and the tone of some of Munting's letters resembles the self-deprecating humor of Wimsey's endless proposals of marriage. Consider the Wimsey-like signature to one of Munting's love letters: "Yours, Bungie, if indeed anything of one's self can ever be anybody else's which, as an up-to-date young woman, you will conscientiously doubt, but, at any rate, with the usual damned feeling of incompleteness in your absence, yours, blast you! yours" (document no. 5). The older and more experienced Wimsey is mercifully not as long-winded, but the tone and attitude is not too far from one of his April Fool letters to Harriet: "*Will you marry me?*—It's beginning to look like one of those lines in a farce—merely boring till it's said often enough; and after that, you get a bigger laugh every time it comes. . . . [signed] Yours, more than my own, Peter Wimsey" (*Gaudy Night* ch. 11). Beneath all the wit, both men display an unusually acute awareness of their egos, especially of their potential for damaging any chance for a genuine relationship with a woman. This uncommon self-awareness makes them particularly diffident and appealing lovers, and opens the male-female relationship to new possibilities.

In a more somber mood, Munting encourages his lover to speak her mind always, because he believes that "married life should be based on mutual frankness" (document no. 6), just as Wimsey later tells Harriet Vane that all he wants from her is "common honesty" (*Have His Carcase* ch. 13). This kind of frankness is a bit easier to envision than to put into action, as some explosive scenes in *Busman's Honeymoon* show (chs. 7, 17), but without it, relationships between men and women are doomed to the manipulative game-playing and deceit that has traditionally defined them.

Since both Munting and Drake are writers, their letters also make *The Documents in the Case* a modernist text in the sense that it is a novel which has as one of its subjects the writing of novels. This corresponds to Wimsey and Vane's serious discussions in *Gaudy Night,* on the subject of how to bring greater realism to the detective story. The most important thing is the respect which Munting accords to Drake's work, which prefigures Wimsey's surprisingly serious regard for Vane's writing. Both are contrasted with the patronizing Lathom and the pompous lover Vane once had (see *Strong Poison* ch. 8). If work is an essential element of any human life, as "Are Women Human?" argues, respect and love for a person must be reflected in respect and love for that person's work. Such respect is a defining characteristic of good male-female relationships in Sayers's fiction, and is, for Harriet Vane, the most persuasive evidence that Peter Wimsey really loves her.

How often Munting sounds like the later Lord Peter, who has been transformed by love. Speaking of Margaret Harrison, for example, Munting concludes: "It is so hard for a woman, isn't it? . . . She said she always felt she could have made herself a happy life by living for and in others. I did not say that she would probably end by devouring her hypothetical family . . ." (document no. 11). This is, of course, one of Sayers's perennial themes, functioning prominently in *Unnatural Death.* Later, in *Gaudy Night,* Wimsey will caution Harriet to remember that "there . . . [is] no devil liked devoted love" (ch. 20), a remarkable speech from a man to his beloved. Reflecting on the Harrisons' bad marriage, Munting expresses a Wimseyian anxiety to his fiancée: "I *see* how these things happen, but how does one insure against them? What security have we that we—you and I, with all our talk of freedom and frankness—shall not come to this?" (document no. 28). This should be compared to the first chapter of *Busman's Honeymoon,* where the new-wedded lord admits to his bride, "I wonder what sort of shot I'm going to make at being decent to you." And for the ultimate in honesty, Munting acknowledges that a lot of the old moss still hangs about him and he fears he will be unable to act upon all of his noble ideas about equality between men and women:

Dearest, do you really want to be married to the sort of unsatisfactory bloke I am? It is extraordinarily brave and dear of you. You will have a devil of a time. I want to warn you now that when I say I want you to keep your independence and exquisite detachment, I don't really mean it. I shall try to mould you into the mirror of myself, fatally and inevitably. When I say I am not jealous, either of your work or friends, I am lying. When I promise to look at things from your point of view, I am promising what I cannot perform. (Document no. 13)

The unusual thing about this statement is not the reality it describes, but the fact that the man sees the problems inherent in the situation and accepts responsibility for his part in creating them. When Elizabeth answers this strange love letter with wit, Munting exclaims, "Thank heaven for a woman with a sense of humour" (document no. 14). This prefigures Wimsey's "code of behavior," or his conviction that "the worst sin—perhaps the only sin—passion can commit, is to be joyless" (*Gaudy Night* ch. 23). In fact with all their high-flown talk about love and work, and men and women, both of these relationships are lightened and made memorable by their wit and capacity for play. It takes Harriet a long time, but by *Busman's Honeymoon,* her relationship with Wimsey, and indeed with the world, is capable of a giddy playfulness. In her insouciant characterizations, Sayers would appear to share W. H. Auden's tendency to love those capable of making him laugh ("Notes on the Comic"). Her fiction also roundly denies the sentimental notion that there is anything beguiling or satisfying about self-sacrificing female behavior. Wimsey sums up the attitude when he announces to the woman he loves, "I will not have surrenders or crucifixions" (*Gaudy Night* ch. 23).

The striking parallels between the Wimsey-Vane relationship and that of Munting and Drake help to illuminate Sayers's intentions in her 1930s novels, especially *Gaudy Night*. In the Munting-Drake alliance, she is contemplating the possibility of a marriage between equals, a marriage that is entered into because of genuine emotional and intellectual affinity, not as a convenience, nor as an irrational surrender to passion. In this relationship, sexual conventions and expectations are examined, rethought, and recast.

It is a paradigm for what Dorothy L. Sayers considered a healthy adult love relationship between a woman and a man: equal, intellectual, passionate, amusing, challenging. Such a relationship is developed in even greater depth in the Vane-Wimsey Quartet.

There is a classical symmetry about *The Documents in the Case:* against the bravely honest and egalitarian alliance of the Muntings is pitted the Harrisons' miserable marriage of convenience and convention, and against them both, the inauthentic and self-indulgent relationship between Margaret Harrison and Harwood Lathom. As is true of Austen's novels, this narrative develops multiple variations on the marriage theme, including even the abrasive presence of Agatha Milsom, who serves as a frightening reminder that celibacy provides no safe refuge from the sexual battlefield.

Margaret Harrison's insipid love letters to Lathom demonstrate the truth of Wimsey's rather unconventional admission to Harriet that he "should like to write . . . [her] the kind of words that burn the paper they are written on—but words like that have a way of being not only unforgettable but unforgivable" (*Gaudy Night* ch. 11). Was there ever a lover more circumspect than Peter Wimsey? To be fair, Margaret Harrison and Harwood Lathom are more naive and less intelligent than Peter and Harriet. This relative inexperience helps explain Margaret's alarming penchant for melodrama, as well as her willingness to declare that all she wants from life is to be free, "worshipping in my hidden temple with my darling Idol, my own dear Petra darling" (document no. 41). Setting her lover up as a false god, she willingly loses herself in his personality and gushes, "the only way I can fulfil any great purpose is in being a little help in your divine work of creation" (document no. 38). This kind of thing appeals to Lathom's overweening pride, and seals their mutual doom. With her debased notion of work, and of herself, Margaret Harrison represents the archetypal Sayers villain, one who makes another person her "job," or one who allows herself to be so used. This corruption of the personal and the ethical indicates that Margaret Harrison is as lost as Agatha Milsom, who chirps tritely, "How true it is that men live for Things and women for People!" (document no. 2). Yet neither woman is as evil as Mary Whittaker. Sayers has made great strides in this book toward realistic characterization and its attendent ambiguities and complexities.

In contrast to Margaret Harrison's sophomoric idolatry is the love shared by the Muntings, who do not expect their relationship to constitute their whole lives, but continue to respect each other as individual human beings. This is to say that each appreciates the sanctity of the other's person and work. In direct opposition to what Margaret Harrison promises her lover, Munting writes to his fiancée: "I don't want to feel that anybody's life and happiness is bound up with mine. What dignity is there in life if one is not free to take one's own risks? . . . People should set their own value on themselves and not 'live for others' "(document no. 14). This is a theme that would emerge not only from "Are Women Human?" but also from *Gaudy Night,* which presents a full-blown version of this problem in both the mystery and the romantic plot. When Harriet realizes that Wimsey acknowledges her right to run her own risks, she also realizes that such an admission of equality means she will have to consider his proposal of marriage in a "new light" (ch. 11). Perhaps with him, marriage will not mean total self-surrender. In the 1986 television adaptation of *Gaudy Night,* in which Wimsey uncharacteristically cautions Harriet to "take care," the delicate balance between these "two independent and equally irritable intelligences" (ch. 22) is destroyed. And when it is destroyed much of the delicacy and subtlety that distinguishes *Gaudy Night* is also lost.

It is possible that Sayers overemphasizes the importance of self-reliance perhaps as a reaction against her own overprotected childhood (Brabazon 27). Yet in cultural and historical terms this is a significant and liberating stance for a woman to take. Women have been imprisoned by polite convention and "protected" into oblivion, a situation Wilkie Collins dramatizes with a vengeance in the predicament of the two half-sisters in *The Woman in White.*

Regarding the mature relationship between Munting and Drake, Lathom is characteristically over-clever and sardonic:

I swear that you and your intelligent young woman are either gods or beasts. Gods, probably—with that dreadful temperateness of the knowledge of good and evil, seeing two sides to every question. You will analyse your bridal raptures, if you have any, and find the whole subject very interesting. You will have, Heaven help you! a sense of humour about the business, and your friends will say how beautiful it is to see such a fine sense of partnership between a man and woman. (Document no. 26)

Without the brittle cleverness, this is, in fact, a description of the kind of relationship that both the Muntings, and later, the Wimseys, struggle to achieve. The bitter sarcasm and feigned sophistication of Lathom's comments demonstrate the wisdom of that helpful parson who once cautioned Munting about the perils of cleverness (document no. 13). This repudiation of too much wit is, in fact, one of the novel's main points: only a fairly clever person could perpetrate this particular crime; only a person entranced with his own intellect would regard people as Lathom does; and a glib, facile cleverness also gets Jack Munting into some difficulties of his own. The repudiation of intellectual conceit is perhaps also a form of self-criticism on Sayers's part. She was certainly very clever, as was her hero, Peter Wimsey, whose early flippancy is also implicitly rejected by such a speech. In *Gaudy Night,* Wimsey has changed enough to astonish Harriet with his declaration, "God! how I loathe haste and violence and all that ghastly, slippery cleverness. Unsound, unscholarly, insincere"(ch. 14). In the context of that novel, and in the view of Oxford it represents, no condemnation could be more damning.

The Documents in the Case is a genuine novel that enlarged the scope and intention of the conventional detective story of its day by taking the issues of life and death seriously. It is also a work of profound psychological realism, presenting a richly varied cast of characters who are so believable and recognizable that they give us the illusion, which is the essence of good fiction, that we are eavesdropping on our neighbors—or on ourselves. There is no Mary Whittaker, no Julian Freke here; flawed rather than fiendish, Margaret Harrison, Harwood Lathom, and Agatha Milsom are regrettably as common as the bland modern landscape they inhabit. Yet this makes the book not only more realistic but more truly frightening, for it shows that in the real world, evil wears a plain face: "It is ironical that Lathom, coming to Suburbia to find raw, red life should have failed to recognise it when he saw it. It was there, all right, in this dry little man, with no imagination beyond beef-steak and mushrooms, but it did not wear bright colours, and Lathom liked colours"(document no. 37). Jack Munting's admission that "it's the silly little things of life that I'm afraid of" (document no. 6) seems a trivial if endearing point at the time, but the narrative shows finally that his fears are well placed.

A deliberate artist, Dorothy L. Sayers realized in retrospect what this book represented, saying in the essay "Gaudy Night" that *The Documents in the Case* was a major step toward writing fiction that was also "a criticism of life" (*Titles to Fame* 78). In drawing real men and women who were neither gods nor beasts, she probed the possibility for marriage to be transformed into a healthy human enterprise full of the potential for encouraging, rather than destroying, individual growth.

This novel is unique in the Sayers canon in that it can be savored and appreciated on its own, without any reference to the Wimsey books. It is unfortunate that it is not better known, although its inclusion in H. R. F. Keating's recent survey of *Crime and Mystery: The 100 Best Books* should alert some readers to what they have been missing. Its being outside the Wimsey saga has presumably discouraged some from reading it; others may be put off by its epistolary form; and the reader who is enamored of Wimsey must agree to forgo his considerable charms in order to enjoy this book. But it is worth attention, not only for the light is sheds upon the eventual transformation of Sayers's great detective into mortal man, but also because it is a landmark in her development as a novelist. *The Documents in the Case* shows Sayers turning the detective story into a serious and subtle consideration of the modern world, with an appropriate emphasis on the relations between men and women in a time of great challenge and change.

9

A Precarious Balance

Love, Work, and Play
in the Vane-Wimsey Quartet

The Sayers novels that are most obviously associated with the so-called women's question are, of course, those featuring Harriet Vane. Although the original plan to use Harriet as a means of marrying off Wimsey did not work in quite the way the author had intended, the romance did point her fiction in a new direction. As the novelist Jack Munting observes in *The Documents in the Case,* "We get somewhere, even if it isn't the place we thought we were aiming for" (document no. 11). In *Strong Poison,* which was written just after Munting's story, DLS began on the path that would take her not only to the climax of her novelistic career in *Gaudy Night,* but also to her fullest treatment of the situation of women in the modern world.

The character of Harriet Vane, and the moral choices she faces, are what Sayers had been aiming toward in all her earlier fiction. One of the more interesting questions implied in her early novels, namely, whether a woman can lay claim to a fully human life that includes work as well as love, pleasure as well as duty without being considered a freak, a monster, or a rebel, is finally answered in the Harriet Vane books. In fact, these four novels focus upon one woman's struggle to integrate the essential human experiences of love, work, and play into one life.

When Sayers considered the whole history of the Wimsey-Vane relationship in the essay "Gaudy Night," she explained why they did not—could not—marry at the end of *Strong Poison:* she had unwittingly put the young woman into a degrading situation. Given the terms on which they met, only gratitude—that hardest of emotions to carry off with grace—could have propelled Vane into a romance with Wimsey. Thus, any relationship between them would have been on unequal, inauthentic terms.[1] The fact that

Harriet, even when benumbed by brutalizing personal experience and the harsh glare of notoriety, refuses to enter into such a relationship shows that her creator did not accept self-abnegation any more readily in a conventional heterosexual relationship than she had in the demeaning lesbian alliance portrayed in *Unnatural Death*. It would take Harriet and her creator two more books to work out a relationship that had begun on the wrong footing. Harriet Vane's search for a relationship based upon equality, honesty, and mutual respect is the compelling story of achieving a precarious, hard-won balance between opposing forces that goes beyond the simple solution of a detective story. And it is the story that Dorothy L. Sayers was born to write.

When we first meet Vane, she is on trial for her ex-lover's murder. A detective novelist, she had been living with a writer of "higher" worth, a man named Philip Boyes, until shortly before his death by poisoning. Their milieu is the literary London of Sayers's day, and her picture of it is not beguiling. It is hard not to detect in Philip Boyes some reflection of John Cournos, the Russian émigré writer who appears to have been the love of Sayers's life (Brabazon ch. 9). Cournos, too, had claimed he did not believe in marriage and his pomposity would seem to be one target of this novel's satire. Both Harriet and her friends indict Boyes especially for not being "the sort of man to make a friend of a woman" (ch. 13). The very antithesis of Wimsey, who Darcy-like says he wants a wife "I could talk sensibly to, who would make life interesting," Boyes essentially demanded devotion from a woman, despite all his self-serving "modern" ideas about love and marriage (ch. 4; cf. *Pride and Prejudice* chs. 8, 60). In its scathing portrait of the Vane-Boyes liaison, the novel underscores how so-called sexual liberation has tended to exact a higher toll on women than on men (ch. 1).

Harriet explains to a besotted Wimsey that she refused Boyes's offer of marriage after living with him because such a proposal made him a liar and her a fool:

> I couldn't stand being put on probation like an office-boy, to see if I was good enough to be condescended to. I quite thought he was honest when he said he didn't believe in marriage—and then it turned out that it was a test, to see whether my devotion was abject enough. Well, it wasn't. I didn't like having matrimony offered as a bad-conduct prize. (Ch. 4)

She is not, that is, as self-sacrificing and weak as Vera Findlater who is quite willing to live in and through the stronger personality of Mary Whittaker. What Harriet does not yet realize is that, in Peter Wimsey, she has

157

found an unusual person who can appreciate her uncommon self-possession and honesty.

When Harriet is unjustly accused of murder, only Miss Climpson's presence on the jury saves her. This redoubtable spinster holds out against the other jurors because she deduces from the prisoner's demeanor that she is innocent. We may chuckle when we glimpse Miss Climpson leaving the jury-box, with "hat askew and her mackintosh dragged awkwardly round her shoulders," but we cheer when she is praised as the "tough, thin, elderly woman with a sound digestion and a militant High-Church conscience of remarkable staying-power" who saves Harriet from a quick verdict of guilty (ch. 4).[2] It is interesting that Miss Climpson reappears in this kind of role in *Strong Poison.* Her function here implies the interdependence of all women, and is an example of the widespread tradition of spinsters aiding young women who will eventually marry and have children.[3]

After Harriet's first trial, which thanks to Miss Climpson ends in a hung jury, the spinster resumes her role as detective with the Cattery, taking on some delicate investigative tasks in the matter of Philip Boyes's death. *Strong Poison* gives us more information about Wimsey's discreet detective bureau, which had been in operation since the time of *Unnatural Death:*

> All the employees were women—mostly elderly, but a few still young and attractive—and . . . . of the class unkindly known as "superfluous." There were spinsters with small fixed incomes, or no income at all; widows without family; women deserted by peripatetic husbands and living on a restricted alimony, who, previous to their engagement by Miss Climpson, had had no resources but bridge and boardinghouse gossip. (*Strong Poison* ch. 5)

The language here invokes the ghost of Austen's Mrs. Bates, who was "past every thing but tea and quadrille." The parallel is apt: who knew better than Jane Austen the lot of the "superfluous female," or rendered it with more sympathy? And who portrayed with more accuracy the spinster's place in the tightly woven fabric of female existence? (See *Emma* chs. 3, 10.)

The relationship between Miss Climpson and Harriet Vane reiterates another common fictional motif described by Nina Auerbach: "in both art and life we find intense alliances between the old maid and the fallen woman, each in her own way an exile from woman's conventional family-bounded existence" (*Woman and the Demon* 151). Although Sayers does not fully endorse such a judgment, society treats Vane as a "fallen" woman in the aftermath of her lover's death. As the crucial juror in Vane's trial, Miss Climpson thus dramatizes the "reclamation of fallen women [which] was one of the few respectable activities available to philanthropically minded Victorian spinsters"(Auerbach, *Woman and the Demon* 153). Although Katherine Climpson herself has no money, she is an agent of the fantastically rich and philanthropic Lord Peter Wimsey. She is also a fine flower of the Victorian era, displaying some of its more attractive values, including duty, propriety, and enterprise. In the broadest cultural terms, Miss Climpson represents those generations of women who "went before" Harriet's time, preparing the way for later women to have fuller lives.[4]

When Peter first offers marriage to Harriet, she is not willing to fall into the trap of comfort and security: "the best remedy for a bruised heart is not, as so many people seem to think, repose upon a manly bosom. Much more efficacious are honest work, physical activity, and the sudden acquisition of wealth." So begins the next Harriet Vane story, *Have His Carcase,* a bulky, brooding book in which she toys with the whole idea of love and marriage. Once again echoing Jane Austen, another woman who knew something about the possibility of work healing personal wounds never acknowledged during her life, Sayers begins the first story in which Harriet is the focus. And this book is more intimate and psychological, more awake to the sensual experience of being alive than anything she had written before.[5] It is almost as if her fiction opens up even as her character does. When Harriet awakens on the beach in the novel's opening scene, she is beginning on a long journey toward a fuller awareness of herself and her world.

Harriet Vane has tried to leave the wreckage of the past behind, and is, in fact, freer than women of previous generations could have been; just the fact of her taking a walking trip alone, with "no responsibilities and no letters forwarded" (ch. 1), would have been unthinkable for a woman a hundred years before. It is difficult for us today to comprehend how literal and complete was the lack of freedom accorded to women of earlier eras, but let this striking example suffice: One of the chief objections to ladies' riding bicycles in their early days was the perception that the new contraptions would give women an unprecedented freedom of movement. This was, of course, a correct perception. By the early twentieth century, the fiercely independent Dorothy Sayers would serve as bicycle secretary at Somerville—and later, even take to a motorcycle!

Harriet's companion on the trip is the deliciously ribald *Tristram Shandy,* an eighteenth-century psychological romp which portrays less genteel days before Victorianism put women on the pedestal, or on the shelf. The book's presence among her few possessions suggests that while romance may have been dismissed from her mind, sex has not. Yet even Mrs. Shandy did not take to the open road. Sayers's distinctively modern heroine is walking a new path, finding no footprints in the sand to follow.

No one can escape the past, however, and Harriet awakens to find herself involved in another mysterious death, with Wimsey soon at her side. She will have to face the unanswered questions of her life after all. Specifically, the novel delineates her agonized, unresolved questioning about whether it is possible for a woman of self-respecting nature to love and be loved, or if she must always sacrifice one to the other.

There is a new level of irony in this book, because while we see all of the action through Harriet's eyes, we understand a bit better than she does the inner turmoil of her heart. She begins by saying that she has dismissed the idea of marriage, but as soon as she is confronted with a lounge full of women who are pathetically trying to attract a man, she begins worrying the old bone: What is it that men really want?

> Men, she thought, like the illusion that woman is dependent on their approbation and favour for her whole interest in life. But do they like the reality? Not, thought Harriet, bitterly, when one is past one's first youth. The girl over there, exercising S.A. on a group of rather possessive-looking males, will turn into a predatory hag like the woman at the next table, if she doesn't find something to occupy her mind, always supposing she has a mind. (Ch. 3)

The interior dialogue that Harriet is carrying on with herself here is almost as old as the novel itself, with famous scenes in *Pride and Prejudice* and *Persuasion* focusing upon just these questions about men and women, especially the attempt to penetrate the mystery of men's attitudes toward women.[6] But as the heroines in those novels discover, women have internalized as many conventional attitudes about gender as men have. When Harriet first glances at the "predatory hag," she assumes that the woman is unmarried, and unhappy as a result. The woman she is scrutinizing has been waiting pathetically for a male companion who never arrives. "Did one come to this, then, if one did not marry? Making a public scorn of one's self before the waiters?" But Harriet soon realizes it is not that simple, for she notices that the woman "wore a wedding-ring. Marriage did not save one, apparently. Single, married, widowed, divorced, one came to the same end" (ch. 3).

Harriet's dilemma is connected to the novel's mystery plot, which grows out of an ill-fated romantic attachment between the "predatory hag" and a younger man. One of the things Harriet is trying to discover is how to survive such disappointment and frustration in her own life. She is actually trying to act on the gigolo's philosophy:

These ladies come and dance and excite themselves and want love and think it is happiness. And they tell me about their sorrows—me—and they have no sorrows at all, only that they are silly and selfish and lazy. Their husbands are unfaithful and their lovers run away and what do they say? Do they say, I have two hands, two feet, all my faculties. I will make a life for myself? (Ch. 15)

This is apparently what DLS herself had resolved to do in the early twenties, when she had been bitterly disappointed in love. The disdainful gigolo continues on the subject of dependent women: "They say, Give me cocaine, give me the cocktail, give me the thrill, give me my gigolo, give me *l'amo-o-ur!*" In her depiction of what Wimsey calls the vulgar "watering-place atmosphere" of Wilvercombe (*Gaudy Night* ch. 14), Sayers is satirizing the decadent cafe society of the thirties, but she is also implying the importance of self-sufficiency and useful occupation in any human life.[7] Unlike the women the gigolo describes, Harriet makes the error of trying to convince herself that love is not important at all, that she needs no one, an error she will correct after much soul-searching in *Gaudy Night*.

Have His Carcase offers Harriet challenging work in the investigation of Mr. Alexis's death. The investigation also forces her to work with Wimsey, to get to know him in a new way. In spite of much sexual tension and anxious sniping, she and Wimsey work the case out together; both "need the work," in different ways: "The nobility ain't much cop these days but Lord Peter is vell known. He does somethings. Nowadays, they all vant somebody as does somethings. A lord is nothing, but a lord that flies the Atlantic or keeps a hatshop or detects murders—there might be a draw in that, vot you think?" (ch. 23). Sayers had, of course, discovered such a draw in these little eccentricities of her great detective (cf. *Gaudy Night* ch. 2 for Harriet on the subject of Peter's "job").

Harriet and Peter's working together, as colleagues, over this case is a necessary first step away from the unequal and artificial situation in which they met. At one point, Harriet is able to forget herself enough to admit that she enjoys the detection, saying that "Time passes when one is pleasantly occupied." Even such a cliché is a bit of a bombshell when it is directed at the man she has harshly rejected again and again. But honest work *is* the best rememdy for a broken heart, and an astonished Wimsey knows when to count his blessings. Lingering over the nuances in the moment, the narrator describes how, in response to Harriet's opening, Wimsey

put his hat and papers down on the table, opened his mouth to speak, changed his mind, took up his belongings again and marched to the door. "Cheerio!" he said, amiably. "Cheerio!" replied Harriet. He went out. Harriet sat looking at the closed door. "Well" she said, "thank goodness he's given up asking me to marry him. It's much better he should put it out of his mind." She must have felt strongly about it, for she repeated the remark several times. (Ch. 29)

The irony here underscores how little Harriet knows her own mind at this point, and how delicate a task Wimsey has before him.

During their time in Wilvercombe, Vane is facing a related struggle in her own novel-writing. Just when she has turned away from romantic entanglements in her personal life, her publisher has started encouraging her to add a love interest to her detective fiction. She finds that she is no more successful in dealing with passion on the page than on the dance floor, and refuses to continue trying.[8] Harriet's difficulty in dealing with romance in her detective stories reflects her creator's uneasy initiation into this different type of mystery. The level of Sayers's discomfort with this subject may be deduced from the pattern of her fiction after Harriet's appearance on the scene. Perhaps because she did not want to deal with the sticky human situation between Harriet and Peter, immediately after *Strong Poison* DLS wrote her most cerebral and least characteristic mystery, *The Five Red Herrings.* What could be further from romance than railway timetables? She returned to human perplexities in *Have His Carcase,* but then went on to *Murder Must Advertise,* a story in which Lord Peter reclaims center stage on his own, and Harriet is barely alluded to. She is also absent from the next novel, *The Nine Tailors,* where an unusually solitary Wimsey addresses questions of eternal import, with no direct reference to the domestic drama of his own life, although his exchange with the young would-be writer, Hilary Thorpe, echoes his attitude toward Harriet's work (see "Lord Peter Is Taken from Lead . . .").

When Vane reappears in *Gaudy Night,* five years after her introduction to the Wimsey saga, she is once again at the center of the action and is finally ready to face the marriage question directly. Here she poses the question in terms of love versus work, and of body versus mind: "Could there ever be any alliance between the intellect and the flesh?" she asks, addressing not only the main question of the novel's detective plot, but also of her own life (ch. 21). The detective plot raises this question through the actions of the Shrewsbury poison-pen, a woman who has disastrously put the claims of the heart and flesh over every other consideration. At the opposite end of the spectrum is the scholarly, relentlessly rational Miss de Vine, the precipitating force who unwittingly set into motion the string of events that led to the malicious mischief besetting Shrewsbury College. Neither Miss de Vine nor Annie Wilson has accomplished "the repose of very delicate balance" (ch. 22) between these two sides of life, between love and work, head and heart. And, as the novel demonstrates, the tension between these two diametrically opposed approaches to life generates the explosive situation at Shrewsbury.

While trying to comprehend the lunacy besetting the college, Harriet herself is torn between these two attitudes toward human experience. Because of her own fear of sexuality and emotion, a fear born of her earlier "unhappy contact with physical passion" (ch. 11), Harriet assumes that the violence must be the result of suppressed appetites, that it is "what happens to one if one keeps out of the way of love and marriage and all the rest of the muddle. . . . Well if Peter fancies I'm going to 'accept the protection of his name' and be grateful, he's damn well mistaken" (ch. 18). Both ways lies madness, or so it seems to her at this point. Because of her fears and unresolved conflicts, Harriet misdiagnoses the Shrewsbury problem, understandably concluding that "I don't know whether I want a doctor or a detective" (ch. 13). This is an appropriate enough confusion in a novel that represents a modern amalgam of the detective story and psychological thriller. Harriet does consider getting help once again from the Cattery, but even this sensible idea falls prey to her inner conflicts and confusion:

> It struck her then as a fantastic idea that she should fly for help to another brood of spinsters; even if she succeeded in getting hold of Miss Climpson, how was she to explain matters to that dessicated and elderly virgin? . . . In this, Harriet did the lady less than justice; Miss Climpson had seen many strange things in sixty-odd years of boarding-house life, and was as free from repressions and complexes as any human being could very well be. . . .
>
> There were plenty of people in London—both men and women—to whom the discussion of sexual abnormalities was a commonplace; but most of them were very little to be trusted. They cultivated normality till it stood out of them all over in knobs. . . . From their bouncing mental health ordinary ill-balanced mortals shrank in alarm. (Ch. 13)

This is all very amusing, with the narrator's comments clearly differentiating Harriet's muddled reasoning from her creator's view of the situation. In fact, this passage demonstrates why, despite the autobiographical elements in Vane's characterization—her educational background and profession, her independent spirit, her tragic personal history—readers must not *equate* this character with Dorothy L. Sayers.[9] Harriet Vane clearly reflects part of the novelist's personality and experience (as does Peter Wimsey), but she is also a creation of the imaginative intellect, and as such, has an identity and life of her own.

This is nowhere more evident than in the subtle distinction between what

163

Harriet chooses to see in the college, and what the novel presents to us. In spite of Harriet's limited perception, the microcosm of the college community reflects a whole universe of female experience, from the compassionate and humane Miss Lydgate, to the man-hating man-trap, Miss Hillyard; from the hapless Cattermole to the elegant Millbanks; from the servants to members of the Senior Common Room. Although the scouts are not studied in any detail, their presence is always felt; their juxtaposition with the dons is most striking in the climactic Senior Common Room scene, where Annie erupts in a excoriating diatribe against educated women (ch. 22). With its richly varied, finely drawn cast of characters, *Gaudy Night* shows that being a woman, even from the rather narrowly defined group known as academic women, means something different for every individual human being.[10] This is an important lesson for Harriet, as well as an effective demonstration of Sayers's major premise that women are fully human creatures, with all the individuality characteristic of the human species. It was precisely this individuality which was obscured in the caricatures of these women presented in the 1986 television adaptation of the novel.

During her time at Oxford, Harriet is driven to ask herself what direction her life and work should take. As a human being, she alone is responsible for this decision, although she admits that even an independent nature like hers is sometimes tempted to abdicate responsibility (ch. 22). Such ambivalence makes her not only more sympathetic but also more believable. One of the most astute points in Harriet's portrait is that she has internalized society's conventional attitudes toward her sex—e.g., a community of women must be plagued by sickness, or women should expect to be "ridden roughshod over" by men—and indeed must fight her battle for independence and self-respect primarily within herself, rather than with Wimsey or the world at large.

A successful career woman in her thirties when she returns to her old college, Harriet Vane is at the right age, and in the right environment, for self-scrutiny to reach a crisis. Who among us has not reconsidered original choices and wished for another chance, especially when we have been "visited by an enormous nostalgia" (ch. 1) in being transplanted to a happy place of our youth? Nostalgic reactions are human, of course, but there is perhaps a special poignancy about a woman's return to such a place. For many women, the college years provide a brief glimpse of what life could be without the relentless reference to gender and family that characterizes most of society: a real taste of independence, of intellectual and psychological freedom, before taking a place in the gender-bound world. This was even truer in Sayers's time than it is today. In a history of Somerville College, Muriel St. Clare Byrne and Catherine Hope Mansfield describe the significance of the college years in a young woman's life: "As the conditions of women's work now are, the years at college, with all their hard work, their plain living, their gaiety, their varied interests, their vivid friendships and aspirations and clashes of thought, seem to the memory of many an older woman like an oasis in a rather dusty landscape" (*Somerville College 1879–1921* vi). They go on to say that "College life to a girl is rather like the best side of public school life to a boy; it is the first taste of freedom combined with the discipline of training" (82). It is not surprising that Harriet Vane was moved to reassessment and recommitment by her return to Oxford, just as Dorothy L. Sayers had been when she returned for the 1934 Somerville Gaudy, a fact she discusses directly in "What Is Right with Oxford?"

Through its explication of Harriet's dilemma, *Gaudy Night* gives serious consideration to the work of women, while challenging the prevailing notion of "women's work." The setting of a women's college is ideal for this subject: it provides ample opportunity to scrutinize the work of the female dons and scholars, as well as time for the dons to scrutinize themselves, a favorite hobby of both fiction-mongers and academics. But apart from theoretical ruminations on the subject, the Shrewsbury community also represents the reality of individual women leading happily work-filled, unmated lives. This provides an important contrast to the unhappy spinsters in some of Sayers's other books.[11] I cannot go so far as Carolyn Heilbrun has, however, and conclude that this novel appeals to American women because such a community is outside of their experience (DLS Society 1985 Seminar Proceedings, 33). It is not outside the experience of those who have studied or taught in women's colleges.

The setting is curiously appropriate to Harriet's consideration of marriage and its implications. A women's college, one of the few places where women are not perforce regarded simply in reference to men, gives her some space away from Wimsey's insistent proposals, and serves as a concrete example of another way of living. Yet the novel is saturated with references to the institution of marriage, even among the dons. At the Gaudy, Harriet betrays her anxiety on this topic by immediately classifying people as married or unmarried, studying them for any evidence of loss or gain tied to their marital status. In Phoebe Tucker, she recognizes a woman who has retained her selfhood in spite of being married, while Catherine Freemantle typifies the more common case of losing one's identity through marriage (chs. 1, 3). The latter's surname suggests that she has taken on such a mantle freely, however: as human beings, women must accept responsibility for their actions. Freemantle's lament, "Once I was a scholar" (ch. 3), echoes in Harriet's mind as she questions the validity of her own work since leaving Oxford. This was perhaps becoming a pressing question in Dorothy Sayers's own mind, for although she did not try to return to the cloister, soon after *Gaudy Night* she began focusing on work of a more ostensibly serious nature. Without overdoing it, we might suggest that this amazingly versatile writer decided, as Harriet Vane considers doing in this novel, that she would "like an academic and meaty egg to my tea for a change" (ch. 10), and proceeded to make that change. It should be noted that the world changed a good deal in these years, also, forcing many serious-minded people to reevaluate their lives. In addition, regardless of the state of the world at large, success often breeds self-criticism and change in writers, a generally healthy situation which can stimulate risk-taking and growth.[12] The irony is that *Gaudy Night* itself is a profound consideration of human life and a book that only a scholar could have written, Leavis's critique notwithstanding.

By bringing the friendly outsiders Vane and Wimsey into the collegial circle for a time, the question of the role of work in human life is further elaborated, because the surroundings force the characters to ponder the relative merits of academic work versus the ways of the world outside the university walls. All of this questioning about kinds of work implies the wider range of possibilities enjoyed by twentieth-century women, while Harriet's well-wrought inner turmoil poignantly dramatizes the dilemma faced by many women during the last century. Because of revolutionary changes in women's education and employment opportunities, a modern woman faces not just the choice between love and work, but also the more subtle one of what kind of work is suitable for her. The agony of choice, with all of its moral implications, is reflected in Harriet's troubled mind, and nothing by Dorothy L. Sayers seems more relevant to readers today, many of whom are still struggling with the dilemma faced by her heroine a half-century ago:

> Now, it is frequently asserted that, with women, the job does not come first. What (people cry) are women doing with this liberty of theirs? What woman really prefers a job to a home and family? Very few, I admit. It is unfortunate that they should so often have to make the choice. A man does not, as a rule, have to choose. He gets both. In fact, if he wants the home and family, he usually has to take the job as well, if he can get it. (*Unpopular Opinions* 110)

Sounding as if it could have been written yesterday, this fifty-year-old passage from "Are Women Human?" puts succinctly the choice faced by Harriet Vane in *Gaudy Night* and by countless other women since.

As it turns out, Harriet is fortunate because she does not have to choose *between* love and work, but gets both, largely because Peter Wimsey is an extraordinary man who can treat her as a human being who needs both to survive. It is, in fact, his demonstration of taking her work seriously, and of acknowledging thereby her equality with him, that finally convinces Harriet that she can "risk the adventure" of marriage with him (*Titles to Fame* 87). When he admonishes her that she has not yet written the book she could write, that she must take the chance of infusing real people with real problems into the tidy little world of her detective stories, he is both complimenting and challenging her. He is also demonstrating a readiness for taking the kind of risks that DLS was herself hazarding in the Vane-Wimsey quartet. Certainly no timid or self-indulgent lover would choose to live through such an ordeal, but as Harriet finally realizes, Peter does not expect "to be quiet, or to be spared things, or to stay put. All he wanted was some kind of central stability, and he was apparently ready to take anything that came along, so long as it stimulated him to keep that precarious balance" (ch. 18).

When Harriet finally realizes that a middle way is possible, that life may give her a chance to gratify both her intellectual and emotional needs, she is ready to try for "that precarious balance" between opposing forces that Wimsey's completion of her sonnet images as the essence of the fully lived life. And in this elegantly elaborated novel, which is the richest explication of Sayers's definition of human life as a composite of love, work, and play, Harriet and Peter are at last playful with each other. The rapturous high spirits of their afternoon of singing in the antique shop, after she has signalled her new willingness to accept love by allowing him to give her the chess set, prefigures their happy union. Later, at the Bach concert on their last night in Oxford, Peter emphasizes that he does not want to be a solo performer, but wants instead to share life with another musician who can play counterpoint to him. This is an implicit repudiation of the idea that every lady should play "a little," as she should paint "a little," and perhaps even scribble "a little."

The novel's musical imagery is apt. Bach was always Wimsey's favorite, but the musical background works especially well here: the imminent union of these two distinct personalities must be played out polyphonically. " 'This kind of thing,' said Peter, as tenor and alto twined themselves in a last companionable cadence, 'is the body and soul of music. Anybody can have the harmony, if they will leave us the counterpoint' " (ch. 19). Such a relationship offers the only kind of peace possible in this world, where the best hope is that human lovers "Poised on the perilous point, in no lax bed/ May sleep, as tension at the verberant core/ Of music sleeps" (ch. 18).

As a metaphysical conceit, Peter's sestet embodies the integration of mind, heart, and passion that Harriet has struggled to comprehend and that their marriage will signify. Given this parallel, it is interesting that the sonnet itself came out of Sayers's attempts to draft the last scene of the novel, where Harriet finally accepts Wimsey's proposal (Brabazon 156).

When Wimsey first learns about Harriet's mysterious assignment at Shrewsbury, he shocks her by acknowledging

> that she had the right to run her own risks . . . [for] that was an admission of equality, and she had not expected it of him. If he conceived of marriage along those lines, then the whole problem would have to be reviewed in a new light; but that seemed scarcely possible. To take such a line and stick to it, he would have to be, not a man but a miracle. (Ch. 11)

But of course Peter Wimsey has become a very human man in the course of these books, neither a god nor a beast. A thoroughly unconventional lover, he has chosen for a mate a woman who is neither beautiful, young, coquettish, nor virginal, saying that his love for her is based upon her "devastating talent for keeping to the point and speaking the truth" (ch. 17). A love based upon such a trait suggests the relationship between heart and mind in a mature, integrated personality. It is also Wimsey's tribute to "that habit of intellectual integrity" which DLS identified as the novel's theme (*Titles to Fame* 81), and as her own greatest debt to Oxford ("What Is Right with Oxford?"). As creatures blessed and cursed with both hearts and brains, Harriet and Peter ultimately accept their heritage of "all the rest of the muddle" freely and deliberately, as only rational creatures can.

DLS admitted having trouble writing the last scene of *Gaudy Night*— "too, too shy-making for words," she declared in a letter to Muriel Byrne— just as Harriet is unable to deal with a detective novel "gone sticky" (Brabazon 156; *Gaudy Night* ch. 15). *Strong Poison* ended in a stalemate between Wimsey and Vane because according to their creator, she could find no form of words for Harriet to accept his proposal. This is a problem she seemingly shared with Jane Austen, whose novels culminate in marriage but notoriously shy away from love-scenes. Yet a mid-twentieth-century novelist, especially one dealing with two experienced people, could not get away with the equivocation of *Emma*'s narrator, for example, who at the crucial moment of Knightley's declaration of love, provides only the teasing remarks, "What did . . . [Emma] say?—Just what she ought, of course, A lady always does" (ch. 49). In *Gaudy Night,* Sayers finally found the form of words in which Harriet could accept Wimsey, a form appropriate to the situation, suggestive of the partnership Wimsey envisions, and remembered from her own college days:

> She laid both hands upon the fronts of his gown, looking into his face while she searched for the word that should carry her over the last difficult breach.
> It was he who found it for her. With a gesture of submission he bared his head and stood gravely, the square cap dangling in his hand.
> *"Placetne, magistra?"*
> *"Placet."*

This one act symbolizes the equality of these two people. As Wimsey admits with true insight and humility, "I set out in a lordly manner to offer you heaven and earth. I find that all I have to give you is Oxford—which was yours already" (ch. 23). In his last proposal, which is notable for both its seriousness and its simplicity, Wimsey's invocation of the *pro forma* Latin question that is part of the University's graduation ceremony signifies Harriet's full citizenship in no mean city.[13] Borrowing his language from the democracy of the collegium, Wimsey acknowledges that Harriet is free completely and at last: she may do as she pleases. This same freedom, paradoxically, enables her to accept him, to make a free decision to take and to be bound to another in love: "She must come to him as a free agent . . . and must realize that she was independent of him before she could bring him her dependence as a willing gift" (*Titles to Fame* 87). Nina Auerbach's observation about the climax of *Persuasion,* which represents the one "emotionally charged" love scene in Jane Austen's fiction, is also germane here: "the heroine speaks obliquely for her right to exist in something more than love" (*Romantic Imprisonment* 53).

The parity achieved between Wimsey and Vane in the final moment of *Gaudy Night* is prefigured earlier, atop the Radcliffe Camera, where the mood promises a bit more than it delivers, and the language suggests the great reconciliation scenes of earlier novels, notably *Pride and Prejudice.* Again, the language of the exchange is most interesting:

> "Harriet," said Peter, "I want to ask your forgiveness for these last five years."
> "I think," said Harriet, "it ought to be the other way round."
> "I think not. When I remember how we first met—"
> "Peter, don't think about that ghastly time. I was sick of myself, body and soul. I didn't know what I was doing."
> "And I chose that time, when I should have thought only of you, to thrust myself upon you, to make demands of you, like a damned arrogant fool—as though I had only to ask and have. Harriet, I ask you to believe that, whatever it

looked like, my blundering was nothing worse than vanity and a blind, childish impatience to get my own way. . . ."

"It has taken me a long time to learn my lesson, Harriet. I have had to pull down, brick by brick, the barriers I built up by my own selfishness and folly." (Ch. 23)

He goes on to ask her leave to "begin again," to start over with a clean slate. She demurs at the possibility of forgetting "this unhappy interval," but says that now she "could be glad to remember it" (ch. 23).

This is very like Elizabeth Bennet's assurances to Darcy, who has similarly apologized for "unpardonable" and "ungentleman-like" behavior: "Think only of the past as its remembrance gives you pleasure," she tells him, since "the conduct of neither [of us], if strictly examined, will be irreproachable; but since then, we have both, I hope, improved in civility." At the climax of the scene, which represents their mutual triumph over the barriers erected between them by pride and prejudice, Darcy declares, "What do I not owe you! You taught me a lesson, hard indeed at first, but most advantageous. By you, I was properly humbled. I came to you without a doubt of my reception. You shewed me how insufficient were all my pretensions to please a woman worthy of being pleased" (*Pride and Prejudice* ch. 58). In other words, in these two novels the romantic plot's resolution depends upon both the man and the woman taking responsibility for earlier errors and being willing to make themselves anew. Both books end with a classical resolution of opposites, an establishment, for the moment, of a delicate balance between the sexes. And of both couples it could be said that "by an exercise on both sides of a strict intellectual integrity, . . . [their] situation is so modified that they are enabled to enter into a new relationship, presenting fresh situations with the prospect of further errors and misunderstandings" (*The Mind of the Maker* 190). The culmination of the lovers' struggle for relative equality, openness, and honesty is not expressed in a conventional love scene, though such is parodied in Reggie Pomfret's absurd behavior in *Gaudy Night* and in Mr. Collins's equally ridiculous proposal in *Pride and Prejudice*—but in a delicate dissection of the male-female relationship.

These parallels do not necessarily argue that Austen's fiction was a conscious model for the Harriet Vane novels, even though Sayers undoubtedly knew and admired the great Regency novelist.[14] The similarities between Austen's novels and the Vane-Wimsey quartet may suggest something more subtle and profound than direct literary influence: the role of mythmaking in the traditional English novel which focuses on marriage. It is almost as if these novels were purposefully imaging a possible way of living, a pattern for humane relationships between the sexes, where reason and passion are linked, and individual needs can be accommodated within the existing social framework.[15] Harriet Vane resembles the intelligent, strong Austen heroines who, if they are to be loved at all, must be so for "the liveliness of their minds" (*Pride and Prejudice* ch. 60). Both their intellectual playfulness and their marriage endings ally these novels with the comic tradition. In Sayers as in Austen, a comic plot is accompanied by a humorous voice and the embracing acceptance of life that is the wellspring of the greatest comedy. This is in keeping with Sayers's generally affirmative way of looking at the world, and even with the subgenre of fiction in which she worked. Classic detective stories, which end with the solution of a crime and a restoration of order, have an essentially comic plot structure.

Gaudy Night has sometimes been sneeringly dismissed as a "women's novel."[16] While I am not sure exactly what is meant by this term, I would agree that it is a woman's novel in the sense that *Emma* is a woman's novel, or *Jane Eyre* is: they are all novels about women's searching and becoming, narratives that explore ways of being for the female of the species.

The English novel has, of all forms of Western literature, been distinguished by such concerns, and its preoccupation with the marriage question has suggested to at least one critic that all heroines in this tradition are "Pamela's daughters."[17] But Harriet Vane is neither Pamela Andrews nor Clarissa Harlowe. She neither barters her way into Wimsey's "old oaks and . . . family plate" (*Strong Poison* ch. 4), nor suffers harm from being the object of his passion. Although the Vane-Wimsey romance is typical of the traditional English novel in the sense that it presents a man of higher social standing marrying a woman of somewhat lower standing, a fact Harriet acknowledges by referring to Wimsey as "Mr. Rochester" in *Busman's Honeymoon,* it is hard to imagine a lover more different from Mr. B_____, or from Lovelace.[18] Not only does Wimsey refuse to abuse power, he seems terrified of it. If anything, Wimsey's wealth and social position just complicate Harriet's reaction to him, and make it harder for her to accept him (see the "Prothalamion" to *Busman's Honeymoon* for details of this). Power may be an aphrodisiac, but the novels in the Vane-Wimsey quartet reveal the beauty, and, yes, the undeniable power of a power that is not invoked. Isn't this also part of what makes Darcy such a beguiling figure?

For all its links to the past, however, *Gaudy Night* is a modern woman's story. The romance between Wimsey and Vane is complicated because Harriet has options and possibilities that an Emma Woodhouse or a Jane Eyre could not have striven for in her most energetic moments. As a liberally educated freewoman of the holy city of learning, Harriet enjoys an equality possible for her sex only in the last hundred years. She is also a mature, experienced person who understands the marriage commitment as only a woman of the world can. All of this makes her choice more difficult and more real. Although many English novels feature heroines of extraordinary intelligence, *Gaudy Night* is a rare variation on the tradition, a love story about an intellectual, accomplished, mature person who also happens to be female. Perhaps this partially accounts for its singular appeal to many such women, even today, when marriage is often considered a negative step in a woman's life.[19]

From time to time Harriet is tempted to side with others because they are female, but she ultimately refuses to do so. In *Busman's Honeymoon,* for example, she identifies for a moment with Aggie Twitterton and reacts against Peter (ch. 16). Nina Auerbach regards the end of *Gaudy Night* as a rejection of the community of women that the college represents and is therefore disappointed by its resolution, although she admits that "even when *Gaudy Night* disappoints . . . it retains its inspiration" (*Romantic Imprisonment* xxii). But if marriage is not, *ipso facto,* a loss for a woman, such an ending does not have to disappoint. Rather, this unusual and interesting love story may be regarded as a compelling argument for the possibility of reforming the institution of marriage in the context of the modern world. Perhaps this reading flows from seeing the "community of women" portrayed in this novel, not as an unalloyed good, but as a mixed group of finite human beings. Their handling of the case of the Shrewsbury poison-pen, while demonstrating an attractive, if somewhat naive loyalty to frankness and fair play, also reveals what an abominable mess basically good, well-intentioned, educated people can (and do) make. This is especially underscored in the Senior Common Room scene, when the Warden insists on bringing Annie into the group to face the charges against her, over the objections of the more worldly and practical Wimsey. The ensuing debacle is only too realistic, showing as it does the potential deadliness of principle when it is acted upon without regard to the particulars of a situation. Following closely upon the display of raw emotion in this scene, Harriet's decision is not simply to wed a man rather than join a cloister; it is a choice for the individual over the group, and more importantly, a choice to live in the world outside the college walls.

As Sayers's last novel, *Busman's Honeymoon,* makes clear, any balance achieved between men and women, and between the competing claims of mind and heart, is ever precarious. Few writers have ventured into the inner workings of a happy marriage, but this look is both believable and provocative.

In the Wimseys' honeymoon story, which should be regarded as a companion piece to *Gaudy Night,* we see Peter's once "imperious" desire for Harriet turn into a relationship of enormous importance:

> for the first time in his experience, it really mattered to him what his relations with a lover were. He had somehow vaguely imagined that, the end of desire attained, soul and sense would lie down together like the lion and the lamb; but they did nothing of the sort. With orb and sceptre thrust into his hands he was afraid to take hold on power and call his empire his own. (Ch. 14)

This is because, as a human being, Harriet is really important to him. The precarious balance they achieve from time to time in this book is pitted against the miserable conflict between Aggie Twitterton and Crutchley—she who promises endless self-sacrifice and humiliating devotion, he who abuses it. In fact, the entire Vane-Wimsey romance is a subtle rendition of what Ian Watt has called "the all but unendurable disparity between expectation and reality that faces sensitive women in modern society, and the difficulties that lie before anyone who is unwilling either to be used, or to use others, as a means" (*The Rise of the Novel* 225).

When Harriet objects to her new husband's involvement in a murder investigation, his easily giving in frightens her because it reveals how much power she has over him. Quickly, she relents: "Whatever marriage is, it isn't . . . letting your affection corrupt your judgement," she says. Wimsey is aghast at her position, saying most women would count such devotion a triumph. She answers: " 'I know, I've heard them.' Her own scorn lashed herself—the self she had only just seen. 'They boast of it—"My husband would do *anything* for me. . . ." It's degrading. No human being ought to have such power over another.' " A shaken Peter calls this "love with honour" (ch. 17). It is that, and more. It is an expression of the woman's unwillingness to become the abuser in a relationship where she has often been the abused. This is real freedom from the sexual fetters of the past. And it shows how this book is integrally related to the story of their courtship, for in *Gaudy Night,* it is just this type of mindless devotion, and manipulation, that is exposed for the destructive force it is. As Wimsey says there, he has deliberately rejected the age-old game-playing between the sexes because he objects "to being tactfully managed by somebody who ought to be my equal" (ch. 16).

In their honeymoon story, Harriet has to learn not only not to be possessive, but also to accept love and to admit emotional need. This is particularly difficult for many educated, self-respecting women, who learn early that to survive in this world, they have to be strong and self-reliant and rational—more relentlessly than any man—to counteract any suspicion of emotionalism or weakness. DLS shows great insight into this aspect of Harriet's personality, as well as its metamorphosis. Eventually, Harriet is capable of looking at the evidence and admitting the awful truth that "she must be completely besotted about Peter. . . . 'Very well,' said Harriet aloud to herself, 'I will *be* besotted' " (ch. 19). To show that this is not a quirk of Harriet's (or Sayers's) personality, Harriet's words should be compared to chapter 59 of *Pride and Prejudice,* where the narrator says that even after Elizabeth has come to terms with Darcy, she "rather *knew* that she was happy, than *felt* herself to be so." That these women are completely besotted about the novels' heroes is, as Miss de Vine says dryly at the end of *Gaudy Night,* "moderately obvious" (ch. 22). But, with all her defenses in place, it has not been obvious to Harriet herself. It is almost as though Miss de Vine, representing the intellectual side of life, functions as Harriet's brain, telling her what her heart feels.

For this reason, Harriet Vane represents more than a woman with a bruised heart or a tragic personal history. She is the woman who is bright enough to realize the risks involved in feeling deeply, or in relinquishing whatever power she has managed to take over her experience. When she finally gives in and relinquishes the power that is hers to give, she is liberated in a different way: "That's right, laugh! I did kill my pride—but, oh, Peter! it had a lovely death" (*Busman's Honeymoon* 14). This is not a conventional case of female submission, however, because in the same scene, Peter also admits to a totally new emotional vulnerability. This constant give and take between them creates the novel's real suspense and its mood of psychological realism.

In the foregoing discussion, the term "play" has usually meant playfulness, as in the ebullient humor with which Miss Climpson lives her life or the joking between Harriet and Peter once she loses sight of her indebtedness to him—especially in the early part of *Busman's Honeymoon,* when they take their first meal at Talboys (ch. 3). Play also suggests the riotous enjoyment of language and ideas, in the free play of mind, which informs all of Sayers's writing with wit, humor, and an effervescent *joie de vivre.* Dorothy L. Sayers's personal life may have been unhappy in some ways, but her books reveal her great capacity for fun, her essential joy in being alive. Such genuine happiness is, in her view, the result of satisfying work and love, not an end in itself. For example, DLS knew well the "emotional excitement" that flows from writing good prose, as she has Harriet Vane describe it: "when you get the thing dead right and know it's dead right, there's no excitement like it. . . . It makes you feel like God on the Seventh Day—for a bit, anyhow" (cf. *The Mind of the Maker*). When satisfied, this excitement results in "the release that all writers, even the feeblest, seek for as men seek for love; and having found it, they doze off happily into dreams and trouble their hearts no further" (*Gaudy Night* ch. 11).

It is significant that the passage implies a similarity between a successful writing experience and a sexual one, for Sayers's third requisite for a fully human life, "reasonable freedom for . . . pleasures," or what we have been calling "play," also means physical passion. It is refreshing that she deliberately and unsentimentally separated love and pleasure, a fact all the more remarkable because of the time in which she considered this subject. Peter Wimsey makes the point explicitly: "Passion's a good, stupid horse that will pull the plough six days a week if you give him the run of his heels on Sundays. But love's a nervous, awkward, over-mastering brute" (*Gaudy Night* ch. 20). In *Gaudy Night*, the story of one woman's journey into joy,[20] Harriet Vane is reawakened physically as well as emotionally: after all, "if people will bring dynamite into a powder factory, they must expect explosions" (ch. 19). This is a sardonic comment upon her allowing Wimsey not only into the college, but into her life. An experienced lover, he senses her gradual reawakening, which is subtly drawn:

A rich, damp fragrance gushed out upon them as they turned into the Market, and she was overcome by a sense of extravagant well-being. 'I love this smell—it's like the cactus-house in the Botanical Gardens.' Her companion opened his mouth to speak, looked at her, and then, as one that will not interfere with fortune, let the name of Robinson [the case they were supposed to be discussing] die upon his lips. (Ch. 20)

Later, the narrator explains that Harriet

had first met Peter at a moment when every physical feeling had been battered out of her by the brutality of circumstance; by this accident she had been aware of him from the beginning as a mind and spirit localized in a body. Never—not even in those dizzying moments on the river—had she considered him primarily as a male animal, or calculated the promise implicit in the veiled eyes, the long, flexible mouth, the curiously vital hands. (Ch. 21)

Carolyn Heilbrun has suggested that such a treatment of the male as an erotic object for the female is almost unique in Western literature (DLS Society 1985 Seminar Proceedings 35). It is certainly not common. In the Senior Common Room scene, Harriet looks at Wimsey and realizes that "Everything that was alive in him lay in the palm of her hand, like a ripe apple" (ch. 22). The question is, then, will she continue to try to live in her idea of the celestial city, or will she take up the life of the flesh, living as human beings do, east of Eden? By the end of this scene, we are told that

Harriet, along with the rest, "looked stupefied with the shock of seeing so many feelings stripped naked in public," but her retreat from feeling is short-lived. She is ready to try to live without repressing her mind, her heart, or her passion. And it is significant that freeing herself to feel also frees her mind from the confusions and prejudices that have made it impossible for her to solve the mystery: an impairment in one vital part of life may damage the others.

If *Gaudy Night* implies the gradual reawakening of passion, *Busman's Honeymoon* is an intensely sensual, erotic book, its subtle characterizations suggesting rather than presenting the play of passion between these two lovers. Of the "interesting revelations of the marriage-bed" we get but a few brief glimpses, which are quite sufficient. They are rendered mainly in stream-of-consciousness flashbacks: "He spread out his hands as though challenging her to look at them. It seemed strange that they should be the same hands that only last night . . . Their smooth strength fascinated her. License my roving hands and let them go before, behind, between— His hands, so curiously gentle and experienced" (ch. 17). Examining the relationship from Wimsey's point of view, we learn of his own happy realization that Harriet "could render back passion for passion with an eagerness beyond all expectation" (ch. 14).

Although the creative imagination covers a great deal, I would judge this book to be the work of a woman who had experienced happy, satisfying passion.[21] A younger Dorothy Sayers once admitted to John Cournos, who had spurned her, that she had "a careless rage for life" and wanted "a man that's human and careless and loves life, and one that can enjoy the rough and tumble of passion. . . . If you had chosen, I would have given you three sons by now . . ."(Brabazon 110). Considering this statement, it is a poignant moment in the short story, "Talboys," when we learn that DLS has given the Wimseys, to whom she had already given so much, three sons.

In the context of a letter to Charles Williams about Dante, whom DLS guessed to have been a good lover based upon the evidence of his poetry, she rather unexpectedly outlined what she considered "the distinguishing marks of True Bedworthiness in the Male." Her idea of "bedworthiness" was based upon "Three Grand Assumptions": "1. That the primary aim and object of Bed is that a good time should be had *by all*. 2. That (other things being equal) it is the business of the Male to make it so. 3. That he knows his business" (Brabazon 112). Although tame by today's standards, this passage would probably have been considered shockingly vulgar by Q. D. Leavis, who accused DLS of being no lady because of the rather timid sexual revelations of *Gaudy Night* and *Busman's Honeymoon* ("The Case of Miss Dorothy Sayers"). I would add that both scholarship and novel-writing are quite unsuitable jobs for a "lady." A "lady" does not display a devastating talent for speaking the truth at all costs, nor does she inquire into the motives and most private actions of others—at least not in public, or as a matter of course. As Peter Wimsey says, being a detective is no job for a gentleman, either. (*Gaudy Night* ch. 17). And yet, would anyone with any pretensions to being a serious critic ever fault a male novelist for being "no gentleman"?[22]

DLS hinted at this problem early on, in an essay entitled "Eros in Academe," where she decried the tendency among educated women to deny that "nice girls" have sexual questions and difficulties.[23] Although the context of her treatise on "Bedworthiness in the Male" may be a bit surprising, I find its inversion of expectations refreshing. Surely there is some scope for addressing, with reason and wit, the reality of women's sexual needs. Taking up such a subject was a direct result of Sayers's ideas about women, which represent a final denial of Victorianism. As she wrote in "The Human-not-quite-Human":

> The period from which we are emerging was like no other: a period when empty head and idle hands were qualities for which a man prized his woman and despised her. When, by an odd, sadistic twist of morality, sexual intercourse was deemed to be a marital right to be religiously enforced upon a meek reluctance— as though the insatiable appetite of wives were not one of the oldest jokes in the world, older than mothers-in-law and far more venerable than kippers. When to think about sex was considered indelicate in a woman, and to think about anything else unfeminine. When to 'manage' a husband by lying and the exploitation of sex was held to be honesty and virtue. (*Unpopular Opinions* 120)

This passage is Dorothy L. Sayers at both her most playful and most serious, and it points to what I consider the most liberating aspect of her views on women: her unwillingness to settle for an incomplete life, a life without play or pleasure.

Amid all the (often grim) talk in our day about women and work, and about ambition and achievement, it is the fun, the pleasure in living that is still most often left out of women's lives.[24] With Nina Auerbach, I too hope women aspire to "the larger world of fun and power" that has traditionally been exclusively male (*Romantic Imprisonment* xiv). For what is the world without a bit of whimsy? Sayers's own Wimsey understands this, acknowledging that "it is better fun to punt than to be punted, and . . . a desire to have all the fun is nine-tenths of the law of chivalry" (*Gaudy Night* ch. 14). He also suggests a link between physical pleasure and playfulness when he says that passion "must lie down with laughter or make its bed in hell"

(*Gaudy Night* ch. 23). There had been a good deal of laughter in Sayers's work from the beginning, but it was only with the creation of Harriet Vane that passionate love became part of her fictional world.

In the unfinished novel, "Thrones, Dominations," Harriet finds it hard to concentrate on writing fiction while happily married. Since it is clear from both *Busman's Honeymoon* and "Thrones" that there is much happy passion in the Wimseys' relationship, perhaps the point was to be that sexual satisfaction ruins the imagination. It is also true that happy marriages, like other happy relationships, do not in themselves generate enough tension for a plot, although the constant redefining and renegotiating of any marriage can surely generate suspense in art as well as in life. But even more importantly, Harriet realizes that her next novel is going to be a different kind of story, a tragedy. She peers down into her fictional world and sees characters acting out their own drama, and is both frightened and exhilarated by the prospect (Wade ms. 89). This image suggests the kind of fully realized world that is the domain of great fiction. Perhaps "Thrones" would have been a "straight" or non-detective novel. If so, Sayers faced the tremendous difficulty of using Lord Peter in a story that had no detection. Because of its incomplete state, we cannot know what the book would have contained; thus, all is conjecture. But I do wish Sayers had written such a book. It would have been an opportunity to explore the possibility of combining love and work in a happy marriage. Perhaps if the war had not intervened, if Dante had not been discovered, if the theater had not beckoned—but all that remains a grand "perhaps."

DLS would take up the women's question once again in the lighter mode of a West End comedy, a play entitled *Love All,* which was produced in April of 1940. This story of a recently successful woman playwright, who has turned to her work for romance and satisfaction because of an unhappy marriage, is perhaps closer to Sayers's personal experience than is the Vane-Wimsey quartet. Beside the subtlety and depth of *Gaudy Night,* however, the play's reflections on men and women seem both arch and glib. For example, when her husband's mistress invokes the cliché that "every great man has had a woman behind him," the play's female protagonist asserts, "and ever great woman has had some man or other in front of her, tripping her up" (185). This is witty enough, but there is a difference between this sort of repartee, which has all the depth of a typical drawing room comedy from whatever period, and the careful dialogue of Sayers's later novels. Her fiction is often praised for being in the comedy of manners tradition, but at its best, it is much more than this, reflecting as it does upon the meaning of human life that resides beneath the display of mannerisms. The Vane-Wimsey quartet, especially its last two books, remains Sayers's most serious and subtle treatment of sexual politics and the predicament of modern women.

Dorothy L. Sayers was one of the first twentieth-century writers to tackle this fatal subject. Because she brought to bear upon it all of her intelligence, learning, and honesty, as well as her good humor and genuine sympathy with the human condition, her writings on women remain provocative, insightful, and inspiring. Her approach to this subject was truly radical, in the sense that it struck at the root of sexual definition and limitation—the question of whether one half of the human race was really human at all. Pointing the way toward a gender-blind regard for the humanity of all people, her writings effectively demonstrate the power of "the brain, that great and sole true Androgyne, that can mate indifferently with male or female and beget offspring upon itself, the cold brain [that] laughs at . . . [the] perversions of history" (*Unpopular Opinions* 120) and corrects them by way of such laughter.

As Sayers's novels show, achieving any balance between the essential elements of human life, or between the two sexes, is ever-precarious. Yet out of the tension created by these competing forces can emerge not only genuine art, but also fully lived human lives—two adventures manifestly worth the risking.

III

A Witness of Universal Truth

The Religious Dimension of Sayers's Art

> "As we *are* so we *make*."
> —"Why Work?"

> "Where there is a church, there is civilization."
> —*The Nine Tailors*

10

The Religious Background

According to one of many legends surrounding Dorothy L. Sayers, an English schoolboy is said to have declared that the famous mystery writer "turned from a life of crime to join the Church of England."[1] Ah, that it were so simple!

Like the schoolboy, we search for a pattern in anything we wish to understand. It is tempting, especially for those of a literary bent, to look for a clear progression of plot even when considering the story of an actual human life. How much more dramatic and satisfying to find in the outline of that life the sudden turning, the definitive action that explains the riddle and predicts the story's final resolution.

There is a sort of pattern to Sayers's career that perhaps makes it even more attractive than usual to attempt an explanation of her work in terms of some fundamental change. It is undeniable that she focused upon writing detective fiction for roughly the first half of her career; that she then became involved with the theater, writing plays that were primarily religious in nature, and emerged as an important essayist and lecturer on political and theological questions; and that, in the last phase of her life, she was absorbed in the translation and interpretation of one of the greatest Christian poems, Dante's *Commedia*. These bare facts of her writing life tell us that she ended where she began, as a writer of verse and a medieval scholar.

The interpretations of these facts have been varied, but most can be summarized in one of two ways: The first holds that DLS wrote a series of popular novels for the simple purpose of making money and, after accomplishing that goal and tiring of the genre, moved on to do the "serious" work she had always wanted to do. This explanation begs the question of why she chose the uncertain life of a freelance writer as opposed to, say, the relative security of a teaching appointment, which would have promised not only a steady income but an ostensible use for her education and a natural base for scholarly work. In the last interview of her life, she said that it was just that she enjoyed writing more than the other forms of work she tried. She sometimes encouraged an easy denigration of her fiction, saying that she considered herself "a scholar gone wrong" or a poet who had abandoned poetry because there was no money in it.[2] Yet it is hard to imagine that Sayers herself, upon reflection, would have held to such a definition of a poet. If the unreliability of income from writing poetry could stop its practice, we should certainly have no poets.

Looking at the pattern in Sayers's work, another school of thought laments that the superb novelist was somehow side-tracked in mid-career, and considers her later work in religious drama, social criticism, and medieval scholarship to be an unfortunate abandonment of her real vocation. Since the type of work to which she turned in the late 1930s was often overtly religious in content or intention, the change is also sometimes taken to signal either a conversion (the best possibility if one seeks to discern a strong dramatic curve in the action of her life), or at least, a new affirmation of Christian tradition.[3] As with all criticism, the attitudes of Sayers's commentators toward her aesthetic, religious, and moral development reveal at least as much about the critics as they do about the subject under consideration. For this reason among many, literary criticism is indeed a dangerous art.

As demonstrated in the first section of this book, Dorothy L. Sayers approached the writing of novels with the same intelligence and integrity she would later bring to more manifestly serious work. One does not write excellent books in any genre by happenstance. As works of art, *The Documents in the Case, The Nine Tailors,* and *Gaudy Night* compare favorably with the best of her later work. Although there was a change of emphasis during her career, that change was neither as simple nor as radical as the general outline might suggest; upon close consideration of the entire body of her work, there emerges a strong sense of thematic unity running throughout the diverse genres and moods.

Dorothy L. Sayers was a rather unusual modern artist in that she appears to have been a committed, orthodox Christian from the beginning of her career. By this I mean that, at least from early adulthood, she accepted the basic Christian creeds as statements of truth. James Brabazon notes that she questioned some aspects of her religious background briefly in adolescence (69–70), and Sayers herself once acknowledged that G. K. Chesterton influenced her profoundly when, as "a sullenly unreceptive adolescent," she was confronted with his irresistible presentation of the central

184

drama of Christianity as the most exciting story ever told. This comment is especially interesting, because she was to perform the same office for a later generation.[4]

In 1954, she wrote to John Wren-Lewis: "If I am not now a Logical Positivist, I probably have to thank G. K. C. Because . . . I am not religious by nature."[5] In the context of this lengthy letter to Wren-Lewis, a fellow Christian known to DLS at St. Anne's House, Soho,[6] her perhaps surprising statement that she is not religious by nature becomes clear. What she means is that, while she is deeply affected by the rational argument of Christianity, of its truth to the human condition, she does not know religious emotion: "Since I cannot come at God through intuition, or through my emotions, or though my 'inner light,' (except in the unendearing form of judgement and conviction of sin) there is only the intellect left. And that is a very different matter."[7] Far from being an unendearing admission, one might very well ask if there could be anything more conducive to genuine religious experience than such a realization of one's limitations combined with a receptive intellect. As the English theologian E. L. Mascall has observed:

> it should be noticed that when she [DLS] singles out the moral sense as the only aspect of her experience that she allows as having evidential value, the moral sense does not mean consciousness of being comfortably at home with absolute goodness but consciousness of being alienated from absolute goodness through sin.[8]

Need we add that her experience is thus in concert with the Christian conception of human nature?

There is no evidence that Dorothy L. Sayers experienced a major spiritual change in the manner of other twentieth-century writers, including such famous examples as T. S. Eliot, C. S. Lewis, and Evelyn Waugh. Her boldly frank letter to Wren-Lewis, written just three years before her death, states unequivocally that she has never undergone a religious conversion (Brabazon 262; cf. "Strong Meat"), a statement supported by her early letters, poems, and stories. In fact, the earliest of her writings are interpenetrated with Christian belief and form the basis for understanding her later patently theological work.

None of this is meant to suggest that DLS was a pietistic person, or that she automatically and uncritically accepted the conventions of her upbringing. Indeed, she seems to have been less influenced by her father's being an ordained minister in the Church of England than one might expect.[9] What she said about the heroine of her thinly veiled autobiographical novel, "Cat O' Mary," would appear to have been true of the young Dorothy Sayers herself: "For a daughter of the parsonage Katherine was oddly uninstructed in Christian dogma" (Brabazon 23). Yet one of the most intriguing scenes in that unpublished fragment depicts the young girl's grandmother remarking, with a certain chagrin, about overhearing the child talking to herself in bed, carrying on as if she were preaching a sermon to herself (Wade ms. 27). It is interesting that this manuscript was written in the early 1930s, before Sayers had actually taken on the role of lecturing about Christianity; the derision with which she regards the young girl in this scene foreshadows the discomfort the writer was to experience when she took on that role in real life. Subtitled "The Biography of a Prig," the work presents a bitterly critical self-portrait.[10] In fact, the self-criticism in "Cat O' Mary" is so unrelieved that one senses the author is being too hard on herself, almost in the spiritually proud vein of an Arthur Dimmesdale proclaiming himself "the one sinner in the world." Such a tone was not typical of Dorothy L. Sayers and it is possible that the manuscript was abandoned when the self-flagellating mood lifted. In addition, "Cat O' Mary" evolved eventually into *Gaudy Night,* which is on one level the story of Harriet Vane's learning to accept herself, and others, in spite of past transgressions.

Despite her healthy misgivings about taking on the role of religious spokesman, Sayers's faith and her concern for the future of Western civilization eventually motivated her to comply with requests that she speak out on theological matters. If nothing else, she wanted to shake complacent church-goers out of their comfortable pews, to disturb "the general air of stained-glass-window decorum" that pervaded the Church in modern England, a country she derided for being only "nominally Christian" (*The Man Born to Be King* 6; *Creed or Chaos?* 20). To approach questions of faith with such liveliness and panache offended many, as DLS must have known it would; in fact, the offense was part of the point. She seems to have always considered primness an unpardonable sin.[11]

Even in childhood, this daughter of the parsonage was repelled by the sanctimonious, by "the awkward stutter and hush that accompanied the word 'Gawd,' " as well as the terms "communion" and "sacrament." As she explains in "Cat O' Mary":

To these rites, which were held in secret, a strong flavour of the indecent seemed to cling. Like the central act of marriage . . . the central mysteries of religion were by common consent exceedingly sacred and beautiful, but on the other hand indelicate, and only to be mentioned in periphrastic whispers. (Brabazon 35)

This is an astute point, curiously reminiscent of the exchange about keeping religion within proper bounds in Shaw's *Major Barbara:*

Lady Britomart: Really, Barbara, you go on as if religion were a pleasant subject. Do have some sense of propriety.
Undershaft: I do not find it an unpleasant subject, my dear. It is the only one that capable people really care for.
Lady Britomart: Well, if you are determined to have it, I insist on having it in a proper and respectable way. Charles, ring for prayers. (16–17)

Although an odd pair, both Sayers and Shaw reject the comfortable false gods of respectability, propriety, and sentimentality. As a believer, she chose to try to rid the Church of these scourges from within, while Shaw took the more common modern approach of satirizing the institutional church from outside.

Sayers's instinctive repulsion over unctuous behavior later motivated her highly original approach to writing about Christianity. She articulated her position in the key 1938 essay, "The Dogma is the Drama":

Let us, in Heaven's name, drag out the Divine Drama from under the dreadful accumulation of slipshod thinking and trashy sentiment heaped upon it, and set it on an open stage to startle the world into some sort of vigorous reaction. If the pious are the first to be shocked, so much the worse for the pious—others will pass into the Kingdom of Heaven before them. (*Creed or Chaos?* 24)

This startlingly ironic essay probes the depths of religious ignorance and apathy in modern society, arguing that it is filled with semi-Christians who know little of what Christ taught and who practice instead the "Seven Deadly Virtues": "respectability; childishness; mental timidity; dullness; sentimentality; censoriousnes; and depression of spirits" (23). The pun on the Seven Deadly Sins gets our attention, as does the remarkably unappealing list of modern "virtues," which would deaden any experience devoted to them. DLS proposes giving the semi-Christians a simple examination to prove her point. Some sample questions from the new catechism:

Q.: What does the Church think of sex?
A.: God made it necessary to the machinery of the world, and tolerates it, provided the parties (a) are married, and (b) get no pleasure out of it.
Q.: What does the Church call sin?
A.: Sex (otherwise than as excepted above); getting drunk; saying "damn"; murder, and cruelty to dumb animals; not going to church; most kinds of amusement. "Original sin" means that anything we enjoy doing is wrong. (23)

This is humorous because the misinformation in these answers is regrettably all too familiar. As the passage demonstrates, no subject remained dull in the hands of DLS, and even her most manifestly serious work is blessed with the playfulness and rich comicality that distinguishes her novels. As one anthology of her theological writing notes in its title, Dorothy L. Sayers was a "Whimsical Christian," and all the more effective for being so.[12]

Long before she was drawn into addressing religious issues directly, however, her work was influenced by a deeply rooted Christianity. James Brabazon has documented the essential religious quality of her mind very well, citing childhood letters in which she discusses with great zest and self-assurance such heady topics as the creation of the universe, the nature of sin and salvation, and the necessary reconciliation between science and theology in the modern world (23, 35). In 1913, while on holiday from Somerville, DLS wrote to her friend Catherine Godfrey, saying that she was composing "an allegorical epic . . . [that was] distinctly Christian" in nature.[13] Sayers's earliest poetry, including that written during her college years and just afterwards, is often based upon Biblical texts and the medieval literature she read at Somerville. This could represent a mere adoption of convention for literary purposes, of course, but there is no hint of unbelief on the part of the fledgling writer. Even at this early date, she seems to have found the images powerful both theologically and aesthetically.[14]

What appears to be her first published story, "Who Calls the Tune?" (1917) is an awkward attempt to portray what happens when a man dies and faces judgment, an idea to which she would return almost thirty years later and develop with subtlety in her Lichfield festival play, *The Just Vengeance*. In the early short story, a millionaire finds that he must enter eternal life with a six-year-old soul. Despite the story's jaunty tone, this severe case of arrested spiritual development is a daunting thought, and one not particularly redolent of the undergraduate temperament.[15] Thematically, the story is precocious: one does not expect a writer to be dealing with the prospect of final judgment at an age when the idea of her own mortality must have seemed a remote conjecture. Over twenty years later, DLS would comment in "Strong Meat" that it pleased her to realize how impressed she had been with St. Augustine's "robust assertion of the claim of Christianity to be a religion for adult minds" while she was still young, "before circumstances rendered it expedient" (*Creed or Chaos?* 14).

Another Somerville friend, Charis Barnett Frankenburg, remembered many years later when writing her own autobiography that DLS had composed for reading at the Mutual Admiration Society a conversation between the three Magi. This early work made a great impression on Frankenburg, and in retrospect seemed to her an adumbration of *The Man Born to*

Be King (*Not Old, Madam, Vintage* 63). Four years after going down from Somerville, Sayers published in *The New Decameron* (1919) a ballad about a master carpenter who is aided by Christ in the building of a shrine. Christ, here described in typically Sayersian language as "a lusty lad" and "a man of strength and skill," comes into human experience and makes the carpenter's pillar straight (1:25–26). This characterization foreshadows not only Sayers's treatment of Christ in later works, especially *The Man Born to Be King,* but also the subject matter and theme of her first full-length religious play, *The Zeal of Thy House* (1937).

In an excellent survey of the religious drama of DLS, Barbara Reynolds has pointed out that Sayers's second collection of poetry, the 1918 *Catholic Tales and Christian Songs,* includes a dramatic poem in the form of a medieval mystery play entitled "The Mocking of Christ," which was presumably her first published attempt at religious drama:

> Despite its figurative presentation and its immaturity *The Mocking of Christ* contains many of the elements she later developed in her articles on Christian belief and on Christian behaviour. Christ is mocked daily by ecclesiastical wrangling, by insistence on certain details in rituals and in the choice of church music by religiosity, by trivialities, respectability, muscular Christianity, self-righteousness, war, sentimentality and facile identification of Christianity with pagan religions and Greek philosophy. (DLS Society 1984 Seminar Proceedings 2–3)

Readers of *The Man Born to Be King* should recognize not only the Sayers approach to Christology in this description, but also her constitutional aversion to such debased ideas of virtue.

When *Catholic Tales* was about to be published in 1918, the young poet wrote to assure her parents that the collection was "*intended* . . . to be an expression of reverent belief"; she was worried that since it was also lively, people might not regard it as suitably serious (Brabazon 68). The book certainly *looks* reverent enough, with an austere drawing of Christ and a title drawn in medieval hand lettering on its dust jacket (see Gilbert 18). At the other end of the spectrum from those pious souls who might have been offended by the book's liveliness, a rather patronizing reviewer in the *Times Literary Supplement* made this astonishing claim: "These pieces reproduce in graceful religious fantasies the childlike spirit and familiar intimacy with Christ characteristic of the Middle Ages" (Hone 30). This statement represents an indirect compliment, although the reviewer obviously did not intend it as such. Certainly Sayers herself never claimed having "a familiar intimacy with Christ." The mere invocation of the words "childlike" and "Middle Ages" suggests a faint, distinctively modern contempt for earlier cultures, although as Sayers would insist, "medieval" is not a term of opprobrium to anyone who really knows anything about the Middle Ages. The review also implies that religious poetry necessarily involves "fantasy," which is presumably opposed to reality. DLS was going against the tide of her times, in both the style and theme of her poetry. Eventually, she would forge a prose style of great freshness, vigor, and flexibility which could more effectively communicate her ideas about tradition and culture.

After the publication of *Catholic Tales and Christian Songs,* the young poet wrote to another Somerville friend, Muriel Jaeger, unabashedly suggesting a way to encourage sales of this reverent book by whipping up a spurious controversy over its theological premises. In this high-spirited stunt, we can perceive the Dorothy Sayers who would later manipulate public opinion to sell everything from mustard to religious drama. James Brabazon comments that

> the most interesting thing about this unashamed attempt to serve God and Mammon at the same time is the discovery that Dorothy was already, at the age of twenty-six, totally informed about the traditional theology of the Roman Catholic Church. She accepted all its tenets save its rejection of the validity of Anglican orders and its acceptance of the supremacy of the Pope. . . . "What I feel is this," she writes to Muriel at one point in the lengthy correspondence, "there is a real truth about everything, which (I believe) Catholicism has got hold of (as far as it is possible for us to grasp the truth about everything . . .)." (69)

Brabazon's interpretation may be justified by something he does not quote here, but in the passage as quoted, DLS does not say specifically that *Roman* Catholicism has got hold of the truth. From this and other statements, I think it fair to consider her a traditional, conservative Anglican who had great respect for the Roman church, especially because of its emphasis on theology (*Creed or Chaos?* 30) and its historical contribution to Western civilization. This is hardly a surprising position for a medieval scholar to assume. In any event, the distinction between the Anglican and Roman communions does not seem to be the point of this statement, which I take to be a straightforward assertion of the orthodox Christian belief that she would later incarnate in stories and plays.

By 1919, then, Sayers had become conversant with, and accepting of, the basic Christian dogma that was apparently left out of her vicarage education. In a world pervaded by what she would later call "an atmosphere of 'odium antitheologicum' "[16] this may seem an unlikely direction for a lively young intellectual to take, but Dorothy L. Sayers was to show just how lively and intellectually challenging Christian dogma can be.

11

Moral Fiction

When DLS decided to try writing detective stories around 1920, did she abandon the theological assumptions of her earlier work? To put it another way, can her work be easily divided into the sacred and the profane? Not exactly. In fact, the novels of Dorothy L. Sayers demonstrate the curious affinity between detection and a belief system which holds that there is something fundamentally amiss in human relations, "that there is a deep interior dislocation in the very centre of human personality" (*Creed or Chaos?* 39). In the most facile and superficial detective stories, whatever is wrong can be righted by an extraordinary human being, the detective. This is possible because the detective problem, whether it be a question of Whodunit? or How Was It Done?, is set in terms solvable by human reason. This radical simplification of experience into a question capable of one and only one answer is part of what makes the detective story appealing to many people: in its purest form, it remains an intellectual exercise unsullied by the complexities of real life (*The Mind of the Maker* 188).

In its most profound incarnations, however, the detective story implies questions about the nature of reality, about life and death, innocence and experience, that cause the genre finally to turn on itself, suggesting the need for a higher power to set things right.[1] There is, in fact, a fundamental irony at the base of detective fiction: while it poses fascinating, answerable questions about a particular death, it distracts us from the realization that it cannot solve the most compelling mystery of all, the riddle of mortality itself. As Sayers notes in *The Mind of the Maker,* although we are confronted with the problem daily, "There is no solution to death" (195). When we move beyond the question of the Body in the Library to questions about the meaning of death, and of life, we have moved into the kind of moral complexity necessary for genuine art. We have also begun asking what are essentially religious questions, "since religious dogma is in fact nothing but a statement of doctrines concerning the nature of life and the universe" (*Creed or Chaos?* 31).

To call great mystery stories "moral fiction" is not simply to assert what Lord Peter meant when he argued that "in detective stories virtue is always triumphant. They're the purest literature we have" (*Strong Poison* ch. 12). This is a description of melodrama, and a novelist whose moral sense is limited to poetic justice cannot lay claim to serious consideration as an artist. Although it is true that classic detective stories seek to punish wrongdoing, the closer these stories come to reflecting real life, the less clear they are about defining what is right and wrong. Moral fiction—that is, fiction that probes the meaning of good and evil—is not limited to writers with a clearly religious slant, of course. A writer can be interested in exploring what constitutes moral action without reference to a supreme arbiter outside of human experience. In the case of Dorothy L. Sayers, however, her fiction is informed by Christian assumptions about sin and salvation, guilt and responsibility, and the implied definition of right conduct that emerges in her created world reflects the Christian dogma she accepted as the essential truth of the universe.

The writer herself once said that detective novelists believe "your sin will find you out" (*Omnibus of Crime III* 2). She was obviously comfortable using the old theological term for humanity's alienation from good, and there is no better genre than the murder mystery for one who believes man to be "very far gone from original righteousness and . . . of his own nature inclined to evil" (*The Mind of the Maker* 17).[2] Perhaps this bracing sense of humanity's essential sinfulness is, ironically, one of the things that makes detective fiction so attractive to moderns. For the better part of two centuries, we have been assured "that progress is making us automatically every day and in every way better, and better, and better" (*The Mind of the Maker* 16), but the thriller and the murder mystery concur with our troubled inner sense of experience, which seems to say, "Oh, no we're not— and here's proof!"

Sayer's religious convictions were implied in her fictional world from the beginning, becoming more patent as time passed. To appreciate fully the religious dimension of her art, we must take another look at her novels, this time in the context of her Christian belief. In her first novel, *Whose Body?*, there is a very clear villain, a man of unrelieved evil, pitted against a detective-hero whose actions seem totally justified. Operating in the stark outlines of a modern morality play, Sir Julian Freke's villainy is compounded because his victim is wholly innocent, one of the few victims in

Sayers's fiction to be so guiltless in his own destruction. Freke's basic flaw is an overweening pride, the greatest and most basic of the Seven Deadly Sins; murder is just one consequence of this disease in his moral nature. Furthermore, his pride is of an intellectual sort, like Satan's. Freke is a melodramatic remnant of Victorian fiction, and as Ralph Hone has said, the stereotypical mad scientist (42). Yet in his cold magnificence, Julian Freke also recalls an archetypal Hawthorne villain eaten up with pride.[3] As Sayers would later argue: "The name under which Pride walks the world at this moment is the Perfectibility of Man, or the doctrine of Progress; and its speciality is the making of blue-prints for Utopia and establishing the Kingdom of Man on earth" (*Creed or Chaos?* 86). This observation from the 1941 lecture, "The Other Six Deadly Sins," was also the theme of her second Canterbury Festival play, *The Devil to Pay* (1939), which was a reworking of the Faust legend. In her lecture on the Seven Deadly Sins, DLS noted with acuity that "the devilish strategy of Pride is that it attacks us, not on our weak points, but on our strong. It is pre-eminently the sin of the noble mind" (*Creed or Chaos?* 86).

The character of Sir Julian Freke, one-dimensional and trite though he is, thus establishes a current of implied self-criticism and examination that runs throughout Sayers's work. As she said of Judas in her introduction to *The Man Born to Be King,* pride is the "besetting sin of highly virtuous and intelligent people" (15). Surely no one as intelligent as DLS could write such a statement without some self-consciousness of its application. And of what are highly intelligent people more proud than their intelligence? Intelligence was something Sayers valued greatly, as both her scholarship and her work in the detective genre, that "sport of noble minds," attest.[4] Her characterizations reveal what her biographers have documented: she did not suffer fools gladly. For all that her detective stories celebrate the power of reason, however, they also question its capacity, in isolation, to discover truth and to motivate right action. In fact, the tension created by this paradoxical attitude toward human reason generates much of her novels' power, especially in *The Nine Tailors* and *Gaudy Night.* It is unlikely that Sayers herself was initially conscious of this critique of human reason, and of the pride often attendant upon it, that is embedded in even her early fiction. Yet, as she says in *The Mind of the Maker,* one of the most mysterious and unexpected results of authorship comes when the writer becomes the reader of her own work, learning what any careful reader can learn from the text (40–41). Both *The Mind of the Maker* and the essay "Gaudy Night" offer ample proof that DLS became a very self-conscious artist indeed.

Sayers's Julian—the apostate—attempts to be as God, not only in the taking of a human life, but in his prideful boast that he, as surgeon and scientist, can make humanity anew in his own image: "The knowledge of good and evil is a phenomenon of the brain, and is removable," concludes this expert on and exemplar of "The Pathological Aspects of Human Genius." Although Lord Peter is no Christian, he is decidedly moral, despite his disclaimers (*Gaudy Night* ch. 23). When confronted with Freke's theory of the ephemeral nature of the conscience, the great detective's own "conscience, instantly allying itself with blind faith," moves him to action against the murderer, an action which outweighs any amount of theorizing on the subject (*Whose Body?* ch. 8). Wimsey's entrapment of this arrogant fool represents a clear victory of good over evil, and of right reason over the corrupted will. Since Wimsey is an intellectual himself, he in a sense represents Freke's better self, the self from which he has become alienated through sin.

Good and evil are rarely so clear-cut in this world, however, and the conflict between them would never again be so simple in Sayers's fiction. As she matured, her novels came to reflect the Christian understanding of the paradoxical relationship between good and evil in human experience. This increased capacity for paradox and ambiguity contributed considerably to her development as a serious novelist, a development most clearly evinced in her hero's evolution into a believable and complex human being.

In *Whose Body?* Wimsey is warned that, as a basically responsible person, he cannot continue to consider sleuthing a mere game. Since it is literally a matter of life and death, detection is serious business and not just an idle occupation to counter his boredom. This warning is issued by Inspector Parker, who is a professing Christian, and whose mind seems to Wimsey well-honed by theology, at least until the theology is turned on him. Being reminded that life is more than a game seems "brutalizing" to the young Peter Wimsey, but the comment pricks him precisely because he is a moral creature who constantly scrutinizes the rightness of his actions, despite the flippant facade he presents to the world (ch. 7).

By the third novel, *Unnatural Death,* Wimsey seeks advice on this matter from a wonderfully named clergyman, Mr. Tredgold. When Wimsey questions the morality of both the crime and his own actions in attempting to solve it, Tredgold realizes that the detective, who is still ostensibly the debonair man-about-town, is a member of "a very difficult class to reach," and thus talks to him in terms of "the damage to Society, the wrongness of the thing," rather than of sin. Yet what Wimsey worries about is not some vague harm to society, but to his own integrity as a human being, or to what a Christian would call his "soul" (ch. 19). Wimsey's creator is developing real subtlety in dealing with moral questions, and Tredgold affirms the greatest of the Christian virtues when he counsels Wimsey to "do what you think is right, according to the laws which we have been brought up to respect. Leave the consequences to God. And try to think charitably, even of wicked people. . . . Bring the offender to justice, but remember that if we all got justice, you and I wouldn't escape either" (ch. 19). Or as Sayers remarks in *Begin Here*, "to make an 'absolute' of justice is a wrong against charity" (139). This may seem an ironic position for a writer of detective stories to take, but from the time of Sherlock Holmes, the great detectives have been concerned not just with serving the letter of the law, but with discovering some higher idea of justice.[5] One of Sayers's contemporaries, Ernest Raymond, put it very well when he reflected on his novel, *We, the Accused,* and tried to explain the peculiar appeal of the detective story to a sinful race: "We are all guilty. We are all fugitives from justice. That is to say, we all stand condemned before our own consciences, whether this judgment is pronounced in the cellar below consciousness or in the open court above; and we all escape and fly from the justice in ourselves" (*Titles to Fame* 189). Through his detective adventures, Wimsey slowly learns the paradoxical truth revealed in *The Just Vengeance.* The revelation is enunciated there by a young airman at the moment of his death: "we are victims together / Or guilty together" (28), sharing as we do, a solidarity in blood.[6] This profound ambiguity is treated with increasing subtlety as Sayers matures as a novelist, until finally in *The Nine Tailors,* hunter and hunted, victim and hero become one in a paradoxical vision of human life that is clearly allied with the Christian explanation of the universe.

This is not to argue that Wimsey becomes a Christian; in fact, we have his creator's assurance that he does not. Several years after completing the last Wimsey novel, DLS reflected on her hero: "Peter is not the Ideal Man; he is an eighteenth-century Whig gentleman, born a little out of his time, and doubtful whether any claim to possess a soul is not a rather vulgar piece of presumption" (*The Mind of the Maker* 131). Despite his similarities to the medieval knight, Wimsey is strangely modern in this regard; he has all the old sense of responsibility and guilt, but no idea of salvation; the prospect of hell with no glimmer of heaven. The Wimsey novels bear out William Butler Yeats's judgment of this "blood-dimmed" century: "the best lack all conviction, / while the worst are full of passionate intensity" ("The Second Coming"). Wimsey is "modern" in the sense that he is a creature of Rationalism who is yet besieged by self-doubt. This tension in his character is part of what makes him so sympathetic to twentieth-century readers. Of course, to a proper medievalist like DLS, an "eighteenth-century Whig gentleman" would be modern in any event.

If Wimsey the nonbeliever is plagued by severe bouts of self-doubt, the

195

thoroughly Christian Miss Climpson suffers a full-blown "Case of Conscience" in *Unnatural Death*.[7] The headnote of the chapter in which this occurs is a quote from *Titus Andronicus,* "I know thou art religious, / And hast a thing within thee called conscience," but unlike this Shakespearean passage, the novel does not mock those who have such a moral censor. The episode is patently religious and Christian: Miss Climpson, who has an exquisitely refined High Church conscience, is leaving church after Vespers, when "a small pentecostal shower of Easter cards" falls in her way. This pentecost presents her with a true moral dilemma: Should she do wrong (by looking at someone's notes for confession) and thus perhaps glean some necessary information about the mystery? Or should she ignore this possibility, follow what she has been taught about the sanctity of such information, and thus risk committing a wrong against her job, which is to find out as much as she can? After much agonizing about the morality of reading these notes, she gives in and hopes for forgiveness. Like any good detective, Miss Climpson decides to go the way of knowledge, even though she fully recognizes the consequences of doing so. In a humorous, engaging way, this scene dramatizes the problem of knowledge in a fallen world, an idea taken up and developed in greater depth in *The Documents in the Case* and *The Nine Tailors.* In fact, these questions of conscience are more interesting than the main plot of *Unnatural Death;* it would be several years before DLS could make the moral predicament of her characters integral to the story.

Many non-Christian novelists present Christian characters, of course, so the inclusion of characters like Mr. Tredgold and Miss Climpson does not in itself make Sayers's novels either religious or Christian. What is important is that the detective action of these novels is played out against a background of religious belief. Sayers's novels portray a post-lapsarian world, a world in which knowledge is both necessary and deadly. In this world, human beings are free moral agents with responsibility for their actions, and transgression results from the divided will, with all human action judged by reference to an authority more powerful than Scotland Yard. It is also significant that Sayersian characters who are manifestly religious are not mocked; this is especially notable when one considers her clergymen— Tredgold, Dawson, Venables, Perry, Goodacre, even Boyes—because of the long, well-loved tradition of satirizing the clergy in English literature. Despite her gift for social satire, nothing in Sayers's work faintly resembles the scathing caricatures of Canon Chasuble, St. John Rivers, or Mr. Collins.[8] It is especially curious how different she is in this respect from Jane Austen, who by all accounts was personally devout. However much these two writers may have in common, it is striking that Sayers does not share

Austen's taste for savaging that group which both women knew intimately from their vicarage backgrounds.[9] Perhaps this difference is related to the different worlds they inhabited; while Austen's comedy assumed a general acceptance of belief, Sayers could make no such assumptions.

As discussed earlier, *The Documents in the Case* represents a turning point in Sayers's career as a novelist. It was her first serious novel, the first that would bear comparison to good "straight" fiction. Since it is also the only novel without Lord Peter and was written in the same year as the first Harriet Vane story, it seems fair to conclude that DLS was in a transition phase at this time. Another clue to this fact is her taking the time, in 1929, to go back to an old project, a translation of the twelfth-century *Tristan* by Thomas the Anglo-Norman. She had first worked on this translation in the early 1920s and her return to it represents a reaffirmation of her scholarly interests in medieval literature. It is also a fair assumption that she was able to get the translation, entitled *Tristan in Brittany,* published at this point because she was an established author. In fact, it could be argued that the remaining scholarly work she was to do was made possible, at least partially, by her growing reputation as a popular novelist. Of course, she had the necessary education, intelligence, and commitment for such undertakings, but she had also become a name in the book trade and in the public mind.[10]

James Brabazon makes an interesting point about Sayers's lifelong passion for translating, saying that "it offered the tantalizing prospect of a problem with a hundred different solutions, none of which could ever be wholly successful" (64). Perhaps such mental gymnastics also made detective fiction and theology attractive to her. It is interesting that she returned to translation around the time she was starting to set higher challenges for herself as a novelist.[11]

Important changes were also occurring in Sayers's personal life around this time, including her father's death in September of 1928, followed by her mother's less than a year later. Between the two deaths, DLS bought the house in Witham, Essex, for her mother's use. After Helen Sayers's death in August of 1929, the house became the Flemings' main residence. They could move into the country because, by this point, Sayers's earnings as a novelist were sufficient to make leaving the London advertising agency possible.[12] Even though her husband's health had begun to deteriorate and he was no longer regularly employed, things eased enough during this period for her to have the chance to reevaluate where she wanted to go as a writer. From 1930 on, there is a general lengthening of perspective, a deepening seriousness about her work. These changes were presumably linked to her expanded freedom to write as she wanted, as well as to a sharpened sense of mortality occasioned by her parents' deaths, her own aging, and her acceptance of a marriage of limited success (see Brabazon 139–47).

A major departure from the puzzle stories of the twenties, *The Documents in the Case* is a deeply philosophical novel about the nature of the universe and humanity's place in it. More particularly, it is an attempt to integrate theology and science, a goal any properly brought-up child of the late Victorian era would recognize, and an inquiry into the possibility for belief in the modern world.[13] For the first time, these questions are intrinsically related to the mystery, rather than merely interesting set pieces.

The novel's main character, the writer Jack Munting, is in some ways a typical modern man who is "tossed about with every wind of doctrine" (document no. 22). Although Munting is an attractive character, he also embodies some of the qualities DLS most sharply criticizes in the modern temperament. The complexity of her characterizations in this and later books is, in fact, an indication of how far she is from being a religious propagandist. By his own admission, Munting has "that kind of vaguely inquiring mind that likes to be told what is going on. . . . A pap-fed, negative, twentieth-century mind, open on all sides and wind-swept by every passing gust" (document no. 52). The novel of which he is the moral center asks what, if anything, is really important in "this universe of infinitesimal immensities" (document no. 31), and what, if anything, constitutes moral action in a world that has lost its faith in itself and its institutions. In Munting, Sayers explores once again the moral and spiritual value of work. He vaguely senses this importance, saying that he wants to do a good job with his current book, "not merely because it will do me good with publishers . . . but for some obscure and irrational motive connected with the development of my soul, if I may so allude to it" (document no. 8). One wonders if this is not, on some level, DLS talking to herself. *Documents* was written in 1930, when she had been working for some time on a biography of Wilkie Collins (just as Munting is writing a "Life") and the deepening seriousness of her fiction suggests concerns that go far beyond the marketplace.

Embarrassed by the word and even the idea of a soul, Munting yet grapples with the problem of how to live in a world that lacks definition and meaning: "if time and space and straightness and curliness and bigness and smallness are all relative, then we may just as well think ourselves important as not. 'Important, unimportant—unimportant, important,' as the King of Hearts said . . ." (document no. 8). But this way lies madness, and Munting does not succumb. A decade later, DLS would assert unequivocally that the only choice for Western civilization is that between creed or chaos, while *The Documents in the Case* focuses upon the common twentieth-century predicament of a people without faith or creed trying to cope with chaotic reality.

Like Wimsey, Munting is intellectually honest and self-effacing enough to be properly humbled by the words of an insightful parson. Munting recalls the incident in a letter to his fiancée:

> "We should pray," said he, making me feel like a very grubby fourth-form infant, "to be delivered from cleverness, because very clever people end by finding that nothing is worthwhile." So I said, rather ungraciously, that probably nothing *was* worthwhile, and he gave the funniest twinkle from under his thick eyebrows and replied: "You must not think that, or you will become a bore." (Document no. 13)

The cleric is himself very clever, warning Munting not of eternal damnation but of what would seem a fate worse than death to a witty young intellectual. Munting admits that he listened to the minister because the man knew his science as well as his theology, and thus could speak with some authority about "the great humility of science, in face of the infinite and valuable variety of Truth" (document no. 13).

All of this seemingly irrelevant talk about the relationship between science and religion culminates in the climactic scene of the novel, where a chemical analysis explains how the murder was committed, and thus provides the basis for punishing the crime. Slowly, Munting comes to realize "that God or Nature or Science or some other sinister and powerful thing had set a trap" for the murderer, adding that "I thought it was ruthless of God or whoever it was" (document no. 52). Ruthless or not, the novel implies that the world operates still by some definite rules, if only we can discover them. Because there is a defining quality about life, because a synthetic chemical differs essentially from a natural one, this murderer is caught and his transgression against traditional morality can be punished. Did chemistry or God trip him up?

As Munting is writing the *Life*, he is drawn into questions about life, and begins "reading a lot of scientific and metaphysical tripe which is of no use to anybody, and least of all to a creative writer" (document no. 22). The irony is that he is asking metaphysical questions all the time, and is most disturbed by the reluctance or inability of modern science and philosophy to deal with "the real question of why or how the thing [life] began at all" (document no. 22). This is a crucial question to Munting, not because of any recognized religious yearnings on his part, but because he is a writer: "You can't really make a novel hold together if you don't believe in causation," he admits, by way of introducing this lovely limerick:

> *Said a rising young author, "What, what?*
> *If I think that causation is not,*
> *No word of my text*
> *Will bear on the next*
> *And what will become of the plot?"* (Document no. 22)

This is, of course, particularly true of detective fiction, with its extreme emphasis upon coherent plot development and rational deduction, but Munting, who appears to be a "straight" novelist, is worried about the encroaching aimlessness of much modern literature. He also voices a realistic fear that an easy cynicism might eventually destroy his ability to create coherent texts, concluding that "if I'm not damn careful I shall end by writing a *Point Counterpoint,* without the wit." A frightening prospect, but a fairly common occurrence in modern letters nevertheless.

Sayers has hit upon an important irony here. No matter what their belief or lack of it, all writers attempt to wrest meaning from experience. Writing is in itself an act of faith—faith in the possibility of discovery, understanding, and communication, in the transcendent power of the word, in the existence of a reader unseen. What happens when a writer communicates clearly the idea that all existence, including the language used to describe it, is meaningless and incoherent? Does not the work itself testify to the existence of meaning, to some meaning in existence?

Like Peter Wimsey, Jack Munting is embarrassed by the very idea of an immortal soul, and he is often ready to run away from the responsibilities of detection, but his insatiable desire to know wins out. In fact, the detective story rests on the premise that not only the detective but also the reader will find the bite into that apple irresistible, echoing the beguiling question in the Garden: "Can it be sin to know, / Can it be death?" (*Paradise Lost* 4.517–18). This is a complicated question because knowledge imparts responsibility, and often in a murder mystery the detective's actions and discoveries lead to other deaths (see *Unnatural Death* and *The Nine Tailors,* for example). Yet the inveterate detective will follow Eve, who plucked fruit from the Tree of Knowledge and "Greedily . . . engorged without restraint, / And knew not eating death" (*Paradise Lost* 9.791–92; or consider Oedipus, for another image of this fateful drive for knowledge in the Western tradition). Even at the end of the story, when Munting already knows more than he can deal with, he articulates the insatiable desire for knowledge that drives not only detective stories, but all fiction. This highly stylized passage, with its careful repetition of the initial phrase, suggests that DLS was deliberately dramatizing the essential curiosity that stimulates detection:

I want to know whether Lathom knows the sort of woman he did it for. I want to know how much she really knows or suspects. I want to know whether, when she wrote that letter which drove him to do it, she was deceiving him or herself. I want to know whether, in all these months, he has been thinking that she was worth it, or whether, in a ghastly disillusionment, he has realised that the only real part of her was vulgar and bad, and the rest merely the brilliant refraction of himself. What is the good? (Document no. 52)

The last question is, of course, the main question, in this book and in life.[14] This novel raises questions about the nature of reality and about traditional conceptions of the universe, but it is not a distinctively Christian book. It does, however, give the churchmen a good chance in various arguments, including one maintaining that the Judeo-Christian account of creation can be squared with Darwin. Curiously, it is a chemist who points out that the author of Genesis seems to have been right when "he put the beginning of life on the face of the waters," and that the modern understanding of heredity actually gives credence to the Biblical idea of the sins of the fathers being visited upon the sons (document no. 52). The novel's theme, which is the possibility of discovering the truth of the universe, is intrinsically linked to its epistolary structure, with each point of view being offered as one way to the truth and all converging in a heightened sense of reality by the novel's end.

If one compares Harwood Lathom to Julian Freke, it becomes apparent how much DLS has grown as an artist. Lathom is both more real and more sympathetic, and one would hesitate calling him a villain. He is young, talented, and passionate, with the kind of hubris very gifted but untried people often have in youth. With Munting, the reader regrets that Lathom will not live to overcome his flaws, to reach his potential as an artist or see the emptiness of his own wit. Our ability to sympathize with him only makes the narrative of his destruction more powerful, of course. The compassion with which both he and his victim are regarded reflects their creator's Christian apprehension of a world in which "we suffer for one another, as indeed, we must, being all members of one another" (document no. 52). Lathom is also manipulated into commiting the crime, which makes him less despicable, although the motivation is not thoroughly convincing.[15]

Once again, the murderer is infected with pride. He considers himself a better artist than the man he kills, and so justifies his action: "Harrison was a brute. . . . the man was unfit to live. He deserved to be murdered for his rotten paintings, let alone for his cruelty to his wife" (document no. 37). This justification is overly ingenious. As Munting remarks, "What devilish things we do when we try to be clever" (document no. 37). In reality, Harrison's paintings are not rotten, but unassuming and craftsmanlike; his "cruelty" to his wife consists largely in a lack of warmth and imagination. He is a drab, limited little man, but such lackluster limitations do not merit harsh treatment, let alone punishment by death. When Munting eventually sides with the law and traditional morality in assisting the conviction of Lathom for Harrison's murder, the novel implicitly rejects the notions of a special morality for artists and of Art as God.

The story also questions the turning of another human being into one's god, an idea that first appeared in the idolatrous attachment of Vera Findlater to Mary Whittaker in *Unnatural Death*. In *The Documents in the Case*, Margaret Harrison's indulgent self-dramatization and rampant self-pity conspire to convince Lathom that they should grasp whatever pleasure they can and do whatever it takes to be happy. Sin is an outmoded idea, she argues, while human love (or the lust and egotism that often masquerade as love) is the only proper object of existence (document no. 43). In one of her letters to Lathom, Margaret babbles on condescendingly about "a funny sermon about the Law and the Gospel" in which the priest said that punishment by the Law "didn't mean that God was vindictive, only that the Laws of Nature had their way, and worked out the punishment quite impartially, just as fire burns you if you touch it . . ." (document no. 43). In her self-absorption, Margaret does not see the relevance of this commonsensical point to her own situation, but her very next letter informs her lover that she has learned the hard way that nature can be inflexible in the enforcement of her laws: it seems that their adulterous behavior has resulted in the "unthinkable," a pregnancy. Perceiving herself as the victim of her experience, she bleats: "How cruel God is! He must be on the conventional people's side after all" (document no. 44), never stopping to consider the possibility that some conventions were based upon natural law, not in spite of it. As Lathom is caught by the modern understanding of chemistry, so Nature, or God, or What You Will continues acting through the universe: there are some intractable laws of reality, after all. To deepen the irony, we find that while arguing for the propriety of her behavior, Margaret refuses to break the most sacred law of Respectability; she will not admit her adultery to a world she holds in so much contempt (document no. 39).

This 1930 novel was Sayers's first extended attempt to consider the relevance of Christian doctrine to the modern world and to apply rigorous intellectual standards to the question of belief. *The Documents in the Case* dramatizes what she would later argue: that belief is enhanced by knowledge and rational questioning, and that all the disciplines, when properly employed, can help make sense of an often forbidding and mysterious universe. This is not to say that the book is a piece of religious propaganda or that it was written to make a theological statement. The moral questions raised in its pages derive from realistic human situations and subtle characterizations created by a novelist who was reflecting and examining the world in which she lived.[16]

Four years later, *Murder Must Advertise* again considered the emptiness of the modern world and its shaky basis on corrupt values. This book attacks particularly the false god of materialism, which is the antithesis of Judeo-Christian morality, no matter how fervently many so-called Christians may worship it. By the use of parallel plots, the novel suggests that the rampant materialism of modern culture corrupts souls as much as dope-dealing does. Both are anti-human and anti-creation, because materialism leads to a debased notion of work and the person, while drug addiction leads to sloth, diminished moral capacity, and death. Although the book is often regarded as a period piece about the Roaring Twenties, it is painfully relevant to American culture today, with its haunting images of the seduction of the masses by advertising and drugs into a death-in-life existence.

DLS judged this book an uneven success, largely because its depiction of the advertising business is more authentic than its parallel study of The Bright Young Things (*The Mind of the Maker* 77). This is an understandable gap, since of the two, she knew only the advertising world at first hand. But the idea of linking them was sound. It is not just that "Death Comes to Pym's Publicity" in the sense that a violent death occurs there. *Murder Must Advertise* presents a decadent modern culture that is being destroyed from the inside by advertising's pandering to the baser human drives, engendering a veritable "hell's-dance of spending"(ch. 11). Mr. Ingleby justly characterizes his work as a "soul-searing profession" (ch. 1), while Inspector Parker, whose moral instincts are always right, tells Wimsey bluntly that "all advertisers are dope-merchants" (ch. 15). Later, Wimsey muses to himself about the awful disparity between reality and what is sold at Pym's, and between the people who do the writing there, and the writing they do:

In this place, where from morning till night a staff of over a hundred people hymned the praises of thrift, virtue, harmony, eupepsia and domestic contentment, the spiritual atmosphere was clamorous with financial storm, intrigue, dissension, indigestion and marital infidelity. And, with worse things—with murder wholesale and retail, of soul and body, murder by weapon and murder by poison. These things did not advertise, or, if they did, they called themselves by other names. (Ch. 17)

This shadow existence, wherein nothing is what it appears to be, is dramatized in Wimsey's double persona. He appears in disguise in both worlds of the story, first as Death Bredon, who works undercover at Pym's Publicity, and then as the masked Harlequin disporting himself with the decadent de Momerie crowd. The pattern of light and dark in his Harlequin costume embodies the novel's theme of deceit and confusion, just as the de Momerie name suggests the masquerading of mummers or the empty show of mummery (from the Middle English "mommer"). Both are apposite to the novel's portrayal of the "gloom and gleam" of modern London, which is more than a pleasing piece of alliteration. Like Dante's Inferno, the book looks beneath the glittering facade of much that is taken for beautiful, desirable, or cultivated, and discovers the ugly face of corruption lurking there. In fact, the London of *Murder Must Advertise* is the closest Sayers gets to the sense of the city presented in the Sherlock Holmes canon, which characterizes it as "that great cesspool into which all the . . . Empire [is] . . . irresistibly drained" (*A Study in Scarlet*), or to the vile metropolis facing American detectives like Chandler's Philip Marlowe. Wimsey slips in and out of various disguises in this "Phantasmagoria—a city of dreadful day, of crude shapes and colours piled Babel-like in a heaven of harsh cobalt and rocking over a void of bankruptcy—a Cloud-Cuckooland, peopled by pitiful ghosts . . ." (ch. 11; cf. the "unreal city" of Eliot's *The Waste Land*). The language of this passage reminds us that, although DLS was writing about her experiences in an advertising agency during the twenties, she was doing so in the early 1930s, after the crash of world markets, and from the enlightened perspective of time.[17]

The novel asks implicitly whether pleasure, physical comfort, and entertainment are the proper goals of human experience, and suggests that the value of human activity must be judged by some standard outside the human being. Sayers saw this reference to universal truth as the only way to spiritual peace, for as she once observed, "whenever man is made the centre of things, he becomes the storm-centre of trouble" (*Creed or Chaos?* 61), an assertion that is supported by much of modern history. The narcissistic Dian de Momerie is such a storm-center of trouble, typifying what DLS says about the sin of Luxuria, or Lust, which is so common in the modern world. In her essay on "The Other Six Deadly Sins," Sayers argues that lust often runs rampant "in periods of disillusionment like our own, when philosophies are bankrupt and life appears without hope—[then] men and women may turn to lust in sheer boredom and discontent, trying to find in it some stimulus which is not provided by the drab discomfort of their mental and physical surroundings" (*Creed or Chaos?* 66). This description of the vague emptiness of life as it is lived in the relative affluence and ease of the postindustrial world is only too telling.[18]

Although it has always been acceptable to decry the drug culture and its obvious effects on traditional moral values, DLS is more provocative regarding another common modern vice. As she argues in her lecture on the Seven Deadly Sins, true Christian morality goes far beyond prohibitions against the "warm-hearted" or "generous" sins of the flesh and presents more radical challenges to the materialistic basis of modern culture. Whereas everyone is ostensibly "against" drugs, one would have a harder time garnering support for the other kind of social criticism implied in *Murder Must Advertise* and made explicit in Sayers's later essays. This is because we have actually made a virtue of the vice, or have come to know the evil as good. To show this, in "The Other Six Deadly Sins" DLS adopts the debased language of a thoroughly materialistic attitude toward life:

> It was left for the present age to endow Covetousness with glamour on a big scale, and to give it a title which it could carry like a flag. It occurred to somebody to call it Enterprise. From the moment of that happy inspiration, Covetousness has . . . never looked back. It has become a swaggering, swashbuckling, piratical sin. . . . its war-cries are 'Business Efficiency,' 'Free Competition,' 'Get Out or Get Under!' and 'There's always room at the Top!' It no longer screws and saves—it launches out into new enterprises; it gambles and speculates; it thinks in a big way; it takes risks. . . . It looks so jolly and jovial, and has such a twinkle in its cunning eye, that nobody can believe that its heart is as cold and calculating as ever. (*Creed or Chaos?* 75)

These words, written in the war year of 1941, are if anything truer today than they were fifty years ago, when such delights as the junk bond business were as yet undreamed.

A master of the provocative title, DLS knew very well that there was not one reader in a thousand who would misunderstand the meaning of her title "The Other Six Deadly Sins"; neither would it be misunderstood that, in the terms "sinner" or "immoral," the transgression being alluded to is almost always a sexual one. But as the essay insists, there are worse sins than Lust, sins that are held in such high regard as to be effectively institutionalized in so-called advanced cultures. Of these cold, pinched, and hardhearted sins, none has a higher place in modern Western culture than avarice and envy.

It is a beguiling if dangerous game to attempt to judge the sinfulness of others and the corruption of the world at large. The most difficult and necessary task for a moral creature is to look into his or her own heart and try to perceive what lurks there. For this reason, the most compelling and courageous aspect of *Murder Must Advertise* is its implicit criticism of Sayers's own work in advertising, the industry which fuels the pyre of materialism. The book accomplishes this by giving Lord Peter the only "honest" job of his life: one curious result of our materialism is that we call a job "honest" or "real" if we are paid for it, no matter how dishonest we may be in the job's execution, or how unreal its results. In the course of the novel, we watch Wimsey working at the advertising game, a game that becomes so interesting to him that he almost forgets his real job, which is the investigation of a death. In Wimsey's debasement, DLS criticizes the facile and the fake, and reveals the ease with which any one of us may be seduced by our own wits.

While working as a copywriter, Wimsey becomes so enamored of the Whifflets campaign that Parker taunts him with the accusation that he is "developing a kind of business morality." Wimsey responds petulantly: "Dash it all, Charles! You don't understand. It's a really big scheme. It'll be the biggest advertising stunt since the Mustard Club." And of course that's exactly the point. DLS herself was present at the creation of "The Mustard Club," a stunt that has been called "the campaign of the century."[19] Wimsey's excitement reveals the strong appeal of such whiffling activity to a literate, witty, and highly verbal creature like himself—or his creator. Playing with language is fun, and yet this is not simply a game. Real people squander real resources on the trash that is marketed by the clever advertiser: "A society in which consumption has to be artifically stimulated in order to keep production going is a society founded on trash and waste, and such a society is a house built upon sand" (*Creed or Chaos?* 47). Sham work creates sham works, and both corrupt the human beings touched by them. As DLS would say about the deadly sin of Acedie, or Sloth: "it is one of the favourite tricks of this Sin to dissemble itself under cover of a whiffling activity of body" (*Creed or Chaos?* 84). Thus, much of the business and busy-ness of the modern world, a world of consumerism and manufactured needs, actually obscures the fact that little genuine activity is going on, and that the edifice being erected is hollow indeed.

The social criticism in *Murder Must Advertise* may be regarded as Sayers's attempt to come to terms with the work she had done in the twenties to keep body and soul together. In the tragic character of Tallboy, an essentially decent chap who is crushed by the system he helps perpetuate, she acknowledges that such work can be as deadly to those who practice it as it is to those who are unwittingly manipulated by it. Wimsey is brought back to reality at the end of the novel, when he sees his own handiwork on the side of a bus: "He contemplated his work with a kind of amazement. With a few idle words on a sheet of paper he had touched the lives of millions" (ch. 21). What writer, however humble, has not been so startled by the results of his work, its extension in time and space beyond anything dreamed of? This image reveals Sayers's growing recognition of the awful power of the word, a recognition that would be sharpened as she watched the rise of the Third Reich. Eventually, in *The Mind of the Maker,* she would deal with the full theological and moral implications of this power, as she explored the meaning of human activity.[20]

Murder Must Advertise is not Sayers's most effective fiction, largely because its thematic material is presented in what are almost mini-essays within the text, rather than emanating from dramatized situations. Indeed, most of the ideas in this novel were later stated explicitly in essays of trenchant social criticism. Yet the office scenes remain vivid and the novel's indictment of modern vapidity, commercialism, and greed are still fresh. The book also reminds us that Sayers's ideas on work were not abstractions born in the study, but the fruit of experience.

Murder Must Advertise was written while she was finishing *The Nine Tailors,* a novel that directly confronts the problem of judgment and looks to a reality outside of human beings for answers. If the advertising story reflects her experiences of a decade earlier, the fenland mystery harks all the way back to her childhood. In its setting, theme, and structure, the novel looks to the past, to the Scriptures, to the meaning of ritual and tradition for answers to present problems. In the unpublished novel, "Thrones, Dominations," Harriet Vane affirms joyfully that "we are what our past has made us" (Wade ms. 1). In *The Nine Tailors,* as in *Murder Must Advertise* and *Gaudy Night,* DLS tries to discover the meaning of her own past.

Since part 1 of the current study includes a comprehensive discussion of *The Nine Tailors,* suffice it to say here, in the context of Sayers's religious outlook, that it is of all her novels the one that is most clearly Christian, in its setting, theme, imagery, even time sequence, which follows the church calendar. The fact that the novel's setting is an ancient church is only one facet of its religious nature. Even more important is the novel's working out a distinctively Christian theme, in which good is seen as paradoxically related to evil, and human suffering is imbued with redemptive meaning. In the course of his investigation, Peter Wimsey learns more from his own pain than his reason could ever teach him. Since he is almost killed in the process of solving the mystery, his mortality is brought home very clearly to him; as he solves the mystery by almost dying in the way Deacon died, the distinction between pursuer and pursued, and between crime and punishment, also becomes richly ambiguous.

Similarly, the bells at Fenchurch St. Paul, which are rung for both weddings and funerals, in celebration and in crisis, seem to stand ambiguously for both life and death, good and evil.[21] The whole question of good versus evil is in fact quite complicated in this novel, for if there is a villain in the book, he is the man who was killed, not the killer—and it is the sound of holy bells that kills him. His death was an accident, assisted unwittingly by Wimsey and permitted by Providence, but the world is better off without him. And yet, the irony deepens further, because the investigation of his death hurts some innocent people and presents Wimsey with another dilemma about the moral implications of his actions. Despite its maze of coincidences, the novel embodies the compounded ironies and ambiguous triumphs of real life: "Once you starts interferin' with things you got to go on. One thing leads to another. . . . Dig up one thing and you got to dig up another" ("The Slow Work"). So says the philosophical sluice-worker as he discusses the difficult task of trying to cope with nature in the fenland water control system. But the statements are equally true of any human action in a world where gain is always attended by loss and we often cannot tell our curses from our blessings. In its elegant elaboration of plot and rich accumulation of imagery and symbol, *The Nine Tailors* powerfully demonstrates the relevance of Christian doctrine to everyday life.

It is in this novel that we most clearly glimpse the Reverend Henry Sayers's daughter, catching a whiff of the ecclesiastical smell of the old church, watching the arranging of flowers for feast days, scurrying to and fro in the churchyard, itself the most obvious and implacable reminder that we are not here forever. In this story, DLS abandons the "gloom and gleam" of London and the temporal world for a return to the timeless center of childhood. She returns to find the church unchanged, inviolate—literally on higher ground—succoring a wandering and frail humanity. Like all rural places, there is a timelessness about Fenchurch St. Paul which suits the novel's theme of the mutability of human life within the timeless arc of eternity. History is preserved here, along with life. Here, the question of mortality, and the prospect of eternity, are more important than the mystery of one man's death. Lord Peter's offhand remark in the first scene, "Where there is a church, there is civilization," is more than a comment on the ancient buildings that dot the English landscape and suggest some settlement of people nearby. It is the most succinct statement of his creator's conception of Christianity as the foundation of Western civilization.

Preparing for the flood at the novel's end, the rector recalls the Great

War of 1914–18, because the church bells were used then to sound the alarm, and the scattered people in the countryside learned where to go in an emergency. He realizes that they will remember to do this when the bells are rung again to signify that the flood has hit, and interprets this knowledge as one more example of the possibility—even the necessity—of good coming out of evil in a fallen world. This is one of the real mysteries of life which remain insolvable by human means: "The first thing to do is to ring the alarm. They know what that means, thank God! They learnt it during the War. I never thought I should thank God for the War, but He moves in a mysterious way" ("The Waters Are Called Home"). As Europe began hurtling toward another war, Sayers would argue insistently that the Church, and the Creeds upon which it was based, offered the only hope for a survival worth the name.

Early in the story, Wimsey wonders if the men who built the beautiful old church believed: "Did the old boys who made that amazing roof believe? Or did they just make those wide wings and adoring hands for fun, because they liked the pattern? At any rate, they made them *look* as though they believed something, and that's where they have us beat" ("Lord Peter Is Taken from Lead").[22] DLS said that she purposely gave the mature Lord Peter "the rudiments of a religious outlook" (*Titles to Fame* 80), and we can see him acquiring such a dimension in this scene. It is interesting that he raises the question of belief in a stream-of-consciousness passage where he once again questions the morality of his own "interfering ways," his pursuit of the sins and secrets of others: "why should I, Peter Wimsey, busy myself with digging them up? I haven't got so very much to boast about myself, if it comes to that. . . ." In a way, he is repeating the questions of *The Documents in the Case,* asking about the possibility of belief, about what anyone can believe, and about what, in the absence of belief, can provide moral guidance for human action. Is there an unerring, eternal measure by which human beings are judged? Like Mr. Tredgold in *Unnatural Death,* Mr. Venables here encourages Lord Peter to go on with his work and leave the consequences to God, because only He has "all the facts" in the great case of life ("The Quick Work").

When Wimsey asks if the men who built the church believed, he is pointing to the necessity of something outside the work to give it meaning. The questioning by Wimsey, as well as the insistent references to the bells, to time, death, and eternal judgment, imply that the final explanation of the mystery of human life resides absolutely elsewhere. If the detective novelist is, as DLS once claimed, "a *momento mori* in the high Roman fashion" ("Detection Club Speech"), it is hard to imagine a book that better typifies this function than *The Nine Tailors.*

In retrospect, DLS judged that her hero was too far removed from the spiritual conflicts set up in *The Nine Tailors* (*Titles to Fame* 77), but she was to rectify this in her last two novels. One may regard Lord Peter's fenland adventure as preparation for the supreme tests he would face in the final episodes of the Wimsey saga. Without his trials in the tower at Fenchurch St. Paul, and the development of his newly humanized persona, Peter Wimsey would not have been ready to face the greatest mystery of his life, the enigma that engaged his entire being and shook his personality to its very foundations—the mystery of human love.

The theme of *The Nine Tailors,* which is the necessity of forging good from evil in an imperfect world, also informs the Vane-Wimsey quartet, but in these books, the idea is made powerfully personal. Wimsey hints at this idea in what seem to be purely aesthetic and psychological terms in *Gaudy Night,* when he tells Harriet to use her mistakes to make a good book (ch. 15). But it is in *Busman's Honeymoon* that his new wife best articulates this theme, with the simple assertion that something good can be redeemed from life, even though it often seems that "everything [is] wrong and wretched." She has always believed this to be possible, she says, that "things . . . [would] come straight . . . if one hung on long enough, waiting for a miracle," but now her experience verifies it ("Epithalamion" 3; ch. 14). In this expression of eternal hopefulness, Harriet signals an openness to redemption: "You *will* see signs and wonders. But you won't believe because you have seen wonders; you will see the wonders because you have believed" (*The Man Born to Be King* 70).

On the day of Crutchley's execution, Harriet must answer Peter's familiar fear that he has meddled too far, played with human lives too much, in sending another man to the gallows. When he realizes that the condemned is totally unrepentant, Wimsey asks the old question: "If there *is* a God or a judgment—what next? What have we done?" ("Epithalamion" 3). The detective thereby acknowledges a terrifying responsibility, but as Harriet reminds him, there is no unalloyed good (or evil) in human life. She offers the most persuasive argument for this idea: if he had not "meddled" a few years earlier, they never would have met, she would have died for a crime she did not commit, and they would never have had this chance for happiness. They are happy, not in spite of the past, but because of it, and happier still than they could have been without past failures and mistakes. Harriet had implied as much in the final chapter of *Gaudy Night,* when she said that, although she could never forget the "unhappy interval" of her recent past, she "could be glad to remember it."

These novels thus implicitly endorse the idea of the Fortunate Fall, the *felix culpa,*[23] to which Peter laughingly alludes when Harriet admits she has tempted him to stray from his job (ch. 17). The Miltonic overtones of this reference, along with Wimsey's earlier allusion to Paradise Lost (ch. 4), remind us that Sayers planned to call the next (and unfinished) Wimsey novel "Thrones, Dominations," after a phrase from Milton's great epic of heaven and hell.[24] At the end of *Busman's Honeymoon,* her lovers seem as vulnerable as Adam and Eve at the end of *Paradise Lost,* when they leave the Garden and face the frightening world east of Eden.

This moving last scene begins with Harriet keeping a vigil in the old house, waiting for her tormented husband to return from his last appointment with the condemned man: "When everything else has perished, love and duty still keep watch . . ."(*The Man Born to Be King* 303). At the end of this dark night, a night in which it seems "there is no answer—no light— no vision: only the dark agony of the mortal flesh" (*Man Born* 246), the dawn begins to break on a new day, imaging the promise of resurrection and new life—of the "dying into life" that is the Christian affirmation (*The Just Vengeance* 75). Like all mortals, Harriet and Peter "have to be shown that 'resurrection and life' mean, not escape *from* death, but the passing through death to life" (*Man Born* 174). As the dawn glimmers its first rays, we are told that through the lovers' anguished minds "there broke uncontrollably the assurance that was like the distant note of a trumpet." They have come full circle from the high-spirited beginning of their wedding journey, when it seemed they were ready to cross Jordan River, albeit prematurely (ch. 3). Yet the assurance, the promise remains. This climactic scene of the Wimsey saga, where the paradisal vision beckons just beyond the horizon, adumbrates the revelation expressed in this litany of paradoxes from *The Just Vengeance:*

> come, receive again
> All your desires, but better than your dreams,
> All your lost loves, but lovelier than you knew,
> All your fond hopes, but higher than your hearts
> Could dare to frame them; . . .
>
> Instead of your justice, you shall have charity;
> Instead of your happiness you shall have joy;
> Instead of your peace the emulous exchange
> Of love; and I will give you the morning star. (79)

Some of Sayers's most effective poetry is in this 1946 play, which shows the influence of T. S. Eliot, in both style and content, as well as of Dante and Charles Williams. *The Just Vengeance* should be in print, if for no other reason than that the writer herself considered it her best work.[25] It is also a crystallization of many religious ideas implied in her fiction.

Harriet and Peter have come so far largely because they have learned to admit their human limitations and need for one another. This was especially hard for Harriet, whose actions in *Strong Poison* and *Have His Carcase* seemed to scream, "I am past relying on anybody," as Sayers's Judas says on his hellbent road to destruction (*Man Born* 222). Lionel Basney has compared the change in Harriet to Dante's portrayal of the "thawing of a hard heart," and I would agree about the parallel as long as we remember that DLS charted this romance long before she "discovered" *The Divine Comedy*.[26] At the beginning of the Vane-Wimsey quartet, Harriet indeed suffers from what *The Just Vengeance* calls in Dantean terms "the frozen charity" (49) that locks so many hearts against the world. That no one is self-sufficient is, in fact, an important implication of these four novels, an everyday reflection of Sayers's belief in the insufficiency of human beings without God's redeeming grace. What is important about these parallels with Dante is that they suggest the affinity between Sayers's mind and that of the great Christian poet and help explain why she eventually became so absorbed in his work.

How does the Wimsey-Vane relationship differ from the many flawed marriages and aborted romances in Sayers's earlier fiction? The key difference is in the respect that each of these lovers has for the other's person. They learn, by a process of defeating the egocentric will, to care really about another human being in that person's distinctly individual character. (As discussed in part 2 of this book, the Muntings from *The Documents in the Case* are prototypes for this kind of humane relationship in Sayers's fiction.) In *Gaudy Night,* Harriet realizes that she has rejected Peter Wimsey without even finding out who he is; because she is so terrified of losing herself, she is blinded both to others and herself. Once she opens her eyes and begins really looking at the other person, however, she not only becomes capable of "thinking more about another person than about herself" (ch. 18), but is also paradoxically freed from the prison of her own mind. This is not to say that, à la Margaret Harrison, Harriet wants to lose herself in Wimsey. It is more that she finds herself by respecting the individuality, the sanctity, of the other person. As *The Just Vengeance* affirms, "the one is the important figure" (15). The Christian concept of duty to oneself and one's God results in a concomitant respect for the personhood of others.

At the end of *Gaudy Night,* when Peter asks Harriet to forgive him for five years of willfully pursuing her with too little attention to her self and her needs, she counters by asking his forgiveness, for she too has willfully misunderstood much. As they acknowledge in *Busman's Honeymoon,* they both must kill their pride and admit their mistakes in order to be together.[27] Finally, "by an exercise on both sides of a strict intellectual integrity" (*The Mind of the Maker* 190), and not a little courage, Harriet and Peter are given the chance to practice "love's strong arts"[28] of patience, humility, and compassion. In so doing, of course, they are putting into action those Christian virtues which make love possible. The contrast between the Wimseys and other lovers in Sayers's fiction shows that it is not loving too much that wreaks havoc, but loving too little, or mistaking possessiveness and sentimentality for love (*The Mind of the Maker* 137).

Wimsey learns that what he once wanted "imperiously" can be had only if the beloved chooses freely to give. Newly married, he reflects on the revolutionary change love has wrought in him: "what was new was the enormous importance of the whole relationship. . . . He had become vulnerable in the very point where always, until now, he had been most triumphantly sure of himself" (ch. 14). His vanity makes him want everything to be perfect for his bride, but this is not to be: envy, violence, and death lurk in the garden, forever challenging the powers of love. Harriet also realizes that "this business of adjusting oneself [to another] was not so easy after all," and an even harder lesson emerges: "Being preposterously fond of a person didn't prevent one from hurting him unintentionally" (ch. 7). This novel powerfully dramatizes, time and again, how often love fails, and how much harm even good people, who are really trying, can do in a fallen world, a world where "We try to do right / And someone is hurt— very likely the wrong person; / And if we do wrong, or even if we do nothing, / It comes to the same in the end. . ." (*The Just Vengeance* 17). A succinct statement of human imperfection, this is strong meat indeed.

And yet the Wimseys make a valiant start at a successful, nonpossessive relationship. The kind of rigorous self-scrutiny we are used to seeing in Peter causes Harriet to back away from her own desire to dominate. As her bridegroom says, "We can't possess one another. We can only give and hazard all we have—Shakespeare, as Kirk would say. . . . I don't know what's the matter with me tonight. Something seems to have got off the chain" (ch. 18). What's "off the chain" is the old self, the egocentric will. This transformation of the self transforms the world. Across the barriers of class and circumstance, Harriet is able to feel real sympathy for the pathetic Aggie Twitterton, while the once-imperious Wimsey empathizes with a lovesick tomcat crying out for his mate. Reconsidering his impulse to drive the cat away, the new-wedded lord voices a mellow acceptance of the world and his place in it: " 'Who am I,' said he aloud, 'to cast stones at my fellow mortals?' " (ch. 18). A man at peace with himself at last, he avers without regret, "I have my softer moments—and my share of human folly" (ch. 10).

When the tension of this busman's holiday causes Peter to have his "old responsibility dream" of war and death, he is visited by images from Eliot's "The Hollow Men," appropriate here because that 1925 poem portrays the bleak emptiness of the postwar world as Wimsey had experienced it. Yet now, when his new wife touches him, the nightmare does not end, but changes into "something about rain and a bunch of chrysanthemums . . ." (ch. 19). Thus do the redemptive powers of love bring life back into the dead land, a land that now offers up the sharply scented flower which blazes into glory only after summer's short lease has ended.[29]

Busman's Honeymoon is not really about "the end of the journey and the beginning of all delight" (ch. 3), much as the besotted bridegroom had wished it to be, but a record of those "interminable ages of emotion" (ch. 17) through which the lovers must pass on their worldly pilgrimage. The story begins where many traditional novels end, with a marriage feast, and follows the tortuous and unending process of love's redeeming fire. This process is dramatized principally in three tableaux of embrace: the first, in the chapter entitled "Jordan River," shows the lovers in the ecstatic bliss of first union. The second appears in "Crown Matrimonial," where the false triumph of possession almost breaks the bond. In the final scene, which is the climax not only of a chapter entitled "Crown Celestial" but of the whole novel, the love has been tempered by adversity into compassion and a transcendent joy that makes even the giddy happiness of the wedding night pale by comparison. Cradled in his wife's arms, Wimsey is able to cry for the man he has helped condemn. As he gives up the last vestiges of his hope for controlling the world of experience, we see real triumph issuing from real surrender: "This is what we have always feared—/ The moment of surrender, the helpless moment / When there is nothing to do but to let go . . ." (*The Just Vengeance* 76; cf. "The Triumph of Easter").

This scene also dramatizes the tough Christian virtue of loving others as they are, in all their humanity and brokenness. This glimpse of the eternal comes in the form it most often takes on earth—in the embrace of a loving heart, the touch of a human hand. As the Recorder puts it in *The Just Vengeance,* those who would know eternal happiness are those

> whose eyes are not shut fast
> Against redemption, drawn to the moment of glory
> By that god-bearing image, whatever it was,
> That carried the glory for them; some, most happy,
> Leaping directly to the unveiled presence
> Of Him that is Himself both image and glory;

Some indirectly—this in a woman's eyes,
that in a friend's hand or a poet' voice
Knowing the eternal moment. . . . (23)

DLS intends us to see the Wimsey marriage in reference to the eternal, for she has Harriet give Peter the perfect wedding gift: a manuscript by Donne on the relationship between human and divine love. The gift is perfect because it is what Peter had wanted to give her, a fact which suggests not only a "marriage of true minds," but also the reciprocity of genuine love.

There are portraits of bad marriages aplenty in fiction, some of the most biting in Sayers's own work, and many novelists chart the course of romance. But I know of no book that better dramatizes the delicate balancing act of a good marriage, that is, a marriage that engages its partners passionately, intellectually, and morally, a marriage that can, and must, be made good every day. This is the life-affirming attitude that shines throughout Sayers's fictional creation, crowned by the story of a love that transformed the world for the lovers. Again, is it surprising that, of all great writers, she came to love Dante best?

Although the novel implies the Christian message of losing oneself in order to find oneself, it is important to note that the Wimseys do not see their love as self-sacrifice. This is not a contradiction but another paradox, because "to feel sacrifice consciously as self-sacrifice argues a failure in love. . . . When the job [or act] is a labor of love, the sacrifices will present themselves . . . in the guise of enjoyment" (*The Mind of the Maker* 134). How different this is from the demeaning attachment of Aggie Twitterton to the murderous Crutchley, a doomed relationship that presents a stark contrast to the Wimsey marriage.[30]

Wimsey is not a believer, but he continually asks what are essentially religious questions about himself and the universe. He also lives out the Christian ethic. This does not make him a Christian, but as Lionel Basney has written of Wimsey, the "lessons he learns are the Christian ones of guilt, self-surrender, and redemption by love" ("God and Peter Wimsey" 27–28). I would add that he also learns something about the value of suffering, patience, and endurance. By the end of *Busman's Honeymoon,* the vain superman has come to resemble the "Man of sorrows, acquainted with grief" (*The Man Born to Be King* 65). Once the agent of justice alone, Wimsey now represents mercy, compassion, and forgiveness as well.

Busman's Honeymoon is a love story for adults, not just because its lovers are too experienced to fight children's games (ch. 10), but because it holds out the eternal promise of another chance at life, while giving uncompromising scrutiny to how we make our own hell, or heaven. *The Nine Tailors* has an austere beauty and its symphonic elaboration of theme is fascinating, but to my mind, of all Sayers's novels, *Busman's Honeymoon* presents the Christian view of human experience in the most poignantly human terms. One may separate oneself from the great detective in the tower at Fenchurch St. Paul, but who among us cannot recognize our failures and desires in the adventures of these two very human creatures?

This story was initially written, with Muriel St. Clare Byrne, for the stage, and in the novel's dedication, DLS says that it adds "but outward limbs and flourishes" to the play. But the novel is much more than that. What has been added is the deep moral and psychological complexity in its study of this elemental human relationship. In its sensitive examination of our treatment of those closest to us, the novel implies a search for the standard by which all conduct is judged. Sayers did not know it at the time, but this was to be her last finished novel—and the play upon which it was based represents the bridge to her new life as a dramatist.

Regardless of her characters' beliefs or lack thereof, Dorothy L. Sayers accepted the Christian explanation of human nature and the universe. These are her assumptions, the attitudes that are so much a part of her way of looking at the world that they inform everything she wrote. A sincere and coherent personality, nothing could keep her created world from reflecting what she regarded as the inalterable laws of reality. As she asserts in *The Mind of the Maker,* "There is a universal moral law, as distinct from a moral code, which consists of certain statements of fact about the nature of man" (9). She goes on to explain that human beings are most free, most in tune with their own natures, when they live in societies where the moral code, established by man, reflects the natural law. For that law will out, no matter what we believe or try to dictate: "If . . . Christian opinion turns out to be right about the facts of human nature, then . . . dissenting societies are exposing themselves to that judgment of catastrophe which awaits those who defy the natural law" (11). To take just one pertinent example, if the Judeo-Christian commandment against murder is based upon the natural law, then murderers, and all societies condoning murder and violence, will be visited with the judgment of catastrophe, an assertion that is certainly borne out in detective fiction. Believe or not as you will, DLS seems to say; your belief will have not one ounce of influence on the intractable nature of reality. And, to the extent that the novelist presents a realistic world, the world of the story must follow the laws of the reality that it mirrors.

With the glaring exception of the hack, it is not possible for a writer to hide what he or she believes: "Insincerity issues in false art" (*The Mind of the Maker* 91). Even though Sayers was not writing about patently religious subjects or settings in most of her fiction, she was a Christian and her created universe was imbued with the elements of her faith: "As we *are,* so we *make"* (*Creed or Chaos?* 63). In her novels, Christian morality is chiefly implied by the use of negative images: envy, hatred, greed, anger, and lust in the place of love; pride instead of humility; destruction instead of creation; the will to death in constant battle with the will to life. This is aesthetically right, not only because wickedness tends to be more interesting than goodness, but because it is more prevalent in the world the novels mirror.

Yet Sayers did not succumb to the fashionable cynicism of the twentieth century. She once noted wryly that many "modern writers . . . indulge in edifying miracles though they generally prefer to use them to procure unhappy endings, by which piece of thaumaturgy they win the title of realists" (*The Mind of the Maker* 81). But every story does not end unhappily, even in real life, and some human activity does issue in creation. Dorothy L. Sayers saw virtue as not just a possibility, but an imperative, and her most sympathetic characters are those who strive after virtue, with varying degrees of self-awareness and success. Like Harriet Vane, she saw life as basically good, if only we can make something out of the difficulties offered to us. In her novels, Dorothy L. Sayers made a shining world.

12

A Crisis in Christendom
and *The Man Born to Be King*

Shortly after completing the stage version of *Busman's Honeymoon,*
DLS was invited to write a play for the Canterbury Festival. Charles Williams suggested her for this commission (Brabazon 160), perhaps because
of his admiration for *The Nine Tailors.*[1] His own *Thomas Cranmer of Canterbury* had been the play for 1936, following T. S. Eliot's *Murder in the
Cathedral,* which had in 1935 inaugurated a series of new plays commissioned by the Friends of the Cathedral. The Canterbury Festival was one of
the most important factors in the revitalization of religious drama in modern England, and Sayers's participation in it began her career as a religious
playwright.

Since it would also be Williams's *The Figure of Beatrice* (1943) which
would inspire her interest in Dante, we might say that, of her contemporaries, this brilliant if eccentric man had the most definitive influence on the
pattern of her later work. Although their styles and temperaments could
not have been more different in most ways, Sayers and Williams were both
scholarly but essentially nonacademic writers of amazing versatility and
originality. Williams's friendship was of great importance to her, even
though they seem to have communicated mainly through letters. Their correspondence was so important to her early work on Dante that, as Barbara
Reynolds has shown, DLS was even tempted to abandon her translation of
the *Commedia* after Williams's death.[2]

Sayers did not initially like the idea of doing a play for the festival, but
agreed when she realized that it could be about the Cathedral's twelfth-century architect, Williams of Sens.[3] She immediately saw in his story a
possibility to explore again an idea that had emerged as the theme of *Gaudy*

Night: the moral implications of work. In the play, entitled *The Zeal of Thy House,* this idea is stated in patently religious terms.

The play dramatizes the architect's literal and figurative fall from grace, a fall that forces him to reassess his attitudes toward work, himself, and God. After a disabling injury in a fall from the scaffolding, William admits that he has made the error of thinking himself and his work equal to God, the sin of pride. In the excited flurry of creation, he had proclaimed: "Man stands equal with Him now, / Partner and rival. . . . / This church is mine / And none but I, not even God, can build it" (70). Echoing the fault of Sayers's earliest villain and reconsidering the theme of *Gaudy Night,* the play represents the thematic bridge between her novels and later work, a fact she recognized in retrospect (*The Mind of the Maker* 207). It also demonstrates her growing recognition that work, however glorious, is not an end in itself. As Laurence Irving says in the play's preface:

> Miss Sayers chooses William of Sens to be the vehicle for her theme of the artist who in the supreme moment of mastery over his craft may be thrown down and destroyed by a consuming and wasting infirmity. . . . Though few may have fallen physically as far and as hard as William, many have fallen away artistically and have perished without the revelation which was granted to him. (6–7)

Perhaps we may regard this play, then, as one way for its author—who had reached the mastery of her craft in *Gaudy Night*—to reconsider the meaning of success, even to stave off the possibility of artistic death and a resulting death of the spirit.

One of the ways artists stay alive is by testing themselves and attempting new things. The Canterbury commission was appealing to DLS partially because it offered the opportunity to develop skills in what was to her a new form. As she later told Joy Lewis, she felt that she had done all she could with the Wimsey novels (C. S. Lewis, "Panegyric" 95). In the late 1930s and early 1940s, Sayers was essentially casting about for a new direction, and the theater was an appealing prospect. Its appeal is not hard to understand. The writer herself said that she found in the theater that sense of community and selfless giving which is often sadly lacking in the institutional church (*Malvern* 59). After years as a novelist, an essentially solitary occupation, the prospect of doing one's work and having human companionship at the same time may have seemed a welcome relief. As we have seen, Dorothy L. Sayers was also a dramatic personality, one who always enjoyed playing a role for an appreciative audience. Perhaps working in the theater was an inevitability for her.

Yet it is not surprising that she was hesitant to write what would be her first Canterbury play. (She would do another, *The Devil to Pay,* in 1939.) As early as 1931, she had been approached by the BBC to do broadcasts on religious topics. She had declined, saying frankly that she considered religion a demanding topic, unless one were willing to risk slipping into heresy or saying something one did not really mean, neither of which appealed to her. She would eventually take to the airwaves on religious topics, but only after much encouragement and never comfortably.[4] Her early poetry had shown that she was capable of dealing directly with religious subjects, but she was throughout her life uncomfortable with the notion of becoming a personal spokesman or apologist for Christianity. I believe this is what she meant when she sometimes impatiently reminded her audience that she had nothing to offer them but the creeds: she was willing to explain Christian dogma, but feared that the subject might be affected by the cult of personality, a reasonable concern when one considers the damage that can be done by cultists and emotional manipulators.

In her 1954 letter to John Wren-Lewis, the writer described her own uncertain transformation from popular novelist to religious dramatist:

> One day, I was asked to write a play for Canterbury about William of Sens. I had just done one play [*Busman's Honeymoon*] and wanted to do another . . . and I liked the story . . . so I wrote the thing and enjoyed doing it. I never, so help me God, wanted to get entangled in religious apologetic, or to bear witness for Christ, or to proclaim my faith to the world, or anything of that kind. . . .

She goes on to explain that she even wrote one of her pivotal religious essays, "The Greatest Drama Ever Staged," for *The Sunday Times* (April 3, 1938) as part of the publicity campaign for the London production of *Zeal.* (We may recall a similar scheme relevant to the publication of *Catholic Tales and Christian Songs,* some twenty years earlier.) She then describes, with some relish, the ensuing furor: "That did it. Apparently the spectacle of a middle-aged female detective-novelist admitting publicly that the judicial murder of God might compete in interest with the corpse in the coal hole was the sensation for which the Christian world was waiting" (Brabazon 165–66). It is interesting to note in this passage not only the characteristic verbal energy and earthiness, but also the writer's ability to make a fairly good assessment of herself as others might have seen her. The statement represents a practical recognition that her status as a popular mystery writer actually made people more interested in her "serious" writing than they would have been otherwise.

The time was propitious in Sayers's life and career for a change, but there was trouble brewing in the world, which also encouraged in her a new willingness to speak out on religious questions. She was certainly not alone; serious-minded believers and nonbelievers alike responded to the growing crisis in world affairs by becoming more manifestly concerned with social and political issues. It is clear from references scattered throughout Sayers's writing during the late 1930s and early 1940s that she was convinced Christians had a special responsibility to respond to the violent currents in the world situation. In January 1939, she called her Presidential Address to the Modern Language Association of Great Britain "The Dictatorship of Words," and raised the pertinent question: "What are we doing, juggling with words at such a time?" (Wade ms. 1). The use of the first-person pronoun suggests that this question goes much deeper than assaulting those, like Hitler, who were abusing language for propaganda, and implicates all who use and misuse the word—an indictment seen in her work as early as Wimsey's participation in the Whifflets campaign of *Murder Must Advertise.*

Since she was speaking to a group of scholars and teachers, another target was the poor educational system responsible for turning out people who were only technically literate, a subject she would pursue further in "The Lost Tools of Learning," published in *The Poetry of Search.* In fact, one of her more astute points in the MLA address is that people who are marginally literate can be manipulated more easily than their illiterate forebearers ever could have been ("Dictatorship of Words" 3). This idea also informs a 1942 lecture entitled "Creative Mind," which laments the fact that few people can "understand and handle language as an instrument of power" and suggests this as the reason for the success of demagogues (*Unpopular Opinions* 57). If some had been naive about the power of language before, the war in Europe demonstrated with a vengeance the "ruthless force" of the word (*Unpopular Opinions* 57).

After England was in the war, DLS would tell fans who wanted to know when they would see another Wimsey novel that, with so much real bloodshed in the world, she thought better of writing murder mysteries (DLS to P. M. Stone, 6 Jan. 1944; cf. "Wimsey Papers" 6). Although, as we have seen, this was hardly the whole reason—if the "whole" reason could ever be determined—for her virtual abandonment of detective fiction, it would be a mistake to conclude that it had nothing to do with the conflagration that came to be known as the Second World War. That war understandably made her more concerned than ever about the moral implications of being a word-juggler, and more reflective about what form her writing should take.

Her youth had been shaped by the Great War that was fought to end war,

221

and she had watched the uneasy peace that followed disintegrating into another bloodbath. The fact that the seeds of the coming conflict had been sown by the peacemakers at Versailles was, for Dorothy L. Sayers, only further evidence of the Christian doctrine of fallen human nature. As she often said, Christians actually have an advantage in times of crisis, because they, of all people, should not be surprised when things go awry ("Making Sense of the Universe" 5). And yet, did these nominal modern Christians really know what they believed? The 1940 essay entitled "What Do We Believe?" states Sayers's position succinctly: "In ordinary times we get along surprisingly well, on the whole, without ever discovering what our faith really is." But in wartime such a cavalier attitude is a luxury, because when we are "cut off from mental distractions by restrictions and black-outs, and cowering in a cellar with a gas-mask under threat of imminent death, comes in the stronger fear and sits down beside us" (*Unpopular Opinions* 17). This vivid image of living in England under siege makes it clear why she was driven at this time to speak out on religious and social issues, and why her approach was to go back to the creeds: how could Christianity play a role in remaking Europe, if Christendom itself did not know its heritage?

The urgency of the message was stated again and again in language calculated to stir the besieged to action. Even if many would not agree with her suggestions for change, few could deny her assertion that Western civilization was in trouble, that "something has gone wrong with the emphasis; and it is becoming very evident that until that emphasis is readjusted, the economic balance-sheet of the world will have to be written in blood."[5]

Because of her conviction that the emphasis in Western culture needed radical readjustment, DLS surfaced at the end of the thirties as a public interpreter of traditional Christianity. Her significance in this regard may be judged from her being invited by William Temple, then Archbishop of York and later Archbishop of Canterbury, to speak at a 1941 conference entitled "The Life of the Church and the Order of Society." Because of its venue, the meeting has come to be known as the Malvern Conference; fear of invasion had forced it to be postponed and then moved farther west in the country, suggesting a powerful image of the embattled situation of the modern church. The only woman on the program, DLS joined other important lay people, including T. S. Eliot, as well as church leaders like Bishop George Bell and Father Patrick McLaughlin, to consider the appropriate Christian response to the war and its aftermath.[6] Shortly after the conference, Father McLaughlin invited Sayers and Eliot to join him in a new outreach program at St. Anne's Soho, which was intended to appeal to skeptical intellectuals, or as James Brabazon has put it, to function "as a sort of mission centre for thinking pagans" (240). Presumably, there was no shortage of such persons in modern London.

The audience at Malvern that January day in 1941 must have been a bit surprised when DLS began her lecture on "The Church's Responsibility" with the statement that "it is always with some embarrassment that I approach any question about the Christian Church. When challenged, I am never quite sure how to identify it or whether, in anything but a technical sense, I feel myself to belong to it." This is the old discomfort, seen as early as her letters to the BBC, rejecting the opportunity to lecture on Christianity. It is also a way of dissociating herself from the official church, which she criticizes for having, on the whole, "very little reverence for intellectual integrity" and for too often identifying itself with secular institutions (*Malvern* 57, 74, 77). Curiously enough, however, it seems to have been this very discomfort that caused her to stay to a rational exposition of basic Christian teaching, a choice that, in turn, has made her theological work appealing and helpful to many different types of Christians through the years. In her Malvern lecture, Sayers recognized that the crisis in Western culture was so great that "we must do . . . the impossible, or perish" (78). In a sense, the impossible happened: without really intending to, Dorothy L. Sayers became a rational voice for Christianity in a world that already seemed to most people who thought seriously about it at all, post-Christian.

Although a shift of emphasis is evident in Sayers's work, it is important to remember that she did not abandon other kinds of writing. At the end of the 1930s, for example, she wrote the drawing room comedy, *Love All* (Brabazon 185), which has more in common with the play *Busman's Honeymoon* than it does with any of her religious plays and essays, or indeed, with her later novels. We can never know what route her career would have taken if the war had not closed the theaters at this point. Perhaps she would have continued writing, among other things, witty comedies of manners for the West End. The Wimsey novels certainly demonstrate her facility with repartee. She wrote a mystery play for radio as late as 1947,[7] and continued to revel in the solemn nonsense of the Detection Club. Before the war in Europe was over, however, she would become immersed in a verse translation of Dante's *Commedia,* a project so monumental that it would occupy most of her time for the rest of her life.

In late 1939, she resurrected Lord Peter for a series in *The Spectator* entitled the "Wimsey Papers."[8] Although originally intended for a longer run, the "Wimsey Papers" ended abruptly in January 1940. The papers that were published offer a fascinating insight into Sayers's motivations and concerns during this period. The series's subtitle, "being war-time letters and documents of the Wimsey family," makes her purpose clear, and every item responds in some fashion to the war. One is the transcript of a sermon on war by Mr. Venables; others indicate the war work of Miss Climpson, Lord Peter, and his sister-in-law, Helen, who is off pestering people at the Ministry of Instruction and Morale, much to the delight of her husband and mother-in-law. Even that lovable old hedonist, Paul Delagardie, is suggesting ways for England to cope with the crisis. It is delightful to find our old friends from the Wimsey saga carrying on so well, and these letters embody the wit and gift for characterization that make Sayers's novels memorable.

The most interesting thing about the "Wimsey Papers," however, emerges in the letters exchanged between Lord Peter and his wife. In one, Harriet writes to her husband, who is "somewhere abroad" on a delicate diplomatic mission:

> I've been trying to write an article about war-aims and peace-aims, though I'm not at all sure that all this definition doesn't end by darkening counsel. . . . We all know pretty well that something we value is threatened, but when we try to say what, we're left with a bunch of big words like justice, freedom, honour, truth and so on, that embarrass us, because they've been misused so often they sound like platform claptrap. (*The Spectator* 24 Nov. 1939)

This language is surprisingly similar to Frederic Henry's rejection of war as a noble cause in *A Farewell to Arms:*

> I was always embarrassed by the words sacred, glorious, and sacrifice and the expression in vain. We had heard them, sometimes standing in the rain almost out of earshot, so that only the shouted words came through . . . and I had seen nothing sacred, and the things that were glorious had no glory and the sacrifices were like the stockyards at Chicago if nothing was done with meat except to bury it. . . . Abstract words such as glory, honor, courage or hallow were obscene beside the concrete names of villages. . . . (177–78)

DLS does not, however, make "a separate peace." In the last letter of the series, Lord Peter urges his wife on, no matter how difficult the task may be:

> You are a writer—there is something you must tell the people, but it is difficult to express. You must find the words.
> Tell them, this is a battle of a new kind, and it is they who have to fight it. . . .
> You must rouse the people. You must make them understand that their salva-

tion is in themselves and in each separate man and woman among them. . . .
Somehow you must contrive to tell them this. It is the only thing that matters.
(*The Spectator* 26 Jan. 1940)

We have seen Harriet and Peter working out aesthetic problems before,
notably in *Gaudy Night,* where he presses her to make her detective stories
more realistic, regardless of the cost (ch. 15). Here we may regard their
letters as a dialogue on the question of how a writer should respond to a
world at war: "It is the only thing that matters."

One of the ways that DLS responded to such a world was an exploration
of the Christian roots of Western civilization. This was not only because
she felt the answers lay there, but because she hoped that "now that we have
seen the chaos of bloodshed which follows upon economic chaos, we might
at least be able to listen with more confidence to the voice of an untainted
and undivided Christendom" (*Unpopular Opinions* 11). She found that
voice in the basic creeds of the historic Christian church, and later, in the
poetry of Dante Alighieri. While she was writing the "Wimsey Papers," she
also composed, at the request of her publisher, Victor Gollancz, "a wartime essay" entitled *Begin Here.* Intended as a Christmas message to the
anxious nation, its position was uncompromising:

the principles to which we are now clinging amid the wreck of the philosophies
are the Christian principles of the Western-Mediterranean civilisation. . . . they
are rocking beneath us because we have knocked away the foundation of eternal
values on which they were built, and . . . unless we can find some eternal basis
on which to rest them, they will founder and our civilisation with them. (126)

Thus, she argued, England had to accept some responsibility for the situation in which it found itself. This was a theme to which she would return
again and again during the war. In a 1943 essay, "They Tried to Be Good,"
she made the case as directly as possible:

I am concerned only to interpret the riddle of the English during the decades of
disaster [those twenty-odd years separating the two great wars]. The answer is, I
think, that we wanted to be good and tried to be good, but that the sincerest
efforts after virtue produce only chaos if they are directed by a ramshackle and
incoherent philosophy. (*Unpopular Opinions* 105)

Yet the Christian creeds stood ready to offer a coherent philosophy, if only
people could learn once again what they really mean. On this assumption,
DLS undertook to explicate Christian teaching in a series of essays and

lectures, most of which were eventually published in *Unpopular Opinions* (1946) and *Creed or Chaos?* (1947). As the title of the second collection suggests, she saw the conflict in Western Europe as "a life-and-death struggle between Christian and pagan" (*Creed or Chaos?* 25), and she was ready to fight the good fight.

In the crisis-laden year of 1941, Dorothy L. Sayers completed her two best works with patently religious import, *The Man Born to Be King* and *The Mind of the Maker,* to help bring the message of Christianity anew to a war-torn world. It is surely no coincidence that these two works were written concurrently, nor that they were products of this particular time in history: "War, by dropping a metaphorical bomb into the structure of our lives, puts our foundations to a critical test, and offers an unequalled opportunity for finding out whether our house was built upon rock or upon sand" (*Begin Here* 20–21). DLS answered the challenge of going to the bedrock of Western culture.

Not only are both works based upon the historic Christian creeds, but the two also depend upon Sayers's earlier experience as a novelist and serve as powerful examples of the idea that one important role of the artist is to recast tradition. Her essential classicism is reflected in this attitude, which is expressed by Harriet Vane in the unpublished "Thrones, Dominations": there is so little real truth in the world, Harriet says, that it is unlikely that any writer will discover anything completely new.[9] This view had its most famous modern incarnation in T. S. Eliot's influential 1919 essay, "Tradition and the Individual Talent," and is reflected in his poetry as well. James Brabazon has noted that both *The Man Born to Be King* and *The Mind of the Maker* are also, in a sense, expansions of something DLS herself had written before, which is perhaps one of the reasons they are so effective, for "she was always at her best when she had plenty of elbow room" (191).

I am at something of a disadvantage for evaluating Sayers's plays because, with the exception of *The Man Born to Be King,* I have simply read them and cannot judge accurately what their dramatic value would be when produced in their original settings, or indeed, in other settings.[10] This may be one of the reasons I find her BBC play-cycle on the life of Christ to be the most powerful of her dramas. A close second is *The Just Vengeance,* which is, despite the author's preface, particularly well-suited to reading because of its poetic form and philosophical nature. Although its figurative form might suggest that *The Just Vengeance* would be difficult to dramatize, we know from firsthand reports of its production in June 1946 at Lichfield Cathedral, that the audience sat spellbound, in spite of the hard chairs on which they had to spend over two hours.[11] The *Times* reviewer actually thought the play's staging more effective than its text.[12] To say that

The Just Vengeance "reads" well is not tantamount to asserting that it would be weak theater, in any case. Some of the best modern drama— O'Neill's *Long Day's Journey into Night* is perhaps the most striking example—is quite powerful when read.

Unlike the Lichfield play, which seems to have been produced only once, *The Man Born to Be King* had a huge audience when it was first broadcast, and has enjoyed steady revivals ever since. The recordings of the plays' original broadcasts give an accurate impression of what that production was like, an indisputable advantage in judging the plays as drama.[13]

The history of this massive project has been detailed elsewhere, and readers interested in its somewhat difficult gestation should consult the Brabazon biography of DLS, as well as Kenneth M. Wolfe's *The Churches and the British Broadcasting Corporation* (1984).[14] As was the case for almost all of Sayers's religious writing, *The Man Born to Be King* was a commissioned work. It was a follow-up to her popular nativity play, *He That Should Come,* which had been broadcast on Christmas, 1938. She spent much of 1940 and 1941 researching, writing, and revising the mammoth play-cycle, which tells the story of Christ's life in twelve, one-act plays that were broadcast every four weeks, beginning in December of 1941 (*Man Born* 13). Like *He That Should Come,* the series was originally intended for the BBC Children's Hour. This proved a poor match, given Sayers's ambitious conception of the project and her fundamental disagreements with the Children's Hour staff. After much negotiation, the venue was changed to allow her to develop the plays as she saw fit. The BBC essentially gave in to many of her demands, because they were convinced that *The Man Born to Be King* was of such great importance they did not want to lose it. Their patience was well repaid when the project was completed. Dr. J. W. Welch, then Director of Religious Broadcasting at the BBC, had commissioned the plays because he "thought a dramatization of the life of Jesus would 'fulfill the obligation of the Corporation to the nation in this time.' " He later judged *The Man Born to Be King* to be "the most important event in religious broadcasting we [the BBC] have ever undertaken."[15] Archbishop Temple called it simply "one of the greatest contributions to the religious life of our time" (Wolfe 234).

It is difficult for us now to imagine the effect that the very idea of such a play must have had on English audiences a half-century ago. We can never duplicate the "theater" the play had, on that day in December 1941, when some two million embattled Britons gathered round their wireless sets to hear a twentieth-century version of the Christmas story.[16] Not only was DLS up against England's long-standing tradition of prohibiting stage representations of Christ, but she was risking offending any number of Christian and non-Christian sects at every turn.[17] There was, in fact, a huge public furor about the plays before they were broadcast, curiously similar to the protests that preceded the screenings of Martin Scorcese's film, *The Last Temptation of Christ,* in the U.S. during the summer of 1988. Since Sayers's plays were written for radio, there was actually no legal problem with their presenting Christ, but some excited citizens likened the effect of the plays' realism to accounts of the recent bombing of Pearl Harbor by the Japanese (Wolfe 226). The English did not identify totally with the Americans, however, as James Brabazon has noted concerning the charge that "U.S. slang" was going to be used in the first play:

> At that time . . . English insularity was putting up a stiff fight against importation of Americanisms, especially those emanating from Hollywood. This particular form of elitism was one which the press was safe in playing on, and the idea of the author of the first Gospel speaking American English was much more dreadful than speaking with any kind of regional accent. (203)

As one might expect, Sayers did not discourage this kind of pre-broadcast publicity. After all, the BBC's Welch had told her "not to spare the dynamite," as if she ever needed such encouragement (Wolfe 219). In spite of all the accusations and fears, many of which were voiced by people who had not seen the script and had no intention of listening to a play they had already condemned, the actual text of *The Man Born to Be King* stays firmly within orthodox teaching about Jesus of Nazareth. For this reason, the vast majority of Christians in the United Kingdom found the plays acceptable, a remarkable feat in itself (Brabazon 204; Wolfe 233). Unlike many other modern approaches to the subject, there is no equivocation about the play's attitude toward its hero. Its subtitle, "A Play-Cycle on the Life of Our Lord and Saviour Jesus Christ," leaves no room for doubt: the play is unambiguously reverent about the divinity of its main character.

Yet Sayers brought much that was fresh to her life of Christ, chiefly in her care to evoke the real world surrounding him during his life on Earth (cf. "Memoirs of Jesus Christ" in *Unpopular Opinions* 26–27). To some, her efforts in this direction may seem vulgar, and there are aspects of the play which do not travel well.[18] For example, some characters, including St. Matthew, speak Cockney dialect. This was perhaps suitable for the play's original audience, because an Englishman hearing this speech pattern immediately recognizes its social significance, even if its use in this context offends him. The use of dialect at least accomplished Sayers's goal of making the story relevant to the world of her listeners, although Americans may find it only an irritating oddity and inexplicable strategy.[19] But one must really question the subtle snobbery which implies that God may be spoken of only in Standard English.

Most readers will have less trouble with another strategy employed to bring the story of Christ home to moderns, a series of analogies the plays draw between the Roman and British Empires (*Man Born* 6). These analogies reveal much about the world inhabited by the historical Jesus, and underscore the point that he lived among real people in a real time and place. His situation was so much like ours, the plays imply, that his story must have something to say to us. Sayers is clearly looking at the gospels as a novelist would, and in fact defines her task as being a writer of "realistic Gospel plays" (*Man Born* 5). Although *The Man Born to Be King* obviously drew upon her recent experience as a dramatist, it also utilized all of her story-telling abilities and her novelistic experience in developing character, constructing coherent plots, and evoking a palpable world. Since Jesus of Nazareth is "the only God who has a date in history" (*Man Born* 5), it is proper that the story of his life should unfold in a richly detailed, time-bound world similar to that found in great realistic fiction, where the delineation of the mundane paradoxically allows us to glimpse something of timeless reality.

Again and again, DLS emphasizes in the play's notes that "this is a thing that actually happened" (1), a position which is both theologically orthodox and aesthetically effective. Her belief in the central drama of Christianity was indispensible for writing these plays, of course, but her ability to evoke "the human Jesus disfigured with blood and grief" (1) was largely the result of her talent, polished through many years of writing fiction, for particularity, or the telling detail. As Kenneth M. Wolfe has said, "she spoke, perhaps uniquely, as an exceptionally gifted storyteller . . . who was also a confident and intelligent believer in the Catholic faith" (235).

The novelist's touch is immediately apparent in the plays' vivid characterizations. When Judas mimics someone's stutter, for example, we grasp the meanness of his mind and spirit more quickly than his own speeches reveal these traits (64). The production notes for the wedding feast at Cana include a witty description of Rebecca that could have come straight out of a Sayers novel: "In every sense a busybody—the indispensable woman with whom everybody would be happy to dispense. A shrill and gabbling voice, an excellent heart, an inquisitive nose, and no tact at all" (77). And the humanity of Jesus comes through strongly in the same scene, when we hear, amidst the "clinking of crockery" (79), his mother excitedly preparing extra places at table for him and his friends, who are unexpectedly coming to the celebration (79–81). Somehow, the earthy reality of such scenes makes the later episodes more moving. Hearing that Jesus enjoyed a good dinner as much as any other man (83) or feeling the joy he brought daily to those around him makes his loss just that much more poignant.

There is, in fact, an almost unbearable tension in "The Road to Calvary" scene of the Eleventh Play, as the sound of the soldiers' whips and the crowd's jeers punctuate Mary's dread of seeing her son at last, bloodied and bearing the weight of the cross (289–94). She could be any mother, at any time, facing the loss of that which is most precious to her. Her lament echoes down through the centuries: "This is the worst thing; to conceive beauty in your heart and bring it forth into the world, and then to stand by helpless and watch it suffer . . . ." (288–89). Because Christian dogma tells us that Mary's son was not only human but divine, the story of his death is supremely shocking. It is the story of "the judicial murder of God," and this play looks unblinkingly at what that means:

> BARUCH:. . . . Going to Pilate, is he? That means the cross. Ever seen a man crucified? There's nothing poetical about it, and it hurts, Judas, it hurts. . . . Will you be eloquent from *that* pulpit of pain? Skewered up there in the broiling sun, like an owl on a barn door, with your joints cracking and your head on fire and your tongue like leather? (263)

At the foot of the cross, the Roman Glaucus, who is described as "educated, vain, heartless, and full of airs and affectations. A very intolerable young man," enjoys noting that "the god is dying." In an almost clinical description that would not be out of place in crime fiction, he observes that the crucified Jesus "has the marks [of death] upon him—the pinched nostrils and hollow face, sunken about the temples, and the skin dry and dusty like parchment. The countenance of death, as old Hippocrates taught" (302).

Sayers's scholarly habit of mind was an important influence on these plays, motivating her to undertake extensive research in preparation for writing them, and to go back to the Greek New Testament for her text. By avoiding the familiar language of the King James version, she was able to make fresh once again many ideas and images that had been dulled by repetition and to shock her audience into a new awareness of what is, after all, an "extremely disturbing story" (9). Her willingness to eschew the beautiful language of the Authorized Version, which she had heard all her life, shows how little she was bound to tradition for its own sake. Her traditionalism is often misunderstood as a kind of unthinking devotion to the past, but she was interested only in reclaiming and perpetuating whatever was living from the past. This is to say, she was interested in discovering timeless truth wherever it may be found.

In *Biblical Drama in England,* Murray Roston praises *The Man Born to Be King* in terms I believe Sayers herself would appreciate, concluding that "her use of realism succeeded, paradoxically, in reaffirming faith in the mystery. In other words, the assumption that realism and miracle were incompatible was . . . challenged" (297). One can see this not only in her depiction of character, but in her recasting of familiar Biblical passages into modern English. For example, consider how a well-worn parable is made more powerful by being restated in the speech of everyday life; the juxtaposition between what we expect and what we hear surprisingly makes Jesus, and his message, more compelling:

> JESUS: The Kingdom of God is like—what shall I say?—it's like a well-to-do merchant, living an easy, comfortable life. And then one day he sees a pearl so rich and beautiful that he feels he can't live without it. So he sells up everything he has, and buys that pearl for his own.
> JOHN EVANGELIST: My father's brother . . . was just like that. . . . Did you know my father's brother?
> JESUS: I know human nature. (67; see also pp. 92–93)

The style of these plays is closer to that of Sayers's novels and essays than it is to the rather stiffly poetical form used in *The Zeal of Thy House,* for example. This plainspoken, colloquial, witty style is undoubtedly one result of the plays' being originally conceived for broadcasting and for an audience composed mainly of children. From the beginning, DLS knew that she was writing *The Man Born to Be King* for a large popular audience, the same kind of audience she had in mind when she wrote fiction. The style appropriate to such an audience seems to have been the one most natural to her; it is, at any rate, the one in which she was most effective. When she wrote the introductions and notes to her translation of *The Divine Comedy,* she would once again employ this style in an unlikely place to powerful effect. For this reason, even those who do not favor her translation of the *Commedia* often enjoy the editorial matter that accompanies it, a rare compliment to a scholarly edition.

One of the main markers of this style is "the juxtaposition of the sublime and the commonplace," which she felt was especially well-suited to "the English language, with its wide, flexible, and double-tongued vocabulary" (*Man Born* 8–9). Thus, we hear a Sayersian John the Baptist proclaiming: "I see a worldly priesthood, a worldly ruler, a worldly people—a nation of shopkeepers and petty bureaucrats, their hearts fixed on cash and credit, and deaf and blind to righteousness" (57). Or Jesus himself, alternating

231

between an outburst like "Fellow, you're a thorough scoundrel . . . but I do admire your thoroughness!" and the more formal and controlled, "Worldly people, you see, use far more wisdom about their trifling affairs than unworldly people do about the affairs of God" (106). Such variation grabs and maintains our attention, as the playwright knew: "sometimes the blunt new word will impress us more than the beautiful and old" (9). It also effectively links the world of the play to the experience of its audience.

The determinedly realistic method, coupled with the choice of modern idiom, carries the plays' thematic weight well—and we should remember that *The Man Born to Be King* was written before the proliferation of modern versions of the Bible. The play's general introduction explains Sayers's purpose, which was to show that

> God was executed by people painfully like us, in a society very similar to our own—in the over-ripeness of the most splendid and sophisticated Empire the world has ever seen. . . . He was executed by a corrupt church, a timid politician, and a fickle proletariat led by professional agitators. His executioners made vulgar jokes about Him, called Him filthy names, taunted Him, smacked Him in the face, flogged Him with the cat, and hanged Him on the common gibbet—a bloody, dusty, sweaty, dirty business. (7)

The statement is similar to Wimsey's insistence that murder is ever a nasty business. To fully appreciate the effect of such a description, we should remember that the plays premiered during the Christmas season, when religious sentimentality is usually at its peak.

The story of that "particular point in history . . . [when] the Timeless irrupted into time" (8), this play-cycle is a product of what William V. Spanos has called "a sense of the contemporaneity of the past" (*The Christian Tradition in Modern British Verse Drama* 82), a sense which would also be fundamental to Sayers's understanding of Dante, following Charles Williams's lead (*The Divine Comedy* 1:9–10). Many of her comments in the plays' notes underscore the similarities between the first and the twentieth centuries: "We have seen something of Caiaphas lately," she remarks wryly about the man who was "the ecclesiastical politician, appointed, like one of Hitler's bishops, by a heathen government, expressly that he might collaborate with the New Order. . ." (7). Later, we are told that "Baruch sees Jesus as the Nazi party may have seen Hitler—the Heaven-sent spellbinder, rather mad but a valuable political tool in the right hands" (125). This authorial commentary on the plays' meaning is helpful to readers and producers of the text, but radio listeners must rely on dialogue to reveal these ideas. To make a modern audience identify with the situation faced by

Jesus two thousand years ago and force them to realize that such a thing *can* happen here, the playwright concludes that "the swiftest way to produce the desirable sense of shock is the use in drama of modern speech and a determined historical realism about the characters" (7). All of this is to enable her listeners to realize that "*We* played the parts in that tragedy"(8), the realization necessary for every Christian. Listening to the clamorous street scenes, with voices from virtually all strata of English society intermingled, one does experience such a sense of immediacy and richly evoked life. *The Man Born to Be King* is written in the fresh, invigorating modern idiom of Sayers's novels, and much of its power is the result of such language.

This play-cycle was, in part, a response to the time and events surrounding its composition, being conceived as a study in kingship during a period when the question of how to rule became critical (14). A wartime work, it looks to traditional Christianity for an explanation of human conflict, failure, and suffering, as well as for a definition of victory that transcends the here and now. In this, as in so much of her work around this time, DLS seems to be arguing that, since war is demonstrating the failure of what we have been trying to rely on, why not seize this opportunity to redefine our assumptions and goals?

She assumed that there was one "aspect of the story which was bound to loom large in the minds of both writer and audience at this moment, namely: its bearing upon the nature of earthly and spiritual kingdoms." In writing the plays, she found that "no force of any kind was needed to bring the story into a form that was sharply topical" (14). Her notes to the plays are peppered with references to a world in chaos: "There is a sense everywhere of disquiet and the breaking-up of old things" (99); "We're sitting on the edge of a volcano" (30); "The underlying note of this play is CRISIS" (225). Although these descriptions are redolent of the time in which the plays were written, they seem remarkably applicable to much of the time since the Second World War as well.

The Man Born to Be King does not imply that war is always avoidable or even that it is the greatest evil. It is chilling to hear Herod assert grimly, "I *will* have order in Judaea," or declare that his country shall have peace at any price (46, 47). In 1941, DLS was most likely thinking of the failed attempts to appease Hitler, but the modern world has seen many instances of the destruction such thinking leads to. The play exposes the whole modern temper to analysis: in the ennui of Herod Antipas—a man doomed to failure in a life he never understands—who sighs, "why does nothing ever happen of the slightest importance in this tedious and intolerable life?" (272), just before the execution of Jesus Christ; or the anxious doubt of

Pilate, who scoffs at the possibility of ever knowing what is right, and asks, "Truth? What is truth?" (270). Early on, one of the three wise men summarizes the modern predicament: "Alas! the more we know, the less we understand life. Doubts make us afraid to act, and much learning dries the heart" (39). In a slightly more modern idiom, this had been an important implication of *The Documents in the Case.*

Baruch's characterization of Rome as "a single benevolent despotism over the whole earth" invokes fearful and familiar images of totalitarian regimes of both the left and the right, and yet he admits that his nation is even more endangered by internal conflict. He predicts that such conflict will wear it down, "till we are disarmed one by one and corrupted away from within. The rot has gone far, Judas, the rot has gone far" (133). The statement evokes a familiar picture, as does the new version of the Sermon on the Mount, which describes much of the modern world: "Unhappy are the well-fed and self-satisfied! There is an emptiness in their souls that nothing can fill. Unhappy are the frivolous and mocking hearts! The time will come when they will mourn and weep and not know where to turn for comfort" (134). In his cynicism, Baruch applies the criticism of false prophets to Jesus. He could be describing many religious leaders today: "They start well—then they get a following, success goes to their heads, and before you know where you are the man who was too unworldly even to earn his own living is accepting presents from rich old ladies, setting up fashionable religious cults, and creeping up the back stairs into politics" (134).

In the plays' general introduction, which bears some similarities to Bernard Shaw's prefaces, DLS argues that "the dramatist must begin by ridding himself of all edificatory and theological intentions. He must set out, not to instruct but to show forth; not to point a moral but to tell a story. . . . As drama, these plays stand or fall" (3–4). In general, the plays do succeed as drama. They manage to make old stories newly interesting, even suspenseful. If conflict is the essence of drama, then the interplay between Judas and Christ, upon which the cycle focuses, is very effective, while the paradoxical nature of the God-Man is drama itself. *The Man Born to Be King* may be regarded as a product of Sayers's entire career to this point, with its emphasis on effective story-telling and upon the integrity of the work itself—apart from any social, religious, or political concerns.

Although one might expect the theological content of *The Man Born to Be King* to overpower its aesthetic qualities, Sayers found just the opposite to be true from her experience of writing the plays. "From the purely dramatic point of view the theology is enormously advantageous, because it locks the whole structure into a massive intellectual coherence" (3). This was the main point she was to argue again and again on the subject of Christianity: that it makes sense of the universe and is itself a rational system of great beauty, power, and internal coherence. In the introduction to *The Man Born to Be King,* she suggests that, while all drama is religious in origin (2), writers in the Christian tradition have an advantage, because if they adhere closely to dogma, they will have a fascinating and moving plot at hand, the story of "the crime of crimes" and "of all examples of the classical tragic irony in fact or fiction . . . the greatest—the classic of classics" (5). As the ritual of the Mass exemplifies, "the dogma *is* the drama,"[20] the mystery of faith in action.

To create a unified work of art, Sayers had to arrange the Gospels into a coherent narrative—not the easiest task, but one which seems deceptively simple when we read the finished plays. In order to do this, she used recurring characters, like Baruch and Proclus. She also had to recognize, as any good novelist would, that the same story told by different narrators takes different forms: "In modern memoirs written by real people about another real person we should expect just that sort of diversity which we find in the Gospels" (19). Because she sees herself as a playwright, not a textual critic, she "does not want to select and reject, but to harmonise . . . to dovetail all these details so that the combined narrative presents a more convincing and dramatic picture than any of the accounts taken separately" (19). This is precisely what an author of epistolary fiction, like *The Documents in the Case* and "The Wimsey Papers," would know.

She also makes the sensible observation that Jesus would have been a poor teacher (a heretical thought) if he had not repeated an effective parable until "his disciples knew it by heart in all its variation." Displaying her characteristic sensitivity to language, Sayers remarks that "the lapidary form in which these teachings have come down to us suggests powerfully that here we have 'set pieces' of teaching with which the transmitters of the oral tradition were verbally and intimately familiar" (17). Although it may seem a surprising vehicle at first glance, the modern medium of radio actually fits the oral nature of early Christianity perfectly. The straightforward, vivid language of these plays provokes strong images of Christ that are not limited by a particular visual presentation, which would have been prohibited in England at that time anyway. Since we are not distracted by the particular features of a particular actor, we can see Christ in our mind's eye. Perhaps this is one of the reasons I find Sayers's portrayal of Jesus Christ more believable than any I have ever seen on film.

Again, this kind of appeal to the imagination is novelistic, and the plays' notes indicate that the author still sees herself as a fiction-writer. Raising the very question which one would expect to be on her audience's mind, she

235

asks bluntly, "What are a detective-novelist and a crew of 'West-End' actors doing in such a place?" (21). Yet the writing of detective stories was not inappropriate preparation for the tasks involved in creating *The Man Born to Be King,* especially those of making a coherent plot from the Gospel accounts of Jesus's life on Earth or creating suspense in spite of the fact that the audience already knows the story's ending. The question of Sayers's suitability for such a job leads to this culminating statement about why she attempted it: "I am a writer and I know my trade; and I say that this story is a very great story indeed, and deserves to be taken seriously . . ." (21). She has approached the subject as a storyteller, not an evangelist, "because it is our craft to tell stories" (22). This is the great strength of these plays: they make the Good News seem new indeed.

Although there is a clear theme in the Gospel story, DLS acknowledges that "theme-structure by itself will not . . . make a play. There must also be a plot-structure, and this was provided by bringing out certain implications in the story and centring them about the character of Judas" (14). In other words, a coherent plot was structured around the conflict between Judas as villain and Christ as hero. Sayers's Judas is, like many of the villains in her detective novels, "an intellectual devil"—the great mind corrupted by pride and over-reliance on self (15). As a literary figure, he is also a complex, or "round" character, just as her fictional villains and hero came to be. This not only makes for better drama—the tension within Judas added to the tension between him and the situation only intensifies the play's power—but also makes sense of the story in theological terms. If Jesus Christ is the living God, he would certainly not choose a blackguard for an apostle. Judas must have great strengths as well as a fatal flaw. The Judas of *The Man Born to Be King* has the temperament, the intelligence, the pride, the fixity, and the petulance of Milton's Satan. Not all readers of these plays have found Sayers's Judas an aesthetic success (Hannay 67–77), and the playwright herself knew that he was a challenge to depict realistically. In the introductions to the individual plays, she spends much time elucidating her view of this enigmatic character: "He seems a strange mixture of the sensitive and the insensitive. One thing is certain: he cannot have been the creeping, crawling, patently worthless villain that some simpleminded people would like to make out. That would be to cast too grave a slur upon the brains or the character of Jesus" (15). It would also be to insulate ourselves from the realization that Judas is one of us, and that his crime is not beyond the best of us.

Baruch the Zealot, the play's only important character created by Sayers, is the "pure politician" (125) who sees that Judas's corrupted virtues can easily be exploited by those wanting to destroy Jesus. Because he, too, is quite clever, Baruch offers a penetrating analysis of Judas, and of the corrupt intellect he represents: "He has a subtle mind and would see through any crude efforts to corrupt him. But, he may be led into deceiving himself with specious arguments. That is the weakness of all clever people. Intellectual dishonesty springing from intellectual pride—the sin by which Adam fell" (116). The age-old question of why, if there is a God, he permits evil to exist at all, is highlighted in Judas. The question takes on a highly emotional, personal dimension in the Gospels, because the story tells us that it was God himself who came down from heaven and accepted the mantle of the world's suffering. Part of that suffering, perhaps its most intense part, was the final failure of friendship, trust, and earthly love. And yet, according to Christian teaching, God permits Judas to exist and to betray him. Sayers offers the Christian explanation of this paradox:

> Jesus "knew all men," and knows well enough the knife-edge of risk that Judas represents. It is the risk that has to be taken, because the Kingdom must always reckon with such men as Judas, who can be the greatest saints or the greatest sinners. The great intellect must be let in, whatever its dangers. . . . Judas is, as it were, the key that will open the door, either on to the way of triumph or on to the way of tragedy. (101)

In this post-lapsarian view of human life, the bitter fruits of knowledge and experience are accepted willingly, as the tragedy of Good Friday must be endured before the triumph of Easter. "The sin of Judas played its part in the great Comedy of Redemption, and if he damned himself, it was because he did not choose to wait for the last act" (11).

The redemption of evil does not excuse the evildoer, however, as Jesus says with the simple directness that characterizes his speech throughout *The Man Born to Be King:* "In a sinful world, disasters are inevitable; but the man who brings them about is guilty none the less" (207). This could serve as a motto for detective fiction, and is especially relevant to the complex moral predicament in which Peter Wimsey finds himself at the end of *The Nine Tailors.* This kind of paradox is sometimes dismissed as contradiction (Hannay 76), but both art and Christian theology flourish on the paradoxical. Indeed, one possible reason that so much Western art has been animated by the Christian mythos—even the work of many modern writers who are nonbelievers—is the richly paradoxical nature of Christian dogma and imagery. Neither literature nor theology created paradox and irony, of course; life itself would be unimaginable without them. How far does anyone have to look to find evidence of the divided will, the human being at war with himself and his environment, regardless of how one should explain this fact? "This contradiction within his own nature is peculiar to man, and is called by the Church 'sinfulness'; other psychologists have other names for it" (*The Mind of the Maker* 10).

Sayers's Judas is cunning, socially advanced, proud, envious, brilliant—recalling Yeats's judgment that "an intellectual hatred is the worst" ("A Prayer for My Daughter"). Suffering from "a peculiarly over-weening loftiness," this Judas is an "intellectual devil of a very insidious kind, very active in these days and remarkably skilful in disguising itself as an angel of light" (15). He is a reformer who forgets the reasons for reform and denies the ultimate reality by which all human action is judged (cf. *The Devil to Pay*). Paul de Voil has said that Judas, the fanatical social reformer, is a creature of the 1930s ("The Theology of Dorothy L. Sayers" 25), but his type reappeared en masse in the 1960s and is with us yet. Judas is the man in love with a concept, a self-described humanitarian who will unhesitatingly walk over any number of human beings in the service of what he considers a noble cause.

In many ways, Judas is representative of the modern temper. He uses a particularly debased modern idiom, sounding for all the world like a cross between gangster, politician, and public relations man: "Herod's only bluffing. . . . There will be great opportunities in Tiberias. . . . Leave it to me. I've established certain contacts . . ." (73). Like "a stunt journalist," he has a clever way of reporting Jesus's words "correctly, but with a false suggestion of context" (230). That Judas understands more than the other disciples only makes him more responsible for his actions, and yet his chief flaw—pride—operates most devastatingly on his great intellect. He sees what Christ means, but is convinced he has to be in control, and is the supreme opportunist. A rationalist who is failed by his reason, and a thoroughgoing materialist, Judas finally rejects both Christ and the community: "I trust nobody. I will believe in nothing but what I can see and handle. All men are liars—only *things* cannot lie" (222). This brand of cynicism is what often passes for realism in the modern world, and the image of Judas, sick to death of himself and his world, is disquietingly familiar.

As Sayers realized, Judas was not the only character in this drama who presented difficulties for a realistic writer. Jesus was even more difficult to render believably, for "perfect goodness is apt to be unsympathetic, and generally speaking permits of little development" (10). Actually, this is why her portrayal of Judas is so effective: by epitomizing the opposite of Christ, or the corruption of human virtues without God's redeeming grace, Judas makes the character of Christ clearer. In this contrast, Judas represents the will to death versus the will to life, despair instead of hope, frenetic anxiety instead of patient self-confidence, hatred instead of love, and denial rather than affirmation (173). This is why he must be the most intelligent, the most imaginative, the most gifted of all the disciples: like Satan, he could have been the highest of his kind, the closest to God, but his pride and egocentric will drive him to want to be *as* God—hence, his fall. He is, simply, "the worst that is the corruption of the best" (101).

Once convinced that Jesus is corrupt, Judas focuses on his own mistakes in judgment about the Nazarene. Notice the relentless reference to self in his speech:

> It is horrible to have been so mistaken in the man. . . . And yet I swear I was *not* mistaken. God meant him for the Messiah, if only he had been true to himself. . . . there was a great man lost in Jesus of Nazareth. The noblest dreams I ever dreamed, the holiest prayer my heart could utter, all my hopes, all my ideals, seemed incarnate in him. . . . Why would he not listen to me? I warned him again and again. (220–21)

While maintaining, irrationally, that he believes Jesus to be the Messiah, Judas's raging arrogance recreates Christ in his own image and cuts him down to his own size. An extreme version of one of the basic tendencies in modern life, Judas's total self-absorption represents the fearful consequences of making man the center and measure of all things.

Since he is the ultimate intellectual, Judas also represents the moral problem of the conflict between head and heart which Sayers considers at length in her fiction, where the villains are often overly clever while the detectives, especially Lord Peter, must work to strike a balance between enlightened minds and hearts.[21] In the first play of the cycle, one of the Magi says that "the riddle that torments the world is this: Shall Wisdom and Love live together at last, when the promised Kingdom comes?" (39). One interesting reflection of Sayers's preoccupation with what Eliot called "the dissociation of sensibility" in the modern world is her imaging each of the three kings who visit the Christ child as the epitome of one aspect of the human being: Caspar, "the wisdom of the intellect"; Melchior, "the wisdom of the bodily senses"; and Balthazar, "the wisdom of the heart" (25). As both the Divine Reason and Love incarnate, Christ represents the unification of head and heart, of love and wisdom, and those who would follow him must strive for this balance in themselves: "To love God with heart and soul and understanding, and one's neighbor as one's self" is the goal of the Christian (216).

In *The Just Vengeance,* such a unification is the essence of the beatific vision. The faithful are promised that in eternity they "shall praise God with the glorious and holy flesh," with "the moving and sensitive heart," and "with the searching and subtle brain" (79, 80). In contrast, earthly existence is marked by a conflict between the mind and the heart. Judas is described as brilliant but cold (52, 206) and hard-hearted (228). His fundamental lack of generosity makes him unable even to forgive himself after betraying Jesus—and it is this inability to forgive himself, and to trust in the forgiveness of God, which seals his fate:

> he cannot be saved because he *will* not be saved. He goes on, down and down to the lowest pit of all, where sits the devil of pride that makes the sin unforgivable because the sinner resents and hates and refuses the forgiveness. At the bottom of that pit is only himself and his self-hatred, and here there is no place of repentance. So he goes to his own place. (254)

Sayers is making a profound theological and psychological point here, one which echoes Milton's images of the fallen Satan in *Paradise Lost* (1.254–55; 4.18–26; 73–80). The haunting picture of Judas descending to the lowest pit of hell is also worthy of the writer who would become one of Dante's most sympathetic modern readers.

Jesus becomes vividly real through these contrasts with Judas, as well as in the words of his disciples. Judas's own memory of the Sermon on the Mount is very moving, and suggests what was lost when Judas was lost:

> The mists were not yet off the hill-tops; it was cool with a little breeze, and so quiet. There was a spring bubbling out of the rock, and he sat beside it, and the rising sun was on his face. If only I could make you see him. If only you could hear his voice as we heard it then, speaking about happiness, and the blessed Kingdom of God. I hear it now . . . it will be in my ears till I die. . . . (133)

Like the audience of a Shakespearean history play or a Greek tragedy, we listen to these lines, knowing full well the outcome of the story. It is as chilling to hear Judas refer to his own death—which we know is not far off—as it is thrilling to hear the voice of Jesus come back from memory, beginning one of the most famous Biblical texts with, "Listen, and I will tell you who are the happy people whom God has blessed. Blessed are the poor . . ." (133).

We see the humanity of Simon Peter when he remembers realizing for the first time that Jesus "wasn't like other men." In the simple language of one who is, unlike Judas, truly humble and truly generous (228), Peter recalls the day that Christ asked them to become fishers of men: "Of course, that's nothing to the things we've seen since: but I'll never quite get over that first moment—the sun on the sea, and the fish leaping and shining, and the shock of knowing that he wasn't—that he wasn't ordinary" (109). An interesting similarity in these two descriptions of Christ is that both memories involve strong images of light, reminiscent of the line from the Nicene Creed, "God of God, Light of Light, Very God of Very God" (cf. Genesis ch. 1, and *Paradise Lost* book 3).

In the ninth play, "The King's Supper," which reenacts the events of Holy Thursday, DLS accomplishes what she saw as her primary task. In the play's introductory notes, she writes: "At no moment must any ecclesiastical associations obscure the fact that this is the greatest of all *human* tragedies" (225). Indeed in this play it seems so, as we feel the anxious dread of separation and abandoment which both Christ, and we, know is inevitable. Like a good father worrying about the future of his hapless children, Jesus says to his followers: "there is so much I want to say to you, but you cannot bear it now; and there is no time . . ." (242). And in the Garden, he poignantly asks Peter to stay with him: "Let me feel you beside me. . . . I have loved you. . . . Oh, children, this moment is bitter—how can the flesh bear it? . . . It is the waiting that is so hard . . ." (245–46). The suffering Christ here feels fully the burden of his humanity, and we recognize the pain: "My soul is full of sorrow—it is like the horror of death. Stay here a little and watch with me, while I go and pray . . ." (246). This is the anguish of one who knows the next act. The playwright advises that the scene "must be played with a very strong and real sense of the human horror at physical death, of the failure of human companionship, and of the apparent vainness of prayer . . . the unbearable thing has to be faced—and is faced with dignity" (230).

The tension in this scene is intensified by the cutting back and forth between the Garden and the high priest's house, where the plot against Jesus is taking final shape. Regardless of one's belief system, it is unthinkable that anyone who has ever loved and lost could read these passages unfeelingly. Later, we again recognize the face of human grief in the apostle John's remark after the crucifixion, when he acknowledges that even the memories of the beloved are painful for a time: "A familiar word—the echo of a laugh—it is like a stab in the heart. Yesterday I found a pair of old sandals, moulded by the feet that wore them" (319)—a human, moving touch.

Since this is a play not only about loss but about fulfillment, Salome's compassionate lines to a grief-striken Mary Magdalen, suggesting the way the dead return to us in memory, adumbrate the Resurrection to come: "We forget the still body and the cold, waxen face, and our dead are given back to our remembrance alive and happy . . ."(322). This, too, resonates with the truth of experience. By dramatizing, in recognizable human detail, the depth of love and awe which Christ inspired in those around him, the play suggests that here indeed was no ordinary man.

In the late summer of 1984, I spent two days at Broadcasting House in London, sitting in a rather cramped office of the BBC's Religious Broadcasting Department, listening to recordings of the first production of this play-cycle. The circumstances were not ideal, and the plays were never intended to be digested in two enormous gulps. Perhaps I should say something about the frame of mind, or the level of expectation, I took with me. I had read the text of the play several times, and felt I knew it, as well as others' responses to it, fairly well. I was going to listen to the original tapes simply to be thorough—it was a scholar's exercise. I had been told that the BBC had recently reproduced the play, because the original was judged to be too "stagey" and old-fashioned for contemporary taste.[22] Although I wanted to hear the production on which the playwright herself had worked, I did not expect any fireworks.

Despite my familiarity with the written text, and indeed with the Gospels on which it is based, the play hit me with all the power of an authentic piece of theater. From the beginning, I felt swept up into the world of Jesus of Nazareth. For the first time, I realized that this play was the creation of the novelist I loved—it had the wit, the suspense, the liveliness, the immediacy of her fiction. By the time the story reached the Garden of Gethsemane, it was as though I was hearing it for the first time. As the narrative built up to the crucifixion, the tension was so great that my disbelief was completely suspended and I forgot that I was listening to a play at all. From this experience, even more than from studying the written text, I can say that these plays are not equally strong, which is to be expected from such a long series. Interest flags from time to time. The work is perhaps too well detailed and defined, and sometimes seems to be just covering necessary territory. Mary, the mother of Jesus, is too sweet, her voice cloying and her dialogue sometimes unbelievable (e.g., 289). The music was, to my taste, a bit maudlin. But my overall response was one of wonder.

Such an effect is, of course, the essence of drama, and can be created only by a very skillful writer. In fact, it reminded me of the first time I saw *King Lear* in a live production, after years of teaching and analyzing the play's text. Because I knew what was going to happen, I found—much to my surprise—the scene that culminates in Gloucester's blinding intolerable to watch. As the play proceeded inexorably to that demonstration of gratuitous cruelty, I became more and more uncomfortable. After years of "understanding" the play intellectually, it was as though I was experiencing it for the first time. It caused a visceral, emotional response for which I was totally unprepared. In the terms Sayers develops in *The Mind of the Maker,* what I learned that night was that Shakespeare's great tragedy encompasses not only "the wisdom of the brain, but the more intimate and instinctive wisdom of the heart and bowels" (176). Almost from the beginning of her career as a detective novelist, she had argued that such power was an attribute of genuine literature.[23] In *The Man Born to Be King,* she takes on the greatest mystery plot of Western culture, the story in which God is both victim and hero, and plays it powerfully indeed.

I do not mean to put Sayers in the uncomfortable position of being compared with the greatest playwright in the English language. Yet my experience tells me that there are sections of *The Man Born to Be King* which have very great dramatic power. At least for this late twentieth-century listener—one who was really not too interested in the subject when she entered the "theater," complacent, detached—the play was capable of recreating the excitement and the glory and the pain of the old story. After years of hearing bits of that story read in weekly installments at church, it became a moving, human story I could not ignore. I must admit that, all theorizing aside, the use of different English dialects and modern idiom was important in creating this effect. If nothing else, the dialects help a listener keep all the different characters straight—and one should not really expect the diverse people surrounding Jesus of Nazareth, in the first century, to have all just come from the Royal Shakespeare Company. As a critic of detective fiction, DLS argued that one of the important distinctions of a real artist is the ability to compel belief in her characters. *The Man Born to Be King* does that with surprising success. It also presents a well-delineated, believable world, as well as a panoply of well-developed minor characters reminiscent of a great novel in the English tradition. More than any other of her plays, *The Man Born to Be King* bears the inimitable Sayers stamp.

DLS says in her introduction to these plays that, as a storyteller, she recognizes that here is a great story, a story that deserves to be taken seriously. She succeeded in making at least this jaded listener do so. Such a response is, of course, also made possible by the superior skill of the actors and others involved in a particular production. They are essential to the manifestation of the author's idea—but the material offered them must be of sufficient power and magnitude for them to create such an effect. A masterful storyteller, Dorothy L. Sayers convinces us, at least for the duration of these plays, that "God died—not in a legend, not in a symbol, not in

243

a distant past nor in a realm unknown, but here, a few weeks ago—*you saw it happen*" (12).

The Man Born to Be King is powerful because it was created by a person who believed deeply in the theology upon which it is based, but it would have been less effective if its creator had not considered it, first and foremost, a story to be told. This play-cycle shows us that Christian dogma is in fact dramatic, compelling, and anything but dull. It is Sayers's best and most representative play.

13

The Mind of the Maker

A Fascinating and Majestic Mystery

Dorothy L. Sayers always maintained that, on the subject of religion, she had nothing to offer moderns beyond the ancient creeds of Christendom. In fact, she felt so strongly about this, and about the ignorance of most people regarding these creeds, that she developed several essays explicating them, including "The Greatest Drama Ever Staged" and "Creed or Chaos?" (both printed in an anthology of the latter title) and "What Do We Believe?" (published in *Unpopular Opinions*). The creeds are also the basis of her most important exploration of Christian theology, *The Mind of the Maker*. Because knowledge of these church teachings is essential to understanding her inquiry into the nature of human creativity, she includes relevant sections from the Athanasian, Nicene and Apostles' creeds at the end of the book. Readers who wish to refresh their memories of these essential Christian texts are referred to the appendix in *The Mind of the Maker*, or to the old *Book of Common Prayer*, which would have been Sayers's primary point of contact with the creeds. Since the language in which an idea is expressed is always important, my quotations are taken from the credal statements in *The Book of Common Prayer* as DLS knew it.[1]

Perhaps I should begin by saying that there is nothing original about the trinitarian theology upon which Sayers's study of the creative mind is based. In fact, originality of that kind would be inappropriate, because she is not questioning the orthodox teaching of the Church on these fundamental points about the nature of God and humanity. Yet, as she often noted with exasperation, so many people misunderstand Christian dogma that just enunciating it clearly may be mistaken for the height of creativity on the part of the explicator (*Creed or Chaos?* 35–36). I should think this distinction especially important for readers today, when there is even more confused thinking about Christianity than there was in her time. Although Sayers's theological premises are not original, what she does with them is. Her contribution in *The Mind of the Maker* is to develop a lucid, extended analogy between the Christian dogma of the Trinity and the creative activity of the human being. In so doing, she not only elucidates "this fascinating and majestic mystery" of the Holy Trinity (*The Mind of the Maker* 149), but also produces one of the most illuminating inquiries into the creative process ever written.

She begins the essay by making another important distinction, saying "this book is not an apology for Christianity, nor . . . an expression of personal religious belief. It is a commentary, in the light of specialized knowledge, on a particular set of statements made in the Christian creeds and their claim to be statements of fact" (ix). This is significant, because too often people confuse matters of fact with personal opinion. The first chapter of *The Mind of the Maker* is thus concerned with distinguishing fact from opinion, and the text proceeds to check the Church's "statements of fact" about the universe against the actual experience of the artist. Specifically, the book considers whether there is anything in the artistic process that parallels the Christian conception of God as Trinity-in-Unity. The author describes her book as a "brief study of the creative mind" and states its thesis as directly as possible:

> The point I shall endeavor to establish is that these statements about God the Creator are not, as is usually supposed, a set of arbitrary mystifications irrelevant to human life and thought. On the contrary, whether or not they are true about God, they are, when examined in the light of direct experience, seen to be plain witness of truth about the nature of the creative mind as such and as we know it. So far as they are applicable to man, they embody a very exact description of the human mind while engaged in the act of creative imagination. (xiii)

Since Sayers takes great pains to tell us what she is and is not doing in this book, it is important to remember the exact terms in which she states her subject and thesis. She is speaking, she tells us, "not . . . 'as a Christian,' but as a professional writer" (xiv). Thus, the book should be judged according to how persuasive its argument is on the subject of human creativity, and especially how well it fits what the reader knows about the experience of writing.

In *The Man Born to Be King,* DLS focused upon the Incarnation, and horrified some pious souls by her emphasis on one part of the Christian affirmation, that Christ was truly Man as well as truly God. *The Mind of the Maker,* which was written during the same period and published in July

1941 (Gilbert 99), takes up another basic teaching of the historic Christian church: the Trinity. These are, of course, interrelated dogmas, for the Church teaches that the second person of the Holy Trinity, God the son, came down from heaven and entered the world of time during the reign of Pontius Pilate. In the Athanasian Creed, or "Quincunque Vult," the relationship between, and relative importance of, these two fundamental teachings is suggested by the creed's organization into two distinct sections. The first begins, "the Catholick faith is this: That we worship one God in Trinity, and Trinity in Unity," and then about halfway through the text, the ground shifts to, "Furthermore, it is necessary to everlasting salvation: that he [who would be saved] also believe rightly the Incarnation of our Lord Jesus Christ" (*The Book of Common Prayer* 65, 67).

If we consider the opening of the more familiar Apostles' Creed, we see these essential teachings asserted together:

I believe in God the Father Almighty,
Maker of heaven and earth:
And in Jesus Christ his only Son our Lord,
Who was conceived by the Holy Ghost,
Born of the Virgin Mary. . . . (48)

With arresting simplicity, *The Mind of the Maker* reconsiders these familiar lines—words said mechanically by millions of Christians every day—and their implication for human life. What does it mean to call God a "Maker," and what does this mean for human beings, who are, the Bible tells us, created in God's image?

The second chapter of *The Mind of the Maker* goes back to the first line of Genesis for the primal image of God as Maker: "In the beginning God created. He made this and He made that and He saw that it was good. And He created man in His own image; in the image of God created He him; male and female He created them" (*The Mind of the Maker* 21). As Sayers notes, there is only one assertion about God in this passage, and it is that he "created." Thus, it is reasonable to conclude that "the characteristic common to God and man is apparently that: the desire and the ability to make things" (22). It is this image of the human being as creator, as "maker," that DLS focuses upon in *The Mind of the Maker,* her most profound exploration of Christian theology as well as her most penetrating work of literary criticism. By examining the dogma of the Trinity, and looking for analogies between it and the world of experience, she attempts not only to explain this most difficult of Christian teachings, but to ascertain its relevance to human life. If God is Trinity-in-Unity, and the human being is, in God's image, a maker, then we should be able to discover some parallels between trinitarian doctrine and the human activity of creation. Discovering such parallels would actually be a great service to Christian teaching, for one of the chief objections made against it is its presumed remoteness from everyday experience. Yet, "if Christian dogma is irrelevant to life, to what, in Heaven's name is it relevant?" (*Creed or Chaos?* 31).

Because she is a writer, DLS examines these parallels mainly by reference to the act of writing, but if the analogy works, it must be applicable to all human creation. The creeds do not say that God made only artists in his image, and Sayers was not one of those modern writers who redefined God as Art. As she explains, "It is true that everybody is a 'maker' in the simplest meaning of the term. We spend our lives putting matter together in new patterns and so 'creating' forms which were not there before." This capacity for creative activity distinguishes human beings as a race. Even so, "it is the artist who, more than other men, is able to create something out of nothing. A whole artistic work is immeasurably more than the sum of its parts" (*The Mind of the Maker* 28). The last sentence can be of help to beginning students of literature, who because of the analytic bias of modern culture, often try to approach art as though it were a problem to be "solved," like a mathematical formula. Focusing the discussion on the artist, as *The Mind of the Maker* does, has the virtue of making the nature of human creativity clearer because it is more clearly manifest in such people. This focus also makes sense given Sayers's own vocation—her experience as writer is the particular form of specialized knowledge that she brings to her study of the mind of the maker. Although references to the writing of mystery novels in such a context might shock some, DLS is wise to stay with what she knows intimately, and the book is full of comments that are helpful to practicing writers.

We do not know with any certainty the particular inspiration for this study of the creative mind. Clearly, as novelist and critic, Sayers had been thinking about the meaning of work and the nature of human creativity for some time. Her shift to writing for the theater in the late 1930s must have also brought some aspects of the creative process into sharper relief. Working in a new form challenges the serious artist to reflect upon the whole process of creation, and it could be that seeing (or hearing) her own word made flesh in drama suggested the analogy between human and divine creators. This would seem especially likely given the fact that she was working simultaneously on *The Mind of the Maker* and *The Man Born to Be King,* a play that seeks to make the Incarnation "really real." Perhaps the playwright herself experienced a "Pentecost of power" (*The Mind of the Maker* 172) in the process of trying to make Christ present for moderns.

Sayers's concern about the moral implications of work, including her critique of the destructive effects of an overly mechanized age, has been compared with similar ideas in John Ruskin and G. K. Chesterton (Hannay 157; Thurmer 51–53). These are appropriate analogues. Like many of her predecesors in the late Victorian period, DLS valued craftsmanship as typified in the medieval guilds.

The Mind of the Maker was written for a projected series entitled "Bridgeheads," which was dedicated to exploring the predicament in which England found itself in the early 1940s and to considering ways to restore it after the war. James Brabazon includes a transcript of the series prospectus, possibly written by DLS, in an appendix to his biography. The points made in that proposal reveal a purpose close to the thesis of *Begin Here,* which argued that all Western values needed to be reassessed in order to understand what brought about the war and what could be done to restore a meaningful peace. The earlier essay also suggested that a new type of creature, which it called "Creative Man," must be developed if we were ever to accomplish the "synthesis of experience" needed to deal with an increasingly fragmented, contradictory, and destructive world (*Begin Here* 126–28; cf. *The Mind of the Maker* ch. 11). *Begin Here* ranges widely, and somewhat superficially, through history, economics, theology, and philosophy, and is consequently not as sound or penetrating as *The Mind of the Maker,* in which Sayers stays close to subjects she knows well and to ideas she had been turning over in her mind for years. *Begin Here* may be regarded as a kind of working paper toward the culminating insights of *The Mind of the Maker.*

It is an indication of the depth and seriousness of her mind that, in the various kinds of writing with which she responded to a world at war, DLS tended to take the long view. *The Mind of the Maker* remains so fresh, in fact, that we have to remind ourselves of the historical context of crisis in which it was written. The text occasionally refers to the war (111, 206), but the focus is on the sweep of history, past and future. As she had argued in *Begin Here,* the time was propitious to decide "how we may use the opportunity of the war to think and plan creatively for the future of our civilisation" (131). This is not merely the pugnacious bulldog of an Englishwoman, taking the most assertive stance in a bad situation; it is also the deeply committed Christian who sees life as a series of possibilities for redemption. And, as *The Mind of the Maker* makes clear, it is the creative artist, attempting to bring order out of chaos and make something out of nothing. The Bridgeheads statement of aims put it this way: "Our aim is to give the people of this country a constructive purpose worth living for and worth dying for" (Brabazon 278). It is significant that establishing a purpose for living is mentioned first, despite the fact that this is a wartime effort. DLS was convinced that, even in peacetime, modern culture offered little to satisfy the real needs of human beings. The statement of purpose continues:

> We believe that peace and stability are not attainable if considered as static in their nature or pursued as ends in themselves. They are the by-products of a right balance between the individual and the community. This balance is attainable only by a ceaseless creative activity directed to a real standard of value. (Brabazon 279)

It is the nature of this "ceaseless creative activity" which must be judged according to "a real standard of value" that *The Mind of the Maker* addresses.

The author herself says that the book is "an expansion of the concluding speech of St. Michael in . . . *The Zeal of Thy House*," and quotes the entire passage. The editorial interpolations are her own:

> For every work [or act] of creation is threefold, an earthly trinity to match the heavenly.
>
> First, [not in time, but merely in order of enumeration] there is the Creative Idea, passionless, timeless, beholding the whole work complete at once, the end in the beginning: and this is the image of the Father.
>
> Second, there is the Creative Energy [or Activity] begotten of that idea, working in time from the beginning to the end, with sweat and passion, being incarnate in the bonds of matter: and this is the image of the Word.
>
> Third, there is the Creative Power, the meaning of the work and its response in the lively soul: and this is the image of the indwelling Spirit.
>
> And these three are one, each equally in itself the whole work, whereof none can exist without other: and this is the image of the Trinity. (37–38)

Or, to use the terms developed in *The Mind of the Maker,* the human act of creation is a trinity composed of "Idea, Energy and Power," which correspond to God the Father, God the Son, and God the Holy Spirit, respectively. Since Sayers came to prefer the word "activity" instead of "energy," that word is used in the following discussion. Quoting a range of thinkers from Augustine and Aquinas to Eddington and Berdyaev, Sayers brings many strains of Western thought together in a new synthesis that seems distinctively hers.

Up to a point, her study of human creativity invites comparison with other treatises on aesthetics. These would include Coleridge's *Biographia Literaria,* which discusses the "primary and secondary imagination" as analogous to divine and human creation, as well as Sidney's image of the poet in "An Apology for Poetry." Closer to Sayers's time, Tolkien developed the concept of a human "sub-creator" reflecting the Divine Creator (see "On Fairy Stories"). It is probable that she knew the Sidney and Coleridge texts, but one would expect her to cite a direct influence if there was one, since *The Mind of the Maker* is filled with allusions to literary, theological, and philosophical sources. Because of the timing of Tolkien's essay, it is unlikely that she knew of his idea before writing *The Mind of the Maker,* but it is interesting that these two writers were mulling over similar ideas at approximately the same time.[2] Since I have found no evidence that they knew each other, this similarity of thought suggests more the existence of a *zeitgeist* than a concrete influence either way, and is especially interesting given the emergence of creation-centered theology after World War II. Neither Sayers nor Tolkien was a theologian, of course; like the great poet-critics, they were writers whose observations about creativity came out of experience. It is not surprising that a number of Western writers have been subtly influenced by the images of God and man in Genesis; indeed, it would be more surprising if they had not. Yet I know of no writer, other than Dorothy L. Sayers, who has gone beyond the basic comparison of human and divine creation and used the Trinitarian model to explicate the creative process itself.

Nancy Tischler and Richard T. Webster have discussed *The Mind of the Maker* in the general context of Western thought (Hannay 153–75). In a fascinating recent monograph entitled *A Detection of the Trinity,* John Thurmer, who is Chancellor of Exeter Cathedral, has attempted to trace more specific roots for Sayers's trinitarian analogy. In line with earlier commentators, he suggests that she borrowed from Augustine of Hippo the idea of a "psychological analogy" between the Trinity and the human soul, which Augustine's *De Trinitate* defines as being composed of memory, understanding, and will. Apparently, this analogy was taken up and developed at the beginning of the twentieth century by the English theologian R. C. Moberly, whose work on it aroused little notice. While Augustine is an obvious source, since DLS quotes him, the Moberly connection is tenuous. Thurmer hypothesizes that she may have heard something of Moberly's work at Oxford, or even from her father (77–79). Observing that she must have also been familiar with Chesterton's view that there is "an analogy between human literary work and God's creation" (52), he concludes that "it was Dorothy L. Sayers's achievement to combine this Chestertonian restatement of a familiar Christian theme with the unique and isolated insight of Moberly" (53), which was that the human personality has a triune structure analogous to the Persons of the Trinity. Finally, *A Detection of the Trinity* argues that, in *The Mind of the Maker,* DLS "has shifted the trinitarian analogy from the human person to the human work" (51). Whatever her sources, this is not a surprising emphasis, for she often argued that it is through the work that we can best know the artist, and it was certainly the work which most interested her.[3]

These suggestions about sources and influence are interesting, but what I find most intriguing is Thurmer's reason for writing a book about Dorothy L. Sayers and trinitarian doctrine. In the preface, he explains, "I learnt most of my theology first from her, and then I relearnt it from more conventional authorities." (One wonders with what dimunition of liveliness.) Then he says that his book, "which explores her insight into the central Christian doctrine of the Trinity is a recognition of what I (and no doubt others) owe to her" (7). This is an impressive tribute to the woman who has spurred countless modern readers to reconsider the doctrine of the Holy Trinity. Although, as Lord Beaumont has observed, few histories of the modern church even mention Dorothy L. Sayers, a number of leaders in the contemporary Church of England have acknowledged debts to her.[4] When one considers these testimonies, alongside the large number of lay Christians and "thinking pagans" who have been influenced by her work, her impact on twentieth-century religious thought is seen to be considerable. How many mystery addicts have unwittingly picked up *The Mind of the Maker* after running out of Sayers novels to read, and thereby stumbled into a compelling argument for Christianity?

It is revealing for DLS to admit that the basic argument of *The Mind of the Maker* is enunciated in one of her plays. The best imaginative literature is not reducible to a single thesis, and I suggest this is one reason her plays are, in general, not as aesthetically pleasing or effective as her novels. To use the critical terminology she develops out of the trinitarian analogy, Sayers's drama tends to be so "father-centered" that its power is not as great as that manifested in her fiction. This is true of *The Emperor Constantine, The Devil to Pay,* and to a lesser extent, *The Zeal of Thy House.* In these plays, one never seems to lose sight of the ideas the author is propounding. If *The Man Born to Be King* reveals the high drama of Christian dogma, most of Sayers's religious plays fall into the error of being merely dogmatic drama.

Although she says that the theme of *The Zeal of Thy House* and the thesis of *The Mind of the Maker* are embedded in *Gaudy Night* as well, it is impossible to point to a single speech or passage in that novel which expresses its theme. Rather, like most good fiction, the story and the dynamic relationships among the characters carry the theme by implying it in a variety of ways. As a genuine novel, *Gaudy Night* is about many things, and cannot be reduced to a single sentence or paragraph of explication. In fact, DLS herself refutes the notion of there being a "thesis" in this novel when she discusses it in *The Mind of the Maker* (191).

Significantly, the speech on the trinitarian nature of human creation comes at the end of *The Zeal of Thy House,* after William of Sens has confessed to the sin of pride and finally acknowledged that his work has value only by reference to his eternal Maker (101–06). Michael the Archangel begins the important speech by asking the assembly to "Laud and magnify God" and to "Praise Him that He hath made man in His own image, a maker and craftsman like Himself, a little mirror of His triune majesty" (*Zeal* 110). This is the lesson that William has learned through bitter experience, and it is an idea implicit in Sayers's work as early as *The Documents in the Case,* where Jack Munting says he wants to write a good book because he has a faint intimation of its being important to his soul (document no. 8). In *The Mind of the Maker,* DLS describes the artist's growing understanding of his or her own work:

> if he looks back along the sequence of his creatures, he will find that each was in some way the outcome and fulfillment of the rest—that all his worlds belong to the one universe that is the image of his own Idea. I know it is no accident that *Gaudy Night,* coming towards the end of a long development in detective fiction, should be the manifestation of precisely the same theme as the play *The Zeal of Thy House,* which followed it and was the first of a series of creatures embodying a Christian theology. They are variations upon a hymn to the Master Maker. (207)

Thus, Margaret P. Hannay has concluded that "the sacramental value of work is the theme which unifies Dorothy L. Sayers's writings in many genres" (*As Her Whimsey Took Her* xi).[5] The key word is "sacramental," which suggests the reason for all of the emphasis on work throughout Sayers's fiction: it is the activity which links human beings to their Maker and the manifestation of whatever is godly in them. That is, "good work well done" (*Creed or Chaos?* 59) is a redemptive action, while corrupted or shoddy work is a certain sign of moral decay. The detective stories dramatize this powerfully by pitting the creative, socially useful work of the detective against the destructive action of the criminal. Many of Sayers's villains wreak chaos in the social order not only through the act of murder, but through a perversion of their vocation: the malignant doctor or nurse, the dishonest solicitor. This emphasis on the meaning of work gives a moral depth and universality to these stories, while *The Mind of the Maker* reveals the theological basis for their world view.

Of special interest in this regard is Sayers's aristocratic detective-hero, Lord Peter Wimsey, who must make a place for himself in a world that has passed his kind by (*Gaudy Night* ch. 14). He does so by finding work that is useful and doing it well. Instead of succumbing to a slow death by boredom, like his contemporary, Jake Barnes,[6] Wimsey exemplifies the Christian injunction to find meaning in life by serving others joyfully. So do Miss Climpson and the Cattery, but they must work out of financial necessity. Thus, the point about work's being a moral and spiritual necessity for every human being is made most forcefully in the character of Lord Peter, who works only for noneconomic reasons and for the love of the job (cf. *The Mind of the Maker* 218).

In the Harriet Vane stories, the meaning of work takes on even greater subtlety. These stories, written just as women were emerging into the world of work, celebrate the possibility of self-actualization and independence through meaningful occupation while daring to question whether that is enough. When Vane returns to Oxford in *Gaudy Night,* she takes comfort in realizing that, despite many mistakes, she has never been untrue to her work (ch. 2). Doing one's proper job with integrity seems an unalloyed gift throughout most of this novel, until we see the human misery resulting from Miss de Vine's so doing. It is not that she was wrong in identifying an academic deceit; she had to do that in order to serve her work and maintain professional integrity. But as she herself finally realizes, serving a principle is not everything; we must give some attention to the human consequences of our actions as well (ch. 22). This is what the contrast between the compassionate scholar, Miss Lydgate, and the steely competent Miss de Vine suggests. And it is this compromise which Harriet must learn, the compromise between head and heart, and between self and other, that is always a matter of most delicate balance in an imperfect world. Sayers's position on work in the Harriet Vane stories, and in her essays on women, is truly liberating. While she rejects the traditional model of female vocation as self-sacrifice, she also suggests that it is not enough to find satisfying work and do it well. Rather, all human beings must ask hard questions about the intrinsic value of their work, and about its relationship to their entire being, not just to their role as workers and wage-earners.

Although *Gaudy Night* puts the question in secular terms, the novel's implication about the necessity of judging human work by reference to something outside the human being foreshadows what William of Sens learns in *The Zeal of Thy House,* written only two years later. Facing death, William readily admits to all manner of transgression, but the greatest of his sins—pride in his work and denial of his need for others, including

God—seem to him virtuous until the very end. Finally, he realizes that, while the work may be good, the human worker is ever flawed. William's imperfection manifests itself not in any defect in his work, but in his prideful attitude toward it and his failure to recognize the only standard by which human work may finally be judged (101). Like Harriet, William must also learn to accept love; he has been too strong and self-important to depend on anyone, until his injury makes autonomy impossible. His new physical and psychological vulnerability, in turn, makes his spiritual development possible: "So works with us/The cunning craftsman, God" (96).

The Mind of the Maker posits an ideal artist for purposes of discussion, but no human maker is perfect or self-sufficient. This was implied in the novels and is made explicit at the conclusion of this book, where the argument culminates in the statement that the "work must be measured by the standard of eternity; or that it must be done for God first and foremost; or that the Energy must faithfully manifest forth the Idea; or, theologically, that the Son does the will of the Father" (*The Mind of the Maker* 225). It is interesting that, in her quotations from the creeds in the book's appendix, Sayers stops in the Creed of St. Athanasius before the lines that set forth the reason for a Christian's being preoccupied with doing good work. At the Final Judgment, the creed says, all "shall give account for their own works. And they that have done good shall go into life everlasting: and they that have done evil into everlasting fire" (*The Book of Common Prayer* 68). This is to say that work, or all human activity, has not only a sacramental value, but a redemptive one as well. When it comes to the final judgment of a writer, the point is even sharper, for "every word—even every idle word— will be accounted for at the day of judgment, because the word itself has power to bring judgment" (*The Mind of the Maker* 111). A chastening warning indeed for any word-juggler.

John Thurmer argues that "*The Mind of the Maker* is unique in being a developed and confident appeal to something in human experience corresponding to, or providing a direct analogy of, the Holy Trinity" (11). "Unique" is a word to be used with great care, yet considering the book from the literary side, I would make a similar point that its greatest strength is its grounding in particular experience. This is something else it has in common with *The Man Born to Be King,* which takes Christ out of the heavens and plants him firmly on earth through insistent references to particular historical and psychological details. *The Mind of the Maker* is not a theoretical defense of an abstract doctrine, but a delicate investigation of the mysterious activities involved in creating a character, writing a scene, developing an idea. From these vivid particulars, which emanate from

Sayers's personal experience as a writer and have all the authenticity of such testimony, we may judge whether the doctrine of the Trinity has parallels in the universe as we know it.

I will not attempt to summarize the heart of this book, or to enumerate its many helpful observations on the artistic process. "The book itself is what the writer means" (*The Mind of the Maker* 57), and a reader who wants to know what Dorothy L. Sayers has to say about human creativity must read her book. Despite its somewhat diffuse structure, there is scarcely a page in *The Mind of the Maker* from which a reader cannot learn something about the craft and vocation of writing, and some aspects of the book have proved particularly useful to me, as a writer and a teacher of writing.

First, the book is indispensable to anyone who wants to understand Sayers's fiction. Its discussions of *Gaudy Night* and *Murder Must Advertise* are particularly enlightening, especially for those who cling to the notion that imaginative literature is the creation of a moment's blinding inspiration, rather than a manifestation of the sweat and passion of an alert and conscientious artist. Equally strong is its analysis of the allusive nature of Sayers's fiction, a characteristic she shares with many other modern writers. Since this is a distinctive quality of her prose, it is fascinating to watch her "raking through" her mind to understand how she came to create such passages as the description of the angel-roof in *The Nine Tailors*. After enumerating an astonishing array of allusions, she concludes that, far from being unwittingly imitative,

> a reminiscent passage of this kind is *intended* to recall to the reader all the associated passages, and so put him in touch with the sources of power behind and beyond the writer. . . . each new work should be a fresh focus of power through which former streams of beauty, emotion, and reflection are directed. . . . The criterion is, not whether the associations are called up, but whether the spirits invoked by this kind of verbal incantation are charged with personal power by the magician who speeds them about their new business. (120–21)

I would judge Dorothy L. Sayers a very good magician in this sense.

By way of discussing the modern propensity for seeing life as a set of problems to be solved, rather than as an unending series of opportunities for creative action, the book even implies why DLS moved away from writing traditional detective stories, a form that reflects the analytical bias of modern culture and its quest for simple answers: "the desire of being persuaded that all human experience may be presented in terms of a problem having a predictable, final, complete and sole possible solution accounts, to a great extent, for the late extraordinary popularity of detective fiction" (188). Yet we must eventually realize that "life is not a candidate for the Detection Club" (202), just as Sayers's own later novels moved away from the puzzle-story to embody the rich ambiguity of real life.

Her discussion of "Free Will and Miracle" illuminates the distinction between genuine art and propaganda, including the kind of "edifying literature" she held in special contempt (see, for example, her essay, "Playwrights Are Not Evangelists"). Like the God in whose image he was made, the human artist must bestow free will upon his characters, even to the point of allowing evil into the world of his creation: "You cannot, in fact, give God His due without giving the devil his due also" (53). Such openness to life is not only a guarantor of literary realism, but a sign of the artist's profound acceptance of reality. It is also the result of a Christian apprehension of the world as being inevitably composed of good and evil: "human situations are subject to the law of human nature, whose evil is at all times rooted in its good, and whose good can only redeem, but not abolish, its evil" (191). Such redemption is accomplished by a creative act, which is to say, by an action that makes something out of the chaotic, flawed material life offers (193). Since the Fall, "the only way to transmute Evil into Good . . . [has been] to redeem it by creation" (107). Thus, the creative work of a human being is analogous, in its way, to the Incarnation which redeemed the world.

Given the shape of her career, one of Sayers's most fascinating comments in *The Mind of the Maker* is that she is "inclined to think that one reason why writing for the stage is so much more interesting than writing for publication is the very fact that, when the play is acted, the free will of the actor is incorporated into the written character" (64). This provides a glimpse of the excitement this particular artist felt when she began writing for the theater. Yet the statement exaggerates the difference between fiction and drama, because all works of the imagination, if they are any good, tend to reincarnate themselves in their audience's imagination. As the chapter on "Pentecost" explains: "once the [writer's] Idea has entered into other minds, it will tend to reincarnate itself there with ever-increasing Energy and ever-increasing Power" (111). This fact of the creative artist's life is properly the source of both joy and terror—joy, because it insures a kind of immortality, and terror, because the artist cannot foresee or control what the unleashed power will do:

Unfortunately his creation is safe from the interference of other wills only as long as it remains in his head. By materializing his . . . [work]—that is, by writing it

257

down and publishing it—he subjects it to the impact of alien wills. These alien wills can, if they like . . . misquote, misinterpret, or deliberately alter [it]. (104)

As the doctrine of Free Will emphasizes, this is the risk every creator takes in the act of creation. But the force of other wills can also give a work expanded life, as the reinterpretation of classics by every generation shows.

One of the most difficult aspects of trinitarian theology, namely that "the whole three Persons are co-eternal together and co-equal" (228), is made surprisingly understandable by Sayers's discussion of the unity of human creation: "Quite simply, every choice of an episode, or a phrase, or a word is made to conform to a pattern of the entire book, which is revealed by that choice *as already existing*" (39; emphasis added). This is an accurate description of a writer's way of working, whether or not she has ever so articulated it. Baldly stated, the point is: how can a writer know what to put into a book, essay, or story, unless the idea of the work already exists, complete in itself? How can the writer know whether a part fits the whole, if she has no idea of the whole already? It is true that untalented or untried writers may work madly and produce only a jumble of unrelated sentences, episodes, or facts, but this is precisely because they have, in the common phrase, "no idea" of what they are doing; we say this, in fact, of any worker whose job is beyond him. Thus, Sayers takes one of the most recondite points of doctrine and shows its truth to the writer's everyday experience. Her ability to do this again and again with the various implications of trinitarian theology is stunning, and I have never discussed *The Mind of the Maker*'s observations on the creative process with a practicing writer who did not find them at once recognizable and useful.

When the discussion turns to the creation of character, that most distinctive and fascinating of novelistic talents, the reader senses being led into the mysterious heart of human creation:

> When making a character he in a manner separates and incarnates a part of his own living mind. He recognizes in himself a powerful emotion—let us say, jealousy. His activity then takes this form: Supposing this emotion were to become so strong as to dominate my whole personality, how should I feel and how should I behave? (51)

This passage suggests the way a writer's imagination transforms the world of experience into an ever-expanding universe, and hints at how DLS herself created such a richly varied fictional world. As a novelist, she was abundantly successful at achieving "that complex end of man's desire—the creation of a living thing with a mind and will of its own" (65); Harriet

Vane is perhaps the prime example of such a creature. Sayers's discussion of characterization is especially enlightening for beginning writers, who often think they are writing fiction when they are only producing poorly masked, and poorly executed, autobiography. I have sent many a creative writing student to *The Mind of the Maker,* often with striking results.

Because even the greatest art made by human hands is flawed, the sections of *The Mind of the Maker* that deal with how a writer can go wrong constitute its most effective practical criticism. Sayers's conception of "Scalene Trinities" seems to me highly original, and it suggests a useful way of talking about imbalances and imperfections in works of literary art. Briefly put, the idea is that a writer fails when his trinity is out of balance, when one of the three aspects of the creative process—idea, activity, or power—is severely deficient or exaggerated:

> Writer after writer comes to grief through the delusion that what Chesterfield calls a 'whiffling Activity' will do the work of the Idea; that the Power of the Idea in his own mind will compensate for a disorderly Energy in manifestation; or that an Idea is a book in its own right, even when expressed without Energy and experienced without Power. (150)

This sentence rings true to every teacher who has ever been told, "Oh, I know what I want to say. I just can't put it into words." A half-formed idea may be in the person's mind, submerged among many others, but until that idea is worked out in the laborious activity of writing and made manifest— until the word becomes flesh—it has no power for the writer or anyone else.

It is the slow, often painful working out of the job, the patient endurance of the "ordeal of incarnation" (92), that distinguishes the writer from the would-be writer: "Everything in the visible structure of the work belongs to the son; so that a really disastrous failure in this person of the trinity produces not a good writer with a weakness, but simply a bad writer" (162). Thus, "*every* failure in form and expression is a failure in the son, from clichés and bad grammar to an ill-constructed plot" (164). The most extreme case of this type of failure is the nonwriting writer who never puts pen to paper. Unfortunately, the world seems to be well-supplied with such people. DLS suggests that they should be not only pitied, but also feared, because they are ultimately dangerous: "the uncreative artist is the destroyer of all things, the active negation." Such destructiveness is rooted in an essential frustration and self-hatred, for these "are the unhappiest of living men, the uncreative artists" (163).

Presumably, a failure in the son can be remedied by the willing devotion of more sweat and toil to the work of incarnation, but a "failure in the ghost

259

is more utterly and hopelessly disastrous than failure elsewhere." As we might expect from a writer and critic who always stressed the affective function of literature, Sayers argues that a "Pentecost of power" is essential to any literary work. Her comments on a deficiency in this power are as withering as they are apt: "Failure in the ghost is a failure in Wisdom—not the wisdom of the brain, but the more intimate and instinctive wisdom of the heart and bowels." Such a failure is the mark of "the unliterary writer and the inartistic artist . . . the men who use words without inspiration and without sympathy" (176). We hardly need to be told that "the deadness of the unghosted hangs like a millstone upon the eloquence of pedestrian politicians and of conscientious parsons who have no gift for preaching" (177). Such deadness is also an attribute of the driest type of detective story, whose appeal is strictly to the intellect, and to much scholarly writing. To her credit, DLS was rarely guilty of this particular sin.

The artistic trinity may be wrenched out of proportion in the other direction as well, so that the writer becomes "ghost-ridden," creating false or empty pentecosts, "thrilling and moving the senses but producing no genuine rebirth of the spirit." The ghost-ridden are "all those . . . whose manner has degenerated into mannerism" (152). This would include mawkishly sentimental writers, as well as the debased rhetoricians of advertising and politics, and the creators of the lowest form of "thriller," where the emotions are manipulated deftly but to no purpose other than producing a vicarious rollercoaster ride. One would automatically associate such abuse of power with writers catering to the popular taste, but oddly, there are also ghost-ridden writers aplenty in the literary establishment today, writers endlessly sharpening their linguistic tools, but with precious little to say.

In a culminating passage, DLS describes the essential similarities she has discovered between the mystery of human creativity and the mystery of the Trinity. The passage is notable for its coolly deliberate tone and careful understatement; the literary detective is obviously striving to avoid any charge of generalizing ahead of her data:

> The artist's knowledge of his own creative nature is often unconscious; he pursues his mysterious way of life in a strange innocence. If he were consciously to pluck out the heart of his mystery, he might say something like this: I find in myself a certain pattern which I acknowledge as the law of my true nature, and which corresponds to experience in such a manner that, while my behavior conforms to the pattern, I can interpret experience in power. (212)

In other words, she perceives in herself a drive to create (or write) and realizes that, by conforming to this law of her nature, she "can interpret experience in power." This is a fairly straightforward description of the process by which a writer creates what we commonly call his "world," a new world brought into being by the force of the writer's mind on the world of experience. It is also the point in the argument where I should think the analogy between human and divine creativity becomes clearest for the general reader, who knows from experience that a good writer does indeed create something that never existed before—a fictional world, a distinctive tone, a way of seeing experience. These comments also resonate with the writer's experience of seeing his work take on a life of its own, quite separate from the mind that made it and capable of effecting incalculable responses in others.

While testifying to "the mysterious and terrible energy of the creative," *The Mind of the Maker* admits that creatures have a certain "resistance to creation" which makes it difficult to be an artist or "those . . . who have the misfortune to live with him during the period when his Energy is engaged on a job of work" (140). I should expect any writer's family to recognize itself, not altogether happily, in this last statement. It is not surprising for so fluent and prolific a writer as DLS to assert that "the urgent desire of the creative mind is towards expression in material form" (42), although few human beings would seem to have been so urgently moved to create as she was. Or perhaps most of us are just better at resisting the urge. Yet it is true that we feel most "like ourselves" when that urge is satisfied, as "What Do We Believe?" argues:

> The men who create with their minds and those who create (not merely labour) with their hands will, I think, agree that their periods of creative activity are those in which they feel right with themselves and the world. . . . There is a psychological theory that artistic creation is merely a 'compensation' for the frustration of sexual creativeness; but it is more probable that the making of life is only one manifestation of the universal urge to create. Our worst trouble to-day [1940] is our feeble hold on creation. To sit down and let ourselves be spoon-fed with the ready-made is to lose grip on our only true life and our only real selves. (*Unpopular Opinions* 18)

As is typical of creative artists, DLS generalizes from her own experience to see a similar pattern in the entire universe. Or perhaps it is more to the point that, as an artist, she is capable of perceiving the universal in the personal. The final step in her argument is to draw a connection between her created world and traditional Christian teaching about the nature of God who, as maker of all things, originates the pattern itself. Again, the crucial insight is expressed with the utmost restraint:

261

> I find . . . that the same pattern inheres in my work as in myself; and I also find that theologians attribute to God Himself precisely that pattern of being which I find in my work and in me.
>
> I am inclined to believe, therefore, that this pattern directly corresponds to the actual structure of the living universe, and that it exists in other men as well as in myself.

Coming to the end result of this line of reasoning, she points to the sweeping implications of her discovery that genuinely creative activity is the essence of human experience and humanity's only means of fulfilling the purpose for which it was made: "I conclude that, if other men feel themselves to be powerless in the universe and at odds with it, it is because the pattern of their lives and works has become distorted and no longer corresponds to the universal pattern—because they are, in short, running counter to the law of their nature" (212). Such a denial of human nature leads inevitably to disaster and perhaps explains the destructive course of modern history, an idea Sayers discusses in *Begin Here*. It is not just that so-called civilized people repeatedly find themselves at war, but that the importance of creative activity, or fulfilling work, for all human beings has been so ignored that they are increasingly alienated, not only from their work, but also from their environment and from themselves.

This is the point at which the aesthetic, the theological, the moral, and the political converge—the final destination of Sayers's magisterial study of the mind of the maker:

> If we conclude that creative mind is in fact the very grain of the spiritual universe—we cannot arbitrarily stop our investigations with the man who happens to work in stone, or paint, or music, or letters. We shall have to ask ourselves whether the same pattern is not also exhibited in the spiritual structure of every man and woman. And, if it is, whether, by confining the average man and woman to uncreative activities and to an uncreative outlook, we are not doing violence to the very structure of our being. (185)

Thus, *The Mind of the Maker* manages to make not only Christian dogma, but also something at least as arcane—aesthetic theory—relevant to everyday life. This accomplishment is quintessential Sayers, linking the cosmic and the mundane, and thereby enabling us to see both in a new light.

It is interesting that here, in 1941, while the war was still in its early years, DLS was already thinking ahead to the problems of peace. This foresightedness was based on her conviction that, far from being an irrational catastrophe, "war is a judgment that overtakes societies when they have been living upon ideas that conflict too violently with the laws governing the universe" (*Creed or Chaos?* 48). She regarded the typical solutions posed by the modern age, including Capitalism and Marxism, to be insufficient because they depend on the wrong definition of the human being as an economic creature. "We cannot deal with industrialism or unemployment unless we lift work out of the economic, political and social spheres and consider it also in terms of the work's worth and the love of the work, as being in itself a sacrament and manifestation of man's creative energy" (*The Mind of the Maker* 218). Considering the course of history since World War II, we might conclude that these were quixotic aims. We do not seem any closer to comprehending work in these terms, and rarely, if ever, take the long view on social issues. Most people today, even in developed, affluent countries, would seem still to work to live, not live to work (*Creed or Chaos?* 55). But this does not mean that reformation in our attitudes toward work is unnecessary, or that the questions Sayers raised fifty years ago are a luxury for a world still caught up in the "whirligig of wasteful production and wasteful consumption," which is driven by a thoroughly materialistic definition of human life (*Creed or Chaos?* 52).

In a March 1941 lecture, entitled "Why Work?" she put forward a thesis similar to that of *The Mind of the Maker:* "what becomes of our civilization after this war is going to depend enormously on our being able to effect . . . [a] revolution in our ideas about work." Such a revolution, which would be more sweeping than those based upon Marxist principles, would mean that work was considered "a creative activity undertaken for the love of the work itself; and that man, made in God's image, should make things, as God makes them, for the sake of doing well a thing that is well worth doing." Without such a fundamental change, she argues, we shall never "escape from the appalling squirrel-cage of economic confusion in which we have been madly turning for the last three centuries or so, the cage in which we landed ourselves by acquiescing in a social system based upon Envy and Avarice" (*Creed or Chaos?* 47). We may question whether it is self-evident, as these comments imply, that the natural universe is the creation of a careful and capable Craftsman. We may wish to declare terms like avarice and envy, and even the whole notion of sin, to be outmoded. But it is impossible not to recognize something of ourselves in the picture DLS drew a half-century ago: "The greatest insult which a commercial age has offered to the worker has been to rob him of all interest in the end-product of the work and to force him to dedicate his life to making badly things which were not worth making" (*Creed or Chaos?* 57).

In Sayers's first detective story, Lord Peter observes that "Most people don't associate anythin'—their ideas just roll about like so many dry peas on a tray, makin' a lot of noise and goin' nowhere" (*Whose Body?* 115). As a detective, his job is not simply to analyze the evidence, but to associate the seemingly disparate pieces of information into a coherent whole—the solution to the mystery. When the solution finally occurs to him, the language of the narrative subtly compares his work to the Creator of the natural universe he is studying:

> It happened suddenly, surely, as unmistakably as sunrise. He remembered—not one thing, nor another thing, nor a logical succession of things, but everything— the whole thing, perfect, complete, in all its dimensions as it were and instantaneously; as if he stood outside the world and saw it suspended in infinitely dimensional space. He no longer needed to reason about it, or even to think about it. He knew it. (*Whose Body?* 127)

As DLS became a more self-conscious artist, she articulated to herself the ideas embedded in her fiction and came to realize the implications of such an image. In her penultimate novel, Harriet Vane remarks that writing good prose makes one "feel like God on the seventh day—for a bit, anyhow" (*Gaudy Night* ch. 9). *The Mind of the Maker* explores this analogy in detail and demonstrates that creativity, in its broadest and most profound sense, is the heart of human experience:

> It has become abundantly clear of late . . . that something has gone seriously wrong with our conception of humanity and of humanity's proper attitude to the universe. We have begun to suspect that the purely analytical approach to phenomena is leading us only further . . . into the abyss of disintegration and randomness, and that it is becoming urgently necessary to construct a synthesis of life. It is dimly apprehended that the creative artist does, somehow or other, specialize in construction, and also that the Christian religion does, in some way that is not altogether clear to us, claim to bring us into a right relation with a God whose attribute is creativeness. (*The Mind of the Maker* 181)

In the entire world of her creation, Dorothy L. Sayers points toward a definition of human life and work that is a reflection of the Creator and Redeemer described in the historic Christian creeds. This is another important link between her story of *The Man Born to Be King* and the doctrine of work propounded in *The Mind of the Maker:* the Christian God is not only the maker of the universe, but a particular man, "Jesu, the carpenter's Son, the Master-builder,/Architect, poet, maker" (*The Zeal of Thy House* 106). Or, as DLS once said in her more characteristic, plainspoken style, "No crooked table-legs or ill-fitting drawers ever . . . came out of the carpenter's shop at Nazareth" (*Creed or Chaos?* 58; see also "Towards a Christian Aesthetic" and "Living to Work" in *Unpopular Opinions*).

The Mind of the Maker is impossible to categorize. Is it, as Ralph Hone suggests, "one of the rare treatises in Christian esthetics"? (127). Is it literary or social criticism? Is it artistic autobiography? My colleagues tell me that the book is sometimes recommended to seminarians, because it is considered by some theologians to be one of the most lucid analyses of Trinitarian dogma ever written. I am not a theologian, but I would say that *The Mind of the Maker* renders that dogma more comprehensible, and yes, more "believable," than any source I have ever encountered. The booksellers and librarians, who have to put the book somewhere, usually label it "religion." Is that what it is? The author herself tells us that it is not an apology for Christianity, nor a declaration of personal faith, but a study of the creative mind.

To use Sayers's own term for some of her other writings on Christianity, we could call *The Mind of the Maker* an essay in "popular theology." This is not to demean it, for as John Thurmer gently reminds us, "Christian doctrine belongs . . . to the common man, and not only to the scholar" (7). And so does art. Perhaps *The Mind of the Maker* is best described as a work in popular aesthetics by way of popular theology. The book transcends genres and definitions. It is a Sayers book, and represents the best that her massive and yet delicate intelligence could bring to bear on the greatest of all mysteries: the meaning of earthly experience and its relationship to that transcendent reality in which she believed.

Before the modern period, most Western art was animated or supported by such belief. The remarkable thing about its role in Sayers's work is that she is a modern writer, reflecting on the modern predicament, but without a fully modern sensibility. Like other twentieth-century artists who were also Christian, including T. S. Eliot and C. S. Lewis, her cleaving to belief was neither a blind acceptance of tradition nor a retreat from reality, but a considered and somewhat courageous choice. By affirming the existence of a reality beyond the here and now, some of the best minds of this century have dared to challenge the orthodoxy of unbelief that characterizes the modern world. In so doing, many of them have also committed the unpardonable sin of making Christianity intellectually respectable. James Brabazon has said that, in *The Mind of the Maker,* Dorothy L. Sayers actually brings human beings closer to God (205), an impressive feat for a writer working in the middle of the twentieth century.

With disarming simplicity, Lewis himself avoided the one-genre fallacy when he reviewed *The Mind of the Maker,* saying that "the purpose of this book is to throw light both on the doctrine of the Blessed Trinity and on the process whereby a work of art (specially of literature) is produced, by drawing an analogy between the two."[7] He also praised it for being "full of

265

illumination both on the theological and on the literary side," comments he could make with special authority. In a recent introduction to the book, Madeleine L'Engle has suggested that only "a totally committed Christian" could have written *The Mind of the Maker* (xvi), but I am not sure this is true. I would say that only a person who understood traditional Christian doctrine could have written it, and perhaps more importantly, only a person who had absorbed and reflected on the Christian view of experience could have conceived it. One thing seems certain: only a writer could have written it.

Although belief may not have been necessary for writing this book, it is possible that belief could result from such a study. I would suggest that, even if its author had not already been a Christian when she started the book, her own argument might very well have converted her by the time she finished it. If, as *The Mind of the Maker* argues, the doctrine of the Trinity is universally applicable to human experience—not just to writing, but to all the making and doing that constitute creative human action—then the book may be a way to faith. The reader of this book is driven, inevitably, to ask: If what it says of the creative process is true (and it seems to be) and if the workings of this human, discoverable process are analogous to the Holy Trinity (as the parallels offered suggest), then what of the dogma itself? After reading *The Mind of the Maker,* we may still choose not to believe the dogma on which it is based. We may conclude that the analogies demonstrated between Christian teaching and human experience are simply proof that human beings have made everything, including the idea of a trinitarian God, in their own image. But we can no longer dismiss the dogma as nonsensical or irrelevant to human life. By linking the human and divine, DLS has achieved her goal of explicating Christianity. This is a worthy goal in itself, for as she once remarked with some asperity, "even if you are going to disbelieve a thing, it is just as well to know what it is" ("Making Sense of the Universe" 13).

Sayers consistently argued that Christianity offers a way of "making sense of the universe." In a lecture of that title, she said: "if you will really apply your intelligence so as to understand, what the Christian revelation means, then I promise you that you will see the pattern of the universe" (13). *The Mind of the Maker* traces a pattern in the universe which images the Christian conception of the universe's Creator.

The Christian affirmation is . . . that the Trinitarian structure which can be shown to exist in the mind of man and in all his works is, in fact, the integral structure of the universe, and corresponds, not by pictorial imagery but by a necessary uniformity of substance, with the nature of God, in Whom all that is exists. (xiii)

Reasoning from "the unknown to the unknowable" (27), *The Mind of the Maker* investigates the mystery of human creativity by reference to the mystery of the universe itself.

The book resembles a detective story in that it similarly demystifies experience, taking something seemingly inexplicable or impenetrable and showing it to be rationally comprehensible. As a mystery writer, DLS worked to bring the detective story back into the tradition of the English novel. So, too, in *The Mind of the Maker* does she reinvigorate Christian tradition. In a sense, she beats the empiricists at their own game: a mid-twentieth-century Thomist, she painstakingly tests dogma by an appeal to verifiable experience. She may be too cerebral for some tastes, too intellectual in her approach, but I find this a welcome antidote to the often overly sentimental and emotional approach to religious questions.[8] It is also refreshing to meet an explicator, rather than an apologist, and to see a writer stay to the main points of Christian teaching.

Sayers's attitude would seem close to that of Lord David Cecil, whom she quotes: "Christianity has compelled the mind of man not because it is the most cheering view of man's existence but because it is truest to the facts" (*The Mind of the Maker* 16). The facts of human existence upon which DLS focuses are not only the essential sinfulness of humanity, but more importantly, the possibility for redemptive action. Placing a characteristically Anglican emphasis on the Incarnation and all its implications, she regards earthly experience as both sanctified and fallen, a blessing as well as a burden. This essential openness to life, this embracing love for the world of matter and time is what fundamentally allies all of her work with the Christian tradition. It is also the quality which most distinguishes her fiction and keeps it fresh. Like Dante and most of the writers she particularly loved, Dorothy L. Sayers went by the Way of Affirmation.[9] Considering the subtle relationship between belief and art in another novelist, Park Honan has observed that "a stoical Christian faith underlies all of Jane Austen's comedies and gives them their moral confidence, a severity and certainty, which in turn allow her comic talent to flourish lightly" (*Jane Austen: Her Life* 275). This paradoxical truth is applicable to the work of Dorothy L. Sayers as well.

Although a crisis in world affairs, accompanied perhaps by "the passion for being useful which attacks the best of us when we're getting past our prime" (*Strong Poison* ch. 12), motivated DLS to take up specifically theological topics in the late thirties, all of her writing is grounded in a deep

267

Christian faith. "Every maker and worker is called to serve God *in* his profession or trade—not outside it. . . . The only Christian work is good work well done" (*Creed or Chaos?* 59). By her own definition, all of Sayers's work is Christian, and a lasting testament to her "true and lively Faith" (*The Book of Common Prayer:* Articles of Religion, 12). She worked out of a love for creation and a desire for truth. A sincere and conscientious artist, she strove to do well something well worth doing. This is why her work is still provocative and still loved. And why it commands our respect: "the seemliness of the ordered work proclaims [her] . . . praise" (*The Mind of the Maker* 142).

In the early years of World War II, Dorothy L. Sayers looked at a world coming apart at the seams and suggested reasons for its dissolution, as well as possible remedies. In order to cope with the crisis in Western civilization, she argued, we must probe the greatest of mysteries: what human beings are, and the purpose for which they were made. And we must reassess all branches of learning, including science, the humanities, and theology, to determine what they can tell us about our predicament. Although she was a traditionalist, what she offered moderns was really much more than an explication of the ancient creeds of Christendom. As her most important consideration of Christian thought, *The Mind of the Maker* represents a truly creative response to tradition. An "imaginative humanist" (*Begin Here* 126), Dorothy Sayers exemplified in her own work that "synthesis of experience" she saw as necessary to the rejuvenation of Western culture (*The Mind of the Maker* 31). "Any witness—however small—to the rationality of a creed assists us to an intelligent apprehension of what it is intended to mean, and enables us to decide whether it is, or is not, as it sets out to be, a witness of universal truth" (17).

The Mind of the Maker is such a witness.

Final Judgment

A Writer First and Foremost

> Some books are undeservedly forgotten; none are
> undeservedly remembered.
> —W. H. Auden, *The Dyer's Hand*

In the case of Dorothy L. Sayers, the evidence points to a serious, conscientious, multifaceted artist who was ever growing and testing herself. She once observed that such experimentation and variation is necessary, because it is fatal for a writer to do the same book over and over again ("Craft of Detective Fiction"). She herself demonstrated this capacity for change and growth, not only in the development of her fiction, but also in the numerous genres she employed throughout her writing life. Although I regret that she did not write more novels, I must respect the courage and conscience which made her explore other forms. And I am happy, for her sake, that she was able to venture into so many of the regions where her whimsy took her. Novelist, essayist, dramatist, scholar, critic, translator, poet—Dorothy L. Sayers may properly be awarded the title few have earned: woman of letters.

There is an essential unity within diversity which characterizes the wide world of her creation. Writing of Charles Williams, she discussed his career in terms equally applicable to her own, concluding that "all the works of his maturity . . . form a closely connected unity, throwing light upon one another. . . ." As we have seen, from the selfsame author came *Gaudy Night*, "Are Women Human?" and *The Mind of the Maker*, works as disparate as her wide interests. *The Man Born to Be King* could not have been written without the experience of writing fiction, especially the kind of fiction at which Sayers excelled: timely, witty, richly detailed reflections on a world that is embraced with both love and wisdom. Knowing all of these texts illumines not only the individual works, but the mind that made them and the artistic process itself.

Of Williams's works, DLS also commented:

> They illumine one another, and illumine also those other great writers of the
> central tradition from whom their author himself derived illumination.
> . . . that which in one of the novels may seem merely entertaining, romantic, or
> fantastical is seen to be but the exposition in action of some profound and chal-
> lenging verity, which in the theological or critical books, is submitted to the anal-
> ysis of the intellect. . . . ("Charles Williams")

Written in 1950, while she was immersed in her translation of Dante's
Commedia, these words are a fitting commentary on her own canon. To
know the work of Dorothy L. Sayers is to understand better not only the
English tradition in literature, especially that of the English novel, but also
the whole tradition of humane letters and the central Christian tradition of
the west.

The world she made is both timebound and universal, a paradox that has
allowed it to survive the many changes in fashion and taste which have
occurred since she first put pen to paper. A novelist at once popular and
literary, a critic scholarly but never precious, Dorothy L. Sayers reminds us
of the real functions of art and learning. Her impeccable craftsmanship and
emphasis upon the timeless truth of human experience have secured a devoted audience spanning many cultures and generations. Wide appeal does
not necessarily prove artistic merit, of course, but the common modern
contempt for writers who have such appeal does not prove the opposite,
either. And wide appeal over time does indeed suggest genuine merit.

Sayers mastered and redefined the art of detection, moving inevitably
into an exploration of the mystery of human nature and finally into the
infinite mysteries of meaning, the universe, and life itself. This thread of
mystery, and of the human being's noble attempts to resolve it, runs
throughout the fabric of her work. In all her guises, she is also a storyteller
par excellence, breathing immortal life into fictional creatures, recreating
Christ's life on earth, describing her own discovery of Dante, tracing the
pattern of the universe. Reading Sayers is an exciting, invigorating experience because she is so full of life herself. It is, in fact, this sense of felt life,
made present through luminous language, that captures our attention and
makes an indelible impression.

Considering Sayers's response to Dante, Barbara Reynolds has pointed
out that "the fragments of *Paradiso* which she chose to translate in advance
are nearly all passages expressing wonder and joy" (*The Passionate Intellect* 214). This should not surprise anyone familiar with Sayers's fictional
world, or indeed, with the exuberance of her prose in general. Dorothy
Sayers found Dante so appealing, in part, because she shared with him a
love for this world, as well as a joyous longing for, and expectation of, a

world to come. Like his, hers was the Way of Affirmation; like him, she seems to echo the laughter of the universe. We love her for this risible nature, and for that "central and abiding sanity" which so often attends a profoundly comic apprehension of the world. It is interesting and revealing that she praised such sanity in Dante when comparing his *Commedia* with the comedy of Jane Austen, the English novelist whose sensibility seems closest to her own (Introduction to *Purgatory* 34).

In another telling comment, DLS suggested that readers should "approach the *Comedy* as though it were a serious and intelligent novel . . . for in the fourteenth century, the allegorical poem was precisely what the novel is to-day—the dominant literary form, into which a writer could pour, without incongruity, everything that he had to say about life and the universe" (Introduction to *Purgatory* 14). This is just what she had done in her own novels.

If a work of art is more than the sum of its parts, an artist is also more than the sum of his or her works. Yet "the sum of all the work is related to the mind itself, which made it, controls it, and relates it to its own creative personality. The mind is not the sum of its works, though it includes them all" (*The Mind of the Maker* 56). Readers return again and again to the works of Dorothy L. Sayers because of the mind that made them; it is an acute, generous, distinctive mind, and we like the view from its particular window.

Sayers's fiction is the best place to discover her perspective on the world, not only because she was an extraordinarily gifted novelist, but also because story is often more effective than exposition or argument. Really superb fiction, like *The Documents in the Case, The Nine Tailors,* and *Gaudy Night,* encompasses a subtlety and ambiguity that enables it to outlast the time and place that generated it. The novels of Dorothy L. Sayers are what first brought me to her spacious world, and they are the part of it I expect to last the longest. In them, we see embedded all of her values, beliefs, hopes, and fears—in them, we come closest to discovering her self.

Turning once again to Sayers's words about another writer, we can see their relevance to her own fate. In 1949, long after she had realized that there would be no more Wimsey novels, she said of a fellow mystery writer:

It cannot be helped. For all the world, and probably for all time, the fame of Conan Doyle must stand coupled with the name of Sherlock Holmes. That Doyle resented this, that he came to loathe Holmes, that he pushed him over the Reichenbach Falls in the vain hope of getting rid of him, is sad but true. . . . ("Conan Doyle: Crusader")

It cannot be helped, and we should not want it to be: Forever, the name of Dorothy L. Sayers will be gloriously linked with that of Lord Peter Wimsey—and of Harriet Vane! And I should expect even their creator would understand this now, as her amused comments on Conan Doyle suggest.

In a witty 1929 essay entitled "The Professor and the Detective," Marjorie Nicolson tried to explain the appeal of this form to scholars, especially professors of literature. After making the somewhat surprising claim that detection appeals to such people largely because it provides an "escape not from life, but from literature," Professor Nicolson goes on to show that this escape is not really from literature, but from some of its peculiarly modernist tendencies in their most exaggerated form. Of detective fans, she says:

> we have revolted from an excessive subjectivity to welcome objectivity; from long-drawn-out dissections of emotion to straightforward appeal to the intellect; from reiterated emphasis upon men and women as victims either of circumstances or of their glands to a suggestion that men and women may consciously plot and consciously plan; from the "stream of consciousness" which threatens to engulf us in its Lethean monotony to analyses of purpose, controlled and directed by a thinking mind; from formlessness to form; from the sophomoric to the mature; most of all, from a smart and easy pessimism which interprets men and the universe in terms of unmoral purposelessness to a rebelief in a universe governed by cause and effect. All this we find in the detective story. (reprinted in Haycraft, *The Art of the Mystery Story* 113–14)

And all this we find in the work of Dorothy L. Sayers. If such an emphasis upon story, upon meaning, coherence and structure, upon life as a moral undertaking and the power of a thinking mind, makes Sayers seem anachronistic or naive, so be it. These were the assumptions of most literature, and of most people, before the modern period. They were certainly the assumptions of the literature upon which she was nourished and which she most admired.

Oddly enough, it seems now, in the waning years of the twentieth century, that traditionalism may have won out after all; that perhaps modernism itself was the aberration, not the norm, even during the period that spawned it (see Hugh Kenner's *The Sinking Island*). In any event, the reports of the death of the novel have been greatly exaggerated. It would appear that the critics failed to tell the readers, who just kept on reading.

Annie Dillard considers this subject in an elegant, provocative collection of essays called *Living by Fiction,* where she argues that fiction keeps its audience by retaining the world as its subject matter. People like the world. Many people actually prefer it to art and spend their days by choice in the thick of it. The world's abounding objects, its rampant variety of people, its exuberant, destructive, and unguessable changes, and the splendid interest of its multiple conjunctions, appeal, attract, and engage more than ideas do, and more than beauty bare. When the arts abandon the world as their subject matter, people abandon the arts. (78)

Dorothy L. Sayers never abandoned the world, which is perhaps the greatest reason it has never abandoned her. She wrote of men and women who engage our interest and our sympathy; she recreated a recognizable landscape and evoked a palpably human world; and she raised many of the questions, large and small, which animate our lives.

Through the years, her work has also demonstrated a remarkable capacity for igniting or rekindling a love of literature and language, even in those whose lives are spent professing an interest in these subjects. Whether she is plotting a detective story, analyzing a text or a personality, ruminating on the state of Western culture, or puzzling over the creation of the universe, Dorothy L. Sayers is always "a writer first and foremost" (*The Sunday Times* 20 Aug. 1933). To her, this was the greatest praise one author could bestow upon another; to me, it is the most appropriate comment on Sayers herself. The Dorothy L. Sayers I know—the person I have met in the pages of her books—is not a strange lady, a curiosity, a social reformer or a preacher, but a writer: a writer of great charm and power, who once told me an unforgettable story.

Like most writers, she also composed her own best epitaph, in the words she gave to the dying William of Sens, a maker and craftsman like herself:

> let my work, all that was good in me,
> All that was God, stand up and live and grow.
>
> (*The Zeal of Thy House* 106)

There is much that is good in the creation of Dorothy L. Sayers: let it grow.

Notes

Preface

[1]Around this time, the first serious academic interest in Sayers was demonstrated by the publication of a scholarly bibliography (in 1978) and the 1979 publication of *As Her Whimsey Took Her,* an anthology which included a number of papers that had been read at various Modern Language Association meetings during the seventies. The Wade Center, then known as the Wade Collection, had begun amassing Sayers's papers and publications and sponsored symposia on her work. A journal, *The Sayers Review,* was published for a few years, and the still-flourishing Dorothy L. Sayers Society was founded in England. All of these things opened the door to informed, scholarly study of her work.

[2]"A Panegyric for Dorothy L. Sayers," *On Stories and Other Essays on Literature* 95.

[3]That study was published in 1988 as *The Passionate Intellect: Dorothy L. Sayers's Encounter with Dante,* by the Kent State University Press.

[4]Janet Hitchman, *Such a Strange Lady—An Introduction to Dorothy L. Sayers;* James Brabazon, *Dorothy L. Sayers: A Biography;* Alzina Stone Dale, *Maker and Craftsman* (Grand Rapids, Michigan: Eerdman's, 1978); Mary Brian Durkin, O.P., *Dorothy L. Sayers;* Ralph E. Hone, *Dorothy L. Sayers: A Literary Biography.*

[5]A word about style: From time to time, I refer to the author as "DLS" or simply "Sayers." I consider this preferable to repeating her full professional name, Dorothy L. Sayers, at every turn, and I could no more call a woman I never met "Dorothy" than I can see my way clear to calling Austen "Jane" or Shakespeare "Will." Sayers herself once commented to R. W. Chapman that no one could properly object to the use of the surname alone because "it is a proof that one has arrived"(Letter of 24 March 1936, in the Bodleian Library, Ms. Eng. lett. c. 469, fols. 175–95). Let *The Remarkable Case of Dorothy L. Sayers* go on record as saying just that.

Chapter 1

[1]Dorothy L. Sayers, "The Modern Detective Story," ms., Wade Center, Wheaton College,

Illinois, unpaginated; according to Colleen B. Gilbert, *A Bibliography of the Works of Dorothy L. Sayers,* this lecture was delivered 27 Oct. 1936.

²The Somerville College Log Book for the years 1911–14 shows that most of its graduates went into teaching, with a few becoming sub-editors or headmistresses.

³DLS, letter to Muriel Jaeger, 8 March 1917; quoted in James Brabazon, *Dorothy L. Sayers* 62. Brabazon also explains that the Reverend Henry Sayers funded this position for his daughter (61–62).

⁴Brabazon 75; cf. Harriet Vane's description of Catherine Freemantle Bendick, who has "wasted" an Oxford education and a brilliant mind as an overworked farmer's wife; *Gaudy Night* ch. 3.

⁵DLS held this job for one year, beginning in 1919; details of her job history clarified by Anthony Fleming, letter to the author, 27 Aug. 1983.

⁶How wrong Colin Watson is, in *Snobbery with Violence,* where he concludes that DLS hates the French (134).

⁷DLS, "Speech Given at Oxford," ms., Wade Center, n.d. but probably 1934. A version of this lecture was published as "What Is Right with Oxford."

⁸DLS, letters to Eustace Barton, various dates, Wade Center, record the exhaustion of these days as well.

⁹She published other poems during this time, including titles in the *Oxford Poetry* volumes for 1915, 1917, 1918, and 1919, and in volumes 1 and 2 of *The New Decameron.*

¹⁰It is interesting that, looking at the subject from a completely different vantage point, Barbara Reynolds notes similarly that "what Dorothy Sayers brought to the story [of *The Divine Comedy*] was the *writer's* eye," *The Passionate Intellect* 57. The Sayers verse translation of Dante has its defenders and detractors. For a brief summary of critical reactions to it, see Mary Brian Durkin, O.P., *Dorothy L. Sayers* ch. 7; and Barbara J. Dunlap, "Through a Dark Wood of Criticism," in *As Her Whimsey Took Her,* ed. Margaret P. Hannay.

¹¹Her habit of self-dramatization is recorded in the fragment of an autobiographical novel, entitled "Cat O' Mary," which James Brabazon uses extensively in his biography. Cf. ms. of "Cat O' Mary" 62–63, and ms. of "My Edwardian Childhood" 14, Wade Center. Based on my reading of these unpublished fragments, I agree with Brabazon that they are revelatory of Sayers's complicated personality and that the one, "Cat O' Mary," is a lightly fictionalized version of the abandoned autobiography, "My Edwardian Childhood."

¹²"My Edwardian Childhood" 7; quoted in Brabazon 5.

¹³Quoted in Brabazon 34; see his ch. 4 for a discussion of Sayers's difficult two years at the Godolphin School, Salisbury. See also Wade ms. of "Cat O' Mary" 153, for the complete passage.

¹⁴"My Edwardian Childhood" 7. In a letter to the author, 31 October 1986, Philip L. Scowcroft has estimated that Shakespeare heads the list of authors quoted in Sayers's fiction, with 155 allusions to 28 different plays; followed by the Bible/Prayer Book, with 115; Dickens, with 11 to *David Copperfield* alone; Lewis Carroll, 40; Tennyson, 25; Donne, 14; Milton, 9. Scowcroft also estimates references to the Sherlock Holmes canon at around 70. See his *Sidelights on Sayers* pertaining to Sayers's allusions (available from the DLS Society). Exact computation of Sayers's allusions is practically impossible, for she buries many of them in puns and even her unpublished manuscripts are filled with quotations.

¹⁵For example, in his influential *Murder for Pleasure,* Howard Haycraft concludes in a generally favorable summary of Sayers's contribution to the genre, that her last books "intruded unwittingly on the dangerous no-man's-land which is neither good detection nor good legitimate fiction," 138. See also DLS, "Novelist's Trade," Wade ms. dated 26 May 1936, which says that *Gaudy Night* was returned by a bookseller because it was not a detective story.

16 See note 14.

17DLS, letter to Catherine "Tony" Godfrey, n.d., Rare Book Collection of Smith College, Northampton, Massachusetts.

18 See, for example, "Departure from Crime," *Newsweek* 46 (22 Aug. 1955): 82–83. She tended to do this in interviews, but perhaps she was just irritated by questions like "When will we get another Peter Wimsey?" while she was laboring on a translation of *The Divine Comedy*. In this connection, it is interesting that Sayers's secretary during the war years, Kathleen Richards of Witham, Essex, does not remember DLS expressing any disdain for her novels, but recalls her appreciation of the fan mail she continued to receive from mystery readers. Interview with author, 21 July 1984.

19DLS, "Trent's Last Case," unpaginated ms., Wade Center; broadcast 24 Jan. 1934, on the BBC and published in *The Radio Times,* 21–27 Jan. 1934.

20There are a number of versions of this idea; the wording I use is from an article by DLS, "A Sport of Noble Minds."

21Kathleen Richards remembers DLS doing many jigsaw puzzles as well. Interview with author, 21 July 1984.

22As of this date, Stephan P. Clarke, *The Lord Peter Wimsey Companion* represents the most ambitious attempt to ferret out the sources of all these references.

23First published in *Pearson's* 60 (October 1925): 355–61; reprinted in *Lord Peter Views the Body.*

24C. S. Lewis, letter to editor, *Encounter* 20 (January 1963): 81–82.

25This can be deduced from the mss. of Sayers's novels in the Wade Center at Wheaton, which owns mss. or fair copies of every novel but *Whose Body?* As far as I have been able to determine, there is no extant manuscript of Sayers's first novel.

26That Byrne's mind worked this way is obvious from their collaborative effort, the play *Busman's Honeymoon;* see Alzina Stone Dale, ed., *Love All and Busman's Honeymoon* xxii, for a discussion of how the two writers contributed to the dialogue of this play. Byrne also wrote to Janet Hitchman, Sayers's first biographer, that she shared this habit with DLS and understood that it irritated many people; letter of 9 June 1967, in possession of the DLS Society. See also DLS, letter to R. W. Chapman, 15 Feb. 1935, Bodleian Library, Oxford; Ms. Eng. lett. c. 469, fols. 175–95, where she says that quoting without verifying is a "disease" with her.

27For example, E. C. Bentley's *Trent's Last Case,* and more recently, the novels of Robert Parker and Martha Grimes. In my opinion this style is not natural for some of the writers who employ it.

28"Religion and Our Reading, Listening and Play-Going," Wade ms. dated 11 Oct. 1938, 2.

29See *The Detling Murders* for his own reaction to this tendency. (U.S. title: *The Detling Secret.*)

30"Detectives in Fiction," Wade ms. of lecture, 1 (n.d.).

31See Watson, *Snobbery with Violence* 134, 145–47, 161, 217, 240, for an especially vehement attack.

32My comments are pertinent not only to novels by these authors of the 1920s and 1930s, but also to those that are intended to evoke this milieu.

33Jessica Mann, *Deadlier than the Male: An Investigation into Feminine Crime Writing,* points out that at the height of Wimsey's detective "career," fewer than one hundred murders and major crimes took place in all of Britain each year. It is amazing that he had enough work to keep busy.

34This judgment is based upon my experiences travelling and living in England at various

276

times since the early '80s. What is striking is the disparity between the general level of interest in DLS in the U.S. and in England.

[35]See, for example, P. D. James's foreword in *Dorothy L. Sayers,* by James Brabazon; and H. R. F. Keating, *Crime and Mystery: The 100 Best Books.*

[36]Recent novels satirizing the Lord Peter Wimsey type—or what the authors construe this type to be—include Elizabeth George, *A Great Deliverance* and Emma Tennant, *The Last of the Country House Murders.* In an entirely different vein, there are the Doran Fairweather mysteries by Mollie Hardwick, including *Parson's Pleasure,* which are also self-consciously in the Vane-Wimsey tradition, but with affection. Hardwick takes for granted that her readers will recognize references to "one other gaudy night" and Harriet Vane, without any further explanation (*Parson's Pleasure* 102, 192). I am indebted to Carol Wise for bringing this series to my attention.

Chapter 2

[1]This is a remarkable record for any novelist. In a letter of 25 March 1986 to the author, Livia Gollancz has written: "I think it is true to say that no novel by Dorothy Sayers has ever been out of print in hardcover except, possibly, for a short time between editions." An interesting wrinkle in this publishing history is that Sayers's first novel was rejected by every London publisher before being bought by an American house (Hodges, *Gollancz* 39). Some of the books were unavailable during 1986, because of litigation within the estate.

[2]See, for example, Christiana Brand, introduction, *Strong Poison,* by DLS, viii.

[3]In *The Thurber Carnival* (New York: Harper & Row, 1945).

[4]*Have His Carcase* and *Gaudy Night* had, of course, implied the passion between Harriet and Peter.

[5]See also Haycraft, *Murder for Pleasure* 135–42.

[6]DLS, "Speech Given at Oxford," ms., Wade Center, 4; the character of Miss Lydgate in *Gaudy Night* is generally considered an affectionate tribute to this well-loved teacher.

[7]DLS, letter to Michael Williams, 2 Dec. 1947, Wade Center.

[8]See Ralph E. Hone, "Dorothy L. Sayers: Critic of Detective Fiction," for a summary of these reviews.

[9]Like all generalizations, this comment about trends in crime fiction is a simplification. Agatha Christie continued to write the classical tale of ratiocination throughout her long career. Ngaio Marsh, P. D. James, Ruth Rendell, and Amanda Cross have each played variations on the type of detective story Sayers created, while Martha Grimes does frank contemporary imitations of the form.

[10]Stories by DLS that emphasize suspense and thereby seem closer to thrillers than detective stories include "The Abominable History of the Man with Copper Fingers," in *Lord Peter Views the Body,* and "The Incredible Elopement of Lord Peter Wimsey," in *Hangman's Holiday.* The stories concerning Montague Egg demonstrate that Sayers could also go beyond the social milieu of her Lord Peter stories.

[11]DLS, *Whose Body?* ch. 1. Early novels which purported to be histories include Henry Fielding's *Tom Jones: The History of a Foundling* and *The Adventures of Joseph Andrews.*

[12]DLS, *Whose Body?* ch. 4. Barbara Reynolds has pointed out Sayers's debt to *Trent's Last Case,* in "The Origin of Lord Peter Wimsey."

[13]See E. R. Gregory, ed. *Wilkie Collins: A Critical Study* by DLS (Toledo, Ohio: Friends of

the University of Toledo Libraries, 1977) 7, for details on dating the projected book, which was left as a fragment and published posthumously. Though he agrees that DLS was doing research on Collins in the early 1920s, Gregory concludes that she did not begin writing the proposed critical-biographical study until 1931 (8).

[14]See Wade file, "Unpublished Lectures by DLS."

[15]I am using the American titles for these collections. The habit of changing book titles for U.S. editions confuses the matter a bit, as does the fact that some of Sayers's works came out earlier in one market or the other. *The Omnibus of Crime* is the U.S. title for a 1929 anthology which came out in England a year earlier as *Great Short Stories of Detection, Mystery and Horror*. A second volume was published, again with different titles for each market, in 1931 (in the U.K.) and 1932 (in the U.S.). According to Gilbert, the contents of the U.S. editions differ somewhat from the British. *Tales of Detection* (1936) mercifully had one edition and one title.

[16]The great detectives were usually male, but not always. Sayers follows the general pattern of detective fiction in that she focuses upon a male detective early in her career, but then develops interesting female sleuths. Today, partially because of her influence, more female detectives are commanding center stage in crime fiction, in both the U.S. and U.K.

[17]See the *Sidelights on Sayers* series published by the DLS Society for a wide-ranging survey of the social history embedded in Sayers's fiction.

[18]DLS, letter to P.M. Stone, 6 Jan. 1944, DLS Society; and "Why Work?," a lecture delivered in 1942 and published in *Creed or Chaos?*: "When paper is scarce we must—or we should—think whether what we have to say is worth saying before writing or printing it" (49).

[19]DLS's letters to Eustace Barton, available at the Wade Center, show that this is just the way she worked on *The Documents in the Case;* other letters indicate similar strategies with *Strong Poison*, where she started with the idea of arsenical poisoning, and *Have His Carcase*.

[20]The English title of the collection was *Great Short Stories of Detection, Mystery and Horror*. Cf. John Milton, *Paradise Lost* 2.746–814.

[21]I am thinking of the emotional and psychological effects of her never acknowledging the birth of her son. While it is impossible to determine precisely what these effects were, it is also foolish to assume that they were not considerable. John Cawelti has made an interesting comment that would seem pertinent to Sayers's situation: "The classical detective story, with its focus on the investigation of mystery, showed a particular fascination with the hidden secrets and guilts that lay within the family circle." *Adventure, Mystery, and Romance Formula Stories as Art and Popular Culture* 77.

[22]"Detective Stories and the Primal Scene," in *The Poetics of Murder*, ed. Glenn W. Most and William Stowe, 13–29.

[23]The ms. of this lecture, entitled "Wilkie Collins 1824–1889" and seemingly intended for a group whose name is abbreviated on the ms. as "Newc. Lit. Phil.," is available at the Wade Center; I have not been able to determine what this group was. Perhaps because it was written on the verso of another ms., this work on Collins was not known when Gregory edited the fragment in 1977. He does acknowledge its existence in his essay on Sayers's relationship with Collins, in *As Her Whimsey Took Her* 53.

[24]DLS, "Wilkie Collins 1824–1889," Wade ms.

[25]For reviews that suggest the importance of humor in detective fiction, see DLS, "Crime Puzzle for Holiday Makers," *The Sunday Times* 6 Aug. 1933; "A Fleet Street Comedy," *The Sunday Times* 14 Jan. 1934.

[26]DLS, "Trent's Last Case," Wade ms. of a lecture, 3.

[27]From *The Mystery Bedside Book* (London: Hodder and Stoughton, 1960) 198; quoted in the DLS Society Bulletin, 70 (April 1987).

²⁸This judgment seems to be confined to English readers. Sheila Hodges reports that Victor Gollancz thought that *The Man Born to Be King* "vulgarised the Bible story and Christ himself" (*Gollancz* 147). C. S. Lewis considered Sayers's contribution to *Essays Presented to Charles Williams* "a trifle vulgar," according to Humphrey Carpenter, *The Inklings* 224. Lewis himself is attacked on this account, along with DLS, in Kathleen Nott's *The Emperor's Clothes*, where both are charged with having "a certain vulgarity, like the Salvation Army" (8). Nott's thesis in this book would seem to suggest that anything remotely religious would be so characterized, however. With her talent for turning what might be perceived as a defect into an asset, Sayers herself celebrated this quality in a lecture with the arresting title of "The Importance of Being Vulgar," which was delivered 12 Feb. 1936, but apparently never published (Gilbert 218).

²⁹G. K. Chesterton, "A Defense of Detective Stories," in *Detective Fiction: Crime and Compromise*, ed. Dick Allen and David Chacko 384—85.

³⁰This image is so widespread that it is held by many people who have never read a Sayers novel. *Gaudy Night* was especially reviewed this way, with undoubtedly the strongest attack being lodged by Q. D. Leavis in "The Case of Miss Dorothy Sayers," *Scrutiny* 6 (December 1937): 334—40. See also Mary McCarthy, "Highbrow Shockers," 142.

³¹DLS was, of course, not alone in trying to enhance the aesthetic qualities of the detective story during this period. In fact, her reviews encouraged other writers to take the genre seriously as a work of art. However, Howard Haycraft's judgment, written just a few years after DLS completed her last novel, still seems accurate: "No single trend in the English detective story of the 1920's was more significant than its approach to the literary standards of the legitimate novel. And no author illustrates the trend better than Dorothy Sayers" (*Murder for Pleasure* 135).

Chapter 3

¹This is also true of George Fentiman, in *The Unpleasantness at the Bellona Club*, who is perhaps more of an autobiographical figure, since he is married and his wife is the breadwinner, which was the pattern of the Sayers-Fleming match after a few years. See the Brabazon biography for details of Sayers's love affairs and marriage (chs. 8—11).

²See Brabazon, especially chs. 6—9, for details of this portion of her life; and Ralph E. Hone, *Dorothy L. Sayers: A Literary Biography*. Brabazon had the advantage of being given access to all the Sayers-Fleming papers, but Hone did well with the material at his disposal, handling the subject with sympathy and insight.

³DLS, letter to Eustace Barton, 7 Feb. 1930, Wade Center. The extensive correspondence between these two writers regarding *Documents* constitutes the most complete history of Sayers's working habits as a novelist that I have been able to discover.

⁴DLS, "Emile Gaboriau—1835—1873 The Detective Novelist's Dilemma," *The Sunday Times* 2 Nov. 1935: 677—78.

⁵DLS, letter to Victor Gollancz, 29 Oct. 1927, DLS Society. For more on her study of English culture, see "The Mysterious English" and "The Gulf Stream and the Channel," *Unpopular Opinions*. I will not take up the question of how Sayers's novels reflect particulars of social history; the *Sidelights on Sayers* series published by the DLS Society has done an exhaustive survey of that subject, much of it summarized in Philip L. Scowcroft, "The Detective Fiction of Dorothy L. Sayers: A Source for the Social Historian?" *Seven* 5 (April 1984):

70–83. See also Alzina Stone Dale, "Fossils in Cloud-Cuckoo Land," *Sayers Review* 3.1 (December 1978): 3–10.

[6]The term "poverty" is, of course, a relative one. What I mean is that both women faced serious financial difficulties in adult life. Brabazon documents this in his biography of DLS, showing that the early years in London were quite difficult financially as well as emotionally. Park Honan has demonstrated "the shadow of hard poverty" which troubled the Reverend Henry Austen and which followed his portionless younger daughter throughout her life; *Jane Austen: Her Life* 17.

[7]DLS, "Thrones, Dominations," unfinished novel ms. in the Wade Center, claims Wimsey is unique in this regard (37A).

[8]I believe this term originated with Robert Graves's book of the same title.

[9]See L. E. Bottiger, "The Murderer's Vade Mecum." After assessing the murder methods in a number of Sayers's novels and finding some of them implausible, he makes this recommendation, which is especially interesting given the context: "Don't bother about a few medical inadvertencies" (1821). He also reports that his pathology professor kept a stack of detective novels in his office, including most of Sayers's mysteries.

[10]In a letter to Eustace Barton, 19 Nov. 1928, DLS indicates that she has deliberately chosen to adopt Collins's style (Wade). Philip Scowcroft has discussed the resemblance between Munting and Wimsey in the *Sidelights on Sayers* series (17).

[11]Joe R. Christopher, "The Mystery of Robert Eustace."

[12]DLS, letters to Eustace Barton, 3 Sept. 1930; 3 Oct. 1932; and 7 Oct. 1932, Wade Center. Of special interest, given the controversy over the forensic accuracy of her mysteries and her employment of scientific details, is the following statement, which was made by a scientist: "Of significance . . . is the extensive background possessed by Sayers, a writer whose penchant for science is clearly displayed in her novel"; Dominick A. Labianca, "The Role of the Humanities in the Teaching of Chemistry." See also: Edwin Crundwell, "Dorothy Sayers's crime" 575; Richard Severo, "Dorothy Sayers's Poison Is a Treat for Chemists"; and Natalie Foster, "Strong Poison: Chemistry in the Works of Dorothy L. Sayers," in *Chemistry and Crime,* ed. Samuel M. Gerber.

[13]She was also an astute judge of what suggestions to accept. For example, she declined writing a "moth-ball story," which Barton also suggested (letter of 15 June 1929, Wade Center).

[14]I am using the name he was given, although he later began calling himself "Atherton." He also elevated his rank to major from captain (Brabazon 113). The DLS Society held its annual seminar in Kirkcudbright during the summer of 1986.

[15]Two other mysteries with effective office settings are Nicholas Blake's *Minute for Murder* and Michael Gilbert's *Smallbone Deceased.* My thanks to Philip Scowcroft for reminding me of them.

Chapter 4

[1]Cf. DLS, "The Mysterious English," *Unpopular Opinions,* and "Wimsey Papers," *The Spectator* 17 Nov. 1939–26 Jan. 1940.

[2]"Cat O' Mary" was announced for publication in the 1935 Gollancz edition of *Whose Body?* but was never published. In a letter to the author, 19 March 1984, Anthony Fleming quoted a January 1932 letter from DLS to her cousin, Ivy, which says that she has started writing her memoirs "in a spasm of middle-agedness."

[3]Quoted in Hone 67.

[4]See "Dante and His Daughter Bice," ms. by DLS in the Wade Center. DLS articulated this in many contexts. Perhaps the strongest is the letter of 2 Jan. 1940 to Anthony Fleming, which Brabazon quotes: "What we make is more important than what we are, particularly if making is our profession" (162–63).

[5]This territory has been covered well in the Brabazon biography (chs. 9–10).

[6]I am not suggesting that DLS was ever alienated from her parents, but the secret of Anthony's birth, along with the struggle for survival in London during the early twenties, must have precluded genuine closeness.

[7]I am indebted to Philip Scowcroft for making me aware of something DLS herself apparently did not realize when she wrote this review: Lorac was a woman!

[8]Edmund Wilson, "Who Cares Who Killed Roger Ackroyd?" in *The Art of the Mystery Story*, ed. Howard Haycraft, 390–97. In his brief introduction to this famous essay, Haycraft welcomes the dour Wilson as "a visitor from another and sadder world."

[9]Mss. of the novels in the Wade Center include evidence that DLS worked out the genealogy for *Unnatural Death*, as well as timetables for *Five Red Herrings*, while she planned and drafted the books. One of the substantive revisions in the manuscript material at the Wade is the simple but significant changing of the heroine's name from Marian Delaney to Harriet Vane (in the ms. of *Strong Poison*).

[10]Brabazon, *Dorothy L. Sayers* 151; his ch. 13 deals with the interplay between Sayers's personal situation and her work during this period.

[11]Brabazon deals extensively with Sayers's intellectualism; see especially ch. 4.

[12]In the course of lecturing on DLS, I have met many people who proudly announce rereading her novels every year or so. The ease with which they quote her words from memory demonstrates that the claim is true.

[13]Bayswater is, of course, very urban today and was perhaps not what most people would describe as "suburban" even in 1930, but this is the word Sayers uses to describe the area and its inhabitants. It is perhaps significant that she never lived in Bayswater, nor in an area that could be properly called "suburban." This is true of most people who use the word as she does.

[14]In a stunning psychological thriller entitled *A Dark-Adapted Eye*, Barbara Vine (Ruth Rendell) has once again demonstrated the fascination of these questions about perception and how to tell a story.

[15]See Bottiger, "The Murderer's Vade Mecum" 1821.

[16]Brabazon stresses this tendency relentlessly (see especially ch. 10), but the novels of DLS reveal her deep capacity for a range of emotion, including love. She writes with passion and affection not only of Wimsey, but of her entire created world: "love is the Energy of creation" (*The Mind of the Maker* 136).

[17]Victor Gollancz once quoted Williams on *The Nine Tailors*, from a letter of 29 Dec. 1933: "It's a marvelous book; it is high imagination . . . The end is unsurpassable. (I daresay I exaggerate, but I've only just finished it and I'm all shaken.)" (Brabazon 225).

[18]I know there is a tendency among Sayers afficionados to apply the standards of Holmesian "higher criticism" to her novels. The DLS Society has published a detailed chronology of Lord Peter's life, for example. Sayers's characters are believable and real to me, but I have my limits: I am considering the development of Sayers's art through her novel sequence, rather than treating Wimsey as an actual person. Therefore, the *order* in which the novels were written is of more importance to my comments than the (presumed) timespan each covers in Wimsey's life. It is, of course, a compliment to Sayers's story-telling abilities that her readers forget that her characters were invented.

[19]Yet Barbara Vine's recent novel, *A Dark-Adapted Eye*, includes elaborate scrutiny of manners and mores as means of unravelling the mystery.

[20]This is the conclusion of Julian Symons, *Bloody Murder: From the Detective Story to the Crime Novel: A History.*

[21]Cf. *Strong Poison* ch. 20 and *The Mind of the Maker* 115–21.

[22]The DLS Society has published excellent guides to Sayers locations, including the fens, Oxford, and London.

[23]Her growth is also reflected in the increasing realism of her settings. *Clouds of Witness, Unnatural Death,* and *Have His Carcase* take place in invented settings and lack the authenticity of her London, Oxford, and Fenland locales.

[24]Examples include Wilkie Collins, *The Woman in White;* Charles Dickens, *Bleak House;* and DLS, *The Documents in the Case, Gaudy Night,* and *Busman's Honeymoon.* The films of Alfred Hitchcock often have this implied theme as well; e.g., *Psycho.*

[25]For example, F. Scott Fitzgerald, *The Great Gatsby* and "Babylon Revisited," and Ernest Hemingway, *The Sun Also Rises* and "Soldier's Home." It is important to place the Wimsey novels in this historical literary context, because they, too, were a product of the period between the wars and reflect much of the history and mood of that time.

[26]Note the Soviet Club (*Clouds of Witness*) and the discussion of relaxed standards in the postwar world (*Strong Poison*). The conservatism of the classic English detective story is savagely parodied in Emma Tennant's *The Last of the Country House Murders,* which also mocks the superficial aspects of Wimsey's character while missing any of its depth. This is yet another thing DLS shares with Jane Austen: both writers have had the fate of being, by turns, loved and hated for the most superficial qualities of their fictional worlds.

Chapter 5

[1]See, for example, Rendell (writing as Barbara Vine), *A Dark-Adapted Eye.* P. D. James's version of the detective story, especially in her earlier books, is in some ways indebted to Sayers. Surely her Cordelia Gray owes something to Harriet Vane. See S. L. Clarke, "*Gaudy Night*'s Legacy: P. D. James' *An Unsuitable Job for a Woman*" and P. D. James, "The Heart-Pounding Pleasure of Whodunits." What DLS and James do not share is something much more fundamental yet ineffable: a way of seeing the world, an attitude toward experience.

[2]DLS foresaw this possibility. In a letter to Victor Gollancz, she characterized the just-finished novel as "this overgrown monster which is neither flesh nor fowl. . . . I do feel rather passionately about this business of integrity of the mind—but I realise that to make a 'detective story' the vehicle for that kind of thing . . . is 'reckless to the point of insanity' " (Hodges, *Gollancz* 44).

[3]Margaret P. Hannay has discussed their relationship in these terms. See "Harriet's Influence on the Characterization of Lord Peter Wimsey" in *As Her Whimsey Took Her.* The essay "Gaudy Night" reveals that DLS was consciously using Harriet in this way.

[4]Alzina Stone Dale summarizes the history of this venture in her introduction to *Love All—Busman's Honeymoon* xviii–xix.

[5]Cf. the description of an Etonian in Helene Hanff's *84 Charing Cross Road* for an American's response to this "type" in actual experience.

[6]See Brabazon chs. 16 and 17.

[7]Brabazon 151. It is a mistake to assume that there was no affection in this marriage. The tone of some of DLS's earlier letters suggests that the marriage was happy for a while. See, for example, her letter to Victor Gollancz (11 Aug. 1928), DLS Society. In "Dorothy L. Sayers: The Holy Mysteries," Alden B. Flanders has speculated about whether there were experiences

of love and "wholeness" in Sayers's life during this period, which could explain the change in her work from 1930 to the end of the Wimsey saga.

⁸See DLS, "Trent's Last Case," Wade lecture ms.

⁹This reference is made in both the "Prothalamion" and ch. 14 of *Busman's Honeymoon.* The parallel is fitting not only because of the inequality of the potential mates, but more importantly, because they are experienced and have painful personal histories which prevent their marriage for some time.

¹⁰ *The Lord Peter Wimsey Companion* suggests another source for the Latinate ending of *Gaudy Night:* Roman civil law (371), but it seems unlikely that this was on Sayers's mind as she struggled to end her Oxford novel. In *The Mind of the Maker,* she refers readers to a book by M. R. Ridley on Keats (120). Does this mean that, like Peter Wimsey, the young man turned out to be a solid scholar who could merit her respect?

¹¹The current secretary of the DLS Society, Christopher Dean, is writing a "biography" of Lord Peter.

¹²DLS did not know whether she had written this poem or simply remembered it (Brabazon 156).

¹³See Ian Watt, *The Rise of the Novel,* and Sandra M. Gilbert and Susan Gubar, *The Madwoman in the Attic,* for two different approaches to this subject.

¹⁴In this 1966 introduction to the Penguin edition of *Emma,* Ronald Blythe called it "the most fiendishly difficult of detective stories," 7.

¹⁵Relevant chapters in each novel would be: *Jane Eyre,* 23, 37; *Pride and Prejudice,* 50, 52, 58, 60; *Emma,* 47, 49; and *Persuasion,* 11.

¹⁶Wimsey acknowledges this himself in *Gaudy Night:* "Our kind of show is dead and done for" (ch. 14). See also "Wimsey Papers," *The Spectator* 8 Dec. 1939. The abandonment of "Thrones, Dominations" seems to confirm this: Wimsey was a creature of the interwar period.

¹⁷DLS, "Speech Given at Oxford," Wade ms. 2.

¹⁸As late as 12 April 1948, DLS wrote to a fan, Doris McCarthy, that she hoped to write more plays and novels when she finished translating *The Divine Comedy* (letter in DLS Society archives). She would die before this opportunity arose. It is interesting that the radio mystery play's proceeds went to the Detection Club, so money-making was not a motive in her taking it on. Barbara Reynolds includes a good account of the fragmentary novel about Dante in *The Passionate Intellect.* The ms. is in the Wade Center.

Chapter 6

¹According to a note by DLS, this lecture was delivered to a "women's society"; it was published later in *Unpopular Opinions* (1946). Page citations are to that collection.

²*Unpopular Opinions* 106. Although she does not explain what she means by an "old-fashioned" and "aggressive" feminism, DLS was no doubt appalled by the anarchic tendencies in the extreme camp of the early twentieth-century British women's movement, with its hunger strikes and occasional street violence. According to Patricia Craig and Mary Cadogan, *The Lady Investigates,* in England by the 1930s "active feminism was considered old hat and soon became a source of irritation to those preoccupied with more pressing issues like the war in Spain and threatening developments in Germany" (207).

³*Unpopular Opinions,* 113. When "Are Women Human?" was reissued in the 1970s, along with "Human-Not-Quite-Human," it was again very popular. The slim volume carried the provocative title, *Are Women Human?* and one wonders how many have picked the book up

because of it. When I have ordered it for classes, I have found that the bookstore has a hard time keeping it in stock.

[4]The two lectures have been published together, in both *Unpopular Opinions* and as *Are Women Human?*

[5]See DLS, *The Comedy of Dante Alighieri The Florentine: Purgatory* 31–38; introduction, *The Moonstone*, by Wilkie Collins; "Eros in Academe," *The Oxford Outlook* 1.2 (June 1919): 110–116; Wade mss. "Cat O' Mary," "My Edwardian Childhood," "Wilkie Collins," and an untitled fragment on Elizabeth I.

[6]The BBC's Written Archives, Caversham Park, Reading, are replete with Sayers correspondence relating to fees and rights. Given the tendency of some critics to regard DLS as overly interested in money, there are two letters of special interest: in one by her agent, dated 6 Nov. 1947, she declines the offer of a higher payment for a serialization of *Whose Body?* because she has already signed a contract for less; in another, the agent reminds the BBC that the profits from the Detection Club series, to which DLS contributed *Where Do We Go from Here?*, go to the Club, not the authors (22 Dec. 1947).

[7]*The Documents in the Case,* document no. 2. Although this thought is expressed by Agatha Milsom, even a disturbed mind is right sometimes and the novel dramatizes the truth of her comment.

[8]DLS refers directly to this in "Human-Not-Quite-Human," (*Unpopular Opinions* 118). Since the essay was originally published in 1941, it is not surprising that the social program of Third Reich was on her mind.

[9]Nina Auerbach, *Communities of Women: An Idea in Fiction* 18.

Chapter 7

[1]Without Lady Mary's confusion about her role in society and her marital future, the death would not occur and the novel's mystery plot would not be set in motion.

[2]Lord Peter is, of course, in this novel and takes the official role of detective, but it is Miss Climpson's detection that makes the solution to the case possible.

[3]I am using the term "hero" to refer not only to the novel's ostensible detective-hero, Lord Peter Wimsey, but also to Miss Climpson herself. She is certainly not a traditional heroine, but functions as a female hero, being an active participant in the plot. Carolyn G. Heilburn has discussed this question of the possibility for female heroes in *Toward a Recognition of Androgny.* The pattern I suggest is established in the first novel, with Julian Freke and Peter Wimsey squaring off in this way. Earlier critics who have noticed the importance of work in the novels include Katherine Keller and Karen Avenish, "Wimsey, Women and Work," and Kathleen Gregory Klein, "Dorothy Sayers," *10 Women of Mystery.*

[4]The population of the United Kingdom was approximately fifty million at this time.

[5]Park Honan has written of Jane Austen's England: "There *was* a vicious new pace in 'matrimonial affairs' in Hampshire these days: music, dancing and dress were more competitively used as men became fewer in wartime" (*Jane Austen: Her Life* 103). For a discussion of the positive affects of such a situation, see Nina Auerbach, *Communities of Women:* "Union among women, perceived by every generation as unprecedented in history, is one of the unacknowledged fruits of war. . . . The force that destroys men brings power and vigor to the community of women and the dream of its postwar inheritance" (161).

[6]Craig and Cadogan, 11; they show the source of this term as Michele Slung, *Crime on Her Mind.* It is important to note that female detectives in American and English fiction had more

in common before the hard-boiled school started in the U.S. In that type of American detective fiction, until very recently, women were most often cast as subhuman vixens who create problems rather than solve them.

[7]This is also true of the general novel tradition, of course, partially because it was the first genre to be heavily written by and for women. Women are perhaps even more dominant in the mystery and crime genre now, with the novels of Amanda Cross, Sara Paretsky, Sue Grafton, and Lady Antonia Fraser featuring strong female protagonists.

[8]See DLS, "The Present Status of the Mystery Story," on these two strains in the history of detective fiction.

[9]P. D. James: "Perhaps because clue-making so often involves the routine and the minutiae of ordinary life, the detective novel can tell us more about contemporary society than many a more pretentious literary form" (Brabazon, xv).

[10]Auerbach, *Communities of Women* 18. There is a strong adumbration of this trend in Jane Austen's novels.

[11]The connotations of these two words are difficult to express, but the point is that, while many of these characters fulfill the legal definition of "spinster" because they are women who have never married, they do not fit the stereotype of "spinster" as an older "maiden lady"—dowdy, fussy, and often sexually repressed.

[12]Austen, *Emma*, ed. Ronald Blythe, 7.

[13]Perhaps the most striking example of such spinsters is in the novels of Barbara Pym.

[14]In *Unnatural Death*, Miss Climpson is described as "middle-aged" (ch. 3), but a short four years later in *Strong Poison*, she is introduced in the first chapter as elderly, which suits her better.

[15]This phrase is used mockingly in Barbara Pym, *Jane and Prudence* 60.

[16]It is interesting to note the difference between Miss Climpson and another member of the Cattery, Miss Murchison, in this regard. Miss Murchison's detective work is also crucial in *Strong Poison*, but she does not suffer the same qualms of conscience that Miss Climpson does (ch. 8). This again demonstrates Sayers's fine detailing of character and her ability to transcend stereotypes.

[17]Brabrazon quotes from the letters of DLS to John Cournos, which show that she was somewhat conflicted on this subject (see ch. 9 of *Dorothy L. Sayers*). "Cat O' Mary" presents the more typical stance (Wade ms. 193).

[18]The early female detectives who were married tended to serve family responsibilities even in their detection, often trying to exonerate a husband or brother. Today, a character like Amanda Cross's Kate Fansler is consciously revising the definition of female experience, especially as it relates to marriage. See *The Question of Max* or *Death in a Tenured Position*.

[19]See Bottiger, "The Murderer's Vade Mecum." Philip Scowcroft, who is a solicitor, has told me that the legal premise of the book, which is crucial to the plot and elaborately developed, is also incorrect.

Chapter 8

[1]DLS, letters of various dates to Eustace Barton, Wade Center. See especially those of 15 May 1928; 29 June 1928; 24 July 1928.

[2]Eustace Barton, letter of 24 May 1928 to DLS; quoted in Brabazon, 130.

[3]Jane Austen, *Persuasion*, ch. 18. It is interesting that in each novel, the victim of such tyranny is also female.

[4]See Jane Austen, *Northanger Abbey,* chs. 6, 7, 11, 13.

[5]Henry James, *The Portrait of a Lady:* "They were strangely married, at all events, and it was a horrible life" (ch. 42).

[6]I should perhaps add that some of the male readers with whom I have discussed this novel have said that they did not find Munting believable.

[7]"Are Women Human?" *Unpopular Opinions* 115. Cf. *The Unpleasantness at the Bellona Club,* where Wimsey says that he has learned much by being "an ordinary person . . . [who has] met women, and talked to them like ordinary human beings" (ch. 18); and Wilkie Collins, *The Woman in White:* "Women can resist a man's love, a man's fame, a man's personal appearance, and a man's money, but they cannot resist a man's tongue when he knows how to talk to them" ("The Second Epoch," 5).

[8]American detectives, especially of the dominant hard-boiled type, often break the law. By contrast, Sherlock Holmes seems to function outside or even above the official arms of the law, bringing justice to those who might elude ordinary policemen and courts. This is true in "The Adventure of the Speckled Band," for example.

[9]Cf. Nathaniel Hawthorne, *The Scarlet Letter,* where Hester Prynne asserts to Dimmesdale that "What we did had a consecration of its own" (ch. 17).

[10]I am not sure how well they are known outside the United States, but I am thinking of such exploitative and sensational films as *The Burning Bed, Fatal Attraction,* and *Extremities.*

[11]The Dowager Duchess compares the Denvers' marriage unfavorably with that between Peter and Harriet in the "Prothalamion" to *Busman's Honeymoon;* the distinction is repeated in the fragmentary novel, "Thrones, Dominations."

[12]This is demonstrated not only in the sharp contrast between Harriet Vane and Helen, Duchess of Denver, but also in the two potential husbands for Lady Mary Wimsey: Cathcart and Parker.

[13]"Are Women Human?" *Unpopular Opinions* 110; Wade ms. on Elizabeth I.

[14]See Philip L. Scowcroft, Dorothy L. Sayers Society Seminar Proceedings, 1983, for a discussion of Munting and Wimsey.

Chapter 9

[1]One wonders how autobiographical this aspect of the Vane-Wimsey courtship is, for DLS knew from experience what a difficult position it was to feel grateful to one's mate. Her husband not only provided her with a name to give her son, but also kept her secret through the years. This could not have been easy for either of them.

[2]Miss Climpson's holding out forces a hung jury and a new trial, which gives Lord Peter time to investigate and solve the case.

[3]The life and works of Jane Austen provide many examples of such women, as do the twentieth-century novels of Barbara Pym.

[4]DLS describes her own mother this way in "My Edwardian Childhood," Wade ms. 7.

[5]Brabazon makes note of this quality (149).

[6]Jane Austen, *Persuasion* ch. 23; *Pride and Prejudice* ch. 8.

[7]Wilvercombe is one of Sayers's invented locations; see John Morris and Philip L. Scowcroft, *Locations in Sayers's Fiction,* 1983 (available from the DLS Society).

[8]The novel employs dancing as a metaphor for the male-female relationship, in much the same way Austen uses the dance. The recent television adaptations of *Have His Carcase* and

Gaudy Night used such scenes effectively to dramatize the slowly developing relationship between Harriet and Peter.

⁹The characterization does, however, provide glimpses of Dorothy L. Sayers, the private woman. Cf. Harriet's lines, "Oh, God, what have I done, that I should be such a misery to myself and other people? Nothing more than thousands of women . . ." (*Gaudy Night* ch. 18), and the author's: "I hope Anthony and I don't come to the workhouse! but it's so hard to work. It frightens me to be so unhappy—I thought it would get better, but I think every day is worse than the last, and I'm always afraid they'll chuck me out of the office because I'm working so badly." (DLS, letter to John Cournos, 22 Feb. 1925, quoted in Brabazon 105).

¹⁰Like most writers, DLS is more successful portraying her own class and type of person. The college servants, for example, are stereotypes, while the dons and students are multidimensional.

¹¹Prominent unhappy spinsters include Agatha Milsom (*The Documents in the Case*) and Aggie Twitterton (*Busman's Honeymoon*); happy ones include Misses Climpson, Meteyard (*Murder Must Advertise*), Lydgate and Martin (*Gaudy Night*). Even the Oxford novel shows that the unmarried state is unhappy for some, like the tortured Miss Hillyard.

¹²It should be remembered that, at the end of the twenties, DLS had gone back to translating the Tristan of Thomas the Anglo-Norman. One cannot fairly say that she ever abandoned scholarship.

¹³In ch. 2, Harriet decides, in a "rather exalted mood," that "in the glamour of one Gaudy night, one could realize that one was a citizen of no mean city"; cf. Acts 21.39. DLS had begun the ms. of "My Edwardian Childhood" with the same line.

¹⁴References to Jane Austen in Sayers's work include *Clouds of Witness*, ch. 4; *Further Papers on Dante* (1957; reprint Westport, Conn.: Greenwood Press, 1979): 21, 30; occasional references in her *Sunday Times* reviews of mystery novels; and this arresting comment in the introduction to her translation of the *Purgatorio:* "When I say that the accents of Dante's Beatrice have much in common with those of Elizabeth Bennet, I intend a compliment, not only to the poet's central and abiding sanity, but also to the sensitive accuracy of his feminine psychology" (34). This statement, of course, also represents an implied compliment to the "central and abiding sanity" and artistry of the greatest female novelist in the English tradition.

¹⁵The key chapter where this is discussed in *Jane Eyre* is 23; the inequality of Bronte's lovers is not resolved until Jane returns, newly wealthy, to find a blinded Rochester, the impediment of his living wife having also been removed, quite dramatically, by the fire. Harriet and Peter do not undergo such extreme, melodramatic reversals, however; their changes are moral and psychological, as is the case in Austen's fiction. See *Pride and Prejudice* chs. 52, 58, 60; *Persuasion* ch. 23; *Emma* ch. 49, for scenes that work out this delicate balancing act between the sexes.

¹⁶Julian Symons, *Bloody Murder: From the Detective Story to the Crime Novel: A History* 128. He does admit that he finds it difficult to write fairly of DLS (13).

¹⁷This pattern was established with Richardson's *Pamela*. Ian Watt postulates that the reason for the pattern is that, if a woman marries below her own class, it is an admission of sexual motivation on her part, since the marriage can do nothing for her social standing or financial future (*The Rise of the Novel* 164).

¹⁸These are, of course, the predatory males in Richardson's *Pamela* and *Clarissa*.

¹⁹See Carolyn Heilbrun, "*Gaudy Night* and Its American Women Readers," Dorothy L. Sayers Society 1985 Seminar Proceedings; and Nina Auerbach, "Dorothy L. Sayers and the Amazons," *Romantic Imprisonment: Women and Other Glorified Outcasts*.

²⁰The word "gaudy" is derived from the Latin, *gaudium,* meaning joy.

²¹It is a mistake to assume that the Sayers-Fleming match was from the beginning unhappy or simply a convenience. See DLS, letter to Victor Gollancz (11 Aug. 1928), in possession of the DLS Society, in which she effusively describes her husband and married life with a kind of giddy affection. James Brabazon reaches a similar conclusion from the evidence of her letters (134).

²²Jane Austen evades this charge by employing a multilevel irony that is at once defense and attack. This is what permits many of her readers to continue to cast her in the role of "lady," despite her biting tongue and unblinking stare. It is also what permits some readers to like her, in spite of what she says.

²³DLS, "Eros in Academe," *The Oxford Outlook* 1.2 (June 1919): 110–16. "The girl when she goes down [graduates] is already a woman, and if she is still socially ignorant it is late for her to begin learning. If she goes straight to the cloister of a girls' school she never will begin . . ." (115).

²⁴In the mid-nineteenth century, the most extreme version of this line of thinking was uttered by St. John Rivers to Jane Eyre, when he told her she was formed for labor, not love or happiness. Jane Eyre takes the revolutionary position that this means she was also not made for marriage (ch. 35).

Chapter 10

¹Quoted in Hone, 94; the source is given as "Death of Miss Dorothy Sayers," *Manchester Guardian Weekly* (26 Dec. 1957).

²Val Gielgud, "Why I Killed Peter Wimsey," *Sunday Dispatch* 22 Dec. 1957: 6. See also Hone 69.

³For example, Richard T. Webster, "*The Mind of the Maker:* Logical Construction, Creative Choice and the Trinity," in *As Her Whimsey Took Her* 174.

⁴Quoted in E. L. Mascall, "What Happened to Dorothy L. Sayers that Good Friday?"

⁵DLS quoted in Mascall, 15; cf. Wade ms. "Cat O' Mary" 166.

⁶This was a venture proposed by the Reverend Patrick McLaughlin, where intellectual Christians were to try to reach nonbelievers.

⁷DLS quoted in Mascall, 10.

⁸DLS quoted in Mascall, 10.

⁹See Muriel Byrne, letter of 9 June 1967, to Janet Hitchman, in possession of the Sayers Society, in which one of Sayers's closest friends objects to the biographer's calling her "intensely religious," adding that Sayers's father influenced her primarily as a classical scholar, not as a cleric. Byrne goes on to say that Sayers's attitude toward religion was "practical and intellectual rather than fervid." This characterization would seem to fit Sayers's own statements on the subject. See also Brabazon 23.

¹⁰Cf. "My Edwardian Childhood," Wade ms. 14.

¹¹DLS, letter to E. V. Rieu, 12 March 1945, Wade Center; the comment is in reference to Dante.

¹²*The Whimsical Christian,* ed. William Griffin. This is a reissue of the collection originally titled *Christian Letters to a Post-Christian World.*

¹³DLS, letter of 29 July 1913, to Catherine Godfrey, Rare Book Collection of Smith College; another letter in this collection, dated "Good Friday, 1913," considers the question of how best to save souls, whether by religious argument or personal example.

¹⁴For example "Lay" and "Hymn in Contemplation of Sudden Death," in *Op. I.*

¹⁵In *The Blue Moon* 1.1 (1917); published for the Mutual Admiration Society. According to the Gilbert bibliography, this was Sayers's first published story.

¹⁶DLS quoted in Mascall, 38.

Chapter 11

¹DLS, "The Religions Behind the Nation," *The Church Looks Ahead:* "The *last* achievement of reason is always to cast doubt on its own validity: so that the final result of rationalism is the appearance of a wholly irrational universe" (77). This is implied in such mysteries as *The Nine Tailors* and *The Woman in White.*

²DLS, *The Mind of the Maker* 17, quotations from the Church of England's *Articles of Religion* 9. It should be noted that both the theological writings of DLS and my discussion of them use the traditional language of the Prayer Book and the Bible, and thus at times employ what is now considered to be sexist terminology.

³For example, cf. Nathaniel Hawthorne, *The Scarlet Letter* (Chillingworth) and "The Birthmark" (Aylmer).

⁴Article of that title by DLS, *The Saturday Review of Literature* 6.2 (3 Aug. 1929): 22–23.

⁵See, for example, "The Adventure of the Speckled Band" and "The Adventure of the Copper Beeches" in the Sherlock Holmes canon.

⁶DLS, "Target Area," *The Atlantic Monthly* 173 (March 1944): 48–50, a poem which speaks eloquently of humanity's essential sinfulness in the context of World War II.

⁷Cf. *Strong Poison* ch. 16, "Even in a righteous cause. . . ," for another moral dilemma Miss Climpson faces.

⁸In Oscar Wilde, *The Importance of Being Earnest;* Charlotte Brontë, *Jane Eyre;* and Jane Austen, *Pride and Prejudice.*

⁹Edmund, in *Mansfield Park,* is an exception to this general comment about Austen's clergy.

¹⁰In *The Passionate Intellect,* Barbara Reynolds explains that DLS was invited to give her first lecture on Dante at Cambridge because she would be "a draw" (54–58). Is there any doubt that Sayers's reputation as a popular novelist was part of the reason she was an appealing choice to translate *The Divine Comedy* for the then-new Penguin series? Or that her familiarity as a mystery writer has motivated many sales of this translation?

¹¹It will be remembered that she was also editing anthologies of the genre and writing critical essays on detective fiction at this time.

¹²Ralph L. Clarke, letter to the author, 3 Nov. 1986, has written that Sayers's father also left her £5,000 (which he estimated was equivalent to $150,000 in 1986). The house in Witham became the Flemings' principle residence until their deaths, his in 1950 and hers in 1957.

¹³Brabazon notes that DLS once gave her father high marks for a sermon in which he showed that science could be reconciled with the Bible, 23.

¹⁴Since the word "good" is derived from "god."

¹⁵Considering the divorce laws of the period, it is not surprising that someone would commit murder as the ultimate way to nullify a marriage, but what I find unbelievable is the attraction between Lathom and Margaret Harrison.

¹⁶I disagree with Carolyn Heilbrun on this. She has written that "for all its virtues, [*The Documents in the Case*] lacks the appeal of the Lord Peter stories; the absence of the moral complexity that Wimsey insured is sadly felt." See "Dorothy L. Sayers: Biography between the Lines."

[17]Cf. F. Scott Fitzgerald's "Babylon Revisited." See also R. C. Stock and Barbara Stock, "The Agents of Evil and Justice in the Novels of Dorothy L. Sayers," in *As Her Whimsey Took Her;* the authors find *Murder Must Advertise* more successful than I do.

[18]Cf. Walker Percy, a contemporary American writer, who speaks eloquently of the difficulty of surviving "the sadness of ordinary mornings"; *The Message in the Bottle* (New York: Farrar, Straus and Giroux, 1975) 7.

[19]Brabazon, 135–38, has a good account of some of DLS's advertising work.

[20]See also DLS, "The Dictatorship of Words," ms. of speech to Modern Language Association, Wade Center; delivered 5 Jan. 1939; reported in the *Times,* 6 Jan. 1939.

[21]See Lionel Basney, "*The Nine Tailors* and the Complexity of Innocence," in *As Her Whimsey Took Her.*

[22]There is a curious similarity between the language of this passage and the words used by those who questioned Sayers's personal belief; see Brabazon, 261–66, where a lengthy letter by DLS to John Wren-Lewis is quoted: "I do not know whether I believe in Christ or whether I am only in love with the pattern."

[23]"He [Christ] takes our sins and errors and turns them into victories, as He made the crime of the crucifixion to be the salvation of the world. '*O felix culpa!*' exclaimed St. Augustine, contemplating the accomplished work"; DLS, "The Triumph of Easter," *Creed or Chaos?* 10.

[24]The source of this allusion is indicated on the first page of the ms. of "Thrones, Dominations," which is in the Wade Center.

[25]The lines quoted from *The Just Vengeance* should be compared with T. S. Eliot, *Four Quartets,* 'Burnt Norton' 2.24–36; 'East Coker' 3.36–47; and 'Little Gidding' 5. During a conversation with the author at the 1984 Sayers Seminar in Witham, Barbara Reynolds quoted DLS as saying she considered this play her best work.

[26]Sayers's "discovery" of Dante dates to 1943, when she read Charles Williams's *The Figure of Beatrice.* Barbara Reynolds has described the history of Sayers's interest in Dante (*The Passionate Intellect* 14–22).

[27]Cf. Jane Austen, *Pride and Prejudice* chs. 52, 58.

[28]This quotation from John Donne's "Eclogue for the Marriage of the Earl of Somerset" closes *Busman's Honeymoon.*

[29]There is a similar pattern in Eliot's poetry, from the sterility of *The Waste Land* to the joyous rejuvenation implied in *Four Quartets.*

[30]The Sellons are most likely miserable, too. The Twitterton-Crutchley alliance is somewhat reminiscent of the Wilsons in Fitzgerald's *The Great Gatsby.*

Chapter 12

[1]Brabazon quotes an effusive 1933 letter from Williams to Victor Gollancz, in which Williams expresses great admiration for this novel (225).

[2]Reynolds, *The Passionate Intellect* 46–47. The quotations from these letters, as well as the lengthy letters exchanged between DLS and E. V. Rieu, which are available at the Wade, suggest that she was sorely in need of someone to "talk with" about her new discovery.

[3]See preface to *The Zeal of Thy House.* William of Sens was actually hired to rebuild the choir after a fire had damaged the church in 1174 (5).

[4]See th DLS corespondence in the BBC Written Archives, File 1B, especially the letters of 5 Dec. 1931; 11 June 1940; and 14 July 1940. In one she says that she is longing to return to less serious work that can compromise only herself, and that she is becoming increasingly uncom-

fortable with being considered a personal spokesman for religion: "the personal angle on religion is getting on my nerves."

[5]This is from an essay published as "Christian Morality" in *Unpopular Opinions* 12; according to the book's foreword, this essay is the text of a lecture that was never delivered, on the assumption that "American readers would be shocked by what they understood of it" (7). This is the patronizing tone DLS habitually used when writing about, or to, Americans.

[6]Brabazon, 188–89; see also Alzina Stone Dale, *T. S. Eliot* (Wheaton, Ill.: Harold Shaw, 1988) 145–47.

[7]Even more interesting is the fact that it is a very conventional mystery. In a letter of 13 Nov. 1986 to the author, Philip L. Scowcroft has written that the play was broadcast in February of 1948, although written in 1947 or even 1946. The play was read at the 1985 Seminar of the DLS Society. On 6 Jan. 1944, DLS wrote to James Sandoe that she might take up Lord Peter again after the war, but for the time being, "a few private murders seem to be rather superfluous"; quoted in Sara Lee Soloway, "Dorothy Sayers: Novelist," 226. Finally, in 1954 she wrote a sketch for the BBC which featured Lord Peter Wimsey as a schoolboy, consulting Sherlock Holmes about a missing kitten (this piece was read at the 1988 DLS Seminar).

[8]She would write a Wimsey short story, "Talboys," as late as 1942. In a July 1984 interview with the author, Kathleen Richards, Sayers's wartime secretary, recalled seeing the ms. of "Talboys" lying around during the early forties. The ms. of this story at the Wade has the note, "This is the unfinished Wimsey," written on the title page, along with the date "1942," in Sayers's hand. This raises the question of what projected work it was to have been part of.

[9]DLS, "Thrones, Dominations,' unfinished novel ms. in the Wade Center, 145–46.

[10]At the 1984 Sayers Society Seminar, persons who had helped produce the entire play-cycle of *The Man Born to Be King* over a twelve-year period reported on that experience (see the Seminar Proceedings for that year, available from the DLS Society, for details). In 1987, the Society Seminar included an anniversary production of *The Zeal of Thy House* at Canterbury.

[11]In an interview with the author, Kathleen Richards recalled *The Just Vengeance* as a powerful theatrical experience. See also Reynolds, *The Passionate Intellect* 92–97, for testimonies about this play's effectiveness.

[12]Unsigned review, *The Times* 17 June 1946: 6a.

[13]I am indebted to David Winter, head of the BBC-Radio's Religious Programmes, for making it possible for me to hear these recordings and for discussing the project with me in August 1984.

[14]In an interview with the author, Kathleen Richards described working with DLS on the extensive timing, cutting, and revising of these scripts as they were prepared for broadcasting. The BBC's Written Archives hold a wealth of information about this project, including letters to and from the BBC and the author, as well as enlightening internal communiqués. Alzina Stone Dale has compared the extant drafts of the plays at the Wade in "*The Man Born to Be King*: Dorothy L. Sayers's Best Mystery Plot," *As Her Whimsey Took Her* 78–90.

[15]Quoted in Wolfe 218, 229; the files in the BBC Written Archives provide ample evidence of the public's overwhelmingly positive reaction to these plays.

[16]Wolfe says that an average of two million people listened to each installment of this play-cycle (234).

[17]As a condition for writing these plays, DLS insisted upon presenting Christ directly, as a speaking character (Hodges, *Gollancz* 146).

[18]Christiana Brand, introduction to *Strong Poison* viii; Hodges, *Gollancz* 146, also notes that the plays have sold 300,000 copies in hardcover.

[19]I have found this to be the case when I have discussed these plays with American students.

[20]See the essay of this title in *Creed or Chaos?* In an untitled, undated ms. in the Wade Center, DLS also discusses "the drama of the Mass" as a celebration of the Christian mysteries. (This ms. has been marked "Christian Faith and the Theatre.")

[21]For a complete discussion of the conflict between heart and mind, especially evident in *Gaudy Night,* see chapters 5 and 9 of the present study.

[22]David Winter, interview with the author, August 1984.

[23]See, for example, "The Present Status of the Mystery Story."

Chapter 13

[1]I am using the Oxford University Press reprint of *The Book of Common Prayer.*

[2]Although the earliest version of this idea was presented in Tolkien's Andrew Lang Lecture at the University of St. Andrews in March 1939, it is highly unlikely DLS knew of it at that time. It was eventually published as "On Fairy-Stories," in *Essays Presented to Charles Williams* (London: Oxford UP, 1947).

[3]Brabazon quotes a 1940 letter from DLS to her son, in which she ridicules people for thinking that meeting a writer in person will reveal who he or she really is, whereas whatever is real and best of that person will actually be found in the person's work. The quotation culminates in the statement, "what we make is more important than what we are, particularly if making is our profession" (162–63).

[4]See Lord Beaumont of Whitley, "Dorothy L. Sayers as a Lay Theologian," text of an address to the DLS Society, 3 June 1978, available from the Society. Christopher Dean, the Society's secretary, has also kindly sent me a transcript of the dean of Canterbury's sermon, which was delivered 2 Aug. 1987, as part of that year's DLS Seminar. In that sermon, The Very Reverend John Simpson spoke eloquently of the effect which *The Man Born to Be King* had upon him and others of his generation.

[5]See also Catherine Kenney, "Dorothy L. Sayers: The Integrity of the Work"; this article was in press when *As Her Whimsey Took Her* was released.

[6]In Ernest Hemingway's *The Sun Also Rises.* Like Wimsey, Barnes is left scarred by the war, but he is unable to function in the world.

[7]C. S. Lewis, review of *The Mind of the Maker.*

[8]What is not appealing is the insularity which sometimes attends Sayers's Christianity. (Sometimes, in fact, it seems that "Christian" is a synonym for "English" in her vocabulary.) This is not the place to discuss the subject in depth, but there is a frightening anti-Semitism which occasionally surfaces in her written statements. Most of this is found in private correspondence (see, for example, her letter to Mrs. R. W. Chapman, 12 April 1945, in the Bodleian Library, Oxford) and in suppressed documents, including some of the cuts made in *The Man Born to Be King* (see the production scripts in the BBC's Play Library). Of course, a stunner remains in the notes to the fourth play, where Matthew is described "as vulgar a little commercial Jew as ever walked Whitechapel." A major document for a study of Sayers's alleged anti-Semitism would be "The Future of the Jews in England Now: Rambling Meditations on the Subject of Christian Duty," which was written by DLS for a 1945 collection of essays, *The Future of the Jews,* but not published in that volume or elsewhere. Galley proofs of this essay are available in the Wade Center. Brabazon gives a brief account of this document, but tries too hard to justify Sayers's position (216–19).

The comments made by DLS in her own voice are more significant than the often-cited anti-Semitic remarks made by characters in her fiction; it is, after all, realistic for some of her characters to be anti-Semites. Yet the question of anti-Semitism among Christians is a serious one, especially for a writer like Dorothy L. Sayers, who was engaged in interpreting the foundations of Christianity. The subject of how anti-Semitism functions in her religious thought and in her work should be investigated in depth. Considering Sayers's fiction, Nancy-Lou Patterson has found her to be anti-Semitic, in spite of the fact that she never created a Jewish villain ("Images of Judaism and Anti-Semitism in the Novels of Dorothy L. Sayers"). This subject is obviously both delicate and complicated, and deserves considered and informed study by reference to the entire written record of DLS.

[9]A representative essay on the relationship between art and the Way of Affirmation is "The Poetry of the Image in Dante and Charles Williams," in *Further Papers on Dante:* "A sure mark of Catholic Christianity is the honouring of the 'holy and glorious flesh,' and indeed of all material things, because they are sacraments and symbols of the Divine glory" (187). This is, of course, the attitude of most poets and novelists toward the world of matter and time, and it is the attitude that characterizes Sayers's fictional creations.

Works Cited

Selected Published Works by Dorothy L. Sayers

Novels

Busman's Honeymoon. 1937. New York: Avon, 1968.
Clouds of Witness. 1926. New York: Avon, 1966.
With Robert Eustace. 1930. *The Documents in the Case.* New York: Avon, 1968.
Five Red Herrings. 1931. New York: Avon, 1968.
Gaudy Night. 1935. New York: Avon, 1968.
Have His Carcase. 1932. New York: Avon, 1968.
Murder Must Advertise. 1933. New York: Avon, 1967.
The Nine Tailors. 1934. New York: Harcourt, 1962.
Strong Poison. 1930. New York: Avon, 1967.
Unnatural Death. 1927. New York: Avon, 1964.
The Unpleasantness at the Bellona Club. 1928. New York: Avon, 1963.
Whose Body? 1923. New York: Avon, 1961.

Short Fiction

Hangman's Holiday. 1933. New York: Avon, 1969.
In the Teeth of the Evidence. 1939. New York: Avon, 1967.
Lord Peter. Introduction by James Sandoe. New York: Avon, 1972.
Lord Peter Views the Body. 1928. New York: Avon, 1969.
"Wimsey Papers," *The Spectator* 17 Nov. 1939–26 Jan. 1940.
"Who Calls the Tune?" *The Blue Moon* 1.1 (1917).

Non-Fiction

Book Reviews

The Sunday Times. 25 June 1933–18 Aug. 1935. Titles and pages for these weekly reviews are enumerated in Gilbert (193–207).

Essays

Are Women Human? Grand Rapids: Eerdman's, 1971.
Begin Here: A War-Time Essay. London: Gollancz, 1940.
"Charles Williams." *Time & Tide* (2 Dec. 1950): 1220.
"Conan Doyle: Crusader." *The Sunday Times* 6 Feb. 1949.
Creed or Chaos? London: Methuen, 1947.
"Eros in Academe." *The Oxford Outlook* 1.2 (June 1919): 110–16.
Further Papers on Dante. London: Methuen, 1957. Westport, Conn.: Greenwood Press, 1979.
"Gaudy Night." *Titles to Fame.* Ed. Denys Kilham Roberts. London: Thomas Nelson, 1937. 75–95.
"How I Came to Invent the Character of Lord Peter." *Harcourt Brace News* 1 (15 July 1936): 1–2.
Introduction. *The Moonstone.* By Wilkie Collins. London: Dent, 1944.
Introductory Papers on Dante. London: Methuen, 1954.
Making Sense of the Universe. London: St. Anne's Church House, 1946.
The Mind of the Maker. 1941. San Francisco: Harper, 1979.
"The Murder of Julia Wallace." *The Anatomy of Murder.* New York: Macmillan, 1937. 157–211.
"Playwrights Are Not Evangelists." *World Theatre* 5.1 (Winter 1955): 61–66.
The Poetry of Search and the Poetry of Statement. London: Gollancz, 1963.
"The Present Status of the Mystery Story." *The London Mercury* 23.133 (November 1930): 47–52.
"The Religions Behind the Nation." *The Church Looks Ahead.* London: Faber, 1941. 67–78.
"A Sport of Noble Minds." *The Saturday Review of Literature* 6.2 (3 Aug. 1929): 22–23.
Unpopular Opinions. London: Gollancz, 1946.
"What is Right with Oxford?" *Oxford* 2.1 (Summer 1935): 34–41.
The Whimsical Christian. Ed. William Griffin. New York: Macmillan, 1978.
Wilkie Collins: A Critical and Biographical Study. Ed. E. R. Gregory. Toledo, Ohio: The Friends of the University of Toledo Libraries, 1977.

Plays

The Devil to Pay. London: Gollancz, 1939.

The Emperor Constantine. London: Gollancz, 1951.
He That Should Come: A Nativity Play in One Act. London: Gollancz, 1939.
The Just Vengeance. London: Gollancz, 1946.
Love All: A Comedy of Manners by Dorothy L. Sayers Together With Busman's Honeymoon, a Detective Comedy by Dorothy L. Sayers and Muriel St. Clare Byrne. Kent, Ohio: Kent State UP, 1984.
The Man Born to Be King: A Play-Cycle on the Life of our Lord and Saviour Jesus Christ. 1943. Grand Rapids: Eerdmans, 1970.
The Zeal of Thy House. London: Gollancz, 1937.

Poetry

Catholic Tales and Christian Songs. Oxford: Blackwell, 1918.
Op. I. Oxford: Blackwell, 1916.
"Target Area." *The Atlantic Monthly* 173 (March 1944): 48–50.

Translations

The Comedy of Dante Alighieri The Florentine: Cantica I: Hell. Harmondsworth, Middlesex: Penguin, 1949.
The Comedy of Dante Alighieri The Florentine: Cantica II: Purgatory. Harmondsworth, Middlesex: Penguin, 1955.
With Barbara Reynolds. *The Comedy of Dante Alighieri The Florentine: Cantica III: Paradise.* Harmondsworth, Middlesex: Penguin, 1962.
The Song of Roland. Harmondsworth, Middlesex: Penguin, 1957.
Tristan in Brittany. London: Benn, 1929.

Books Edited

The Omnibus of Crime. New York: Payson and Clarke, 1929.
The Second Omnibus of Crime. New York: Coward-McCann, 1932.
Tales of Detection. London: Dent, 1936.
The Third Omnibus of Crime. New York: Coward-McCann, 1935.

Interviews

"Departure from Crime." *Newsweek* 46 (22 Aug. 1955): 82–83.
Gielgud, Val. "Why I Killed Peter Wimsey—by Dorothy L. Sayers." *Sunday Dispatch* 22 Dec. 1957: 6.

Selected Unpublished Works by Dorothy L. Sayers

With the exception of *Whose Body?* the Wade Center owns manuscripts, type-scripts, or fair copies of all Sayers's novels. I have cited these manuscripts in the notes to the chapters, as they were relevant.

Titles in brackets were assigned by the Wade Center.

Manuscripts

"Cat O' Mary." Wade Center, Wheaton College.
["Christian Faith and the Theatre."] Wade Center.
"The Comedy of Horror." Wade Center.
[*Dante Alighieri and His Daughter Bice.*] Wade Center.
"Detection Club Speech." Wade Center.
"Detectives in Fiction." Wade Center.
"The Dictatorship of Words." Wade Center.
"The Importance of Being Vulgar." Wade Center.
The Man Born to Be King. BBC Play Library, London.
"The Modern Detective Story." Wade Center.
"My Edwardian Childhood." Wade Center.
"Novelist's Trade." Wade Center.
"Speech Given at Oxford." Wade Center.
"Talboys." Wade Center.
"Thrones, Dominations." Wade Center.
"*Trent's Last Case:* A Critique." Wade Center.
Untitled fragment on Queen Elizabeth I. Wade Center.
Where Do We Go From Here? BBC Play Library, London.
"Wilkie Collins: 1824–1889." Wade Center.

Unpublished Essay

"The Future of the Jews in England Now: Rambling Meditations on the Subject of Christian Duty." Galley proof in the Wade Center.

Letters

DLS to Eustace Barton. 15 May 1928; 29 June 1928; 24 July 1928; 1 Aug. 1928; 19 Nov. 1928; 15 June 1929; 4 Jan. 1930; 7 Feb. 1930; 3 Sept. 1930; 3 Oct. 1932; 7 Oct. 1932. Wade Center.

DLS to the BBC. 5 Dec. 1931, File 1B; 11 June 1940, File 2A; 14 July 1940, File 2A. BBC Written Archives, Caversham Park, Reading.

DLS to R. W. Chapman. 15 Feb. 1935; 24 March 1936. Ms. Eng. lett. c. 469, Fols. 175195. Bodleian Library, Oxford.

DLS to Mrs. R. W. Chapman. 12 April 1945. Bodleian Library, Oxford.

DLS to Maxwell Fraser. 13 Dec. 1934. Sayers Society Archives.

DLS to Catherine "Tony" Godfrey. Good Friday 1913; 29 July 1913; undated letter to same correspondent. Rare Book Collection of Smith College, Northampton, Massachusetts.

DLS to Victor Gollancz. 29 Oct. 1927; 11 Aug. 1928; 20 Sept. 1930; 22 Jan. 1931. Sayers Society Archives.

DLS to Mr. Lakin. 27 Jan. 1935. Wade Center.

DLS to Doris McCarthy. 12 April 1948. 13 April 1948. Sayers Society Archives.

DLS to E. V. Rieu. 12 March 1945. Wade Center.

DLS to P. M. Stone. 6 Jan. 1944. Sayers Society Archives.

DLS to Michael Williams. 2 Dec. 1977. Wade Center.

Works by Other Authors

Auden, W. H. *The Dyer's Hand and Other Essays.* New York: Random, 1962.

Auerbach, Nina. *Communities of Women: An Idea in Fiction.* Cambridge: Harvard UP, 1978.

———. *Romantic Imprisonment: Women and Other Glorified Outcasts.* New York: Columbia UP, 1985.

———. *Woman and the Demon: The Life of a Victorian Myth.* Cambridge: Harvard UP, 1982.

Austen, Jane. *The Oxford Illustrated Jane Austen.* 3d edition. Ed. R. W. Chapman. Oxford: Oxford UP, 1979.

Barzun, Jacques. *The Delights of Detection.* New York: Criterion, 1961.

Basney, Lionel. "God and Peter Wimsey." *Christianity Today* 17 (14 Sept. 1973): 27–28.

———. "*The Nine Tailors* and the Complexity of Innocence." *As Her Whimsey Took Her.* Ed. Margaret P. Hannay. Kent, Ohio: Kent State UP, 1979.

Lord Beaumont of Whitley. "Dorothy L. Sayers as a Lay Theologian." Dorothy L. Sayers Society, 1978.

Bentley, E. C. *Trent's Last Case.* Introduction by Dorothy L. Sayers. New York: Harper & Row-Perennial Library, 1978.

The Book of Common Prayer. Oxford: Oxford UP, n.d.

Bottiger, L. E. "The Murderer's Vade Mecum." *British Medical Journal* 18.25 (December 1982): 1819–1821.

Brabazon, James. *Dorothy L. Sayers: A Biography.* Preface by Anthony Fleming and Foreword by P. D. James. New York: Scribner's, 1981.

Brand, Christiana. Introduction. *Strong Poison* by Dorothy L. Sayers. New York: Bantam, 1985.

Brittain, Vera. *England's Hour: An Autobiography 1939–1941.* London: Futura, 1981.

_____. *The Testament of Youth: An Autobiographical Study of the Years 1900–1925.* New York: Macmillan, 1934.

Brontë, Charlotte. *Jane Eyre.* 1847. New York: Penguin, 1966.

Byrne, Muriel St. Clare and Catherine Hope Mansfield. *Somervile College: 1879–1921.* Oxford: Oxford UP, n.d.

Cantwell, Mary. "The Mystery of Women Mystery Writers." *The New York Times Book Review* 22 March 1981: 22.

Carpenter, Humphrey. *The Inklings.* Boston: Houghton Mifflin, 1979.

Cawelti, John. *Adventure, Mystery, and Romance: Formula Stories as Art and Popular Culture.* Chicago: U of Chicago P, 1976.

Chandler, Raymond. *The Simple Art of Murder.* New York: Vintage, 1988.

Chesterton, G. K. "A Defense of Detective Stories." *Detective Fiction: Crime and Compromise.* Ed. Dick Allen and David Chacko. New York: Harcourt, 1974. 384–86.

Christopher, Joe R. "The Mystery of Robert Eustace." *The Armchair Detective* 13.4 (1980): 365.

Clark, S. L. "*Gaudy Night*'s Legacy: P. D. James's *An Unsuitable Job for a Woman.*" *Sayers Review* 4.1: 1–12.

Clarke, Stephan P. *The Lord Peter Wimsey Companion.* New York: Mysterious Press, 1985.

Coleridge, Samuel Taylor. *Biographia Literaria.* Ch. 13. Ed. George Watson. New York: Everyman's Library, 1967.

Collins, Wilkie. *The Moonstone.* 1868. Introduction by Dorothy L. Sayers. London: Dent, 1944.

_____. *The Woman in White.* 1859–60. New York: Penguin, 1982.

Craig, Patricia and Mary Cadogan. *The Lady Investigates: Women Detectives and Spies in Fiction.* New York: St. Martin's, 1981.

Cross, Amanda. *Death in a Tenured Position.* New York: Ballantine, 1982.

_____. *The Question of Max.* New York: Knopf, 1976.

Crundwell, Edwin. "Dorothy Sayers's Crime." *Chemistry in Britain* 19.7 (July 1983): 575–76.

Curran, Terrie. "The Word Made Flesh: The Christian Aesthetic in Dorothy L. Sayers's *The Man Born to Be King.*" *As Her Whimsey Took Her.* Ed. Margaret P. Hannay. Kent, Ohio: Kent State UP, 1979, 67–77.

Dale, Alzina Stone. "Fossils in Cloud-Cuckoo Land." *Sayers Review* 3.1 (December 1978): 3–10.

_____. *The Man Born to Be King:* Dorothy L. Sayers's Best Mystery Plot." *As Her Whimsey Took Her.* Ed. Margaret P. Hannay. Kent, Ohio: Kent State UP, 1979. 78–90.

De Quincy. *On Murder Considered as One of the Fine Arts.* 1827. New York: Brentano's, n.d.

De Voil, Paul. "The Theology of DLS." Proceedings of the 1978 Sayers Society Seminar.

Dillard, Annie. *Living by Fiction.* New York: Harper Colophon, 1983.

Doyle, Sir Arthur Conan. *The Adventures of Sherlock Holmes.* New York: Berkley, 1963.

————. *A Study in Scarlet and The Sign of Four.* New York: Berkley, 1975.

Dunlap, Barbara J. "Through a Dark Wood of Criticism: The Rationale and Reception of Dorothy L. Sayers's Translation of Dante." *As Her Whimsey Took Her.* Ed. Margaret P. Hannay. Kent, Ohio: Kent State UP, 1979. 133–52.

Durkin, Mary Brian, O.P. *Dorothy L. Sayers.* Boston: Twayne, 1980.

Eliot, T. S. *The Complete Poems and Plays: 1909–1950.* New York: Harcourt, 1962.

Falkner, John Meade. *The Nebuly Coat.* London: Edward Arnold, 1903.

Flanders, Alden B. "Dorothy L. Sayers: The Holy Mysteries." *Anglican Theological Review* 59.4 (October 1977): 366–86.

Foster, Natalie. "Strong Poison: Chemistry in the Works of Dorothy L. Sayers." *Chemistry and Crime.* Ed. Samuel M. Gerber. Washington, D.C.: American Chemical Society, 1983. 17–29.

Foster, Paul. "Dorothy L. Sayers." *Writers of To-day.* Ed. Denys Val Baker. London: Sidgwick & Jackson, 1946. 111–21.

Frankenburg, Charis. *Not Old, Madam—Vintage.* Lavenham, Suffolk: Galaxy, 1975.

Gaillard, Dawson. *Dorothy L. Sayers.* New York: Ungar, 1981.

George, Elizabeth. *A Great Deliverance.* New York: Bantam, 1988.

Gilbert, Colleen B. *A Bibliography of the Works of Dorothy L. Sayers.* Hamden, Conn.: Archon, 1978.

Gilbert, Sandra M. and Susan Gubar. *The Madwoman in the Attic.* New Haven: Yale UP, 1979.

Graves, Robert. *Good-Bye to All That.* Garden City, NY: Doubleday Anchor, 1957.

Gregory, E. R. "Wilkie Collins and Dorothy L. Sayers." *As Her Whimsey Took Her.* Ed. Margaret P. Hannay. Kent, Ohio: Kent State UP, 1979. 51–66.

Hamilton, Edith. "Gaudeamus Igiture." *Saturday Review of Literature* 13 (22 Feb. 1936): 6.

Hanff, Helene. *84 Charing Cross Road.* London: Futura, 1976.

Hannay, Margaret P. "Harriet's Influence on the Characterization of Lord Peter Wimsey." *As Her Whimsey Took Her.* Ed. Margaret P. Hannay. Kent, Ohio: Kent State UP, 1979. 36–50.

————. "Head Versus Heart in Dorothy L. Sayers's *Gaudy Night.*" *Mythlore* (Summer 1979): 33–37.

Hardwick, Mollie. *Parsons's Pleasure.* New York: St. Martin's, 1987.

Hawthorne, Nathaniel. *The Complete Novels and Selected Tales.* New York: Modern Library, 1937.

Haycraft, Howard. *The Art of the Mystery Story*. New York: Simon and Schuster, 1946.

———. *Murder for Pleasure: The Life and Times of the Detective Story*. 1941. New York: Carroll and Graf, 1984.

Heilbrun, Carolyn G. "Dorothy L. Sayers: Biography between the Lines." *American Scholar* Autumn 1982: 552+.

———. "*Gaudy Night* and Its American Women Readers." Proceedings of the 1985 Sayers Society Seminar.

———. "Sayers, Lord Peter, and God." *American Scholar* 37 (Spring 1968): 324–30.

———. *Toward a Recognition of Androgyny*. New York: Knopf, 1973.

———. *Writing a Woman's Life*. New York: Norton, 1988.

Hemingway, Ernest. *A Farewell to Arms*. New York: Scribner's, 1929.

Hickman, H. P. "From Detection to Theology." *Hibbert Journal* 60 (July 1962): 290–96.

Hitchman, Janet. *Such a Strange Lady*. New York: Harper and Row, 1975.

Hodges, Sheila. *Gollancz: The Story of a Publishing House 1928–1978*. London: Gollancz, 1978.

Honan, Park. *Jane Austen: Her Life*. New York: St. Martin's, 1987.

Hone, Ralph E. "Dorothy L. Sayers: Critic of Detective Fiction." *Seven* 6 (1985): 45–71.

———. *Dorothy L. Sayers: A Literary Biography*. Kent, Ohio: Kent State UP, 1979.

James, Henry. *The Art of the Novel*. New York: Scribner's, 1934.

———. *The Portrait of a Lady*. 1881. Boston: Houghton Mifflin, 1963.

James, P. D. "The Heart-Pounding Pleasure of Whodunits." *Family Weekly* 22 Aug. 1982: 6–8.

———. *An Unsuitable Job for a Woman*. New York: Popular Library, 1972.

Rev. of *The Just Vengeance*. *The [London] Times* 17 June 1946: 6a.

Keating, H. R. F. *Crime and Mystery: The Hundred Best Books*. New York: Carroll and Graf, 1987.

———. *Who-Dunit? A Guide to Crime, Suspense, and Spy Fiction*. New York: Van Norstrand Reinhold, 1982.

Keller, Katherine, and Karen Avenish. "Wimsey, Women and Work." *Sayers Review* 2.3: 1–15.

Kenney, Catherine. "Dorothy L. Sayers." *Critical Survey of Long Fiction*. Salem Press, 1983.

———. "Dorothy L. Sayers: The Integrity of the Work." *Listening: A Journal of Religion and Culture*. 15.3 (Fall, 1980): 230–40.

Klein, Kathleen Gregory. "Dorothy Sayers." *10 Women of Mystery*. Bowling Green, Ky.: Popular Press, 1981.

Labianca, Dominick A. "The Role of the Humanities in the Teaching of Chemistry." *Journal of Chemical Education* 61.2 (February 1984): 148–51.

Leavis, Q. D. "The Case of Miss Dorothy Sayers." *Scrutiny* 6 (December 1937): 334–40.

Lewis, C. S. *A Grief Observed.* 1963. New York: Bantam, 1976.

———. Rev. of *The Mind of the Maker. Theology* 43 (October 1941): 248–49.

———. "A Panegyric for Dorothy L. Sayers." *On Stories and Other Essays in Literature.* New York: Harcourt, 1982. 91–95.

———. "Wain's Oxford." Letter to the editor of *Encounter* 20 (January 1963): 81–82.

Malvern, 1941: The Life of the Church and the Order of Society. London: Longmans, 1942. "The Church's Responsibility" by Dorothy L. Sayers. 57–78.

Mann, Jessica. *Deadlier than the Male: An Investigation into Feminine Crime Writing.* London: David and Charles, 1981.

Mascall, E. L. "What Happened to Dorothy L. Sayers that Good Friday?" *Seven* 3 (1982): 9–18.

McCarthy, Mary. "Highbrow Shockers." *The Nation* 142 (8 April 1936): 142.

Milton, John. *The Complete Poetry and Selected Prose of John Milton.* New York: Modern Library, 1950.

Morley, Frank. *Literary Britain.* New York: Harper and Row, 1980.

Nott, Kathleen. *The Emperor's Clothes.* Bloomington: Indiana UP, 1954.

O'Connor, Flannery. *Mystery and Manners.* Ed. Sally and Robert Fitzgerald. New York: Farrar, 1969.

Patterson, Nancy-Lou. "Images of Judaism and Anti-Semitism in the Novels of Dorothy L. Sayers." *Sayers Review* 2.2 (June 1978): 17–24.

Pederson-Krag, Geraldine. "Detective Stories and the Primal Scene." In *The Poetics of Murder.* Ed. Glenn W. Most and William W. Stowe. New York: Harcourt, 1983.

Pym, Barbara. *Jane and Prudence.* New York: Perennial Library, 1982.

Raymond, Ernest. "We, the Accused." *Titles to Fame.* Ed. Denys Kilham Roberts. London: Thomas Nelson. 1937. 189–207.

Reynolds, Barbara. "Dorothy L. Sayers as Dramatist." Proceedings of the 1984 Sayers Society Seminar.

———. "The Origin of Lord Peter Wimsey." *Times Literary Supplement* (22 April 1977): 492.

———. *The Passionate Intellect: Dorothy L. Sayers's Encounter with Dante.* Kent, Ohio: Kent State UP, 1989.

Roston, Murray. *Biblical Drama in England.* Evanston, Ill.: Northwestern UP, 1968.

Routley, Erik. *The Puritan Pleasures of the Detective Story.* London: Gollancz, 1972.

Scowcroft, Philip L. "The Detective Fiction of Dorothy L. Sayers: A Source for the Social Historian?" *Seven* 5 (April 1984): 70–83.

———. Untitled lecture on Sayers's fiction. Proceedings of the 1983 Sayers Society Seminar.

Severo, Richard. "Dorothy Sayers's Poison Is a Treat for Chemists." *The New York Times* 31 Oct. 1981: C1.

Shaw, George Bernard. *Bernard Shaw's Plays.* New York: Norton, 1970.

Sidelights on Sayers. Series available from the Dorothy L. Sayers Society.

Soloway, Sara Lee. "Dorothy Sayers: Novelist." Diss. U of Kentucky, 1971.

Spanos, William V. *Christian Tradition in Modern British Verse Drama: The Poetics of Sacramental Time.* New Brunswick, NJ: Rutgers UP, 1967.

Stock, R. D. and Barbara Stock. "The Agents of Evil and Justice in the Novels of Dorothy L. Sayers." *As Her Whimsey Took Her.* Ed. Margaret P. Hannay. Kent, Ohio: Kent State UP, 1979. 14–22.

Symons, Julian. *Bloody Murder: From the Detective Story to the Crime Novel: A History.* London: Faber, 1972.

———. *The Detective Story in Britain.* London: Longmans, 1962.

———. *The Detling Secret.* New York: Penguin, 1984. U.K. title, *The Detling Murders.*

Tennant, Emma. *The Last of the Country House Murders.* London: Jonathan Cape, 1974.

Thurmer, John. *A Detection of the Trinity.* Exeter: Paternoster Press, 1984.

Tillinghast, Richard. "Dorothy L. Sayers: Murder and Whimsey." *New Republic* 175.5 (31 July 1976): 30–31.

Tischler, Nancy. "Artist, Artifact, and Audience: The Aesthetics and Practice of Dorothy L. Sayers." *As Her Whimsey Took Her.* Ed. Margaret P. Hannay. Kent, Ohio: Kent State UP, 1979. 153–64.

Tolkien, J. R. R. "On Fairy Stories." *Essays Presented to Charles Williams.* Ed. C. S. Lewis. London: Oxford UP, 1947.

Vine, Barbara. *A Dark-Adapted Eye.* New York: Bantam, 1986.

Watson, Colin. *Snobbery with Violence.* London: Methuen, 1979.

Watt, Ian. *The Rise of the Novel.* Berkeley: U of California P, 1957.

Webster, Richard T. "*The Mind of the Maker:* Logical Construction, Creative Choice, and the Trinity." *As Her Whimsey Took Her.* Ed. Margaret P. Hannay. Kent, Ohio: Kent State UP, 1979. 165–75.

Williams, Charles. *The Figure of Beatrice.* London: Faber, 1950.

Wilson, Edmund. "Who Cares Who Killed Roger Ackroyd?" *Classics and Commercials.* New York: Farrar, 1950. 257–65.

Winks, Robin W., ed. *Detective Fiction: A Collection of Critical Essays.* Woodstock, Vt.: Countryman Press, 1988.

———. *Modus Operandi.* Boston: Godine, 1982.

Wolfe, Kenneth M. *The Churches and the British Broadcasting Corporation.* London: SCM Press, 1984.

Yeats, W. B. *The Collected Poems of W. B. Yeats.* New York: Macmillan, 1956.

Letters

Bryne, Muriel St. Clare to Janet Hitchman. 9 June 1967. Sayers Society Archives.

Clarke, Ralph L. to the author. 3 Nov. 1986.
Fleming, Anthony to the author. 27 Aug. 1983; 19 Mar. 1984.
Gollancz, Livia to the author. 25 March 1986.
Scowcroft, Philip L. to the author. 31 Oct. 1986; 13 Nov. 1986.

Index